Consumer Behaviour in Tourism

Now fully revised and updated, the third edition of this bestselling text provides students with a vital understanding of the nature of tourism and contemporary tourists' behaviour in political, social and economic contexts, and how this knowledge can be used to manage and market effectively in a variety of tourism sectors, including tourism operations, tourist destinations, hospitality, visitor attractions, retail travel and transport.

This third edition has been updated to include:

- new material on the impacts of IT on research and marketing communications, the rise and influence of social media and virtual technology, the growth of interest in sustainable tourism products including slow food, the experience economy, and new consumer experiences including fulfilment;
- new international case studies including growth regions such as the Middle East, Russia, Europe, China, India and Brazil;
- new companion website.

Each chapter features conclusions, discussion points and essay questions, and exercises at the end, to help tutors direct student-centred learning and to allow readers to check their understanding of what they have read. This book is an invaluable resource for students following tourism courses.

Susan Horner is Associate Professor in Hospitality Management at the School of Tourism and Hospitality, Plymouth University.

John Swarbrooke is Visiting Professor, Plymouth University and Director, J and S Consultancy Limited.

Consumer Behaviour in Tourism

Third Edition

Susan Horner and John Swarbrooke

Routledge
Taylor & Francis Group

LONDON AND NEW YORK

Third edition published 2016

by Routledge
2 Park Square, Milton Park, Abingdon, Oxon, OX14 4RN
and by Routledge
711 Third Avenue, New York, NY 10017

Routledge is an imprint of the Taylor & Francis Group, an informa business

First edition published by Butterworth-Heinemann 1999
Second Edition published by Routledge 2007

British Library Cataloguing in Publication Data
A catalogue record for this book is available from the British Library

Library of Congress Cataloging in Publication Data
Names: Horner, Susan, author. | Swarbrooke, John, author.
Title: Consumer behaviour in tourism / Susan Horner and John
Swarbrooke.
Description: 3rd edition. | Abingdon, Oxon ; New York, NY : Routledge, is
an imprint of the Taylor & Francis Group, an Informa Business, [2016] |
Revised edition of: Consumer behaviour in tourism / John Swarbrooke and
Susan Horner. 2007. | Includes bibliographical references and index.
Identifiers: LCCN 2015041566| ISBN 9781138013384 (hbk) | ISBN
9781138013391 (pbk) | ISBN 9781315795232 (ebk)
Subjects: LCSH: Consumer behaviour. | Tourism.
Classification: LCC G155.A1 S88 2016 | DDC 910.68/8--dc23
LC
record available at http://lccn.loc.gov/2015041566

ISBN: 978-1-138-01338-4 (hbk)
ISBN: 978-1-138-01339-1 (pbk)
ISBN: 978-1-315-79523-2 (ebk)

Typeset in Helvetica Neue by
Servis Filmsetting Ltd, Stockport, Cheshire
Printed in Great Britain by
Ashford Colour Press Ltd, Gosport, Hants

Contents

Part 7 Conclusions and future

Preface to the third edition

It is now many years since we wrote the first edition of *Consumer Behaviour in Tourism* and nearly a decade since the second edition. In that time the world of tourism and tourist behaviour has changed dramatically in ways we could not have even dreamt of in the late 1990s when the first edition was published.

The events of 11 September 2001 in the USA, in which civilian airliners were used as terrorist weapons, put the travel industry at the heart of the growth of terrorism. Tourists have become specific targets for terrorist attacks in the years since 11 September, with attacks on tourists in countries as diverse as Tunisia, India, Kenya and Indonesia, the former just a few weeks before writing this. Hotels have become popular targets for terrorist groups, which has also helped put tourism at the centre of the upsurge in terrorism. However, as terrorism has sadly become widespread and almost an accepted risk in everyday life, perhaps its influence on tourism and tourist behaviour has declined.

At the same time, over the past decade and a half, tourism and tourists have been faced with one threat and scare after another that has affected confidence, including SARS, the tsunami in South East Asia and hurricane Katrina in New Orleans. To that list in recent months can be added the earthquake in Nepal, a number of high-profile air crashes and the sinking of several cruise ships.

Despite all these threats and problems, tourism has continued to grow since the late 1990s. And the market has been changing in fascinating ways, from the growth of outbound tourism from China and India to the rapid rise of the Gulf States as a major tourist destination region. Over the past few years we have also seen an explosive growth in use of the internet by tourists, as well as the continued rise of budget airlines around the world.

All these changes mean that in recent years tourist behaviour has experienced a scale of change that can truly be called 'revolutionary'. Unfortunately, tourism academics have not been able to keep up with these rapid changes in the tourism market and tourist behaviour. There has been a growing interest in consumer behaviour by tourism researchers, but there are still major gaps in our knowledge, which is a challenge for future researchers. We said this in 2007 when we published the second edition, and it is still true today.

The subject of tourist behaviour and how it is changing is also now more relevant than ever for students, as they will be the future managers and policy-makers who have to grapple with the effects of these changes in behaviour.

When writing this new edition, we have tried to retain much of the core text because the main principles, issues and techniques of consumer behaviour in tourism remain constant. We have even kept some of what we wrote in the late 1990s but it now has an almost 'historical' interest. However, we have also thoroughly updated the data in the text and added new sections on important topics including technology and terrorism. We have updated some case studies, revised others and added a number of new ones.

We must always remember that without tourists there can be no tourism, and recognize that if we are to manage tourism effectively, we need to understand tourists and their behaviour. We hope this book will help develop such understanding and that it will stimulate academics and policy-makers to conduct more research in this field, which is still underdeveloped.

Happy reading!

John Swarbrooke and Susan Horner

Acknowledgements

This book is dedicated to our son, John, who has become an art historian but still our special and much loved travel companion.

We would like to thank the following people for their help in writing this third edition.

The students who have asked difficult questions, which have helped us clarify our own thinking, and the students from many countries who have provided us with interesting insights into national and cultural differences in tourist behaviour.

The many colleagues around the world who gave us positive feedback on the first and second editions and who convinced us of the importance of a book on this subject for tourism academics.

Our friend Judy Mitchell, who helped make a manuscript out of our illegible scribbling in the first edition.

We would also like to thank our colleagues Saskia Faulk and Natalia Lavrushkina, who have helped us with the considerable amount of research necessary for this type of book, as well as writing specific sections, especially the case studies.

Finally we would like to thank our parents, John and Maureen Swarbrooke and Norman and Pauline Horner, who encouraged us to go to university – without that, we would not have written this book or achieved so much in our lives.

Every effort has been made to contact the copyright holders for their permission to reprint selections of this book. The publishers would be grateful to hear from any copyright holder who is not here acknowledged and we will undertake to rectify any errors or omissions in future editions of this book.

1

Context

Part 1 sets the scene for the rest of the book, through three chapters.

1. This introduction includes key definitions and explores the importance of consumer behaviour in tourism as a subject.
2. This chapter provides a history of consumer behaviour in tourism, in terms of both different types of tourism and the various regions of the world.
3. The final chapter in this part discusses the main general concepts in consumer behaviour that were developed from other industries and/or industry as a whole. It also looks at concepts that authors have sought to adopt for tourism. It closes with a brief consideration of the specific characteristics of tourism which make it difficult to apply general consumer behaviour concepts and markets to tourism.

CHAPTER 1

Introduction

The subject of consumer behaviour is key to the underpinning of all marketing activity which is carried out to develop, promote and sell tourism products. Clearly, if we are to optimize the effectiveness and efficiency of marketing activities, we must try to understand how consumers make their decisions to purchase or use tourism products. If we understand their behaviour patterns, then we will know when we need to intervene in the process to obtain the results that we want. We will know who to target at a particular time with a particular tourism product. More importantly, we will know how to persuade them to choose certain products which we will have designed more effectively to meet their particular needs and wants. An understanding of consumer behaviour is therefore crucial to make marketing activity more successful.

The problem with the academic discipline of consumer behaviour, however, is that while many general models of consumer behaviour have been advanced, there has been little empirical research conducted to test these models against actual behaviour patterns. This is especially true in the tourism sector, where research on consumer behaviour is very much in the early stages of development. Despite a lack of empirical research, however, several models of consumer behaviour in tourism have been suggested. It is important that, in this book, we consider these models and the stage that the development of the subject has reached. This will allow us to identify further areas of research and will offer the reader some judgements as to how useful the research is to date for application to practical marketing activities.

Consumer behaviour is a fascinating but difficult subject to research. This is particularly relevant in the tourism field, where a consumer's decision to purchase is of emotional significance. Purchase of a holiday, for example, involves consumers in a large spend. The holiday that the consumer buys will probably provide them with the major highlight of their year – a chance to escape from work and grey skies and to revitalize the spirit. Consumers are influenced in their decision-making processes by many internal and external motivators and determinants when they choose products. It is very difficult to research how these many motivators and determinants affect consumers as they make their choices. They may be affected in different ways according to the type of product or service they are purchasing. The experience of purchasing a holiday, for example, will be very different from the experience of purchasing an everyday food item in a supermarket. It is likely to take much more time and involve more careful consideration and selection, particularly as the purchase of a holiday usually involves a high proportion of income.

Before we get into the detail, however, we need to define some of the key terms.

We can start with a definition of tourism. Definitions of tourism are explained by Horner and Swarbrooke (1996) as having several components and considerable overlap with hospitality and leisure.

Tourism is defined as a short-term movement of people to places some distance from their normal place of residence to indulge in pleasurable activities. It may also involve travel for business purposes. Horner and Swarbrooke (1996) continue to discuss the reasons for tourism not being a simple concept:

> It does not encompass the lucrative field of business tourism where the main purpose of the trip is for work rather than play. We also have difficulty in deciding how far you have to travel to be a tourist or how many nights you have to stay away from home to be classified as a tourist.

Tourism can be described as an activity which is serviced by a number of other industries such as hospitality and transport. The rise of the mass package tourism business with the development of package holiday companies and retail travel agencies is probably the nearest that tourism comes to being an industrial sector.

Tourism also incorporates the hospitality sector. Collin (1994) defined *hospitality* as 'looking after guests well'. The term 'hospitality' is becoming increasingly used in Europe to replace more traditional terms such as hotel and catering. This is because the word 'well' suggests a qualitative dimension which is a fashionable concept in a time when quality management is growing in importance as a discipline. Hospitality therefore includes all organizations that provide guests with food, drink and leisure facilities. Not all hospitality is concerned with tourism, however. It may just involve people going to a leisure centre, or out for a drink.

Horner and Swarbrooke (1996) also suggest that tourism incorporates leisure. According to Collin (1994), *leisure* as a noun means 'free time to do what you want'. He also defines the *leisure industry* as 'companies which provide goods and services used during people's leisure time'. This includes holidays, cinema, theatres, visitor attractions, etc. This shows that, like hospitality, not all leisure organizations are concerned with tourism.

The distinctions between tourism, leisure and hospitality are blurred. A number of examples are suggested by Horner and Swarbrooke (1996) and are shown in Figure 1.1. The best example of the blurring of the distinction between tourism, hospitality and leisure is an American import, the resort complex concept.

The tourism market is very diverse and incorporates a range of market segments, each of which has its own demand characteristics. We will return to this

- The resort complexes such as Club Med and Center Parcs offer both hospitality services and leisure facilities on the same site, under the ownership of one organization. Furthermore, they offer this mixture to a market which largely consists of tourists, in other words, people who have travelled away from home and are spending at least one night away from their normal place of residence.
- Theme park attractions are increasingly offering on-site accommodation units to encourage visitors to spend more time, and thus more money, on site.
- The trend amongst hotels in most European countries is to build in-house leisure facilities for their guests such as gymnasia, spas and swimming pools. This is seen as necessary to attract two very different groups of clients – leisure visitors at weekends and business customers on weekdays.
- Leisure shopping is now highly developed as a tourist activity. Shopping is now used as a way of motivating trips to a wide range of destinations; indeed it could be argued that Dubai's success has been largely built on leisure shopping. In the UK we have Bicester Village Designer Outlet Shopping, which is visited by many international tourists in addition to the famous stores in London's West End.
- Sophisticated catering operations are being developed at visitor attractions to boost income. These can range from fast-food outlets to themed restaurants. Interestingly, many of these current developments in Europe are mirroring earlier ones in North America. At the same time we are seeing fine-dining restaurants becoming tourist destinations in their own right. In the UK this has been seen in Cornwall, where a major motivator for some tourists is to eat at Rick Stein's outlets in Padstow or Nathan Outlaw's two-Michelin-starred restaurant in Port Isaac. Internationally, San Sebastian (in the Basque region of Spain) and Copenhagen have become culinary tourist destinations.

Figure 1.1 Examples of the blurring of tourism, leisure and hospitality organizations

Source: Adapted from Horner and Swarbrooke (1996)

in Chapter 10 when we consider the nature of demand in different segments of the tourism market. It is sufficient here to define the different market segments of tourism, as follows.

- *Business tourism* is a tourist trip that takes place as part of people's business occupational commitment, largely in work time, rather than for pleasure, in people's leisure time (Horner and Swarbrooke, 1996). It incorporates individual business trips; attendance at meetings, training courses and conferences; visiting and organizing trade fairs and exhibitions; undertaking product launches; and incentive travel. There is a blurring of business tourism with leisure tourism, particularly when a business person takes their family with them on business, or extends their business trip to incorporate a relaxing holiday after their work is finished.
- *Hedonistic tourism* involves the tourist in seeking pleasurable activities. The tourism experience is based on physical pleasure and social life. The hedonistic tourist is often younger and often travels in a group with other like-minded people.
- *Educational tourism* involves the tourist travelling for education. This form of tourism is not a new phenomenon, but is still an important segment of the tourism business.
- *Religious tourism* is one of the oldest forms of tourism and involves people travelling often as a sense of duty rather than for pleasure and leisure.

We will expand this analysis of different market segments in tourism further in Chapter 10.

Let us now turn our attention to defining consumer behaviour. Horner and Swarbrooke (1996) have defined *consumer behaviour* in tourism: 'Consumer behaviour is the study of why people buy the product they do, and how they make their decision.'

Before we consider definitions and models that have been adapted for the tourism sector, it is important to consider the general definitions developed by researchers when considering consumer behaviour as a general topic.

The process by which a consumer chooses to purchase or use a product or service is defined as the *consumer behaviour process*. Consumer behaviour has been defined by Engel, Blackwell and Miniard (2001) as 'those activities directly involved in obtaining, consuming, and disposing of products and services including the decision processes that precedes and follows these actions'. This definition emphasizes the importance of the psychological process which the consumer goes through during the pre-purchase and post-purchase stages.

Solomon (1996) incorporates the concept of consumer needs and wants into his definition as follows: 'Consumer behaviour is the process involved when individuals or groups select, purchase, use, or dispose of products, services, ideas or experiences to satisfy needs and wants.' This definition introduces the idea that consumers may make purchase decisions in groups, not simply as individuals. The processes that are highlighted in these definitions are very complex, and for this reason it has been more common to illustrate the consumer behaviour process with reference to models rather than definitions. These are reviewed in the following section.

Before we consider consumer behaviour models in more depth, however, it is important to consider the role of consumer behaviour in the marketing process. An understanding of consumer behaviour is vital if the marketing activity carried out by organizations is to be effective. Marketing is concerned with the relationship between consumer or buyer and seller. Marketing relies on the idea that organizations should have the consumer as the central focus for all their activities.

Organizations often consider their consumer's wants and needs, but also rely on persuading them to buy their products and services. This is often referred to as *consumer persuasion*, rather than putting the consumer at the centre of the organization in a process which is often referred to as *consumer sovereignty*.

The marketing concept does suggest, however, that the overriding inclination of the organization will be to serve the final consumer's wants and needs as the main priority. This will mean that the organization constantly researches consumer demand and the reasons for this demand. The organization will seek constantly to find out what the consumer wants, both today and in the future, and will work hard to produce the products and services that are requested by the assembly of correctly designed marketing mixes. The provision of these well designed products and services will require an understanding of consumer behaviour and the ability to predict how this will change in the future. The organization will also have to understand how and why a consumer makes a choice. This will enable them to persuade the consumer to choose their products and services, rather than those offered by the competition. It will also allow the organization to develop products and services which are correctly *positioned* for their target market.

The definitions of *marketing* demonstrate the different approaches that have been taken to the marketing philosophy. Kotler and Armstrong (2004) define marketing as a 'social and managerial process by which individuals and groups obtain what they need and want through creating and exchanging products and values with others'. Their definition emphasizes the requirement for products and services to reflect consumer wants and needs.

Levitt (1986) emphasizes the fact that organizations must provide consumers with added-value appeal in his definition, as follows: 'a truly marketing minded firm tries to create value satisfying goods and services that consumers will want to buy'. Levitt's definition also highlights the importance of consumer needs and wants as being central to the marketing function. The UK-based Chartered Institute of Marketing's definition also emphasizes the fact that the marketing philosophy involves placing the consumer or customer as the central focus for the organizational decision-making process: 'Identifying, anticipating, and satisfying customer requirements profitably.'

Piercy (2002) suggests that a market-led approach which considers consumer demand is essential for two reasons:

* ultimately, all organizations are forced to follow the dictates of the market (i.e. the paying customer) or go out of business
* the organization can pursue organizational effectiveness by being 'market-led' and focusing on the customer's needs, wants and demands.

Piercy (2002) has also explained the reasons why organizations may find it difficult to adopt marketing. He suggests that there are considerable barriers to the introduction of marketing, such as ignorance of customer characteristics, lack of information, inflexible technology and competitive threats. It can be suggested, however, that the most likely reason for organizations not adopting a truly marketing-led approach is the fact that they do not really understand consumer behaviour in depth. They have simply learnt by trial and error how to persuade consumers to purchase, rather than having a sophisticated understanding of these complex purchasing processes.

Organizations have, however, become very sophisticated at persuading consumers to purchase, despite an apparent lack of understanding. As far back as 1957, Vance Packard in his book *The Hidden Persuaders* portrayed a frightening, manipulative view of the marketing function. He showed how organizations, even at that time, could manipulate consumers, including children, into buying products and services.

This work suggested that the ability to persuade consumers to purchase products may not necessitate a detailed understanding of their behaviour patterns and motives. It may be enough just to have the ability to persuade them to purchase. Despite this view, the authors suggest that a deeper understanding of the consumer behaviour process will help with the marketing of products and services.

Calantone and Mazanec (1991) outline the value of consumer behaviour for the marketing management process in tourism. An understanding of consumer needs, attitudes and decision processes will allow marketing managers to improve their decision-making process. It will allow marketing managers to forecast behaviour in the future and therefore avoid being overoptimistic or underestimating consumer demand. An understanding of consumer behaviour is also important for the *product development* of new tourism products and facilities. It will allow the marketing manager to have a clearer view of the types of benefits that consumers are looking for, and enable these to be reflected in the development process.

The development of effective and efficient *advertising campaigns* also requires an understanding of consumer behaviour. Benefit segmentation is often used here so that managers can design the advertising campaign based on the particular benefits sought by the market segment. Calantone and Sawyer (1978), for example, identify five benefit segments of consumers, which could be used to develop effective advertising campaigns. The use of benefit segmentation also allows marketing managers to understand changes that may occur with time (ibid.) and from season to season (Calantone and Johar, 1984). This will allow the advertising copy to be amended to reflect the different benefits sought during different periods.

Benefit segmentation also allows marketing managers to identify very well defined groups of people and target them with well designed products and services. Several tourist practitioners have recently developed promotions specifically for target groups. Saga, for example, targets the over-fifties market exclusively with well designed direct-mail brochures. Targeting of older consumers has been developing for some time. Companies in the tourism sector have recognized the lucrative over-fifties market. Similarly, PGL has a long history of targeting children and young adults who are looking for an outward-bound type of holiday away from their parents. We will return to the use of benefit segmentation in the marketing process in later chapters.

To finish this section, we consider the marketing planning process and how an understanding of consumer behaviour helps with the process in tourism marketing. Marketing planning was developed as a systematic way of incorporating marketing into an organization. The marketing planning process is defined by McDonald and Morris (2000) as a series of steps which incorporates all aspects of the marketing process (Figure 1.2).

We can use this model of marketing planning to consider the usefulness of an understanding of consumer behaviour in this process. This is explored in more depth in Figure 1.3.

It can be seen from Figure 1.3 that an understanding of consumer behaviour will allow a more effective marketing planning process. Some examples of where this understanding helps include:

- understanding why consumers currently choose products and services and the benefits they seek, including their USP
- forecasting consumer demand, which will bring efficiencies
- targeting particular market segments
- correct positioning of the product

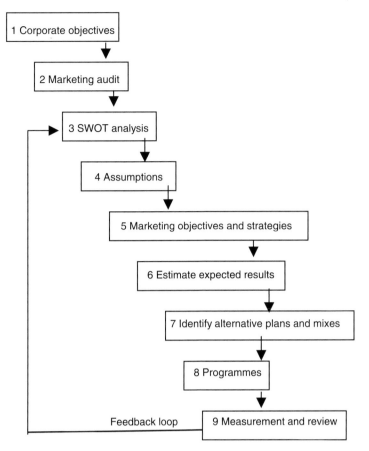

Figure 1.2 A summary of the steps involved in the marketing planning process

Source: adapted from McDonald and Morris (2000)

- designing effective marketing mixes and reflection of consumer behaviour in all elements – product, promotion, price and place (distribution)
- reviewing how new products and services have been received and an exploration of this in relation to consumer behaviour.

We can conclude therefore that the marketing planning process will be helped immensely if the marketing manager has a thorough understanding of consumer behaviour. Whether this understanding is developed as a result of thorough and systematic research or as a result of 'gut feel' and past experience is a matter of opinion and circumstances.

There are many examples of individuals who have spotted an opportunity and developed products to exploit them without much detailed research. These organizations are usually headed by entrepreneurs who, we could argue, have an interest in and understanding of consumers, and who do not require sophisticated research to confirm their ideas. Even these organizations, however, tend to investigate consumer

1.	Corporate objectives	Usually includes a vision or mission statement
2.	Marketing audit	An understanding of current consumers and the benefits they seek from our products/services and the competition
3.	SWOT analysis	Consumer perceptions of our products/services and their unique selling propositions (USPs)
4.	Assumptions	Comparisons with competitor views of brand, consumers
		Forecasts of consumer demands will allow opportunities to be defined
5.	Marketing objectives and strategies	Overall objectives and strategies should reflect consumer demands both now and in the future
		Segmentation techniques will be important here
6.	Estimate expected results	Forecasting models for consumer demand essential here
7.	Identify alternative plans and mixes	Products – should reflect consumer wants and needs
8.	Programmes	Promotion – should target customers with effective and well designed campaigns and understanding of consumers
		Pricing in relation to demand is essential here
		Distribution – an understanding of patterns of consumer purchase essential here
9.	Measurement and review	Market research of consumer responses is essential here

Figure 1.3 The marketing planning process and the usefulness of an understanding of consumer behaviour

behaviour in more depth as the organization reaches maturity and more competitive products arrive on the market.

Now that we have considered the role of consumer behaviour in the marketing process, we will move on in the next chapter to the history of tourist behaviour.

Discussion points and essay questions

1. Discuss the reasons for tourism, leisure and hospitality marketing becoming increasingly blurred.
2. Evaluate the importance of the fact that consumers may make purchase decisions for tourism products in groups, rather than as individuals.
3. 'Tourism marketing relies entirely on the fact that consumers can be persuaded to buy by powerful communication techniques' (Horner and Swarbrooke, 1996). Critically evaluate this statement.

Exercise

Conduct a small-scale survey to investigate the importance of the high-spend nature of tourism products on the purchasing decisions of consumers.

References

Calantone, R.J. and Johar, J.S. (1984). Seasonal segmentation of the tourism market using a benefit segmentation framework. *Journal of Travel Research* 25 (2), 14–24.

Calantone, R.J. and Mazanec, J.A. (1991). Marketing management and tourism. *Annals of Tourism Research* 18, 101–119.

Calantone, R.J. and Sawyer, A. (1978). The stability of benefit segments. *Journal of Marketing Research* 15, August, 395–404.

Collin, P.H. (1994). *Dictionary of Hotels, Tourism and Catering Management*. Peter Collin Publishing, London.

Engel, J.F., Blackwell, R.D. and Miniard, P.W. (2001). *Consumer Behaviour*, 9th edn. Dryden Press, Oak Brook, IL.

Horner, S. and Swarbrooke, J. (1996). *Marketing Tourism, Hospitality, and Leisure in Europe*. International Thomson Business Press.

Kotler, P. and Armstrong, G. (2004). *Marketing Management: Analysis Planning, Implementation*, 4th European edn. Pearson Education, Upper Saddle River, NJ.

Levitt, T. (1986). *The Marketing Imagination*. Free Press, Cambridge.

McDonald, M.H.B. and Morris, P. (2000). *The Marketing Plan*. Butterworth-Heinemann, Oxford.

Packard, V. (1957). *The Hidden Persuaders*. Longmans, Green, and Co, London.

Piercy, N. (2002). Market-led Strategic Change – A Guide to Transforming the Process of Going to Market. Butterworth-Heinemann, Oxford.

Solomon, M.R. (1996). *Consumer Behaviour*, 3rd edn. Prentice Hall, Upper Saddle River, NJ.

CASE STUDY 1: The rise of TripAdvisor

It seems as if TripAdvisor has been with us forever, but it is less than 20 years old, having been founded in 2000 in the USA, one of the earliest websites based on user-generated content.

Based on data from the company for the period April–June 2015, TripAdvisor offers 250 million reviews and receives some 375 million visits per month.

At the beginning the site was based on content from 'traditional sources' such as guide books, but travellers were invited to submit their own reviews, which took off at an astonishing pace. Over time it became a site where travellers share reviews with each other.

In 2004 TripAdvisor was purchased by IAC/InterActiveCorp and in the following years it was put under the Expedia, Inc. name along with the company's other travel-related brands.

In 2009 TripAdvisor launched in China and two years later it was spun off from Expedia as a separate entity. Since then it has been steadily acquiring other online brands including seatguru.com, viator.com, smartertravel.com, vacationhomerentals.com and besttables.com. In this way TripAdvisor has endeavoured to cover pretty well every type of tourism and hospitality product as a way of maximizing its reach within the market.

On its website, TripAdvisor says it 'offers advice from travellers and a wide variety of travel choices and planning features with seamless links to booking tools that check hundreds of websites to find great hotel prices'. This reflects the evolution of the company from an information-sharing, user-generated content site to a booking site and even a price comparison site.

Several surveys have suggested that TripAdvisor is the world's largest travel website, and that consumers generally believe what they read on the site and make use of it when making purchasing decisions.

Academic research has also generally validated the reliability of the reviews published on TripAdvisor, including the work of Ayeh, Au and Law (2013), Tuominen (2011), and Chua and Banerjee (2013).

However, its role has not been without criticism. There has been controversy over the extent to which TripAdvisor has managed to maintain the integrity of reviews on the site and prevent fake reviews. Others have criticized the whole review phenomenon, which gives guests the power to post reviews that can seriously damage a business, although organizations clearly have the right to respond to reviews. On the other hand, a hotel cannot remove its listing from TripAdvisor unless it has permanently closed, and although it can request that certain reviews are removed, it does not have the right to demand this, for obvious reasons.

TripAdvisor has introduced a number of interesting developments in recent years, including:

- a 'Green Leaders' accreditation programme for hotels and their environmental policies; while some would argue there are too many such schemes already, this one could be particularly effective because of TripAdvisor's high profile and large consumer base
- a Travel Forum where travellers can post questions to which other users post responses
- TripAdvisor apps for phones and tablets, which means it can be used easily by travellers when on their trips rather than just at the pre-planning stage
- a link to Facebook so that travellers can see what their Facebook 'friends' have been reviewing
- its own travel awards, including hotels, destinations, visitor attractions, beaches and landmarks.

Through TripAdvisor now one can not only post reviews but also book hotels around the world, flights, restaurants, cruises and holiday rentals.

The website has become increasingly sophisticated and offers the opportunity to reserve via a range of online booking sites for many hotels. In addition it offers a range of other services including latest offers, room tips, photos taken by guests, and the opportunity to ask questions of the hotel management with their responses published on the site.

TripAdvisor has changed dramatically since its inception, but it has very successfully kept pace with developments in consumer behaviour in tourism, and has shaped some of these developments.

REFERENCES

Ayeh, J.K., Au, N. and Law, R. (2013). Do we believe in TripAdvisor? Examining credibility perceptions and online travelers' attitude toward user-generated content. *Journal of Travel Research* Online, 11 February.

Chua, A.Y.K. and Banerjee, S. (2013). Reliability of reviews on the Internet: the case of TripAdvisor. *Proceedings of the World Congress on Engineering and Computer Science* Vol. 1, 23–25 October 2013, San Francisco, USA.

Tuominen, P. (2011). *The Influence of TripAdvisor Consumer generated Travel Reviews on Hotel Performance*, Working Paper. University of Hertfordshire Business School, Hatfield, UK. https://uhra.herts.ac.uk/dspace/handle/2299/5549

The history of tourist behaviour

Introduction

We do not know the name of the first tourist or the era in which the first holiday was taken. This may be because it is so difficult to define what is meant by the words 'tourist' and 'holiday'. Or does it reflect the fact that chroniclers did not believe the phenomenon of tourism was significant enough to be worth recording? Perhaps, but we know that for centuries tourism has existed in one form or another, and has given us a legacy of travel writing dating back to Roman times. It has also stimulated some of the world's greatest literature, such as Chaucer's *Canterbury Tales*. Therefore, while we may talk of mass tourism as a twentieth-century phenomenon, tourism in the broadest sense of the word has existed for centuries.

In this chapter we aim to address briefly the chronological development of tourist behaviour. It is difficult to understand current tourist behaviour, or predict future behaviour, unless we understand a little about the past.

As we shall see, the history of tourist behaviour is a complex subject. Furthermore, there is relatively little by way of empirical data or artefacts from which we can derive a history or chronology of early tourist behaviour. Most historians of tourism have tended to focus on Europe, from the Greeks and the Romans to the railway and Thomas Cook in the UK. However, it is important to recognize that tourism has existed on other continents for centuries. Furthermore, we need to remember that there are many different types of tourism, including business tourism, health tourism, religious tourism, educational tourism and hedonistic tourism. Finally, there is a need to distinguish between domestic and international tourism, together with inbound and outbound tourist flows.

The first tourists

We do not know for certain who the first tourists were or where they lived. It is often thought that the beginnings of tourism date back to ancient Greece and ancient Rome because we have evidence of tourism from these eras in the form of travel writing.

However, as archaeologists know, it is dangerous to be too dogmatic about history based on current knowledge and the artefacts we have found up until now. Who is to say that we will not find, in due course, evidence that tourism pre-dates Greek and Roman times? This has already happened over the years in other areas of history, leading to historians having to rethink accepted ideas on everything from who discovered the USA to who built the so-called 'Roman roads' in England.

Future research may ultimately show us that tourism pre-dates the Greek era and may indeed have developed first outside Europe. To date, little research appears to have been undertaken on the development of tourism outside Europe. Furthermore, in countries such as the USA, which were settled by people from the 'Old World', the study of the history of tourism begins with the first holiday-making activities of these colonists. However, some forms of tourism, notably visiting friends and relatives, undoubtedly already existed among Native Americans long before the Europeans arrived.

Unfortunately, in this chapter, by and large, we must base our comments on existing knowledge rather than hypothesizing about what we may come to know in the future. Nevertheless, it is important to read what follows with the latter two paragraphs in mind.

Regions of the world

We will now look at the chronological development of tourist behaviour, in two respects:

- the varied type and pace of development in the different regions of the world
- the way different types of tourism have developed, including visiting friends and relatives, business tourism, religious tourism, health tourism, educational tourism and hedonistic tourism.

In the first instance we will outline the historical development of tourism in the following regions of the world:

- Europe
- North America
- Central America, the Caribbean and South America
- Africa
- the Middle East
- Asia

- Australasia and the Pacific Rim
- Antarctica.

The emphasis in this section is on international rather than domestic tourism.

Europe

Today Europe is the most popular continent as a destination for international tourists, although it is slowly losing its position in the world tourism market to other regions, such as the Pacific Rim. It is appropriate that Europe should continue to hold this preeminent position, for most commentators consider it to be the birthplace of modern tourism.

The development of tourism in Europe, as elsewhere, rested on two essential prerequisites:

- a desire to travel
- the removal of obstacles that prevented people from taking trips.

As we shall see, the desire to travel, until relatively recently, was based predominantly on religious devotion, concerns over health, or trade, rather than pleasure. The obstacles that needed to be overcome so that people could become tourists of whatever kind were largely related to transport, in terms of both the lack of adequate roads and sea transport, and the risk of attack faced by travellers. Tourism could only begin to develop when these problems were removed or ameliorated.

The earliest recorded tourism in Europe dates back to the time of ancient Greece. It tended to be specialist in nature and related to religious practice. People visited religious festivals and consulted oracles. They also visited sporting events, such as the Olympic Games, which began in 776 BC – but even these had a religious significance.

The oldest recognized travel writing also dates from that millennium. For example, we have the writings of Herodotus, a historian who lived in the fifth century BC, who travelled by sea to Egypt, Persia, Sicily and Babylon. He recorded his experiences in ways that both informed and entertained the reader. Travel writing is thus an activity with a history that stretches back over 2000 years.

It was the Romans who were largely responsible for introducing the idea of tourism for pleasure, rather than for utilitarian purposes such as religious devotion, health or business. They started the hedonistic, sensual tradition in tourism, which has perhaps reached its peak in our age. The Romans were perhaps the first to create purpose-built tourism resorts, both on the coast and inland. These resorts often combined leisure pursuits such as bathing or the arts with health in terms of thermal spas. Such resorts were found not only in Italy, but also in the Roman provinces. They also gained a reputation as places where Romans could escape from the moral codes that constrained their everyday lives. This led to 'loud parties, excessive drinking, and nude bathing' (Sharpley, 1994). So we can see that there is little new in the behaviour of today's tourists. However, the Romans also developed tourism based on sightseeing within their empire, utilizing the roads that had been built for the convenience of troops and trade. Romans visited famous buildings, while young Romans were sent to Greece to be educated.

Yet, although the Romans pioneered the idea of hedonistic tourism, it was an elitist activity beyond the means of most people. It is this fact that distinguishes it from today's mass tourism. The steady march of tourism development in Europe was halted by the Dark Ages. With the end of the Roman Empire came the end of most tourism in Europe, although there was still some business tourism in the form of trade. Historians are now rethinking the so-called Dark Ages and are questioning whether they were as dark as we have been led to believe.

However, one form of tourism, which was to become the earliest form of mass tourism, was born in Europe at this time – the pilgrimage. This form of tourism reached its peak during the Middle Ages, and the numbers travelling were large, given the population of Europe at the time. For example, by 1300 some 300,000 people visited Rome in that year alone (Sharpley, 1994).

Other major destinations for European pilgrims included Jerusalem and Santiago de Compostela. There were also shorter pilgrimages, such as those taken by the English to Canterbury. The pilgrimages were supported by a well developed infrastructure of accommodation, eating places and even guidebooks, and were the forerunners of the modern tourism industry.

Towards the end of the Middle Ages there was a growth in what might be termed educational tourism, where people travelled to see great paintings and buildings, meet famous artists, and learn more about language and culture. Italy was the favoured destination for such trips, which were the origin of the 'Grand Tour'. However, in contrast to pilgrimages, which were more democratic, such trips were largely the preserve of the wealthy and well educated. Both pilgrimages and the Grand Tour were the origins of the tradition of Northern Europeans travelling to Southern Europe as tourists, which continues to this day.

The Grand Tour reached its zenith in the seventeenth and eighteenth centuries, with the sons of aristocrats spending up to four years travelling around Europe. As many as 20,000 young English people could be on the Continent at any one time (Sharpley, 1994). As well as Italy, the tour usually encompassed France, the Netherlands, Germany, Austria and Switzerland. In the latter decades of the eighteenth century, the Grand Tour changed in nature, with more people travelling but taking shorter trips. They tended to be older than previously and more middle class than aristocrat, and were more interested in sightseeing and hedonism than learning. The aristocracy began to desert the Grand Tour and look for more exclusive leisure activities elsewhere.

Nature and the scenic beauty of landscapes started to become a major attraction for some tourists, stimulated by the growth of the Romantic Movement in art. This movement created the perceptions that still determine the way we view rural landscapes and visit the countryside today. At the same time as the rise of the Grand Tour came the rediscovery of the spas which had been so popular with the Romans. The poor sanitary conditions of the burgeoning towns of Europe in the fifteenth and sixteenth centuries stimulated an interest in health among the upper classes. Doctors, such as William Turner in 1562, extolled the medicinal virtues of spa waters. Bath in England was a pioneer in the European spa movement, but there were many others, such as Royal Tunbridge Wells in England and numerous examples in France, Germany and Italy. Many were not new spa resorts but old Roman resorts. In later years, in the nineteenth century, other spas were developed, most notably in Poland, Belgium and the Czech Republic. The spas became major centres of fashion, social activities and gambling. Over time, like the Grand Tour, the spas became less exclusive as middle-class people began to visit them. This process led to the spas' commercialization and to their becoming places to live as well as just visit.

In Britain the early seaside resorts, such as Scarborough, were developed on the premise that people would bathe in the sea to improve their health, rather than for pleasure.

In the nineteenth century we see the real foundations being laid for the development of modern tourism, most notably due to the introduction of railways. This, and the results of the Industrial Revolution in Britain and some European countries, created the conditions for the growth of larger-scale forms of tourism. The seaside resort was the main beneficiary of this change, particularly in Britain, where the Industrial Revolution occurred first. Some of the newly urbanized and industrialized population had some leisure time and disposable income to enable them to travel for pleasure, while the squalor of many towns and cities created a desire to escape for a short time. In Britain this new demand was met by resorts that served largely regional markets. Blackpool catered for Lancashire, Scarborough for Yorkshire, and Margate and Brighton accommodated the needs of London. This pattern of regional catchment areas for many resorts lasted well into the 1950s and 1960s, and has not yet disappeared. However, as rail services improved and journey times reduced, resorts grew up which were further from the major centres of population and industry, such as Torquay. These tended to attract more affluent tourists from all over Britain. The rise of seaside resorts was also seen in continental Europe, where resorts developed to meet the needs of the urban dwellers of France, Belgium, the Netherlands and Germany, from the North Sea to the Atlantic shores of Brittany.

Just as we have seen throughout history, as resorts developed by the upper classes became favoured by the middle classes, the former moved on in search of more exclusive destinations. Thus wealthier Britons, for example, began to visit resorts in mainland Europe. Sir George Young has estimated that 100,000 Britons were crossing the English Channel in 1840, while the number had risen to 1 million by the turn of the century (Sharpley, 1994). These Britons began to choose resorts in southern France, where the climate was better, as places to spend the winter away from the cold of Britain. Here we see the forerunners, albeit a small elite, of today's flow of elderly Britons who travel to Benidorm for several months every winter for exactly the same reason.

It was sun-seeking, affluent Britons who, in the late nineteenth century, stimulated the growth of resorts such as Nice and Biarritz. These resorts were also frequented by royalty from other European countries and became fashionable places. Their image as glamorous, risqué playgrounds for the rich was enhanced by the opening of casinos and the growth of gambling.

Another development in the nineteenth century that was to have a profound impact on the growth of tourism was the creation of the modern tour operator, which traditionally is thought to be the excursion business started by Thomas Cook in 1841, in Britain. This company, which has since become a byword for tourism, started by organizing local rail excursions in Leicestershire, but by the end of the nineteenth century it was taking British tourists to Egypt. It also dealt with the travel arrangements of travellers from many other countries. By taking responsibility for organizing trips for tourists, Thomas Cook made travel accessible to those who lacked the language skills or the confidence to travel independently. It thus laid the foundations for modern package tourism.

By the beginning of the twentieth century, the seeds of long-haul international leisure tourism were taking root. Sharpley, writing in 1994, estimates that in the years leading up to the First World War, up to 100,000 Americans visited Europe each year. Other future tourism markets were also being pioneered in the early years of the twentieth century, including skiing holidays, which have reached their zenith in our time. Tourism continued to develop after the First World War. The 1920s were the heyday of the transatlantic cruise market. Sunbathing also developed as a leisure activity in the hedonistic days of the same decade. A suntan became fashionable rather than being associated with lower-class rural dwellers and manual labourers. From the 1930s onwards, the growing availability of the motor car further stimulated tourism, opening up areas that were beyond the public transport system. During the interwar years, the aeroplane began to play a small role in the tourism market as an option for the wealthier classes, particularly in Europe. These improvements in transport coincided in Europe with an increase in leisure time as a result of legislation on the length of the working week in many European countries. An example of this trend is the Holidays with Pay Act 1938 in Britain. This era also saw the growth of the holiday camp concept, particularly again in Britain, through the activities of entrepreneurs such as Billy Butlin. These camps reached their peak in the early years after the Second World War and were clearly the forerunners of modern inland complexes such as Center Parcs.

The rapid growth of mass tourism in Europe since the late 1940s has been well documented. It has been explained by the coincidence of a number of interrelated factors occurring at the same time, including:

- increases in disposable income
- advances in aircraft technology
- the greater availability of motor cars
- further increases in leisure time
- education
- the growth of tour operators and the package holiday.

The first wave of mass tourism in Europe consisted of annual migrations to the Mediterranean, in search of sun, by the residents of Northern Europe. Until recently this was largely a one-way flow, although now there is a rapid growth in outbound tourism from these Mediterranean countries, notably from Italy and Spain. Furthermore, not all Europeans have shown the same desire to visit other countries even though they can afford to, as we can see from the example of the French, who still show a preference for holidaying at home. This may reflect the variety of tourism opportunities that exist within their own country, as well as being the result of government initiatives designed to encourage people to holiday at home for economic reasons. These initiatives include the development of new purpose-built resorts on the Languedoc and Aquitaine coasts and in the French Alps.

These developments illustrate another major recent trend in the European tourism market – the increasing role of governments as both attraction developers and destination marketers. Governments have also often been the catalyst for the growth of a modern form of tourism in Europe, that is, social tourism, where holiday-taking is viewed as a right and may form part of the social security system. While never popular in Britain, it is an important element of the market in France and Germany.

However, it would be wrong to suggest that the past four or five decades have been a period of growth for all forms of tourism. In the 1950s, 1960s and 1970s the opportunities offered by jet travel and new Mediterranean destinations considerably reduced demand for both transatlantic cruises and the seaside resorts of Northern Europe. Interestingly, in recent years we have seen the renaissance of the European cruise market, but now it is more about mass appeal and budget prices rather than elegance and exclusivity. Nothing typifies better the march of mass tourism and the democratization of travel than this.

It would also be incorrect to imply that the growth of tourism has been a pan-European phenomenon. Until the political change of the late 1980s and early 1990s in Eastern Europe, the countries of the east were locked in their own tourism world. Domestic tourism existed on a large scale and cross-border tourism also existed, although it largely took place wholly within the Eastern bloc. Visits to Western Europe were rare and reserved for the political elite. This process is now changing and new markets are opening up for Mediterranean resorts, just as European tourists are starting to look further afield to the USA, Asia and the Caribbean for their holidays.

The final trend we should note in the historical development of tourism in Europe is the fact that Britain is no longer at the forefront of developments. Germany is the world's largest generator of international trips, and the Dutch, Belgians, Swedes and Danes take more holidays per head than the British. Even the most successful tourism developments in the UK are now often imported, such as the Center Parcs concept from the Netherlands, or the waterfront developments based on experience in the USA. Perhaps the most significant example of this trend is the fact that the largest tour operators in the UK are German-owned.

However, the future of tourism in Europe may not be about what happens in different European countries, but rather about events in the rest of the world. Tourism is increasingly a truly global market, but it is a market in which Europe is losing its dominant position.

North America

Some histories of tourism in the USA and Canada begin in the nineteenth century, but clearly the first peoples, the Native Americans, had been travelling around the continent of North America for centuries before the colonists arrived. This travel, while not often recorded by historians, must have been motivated by religious devotion, the desire to keep in touch with relatives and the need to look for new hunting grounds. We should also recognize the role played by these Native Americans in helping the early settlers find their way around their newly adopted homeland. However, it is correct to say that the modern tourism industry in the USA only dates back to the mid-eighteenth century. It is not surprising that the earliest growth of tourism in the USA should have occurred in New England, one of the first areas of the country settled by Europeans. In the latter half of the century, coaching inns and taverns began to develop to meet the needs of tourists. An early example is now part of the Historic Deerfield museum complex in Massachusetts. City centre hotels began to develop later, with the first-recognized such hotel being the Tremont in Boston, which opened in 1829.

However, it was the railway which first really stimulated tourism in the USA, both for pleasure and for business. It particularly opened up the 'wild west' to settlers, commercial travellers and curious tourists. In 1830 there were only 23 miles of rail track in the USA, but by 1880 the figure was 93,267, and by 1920 it had reached 240,293. The railway companies also contributed to the growth of tourism through the building of hotels and resort complexes in New England. They were heavily involved in the development of Florida from the turn of the twentieth century.

The next major phase of tourism growth in the USA was stimulated by the growth of car ownership. In 1914 there were already 2 million private cars on the roads but by the 1930s, at the height of the Depression, there were some 25 million (Lundberg, 1990).

Car ownership stimulated two new developments in US tourism:

- the creation of roadside motels, offering accommodation that was convenient for motorists – while the motel concept did not extend to Europe until the 1980s, it dates back to the 1920s in the USA
- a growing number of visitors to remote national parks that were beyond the public transport network – this started what has become a major theme of US domestic tourism, visiting wilderness areas in a private car or recreational vehicle (RV).

The development of US tourism was also stimulated by the creation of travel agency chains, beginning with 'Ask Foster' in 1888 and American Express three years later. Since the Second World War, both domestic and outbound tourism have increased in the USA. Indeed, for many Europeans the stereotype of a tourist is normally an American. Yet the truth is that, given the size of the population, Americans are not great world travellers. Relatively few possess a passport and the majority exhibit a preference for domestic holidays. This may well reflect the great size and diversity of their own country, but it may also be related to other issues such as the notably modest level of skill in foreign languages possessed by most Americans.

In recent decades, the USA has pioneered a number of new forms of visitor attraction which have been adopted elsewhere in the world. These include:

- theme parks, beginning with Disneyland in California which opened over forty years ago
- leisure shopping
- open-air museums with live interpretation, such as Old Sturbridge Village, the Plimoth Plantation, and Mystic Seaport in New England
- waterfront redevelopment projects, for example those of Baltimore, Boston and San Francisco.

Furthermore, they have led the way in the development of some new tourism markets that have spread to Europe. For example, the 'snowbirds' who travel to Florida and the South West from the North to escape the harsh winter are now being imitated by Britons who winter on the Spanish and Portuguese coasts. The USA also provided the model for the development of destination marketing agencies around the world, based on the principle of public–private sector partnership, through the visitor and convention bureaux that are found in most US towns and cities.

Turning our attention to Canada, much tourism has traditionally been based on the beauty of the natural environment. In the late nineteenth and early twentieth centuries it was the railroad that stimulated the growth of Canadian tourism. Rail companies such as Canadian Pacific developed hotels as well as providing the transport for tourists.

In recent years, however, Canada has started to broaden its tourism appeal in a number of ways, notably by:

- becoming a destination for skiers from Europe
- offering city breaks that explore the different linguistic cultures, such as English-speaking Toronto and French-speaking Montreal.

Central America

Tourism in Central America (including Mexico) has a relatively long history, but it has experienced rapid growth since the 1960s. In 1960 the region received 749,000 international arrivals, according to the World Tourism Organization, but this figure had risen to 2.9 million in 1970 and more than 7 million by 1989. According to the World Tourism Organization, in 1990 there were major differences in the place of origin of tourists visiting different countries within the region. Mexico, for example, received 92 per cent of all its visitors from the USA and Canada, and only 3 per cent came from other Latin American countries. On the other hand, the equivalent figures for Guatemala were 26 and 56 per cent, respectively. Mexico's situation is clearly explained by its proximity to the USA.

However, while Mexico has focused on beach and coach tour holidays, other countries in the region have pioneered new forms of tourism, notably eco-tourism. It is in this field that Belize and Costa Rica have built their fledgling tourist industries in the past decade.

The Caribbean

The Caribbean is a single name that covers hundreds of very different islands. It includes countries with different colonial histories, including Dutch, French, Spanish and British colonies, and countries with distinctly different modern political histories. Cuba is part of the same region as the American-influenced capitalist 'tax havens' of the Virgin Islands and the Bahamas. So it is no surprise to learn that its tourism takes many different forms, but two factors we have already mentioned have determined the tourism history of the area – colonial history and modern politics. The first point is evident in the markets for different Caribbean Islands. Former British colonies such as Jamaica and Barbados attract British visitors, while former French colonies and French *Outre Mer Départements* such as Guadeloupe and Martinique attract mainly French tourists. At the same time a shared history and language draws Spanish tourists to the Dominican Republic. However, this pattern is showing evidence of breaking down, with upmarket British tourists being attracted to the French-speaking Caribbean and those in search of value for money visiting the all-inclusive resorts of the Dominican Republic.

Cuba perfectly illustrates the second point, about modern politics. Seaton recognizes that 'up to the 1958 revolution, Cuba was the most successful Caribbean destination with a thriving tourism industry primarily controlled by US interests and made up of US visitors' (Seaton, 1996). Gambling was perhaps the major motivation for these tourists. After the revolution, the US government introduced a trade blockade of Cuba and the flow of American tourists dried up. To some extent they were replaced by visitors from Europe who were sympathetic to the politics of the new regime of Fidel Castro. The story continues today with Cuba trying to broaden its appeal and attract mass-market package tourists to offset its loss of financial support from the old Soviet Union. Interestingly, though, while we have seen that the Caribbean is a very diverse region, its countries have a long tradition of working together in mutually beneficial destination marketing campaigns. This has been achieved largely through the Caribbean Tourism Organization, a government agency dating back to 1951, which has an office in New York.

In recent years the Caribbean has attracted primarily three types of tourism – cruises, beach holidays, and visits from people who emigrated or whose parents emigrated from the region.

However, at the time of writing the thaw in relations between Cuba and the USA is opening up the prospect of tourist flows between the two after many years of travel bans and boycotts. It will be interesting to see if the Americans who visit Cuba in the future will be like those who visited in the past, seeking illicit pleasures not easily available in their own country.

South America

Tourism to South America has a history that dates back decades, but it did not really grow dramatically until the 1960s. The World Tourism Organization in 1991 reported that between 1950 and 1960 the number of international arrivals grew only from

410,000 to 426,000. However, by 1970 the figure was 2.4 million and by 1989 it was up to around 8 million arrivals. In the early days of tourism in South America, cruises were a major product and air travel developed rapidly in the region between the First and Second World Wars, at a time when cities such as Buenos Aires were seen as sophisticated places to visit. Business tourism has existed in the region for decades, based on, for example, the exploitation of crops such as coffee, vital raw materials such as the nitrates required by the fertilizer industry, and the mining of tin.

Recent decades have seen the rise of newer forms of tourism in South America, such as visits to the cultural heritage sites of Peru and trips to the carnival in Rio de Janeiro, Brazil. Political instability has always been an inhibiting factor for the development of tourism in some countries, such as Bolivia and Paraguay. However, this very instability has become quite a motivator for a small niche market of adventure travellers. The market for South America has developed considerably in Spain and Portugal in recent years owing to the common shared language and the growth of foreign holiday-taking by Spanish and Portuguese tourists.

Recently Brazil has made a major effort to attract tourists for mega events such as the 2014 World Cup and the forthcoming 2016 Olympics. However, this has not been without its controversy over the costs, or concerns over safety on the part of tourists.

Africa

The continent of Africa is so diverse that making generalizations about it is at best problematic and at worst meaningless. But we can say that tourism has existed in Africa for many centuries. We know, for instance, that the Greeks and Romans visited the sights of Egypt. There has also been more outbound tourism from some parts of Africa over the centuries than one might think, particularly in terms of business tourism and religious tourism. For example, for a very long time Nigerians who are Muslims have made pilgrimages to the Middle East. However, Africa is undoubtedly largely a receiver rather than a generator of international trips, and has been since the nineteenth century. We should remember that Thomas Cook was offering tours to the historic treasures of Egypt at the end of the nineteenth century. During the first half of the twentieth century, the British played a major role in opening up Africa as a tourist destination, particularly in the countries which were then still part of the British Empire.

In the 1920s and 1930s the two main regions that attracted foreign visitors, apart from Egypt, were:

- Kenya, where the appeal was big-game hunting
- Morocco, which was a popular winter sun destination, favoured by, among others, Winston Churchill.

After gaining their independence, many African countries sought to attract tourists to help develop their economies. Between the 1960s and 1980s, a number of African countries began to attract foreign tourists. Tunisia and Morocco became popular summer sun destinations, and wildlife holidays were being offered in Tanzania and

Botswana, for example. In the 1960s Scandinavian tourists discovered Gambia, which in the 1980s was to become a popular winter sun destination for British tourists.

Africa also saw some early experiments in what is now termed sustainable tourism. For instance, there were experiments in small-scale rural tourism in the Casamance region of the former French colony of Senegal. However, the growth of tourism in Africa has been constrained by political instability and poverty in many countries. For instance, in the past three decades tourism has been disrupted by a range of problems, including wars and civil strife, genocide in Rwanda, and Ebola in West Africa. Rwanda is an example of how a destination can rebuild after such terrible events.

The link between politics and tourism is seen most clearly in regions of South Africa. After the country was ostracized by the international community because of its apartheid policies, relatively few international tourists visited South Africa and few residents of the country travelled abroad. Only the white minority could participate actively in the well developed domestic tourism industry. At the same time, some whites travelled to the so-called 'tribal homelands', for example Bophuthatswana, and resorts such as Sun City where mixed-race relationships were tolerated.

With the end of apartheid and the election of a new government, South Africa has begun to attract large numbers of foreign tourists. Indeed, buying property in the country has become popular among Europeans and Americans. There has also been a large growth in business tourism with the resumption of normal trade relations between South Africa and the rest of the world. On the other hand, fears remain over safety, and the legacy of hosting the 2010 World Cup has been disappointing.

Finally, as some African economies have developed, most notably that of Nigeria, outbound tourism from these countries has grown in terms of both business and leisure tourism.

The Middle East

The countries of the Middle East have a long history of involvement in the tourism industry, most notably in terms of religious tourism. This region is the most important pilgrimage destination in the world for three major religions:

- Mecca and Jerusalem are very sacred places for Muslims; the tourist flow to Mecca is probably the largest single annual movement of tourists in the world
- the cities of Nazareth, Bethlehem, Jerusalem and Jericho, which are the most important religious cities for Christians
- Jerusalem, which is the holiest city for Jews.

However, it is not only religion that has brought tourists to the region. The Middle East has always been an important crossroads for business travellers. Some Silk Route caravans used to be routed through Syria and Jordan to the Mediterranean coast, for instance. Until its civil war, the Lebanon, and Beirut specifically, was one of the world's most fashionable and sophisticated tourist destinations. This is clearly illustrated by an advertisement placed by the British airline BOAC in 1962 which described Beirut as an 'international playground'. It offered a return flight for £105 – a fortune in 1962 – and promised passengers 'exotic night spots', great skiing and 'fabulous beaches'. The wars between Israel and her neighbours in 1962 and 1973, and the civil war in Lebanon in the 1970s and 1980s, greatly hindered the rise of tourism in the region. However, in recent years the Middle East peace process has helped stimulate a rejuvenation and growth of the industry. It has particularly stimulated the development of cross-border tours of the region's heritage, typically featuring Jordan, Israel, Palestine and Egypt. At the time of writing, tension still exists in Israel and the Palestinian territories, which is threatening the future of pilgrimage and cultural tourism in the region. Nevertheless, Israel is still seeing its tourism arrivals growing on its Red Sea coast in resorts such as Eilat, particularly in relation to winter sun packages and water sports holidays.

Over the past 30 years the so-called Middle East has contained perhaps the most impressive examples of rapid tourism growth in the world, first in Dubai and later in Abu Dhabi and Qatar.

Meanwhile the rest of the region has tended to underperform, largely as a result of the political situation and the threat of terrorism, most notably now with the phenomenon of the Islamic State.

Asia

Clearly, Asia is a large continent which encompasses a wide variety of national tourism markets with very different characteristics. In countries such as Thailand and the Philippines, inbound tourism began with visiting sailors, followed by the arrival of package tourism in the 1980s and 1990s. For example, according to Richter, writing in 1989 (in Hitchcock, King and Parnwell, 1993), Thailand's market grew as follows:

- 1960: 81,340 arrivals
- 1970: 628,671 arrivals
- 1980: 1,858,801 arrivals
- 1986: 2,818,292 arrivals.

Thailand's resorts are now a cheap, good quality destination for Europeans seeking a sun, sand and sea holiday, but Bangkok has still maintained its reputation for sex tourism, which dates back to its days as a shore trip for sailors.

In India, there is a strong tradition of domestic tourism of two types:

- trips to hill stations during the hot summer months
- visits to religious festivals.

Inbound tourism has tended to focus on historic cities, but coastal resorts such as Goa and Kerala have become major destinations for foreign package tourists looking for winter sun holidays.

While most Asian countries have been trying to attract foreign tourists, Japan, for example, tried to encourage its population to holiday abroad 'as a way of alleviating trade friction with neighbouring countries' (Mackie in Harrison, 1992), and in 1986 some 5.5 million Japanese were taking foreign holidays (Choy, 1995). However, in recent decades in Japan the holiday market has been constrained by the Japanese habit of working long hours and taking fewer holidays than other nationalities. The tastes of Japanese tourists and their tendency to demand familiar food, drink and accommodation can be a controversial issue, as for example on the Gold Coast in Australia. They also show a preference for other Asian countries with cultures similar to their own, such as South Korea.

More recently the newly industrialized nations of Asia, such as South Korea and Singapore, have started to become significant generators of international tourist trips.

In recent years, some countries in Asia have begun to attract foreign tourists in significant numbers, including Cambodia and Myanmar, but one of the most spectacular growth rates in international arrivals has been seen in Vietnam. This growth can be seen with reference to figures for the 1990s, quoted by Hitchcock *et al.* (1993), when visitors to Vietnam rose from just 20,000 in 1986, to 500,000 in 1995, to 7.8 million in 2014 (based on Vietnam government data). This growth has been fuelled by political change in the country and a desire by foreigners to see its cultural and heritage attractions.

Across the region, special interest and beach-based tourism have taken over from the 'travellers' of yesterday.

Australasia and the Pacific Rim

Australia and New Zealand, although they have relatively small populations, have a long tradition of outbound tourism, particularly among the younger population of both countries. This growth in outbound tourism occurred steadily from the 1960s to the 1990s. Early research offered the following figures on the growth of outbound tourism from Australia:

* 1965: 161,692 departures
* 1975: 911,815 departures.

These tourists have traditionally taken relatively long trips to Europe and North America, but Asia is now attracting large numbers too. At the same time, the main market for inbound tourism to Australasia has traditionally been people from Europe visiting friends and relatives (VFR) who have emigrated to the region. In the early days this market was largely English-speaking, but it increasingly reflects the multicultural nature of Australian society. Many VFR tourists are now equally likely to be Greek or Asian. Australia has also attracted considerable numbers of leisure tourists from Japan, who have shown a particular preference for the Gold Coast of Queensland. This has led to the growth of infrastructure that is geared to the tastes of Japanese visitors. Australasia is also attracting growing numbers of tourists from Europe and North America, who are attracted by the natural beauty. For example, there are trips to the Kakadu National Park in Northern Australia and whale-watching in New Zealand. The islands of the

South Pacific have long held an appeal for Western tourists as they are perceived to offer exotic 'paradise' experiences, although tourist numbers are still relatively small.

Antarctica

Antarctica is unique in the tourism world in that its lack of a permanent resident population means that the only tourism is inbound, rather than outbound or domestic. The region did not begin to attract tourists until the 1950s. However, while numbers are still small, the growth rate has been dramatic. Statistics quoted by Hall and Johnston (1995), in an edited work on Polar tourism, present the following picture of the growth of arrivals in Antarctica during the period from 1957 to 1993:

- 1957–58: 194 arrivals
- 1967–68: 147 arrivals
- 1977–78: 845 arrivals
- 1987–88: 2782 arrivals
- 1992–93: 7037 arrivals.

The same text tells us that more than 90 per cent of visitors to the region arrived by sea, on cruise ships, as they still do today. However, according to data from the International Association of Antarctica Tour Operators (IAATO) more than 35,000 people visited during 2014–15.

   These cruises originate principally from ports in Australasia, Argentina and Chile. While the cruises may last for an average of 12 to 15 days, most cruise passengers spend only a few hours on land in the Antarctic, and some do not even land.

Inter-regional comparisons across the world

There have clearly been considerable differences in the nature and volume of tourism demand between different countries and regions of the world. Some have been generators of international trips while others have generated very few such trips. Certain regions have traditionally been popular tourist destinations while others have until recently attracted relatively few tourists. There are also very different levels and patterns of domestic tourism between different countries, even within the same region of the world. For example, French people take far more domestic holidays than their neighbours in Germany.

   The nature of tourism in different countries has been influenced by a myriad of factors, including:

- climate
- geographical location
- history
- language

- development of transport systems
- levels of economic development
- quality of landscapes and townscapes
- government policies towards tourism
- degree of economic and political stability.

However, in recent years the picture of world tourism demand has begun to change dramatically. Newly industrialized countries such as South Korea have started to become major generating countries for tourism trips. At the same time, countries renowned for receiving tourists, such as Spain, have also begun to generate tourist trips. Political change has created opportunities for Eastern Europeans to travel outside their own region. However, the recent economic crisis in the eurozone has certainly slowed the trend in outbound tourism from Spain.

At the same time, there has been a general growth in long-haul travel which has taken tourists to countries where they did not travel before, outside their own continent.

The most significant trend in the period from 1950 to 1990 was the relative decline in the share of tourist arrivals in the Americas and the increase in the share of arrivals in East Asia and the Pacific. However, we must put this in context. According to the World Tourism Organization, while the Americas show a reduction of a third in their share of international tourist arrivals between 1980 and 1990, their number of visitors actually grew from 7.5 million to 84 million over the same period. In other words, these figures have to be seen in the context of the phenomenal rise in international tourism experienced between 1980 and 1990. Nevertheless, there was a clear trend towards the Pacific Rim, and to a lesser extent Africa, which is evident in the history of international tourism over the past few decades, and particularly during the period from 1970 to 1990.

Different types of tourism

Having looked at the chronological development of tourism from a geographical perspective, it is now time to consider it in terms of different types of tourism. Dividing tourism up into subtypes is always subjective, but the authors believe that the approach chosen here allows interesting points to be made about the growth of tourism and the development of tourist behaviour. This section covers the following types of tourism:

- visiting friends and relatives
- business tourism
- religious tourism
- health tourism
- social tourism
- educational tourism
- cultural tourism
- scenic tourism

- hedonistic tourism
- activity tourism
- special interest tourism.

Visiting friends and relatives

This phenomenon clearly dates back to the earliest days in pre-history when migration first separated families. Notwithstanding the immense difficulties of travelling in ancient times, it is natural that, from time to time, family members would have wanted to see each other. The same is true of friends who were permanently or temporarily parted by migration and nomadic lifestyles. Weddings and religious festivals provided opportunities for the earliest form of VFR tourism.

In recent centuries this form of tourism has been further stimulated by a range of factors, including:

- increased leisure time
- improved transport systems
- better housing so that people can now accommodate their friends and relatives more comfortably in their own homes.

The VFR market is notoriously difficult to measure, for two main reasons:

- much of it is domestic and no national boundaries are crossed
- VFR tourists do not usually make use of commercial accommodation establishments where visitor data could be collected.

However, the growth of economic migration in recent decades, around the world, has given a new impetus to this market. The families or individuals who migrate permanently or temporarily to improve their economic wellbeing create markets for VFR trips. While such trips bring little benefit for accommodation suppliers, they can bring considerable new business for transport operators and travel agents, as the following examples illustrate:

- so-called 'guest workers' in Germany returning home by air and rail to Turkey to visit friends and family
- trips to India, Pakistan and Bangladesh from the UK
- Moroccan and Algerian people, who live in France, using ferries and flights to visit their families in North Africa
- expatriate British workers returning home for brief visits to the UK from Middle Eastern countries such as Saudi Arabia and Kuwait.

Clearly, the demand for visiting families is potentially greater among those communities where the extended family, rather than the nuclear family, is the norm.

Business tourism

We are inclined to think of business tourism as a fundamentally modern phenomenon. In our minds it involves purpose-built convention centres, business people jetting around the world, product launches, training seminars and incentive travel packages. Yet business tourism is one of the oldest forms of tourism; it is just that the type of business tourism has changed over time.

Until this century, business travel was largely related purely to trade, to selling and transporting goods to customers who resided outside the area of production. It thus involved:

- visits to potential customers by 'sales people', so-called commercial travellers
- the transporting of goods to the customer.

This activity has been going on for longer than we often imagine, and each new piece of archaeological research seems to indicate that its history extends even further back into the mists of prehistory. Furthermore, early business tourism is not restricted to any single continent. Evidence of business tourism has been found, in terms of artefacts discovered by archaeologists that could only have been produced elsewhere, all over Africa, the Americas, Asia, the Middle East and Europe. There is evidence of trade taking place in all these countries. There is a tendency to believe that, because of the poor state of transport systems until the modern era, most trade generally only involved short-distance movement. That clearly is not true.

Not only were ships used widely for longer-distance trade, but also well developed, long-distance overland routes existed many centuries ago. Perhaps the greatest example of this phenomenon is the former Silk Route, which brought silk from China to Europe by way of such magically named places as Samarkand and Constantinople. This route, or more accurately set of interconnecting routes, covered thousands of kilometres and was used for hundreds of years.

From its early days, business tourism developed its own infrastructure, reflecting the needs of the business traveller. In the case of the Silk Route this revolved around food, accommodation for the travellers, and the supply of water for their beasts of burden in the arid regions of Central Asia. Many of the buildings that served these travellers, such as the *caravanserai* where caravans of merchants would stop for rest, remain today as a memorial to early business tourism. Some are now being restored as tourist attractions, for example in Turkey. Indeed, one of the authors recalls a meal taken in a fourteenth-century *caravanserai* in the Azerbaijani city of Baku more than a decade ago. The desire of merchants to travel together for safety led to the growth of caravans, and thus the development of a new type of professional, the caravan master. But early trade and business tourism also led to the growth of a range of professions over the years, including sailors, carters and canal boat operators, all with their own unique lifestyles. Alongside individual business trips and the activities of those involved in transporting goods, the third major stream of business tourism has been the trade fair. Here people from a region or a specific industry gather together to sell to each other and exchange professional news. Such trade fairs are not a recent invention; they date back hundreds of years. For example, in the Middle Ages there was a famous annual fair at Beaucaire, on the banks of the Rhône, which was known all over the Western world.

In Europe, at least, the growth of business tourism was greatly stimulated by the Industrial Revolution, and throughout the world it was made easier by the introduction of the railway. However, like leisure tourism, the real boom in business tourism did not occur until after the Second World War. Its rapid growth has been fuelled by a number of factors, including:

- improvements in transport technologies
- the rise of the global economy
- the growth of supra-national trading blocks such as the European Union and the trade agreement between the USA, Canada, and Mexico, the North American Free Trade Agreement (NAFTA)
- the efforts made by governments to attract high-spending business tourists to their country
- the development of new forms of business tourism such as incentive travel.

Business tourism is no longer just about sales trips and the transport of goods. It now involves conferences where information is exchanged, lavish events to launch new products, survival weekends to motivate or reward staff, and intensive training courses. New types of business tourist have appeared, linked to these developments in business tourism, including the company trouble-shooter, the trainer and the conference circuit traveller. However, certain traditional types of business traveller are declining in numbers, notably the commercial traveller, who has been made increasingly obsolete by developments in communication technologies. Their passing has been the death knell for many small, privately owned commercial hotels in the UK. A whole new industry has arisen to serve these modern types of business tourists, as well as the 'traditional' individual on a business trip. It is an increasingly specialist field, with major corporations seeking to achieve competitive advantage in this most lucrative of tourist markets.

It is important to recognize that throughout history there has been a strong link between leisure tourism and business tourism. Business tourists become leisure tourists when the working day is over, and they are often accompanied by partners who are full-time leisure tourists. Furthermore, as they are often travelling at someone else's expense, business tourists can represent a particularly high-spending segment. The way business tourists have chosen to spend their leisure time has, however, often been controversial. For example, business tourists have often been the stimulus for the growth of red-light districts and prostitution, from Amsterdam to Bangkok.

Religious tourism

We saw earlier in this chapter that, in Europe for example, religion was a major catalyst for early tourism. Religious tourism usually involves visiting places with religious significance such as shrines, or attending religious events such as saint's day festivals. However, it would be a mistake – one often made by tourism historians – to talk about religious tourism mainly in terms of Christian pilgrimages in Europe. Religious tourism undoubtedly existed long before Christianity. Devotion to a religion motivated trips by ancient peoples including the Egyptians, Greeks and Jews. Travel for religious reasons existed in India and Asia, for example, before Christ was born. Many early religions that encouraged pilgrimages in ancient times are now marginal or forgotten, such as the fire-worshippers or Zoroastrians. At a time when Europe was in the Dark Ages the Islamic religion came into existence. We in the West often forget that the Islamic pilgrimage to Mecca is still perhaps the greatest single tourist flow in the world, eclipsing in size modern Christian pilgrimages. Having made this important point, we now return to Christian tourism in Europe.

It is often said that the difference between tourism in the past and modern tourism is that the former was small-scale and elitist while the latter is on a mass scale and more democratic. Yet if we look at the European Christian pilgrimages, we can see a very different pattern. We can observe that this form of religious tourism peaked in the Middle Ages and has since declined, as religious observance has declined, particularly in Northern Europe. It also reflects the rise of Protestantism in Europe, which has never placed the same emphasis on pilgrimages as has Catholicism. Where the latter religion is still practised by the majority of the population, such as in Ireland, the pilgrimage is still popular. For one market segment there is a strong link between religious and health tourism. These are the people who visit more modern shrines such as Lourdes in the hope that they will be cured of their ailments. Finally, religious tourism in Europe is a good example of how infrastructure that developed for one form of tourism can be used in the future for another type. The great cathedrals that were built as symbols of, and places for, religious devotion and pilgrimages are now merely another sightseeing attraction for the package tourist. Events with great religious significance, such as processions parading a town's patron saints through the streets, become entertainment for tourists. Pilgrimage routes, such as Santiago de Compostela, become themed tours for non-religious tourists, while accommodations built to shelter pilgrims become trendy stopovers for tired cyclists. However, this can only happen when the original fundamental purpose has largely become obsolete or of relatively minor significance. This is therefore not happening to Islamic infrastructure, in an era when the Islamic religion is growing and flourishing.

Health tourism

As we saw in the context of Europe, health tourism laid the foundations for the development of much of the modern tourism industry in Europe. While it was pioneered by the Romans, it did not become popular again until the sixteenth and seventeenth centuries. It grew then as a response to the unsanitary conditions in many towns and cities. At first, health tourism was simply about exploiting natural phenomena for their medicinal benefits, for example mineral springs and sea water. However, as time went on, these resorts also became centres of fashion and social activity. The history of these spas and resorts was described in more detail earlier in this chapter, in the section on Europe; however, it would be wrong to suggest that this development was confined to Europe. Spa resorts also grew up in other continents, such as those found in the USA in upstate New York.

It would also be incorrect to give the impression that seaside bathing and spa visiting were the only forms of health tourism. In the seventeenth and eighteenth centuries, many wealthy Europeans paid lengthy visits to reputed doctors at renowned medical schools, such as at Montpellier in France. These visits resulted in some of the most famous travel writing of the era, for example Smollett's account of his visit to Montpellier in 1763. Also, for centuries climate has played a major part in health tourism. While in Northern Europe this usually means travelling in search of the sun, it has motivated very different types of tourism flow. Particularly during the age of colonial expansion, European colonists often sought to escape summer heat by moving up to the cooler hills. An excellent example was the practice in India of spending the summer at hill stations such as Shimla. In doing this, the colonists were continuing a much earlier tradition established by the Maharajas.

Health tourism, in Europe at least, is an excellent example of fashion cycles in tourist behaviour. Many of the spas that were so popular between the sixteenth and nineteenth centuries in Europe went into decline in the first half of the twentieth century. They ceased to be socially fashionable, and improvements in health care standards made them less necessary. In some resorts, political instability and the onset of war made them less accessible to their former markets. While this is generally true, there are exceptions, for example Germany, where the involvement of trade unions and social tourism organizations in spa tourism has meant that some have maintained their position. In France, although not in the UK, spas have enjoyed a renaissance in recent years with tourists' growing interest in health. They have again become smart places where health care is combined with leisure facilities and entertainment. The Auvergne region of France, in particular, is exploiting this new interest in spas to develop high-spending forms of health tourism. In recent years the interest in health has led to a rediscovery of seawater bathing as a health-enhancing activity. Thalassotherapy is very popular in France, for example, where companies such as Accor have invested heavily in the necessary facilities. We have also seen the rise of health farms in Europe and the USA, where many men and women take a short break to lose weight and improve their fitness. The most sophisticated modern form of health tourism is that where people travel abroad for medical treatment, to institutions which are perceived to be world leaders in their field, or which offer cheaper treatment than their own country. This cost advantage has been very attractive to health insurance companies in recent years. A case study at the end of this chapter considers the international spa and wellness market.

Social tourism

In general, the holiday market is a commercial market where consumers are asked to pay a full market price for their vacation. However, in a number of countries, tourism and holiday-taking is also encompassed within the realms of welfare policy. Holidays are subsidized in some way, either by government or voluntary sector agencies such as non-profit-making organizations or trade unions. This may be termed social tourism.

This form of tourism is largely absent from the UK, where its only manifestation is in the area of subsidized holidays for carers, offered by some charities and local authorities. However, it is much more prevalent in other countries, notably Germany, Spain and France. In the latter country, social tourism is well developed and its 'infrastructure' includes:

- Chèques-Vacances, which can be exchanged for tourism services
- social tourism holiday villages and centres, operated by non-profit-making associations.

This provision is subsidized by employers, trade unions and the government. However, pressures on public spending are currently casting a shadow over the future of social tourism in France.

While not strictly speaking social tourism, in recent years we have seen attempts by the tourism industry to provide a better service for groups in society who have been largely ignored, or even discriminated against, by the industry. These groups include two in particular:

- consumers with disabilities, including those with mobility problems, impaired sight or hearing difficulties
- single-parent families who are often unable to take advantage of the usual 'family' offers that stipulate that a family means *two* adults and a number of children, which is clearly discriminatory in a world where an increasing number of families have a single parent.

As yet, however, little effort appears to be being made, overall, by the tourism industry, in Europe at least, to encourage people from ethnic minority communities to participate in the mainstream tourism market. In many European countries these communities represent markets that run to hundreds of thousands of consumers. Perhaps, however, the situation reflects the feeling that many ethnic communities have their own established patterns of tourism demand, such as visiting friends and relatives in the country from which their parents and grandparents came. This market is often serviced by specialist suppliers drawn from within the communities. The USA shows that in due course such communities do develop a demand for mainstream travel services, but these may still be met by specialist operators drawn from these communities. This is true, for instance, of the African American market.

Educational tourism

Educational tourism, or travelling to learn, has a long history, from the days when wealthy members of the Greek and Roman elites travelled to increase their understanding of the world. Centuries later came one of the greatest manifestations ever of educational tourism, in Europe at least – the Grand Tour.

In recent decades, educational tourism has developed in a number of ways, of which two are perhaps particularly worthy of note.

- *Student exchanges*, where young people travel to other countries to study and learn more about the culture and language of other people. Such exchanges have developed strongly between educational institutions in North America and Europe. For example, many Americans travel to Aix-en-Provence in France to attend special courses put on for them by the local university. Exchanges between European universities are highly developed between member states of the European Union, thanks to the Erasmus exchange programme. In addition to exchanges, we have also seen a massive growth in young people, particularly from Asia, travelling to Europe, North America and Australasia for their higher education.
- *Special interest holidays*, where people's main motivation for taking a trip is to learn something new. This market has grown rapidly in recent years and now encompasses everything from painting holidays to cookery classes, gardening-themed cruises to language classes. The market is particularly strong among early retired people, the so-called 'empty-nesters'.

Cultural tourism

Cultural tourism is clearly linked to special interest tourism (discussed below), but is broader in scope. The desire to experience other current cultures and to view the artefacts of previous cultures has been a motivator in the tourism market since Greek and Roman times. Today it is extremely popular, and is often viewed positively by tourism policy-makers as a 'good' form of tourism, as 'intelligent tourism'.

Cultural tourism encompasses many elements of the tourism market, including:

- visits to heritage attractions and destinations, and attendance at traditional festivals
- holidays motivated by a desire to sample national, regional or local food and wine
- watching traditional sporting events and taking part in local leisure activities
- visiting workplaces, for example farms, craft centres or factories.

Cultural tourism is the core of the tourism product in many countries and is the main reason why tourists visit these countries. However, concern is often expressed about the impact tourists may have on the cultures they wish to experience, making this a very sensitive sector of the tourism market.

Scenic tourism

The desire to view spectacular natural scenery has stimulated tourists since time immemorial. However, it perhaps really came of age in the nineteenth century, through the influence of the Romantic Movement in the arts. Artists and writers drew inspiration from the natural environment and created popular interest in landscapes. Tourists then began to come to view these same landscapes for themselves, and to follow in the footsteps of the artists.

An example of this phenomenon in the UK is the way in which William Wordsworth's poetry stimulated tourism to the Lake District. Today his houses in the heart of the area, Dove Cottage and Rydal Mount, attract tens of thousands of tourists. Scenic tourism grew dramatically in the previous century both in Europe, particularly in the Alps, and in the USA, where the steady growth of tourism was one of the factors that led to the creation of the world's first national park in 1872. As well as mountains, water-related scenery also became a draw for tourists in the nineteenth century. The Lakes region of Italy and the dramatic coastal scenery of Brittany and Cornwall became popular during this era. We must remember that the original appeal of seaside resorts that we now see as urban areas was often their natural scenery.

Hedonistic tourism

We tend to believe that hedonistic tourism, motivated by a desire for sensual pleasure, is a modern creation, encapsulated in the now classic four s's: sea, sun, sand and sex. However, hedonistic holiday-making has a much longer history. We saw earlier that the Romans practised this form of tourism in their resorts. In the UK such tourism has given rise to the term 'dirty weekend', often associated with the south coast resort of Brighton. In the strict Victorian era, Londoners might take their 'partner', or someone else's partner, off to Brighton where they could behave in ways that were not acceptable in London.

Paris, from the nineteenth century onwards, developed as Europe's first capital of hedonistic tourism. Young men from affluent families were sent there to complete their 'education' in the ways of the world. This often involved visiting brothels, going to risqué shows and gambling. However, other cities also based much of their appeal on hedonism and pleasure-seeking. Writing about Vienna, Steward said 'By far the strongest component of the city's place image was its reputation for frivolity [and] the pleasure-loving nature of its inhabitants' (Steward, 1996).

Hedonistic tourism has reached new peaks in the current era with the rise of the 'sea, sun, sand and sex' package holiday from the 1960s onwards. The promise of hedonistic experiences is now the core offer of some operators, such as Club 18-30, in the UK market. We have also seen the rise of distinct hedonistic market segments in recent years, such as the so-called 'Shirley Valentines', Northern European married older women who travel to Mediterranean resorts in search of romance with local men.

Hedonistic tourism is not a purely European phenomenon; the USA has its notorious 'Spring Break' market which is experienced in many destinations within the USA, Mexico and the Caribbean.

Though often harmless fun, hedonistic tourism is often seen to have a negative impact on both the tourists themselves and the host community: both are at risk from diseases such as AIDS, while the hosts are often offended by the tourists' behaviour.

There is currently considerable international debate about sex tourism, particularly involving Europeans travelling to developing countries for sex with children. This is clearly far from harmless and represents the morally unacceptable face of hedonistic tourism.

Activity tourism

Activity holidays are a more recent development, and are a rapidly growing market. They are based on the desire for new experiences on the part of ever more sophisticated tourists, and are also a reflection of growing social concerns about health and fitness.

Activity tourism is a broad field that encompasses, for example:

- using modes of transport to tour areas that require effort on the part of the tourist, such as walking, cycling and riding
- participating in land-based sports such as golf and tennis
- taking part in water-based activities such as diving and wind-surfing.

Some forms of activity holiday can be criticized in terms of their impact on the physical environment. Golf courses take up valuable greenfield sites, while walking and riding cause erosion. On the other hand, activity tourism is often viewed positively because it improves people's health.

In recent decades we have seen a growth in adventure activities such as bungee jumping and canyoning; destinations such as Queenstown in New Zealand have come to international prominence because of their suitability for adventure activities.

Special interest tourism

Recent years have seen the growth of special interest tourism, where the motivation is a desire to indulge in an existing interest in a new or familiar location, or to develop a new interest in a new or familiar location. Like activity-based tourism, special interest tourism can be either the focus of the whole holiday, or a way of spending one or two days during a holiday.

Special interest tourism is a niche market, somewhat like activity tourism, but different in that it involves little or no physical exertion. The types of interest are diverse, some of the most popular being:

- painting
- gastronomy, both learning to cook and enjoying gourmet meals in restaurants
- military history and visiting battlefields
- visiting gardens
- attending music festivals.

Summary

The list of types of tourism we have just examined is clearly subjective, but it does demonstrate the breadth of the tourism market. It illustrates too that the different types of tourism are linked. For example, religious tourism can also be seen as cultural tourism. It also demonstrates that few forms of tourism are new.

But what about the future? Perhaps the next major development in tourism will be the rise of techno-tourism, that is, tourism based on new technologies such as virtual reality. This could be a revolutionary change where tourism no longer involves travel, and tourism experiences of a kind can be enjoyed from the comfort of the tourist's own home.

Conclusions

To understand present and future tourist behaviour, it is essential that we have an appreciation of the history of consumer behaviour in tourism. For that reason we have focused on discussing the history of tourism demand. However, it is important to recognize that this chapter offers only an outline, full of generalizations, where whole countries have been reduced to a paragraph or less.

Nevertheless, hopefully the reader will have identified a number of key points, notably:

- tourism is older than we often appreciate
- tourists have existed for centuries in many countries, not just in Europe and the USA.

The emphasis of this chapter has been on international tourist flows, but we must also recognize that domestic tourism has, perhaps, a longer history, and is certainly much greater in volume. However, it is harder to measure, and it is the growth of mass international tourism that has been at the forefront of the rise of modern tourism.

Discussion points and essay questions

1. Discuss the ways in which Britain played a major role in the growth of modern tourism.
2. Critically evaluate the contention that 'tourism history was born in Europe but its future lies in Asia and the Pacific' (Horner and Swarbrooke, 1996).
3. Discuss the ways in which business tourism demand has changed over the past 2000 years in terms of both the types of business tourism and business tourism destinations.
4. Using examples, evaluate the suggestion that 'few, if any, tourism markets are new' (Horner and Swarbrooke, 1996).

Exercise

Choose a country from *each* of the following regions of the world:

- Europe
- the Americas
- Africa
- Asia.

For each country, produce a summary of its history as a destination for inbound foreign tourists, using statistics wherever possible.

Finally, compare and contrast the situation in each country and suggest reasons for the similarities and differences.

References

Choy, L.-K. (1995). *Japan – Between Myth and Reality*. World Scientific, Singapore.

Hall, C.M. and Johnston, M.E. (1995). Introduction. Pole to pole: tourism issues, impacts and the search for a management regime in the polar regions. In *Polar Tourism: Tourism in the Arctic and Antarctic Regions*, eds C.M. Hall and M.E. Johnston. John Wiley & Sons, Chichester.

Harrison, D. (1992). *Tourism and the Less Developed Countries*. Belhaven Press, London.

Hitchcock, M., King, V.T. and Parnwell, J.G. (1993). *Tourism in South East Asia*. Routledge, London and New York.

Horner, S. and Swarbrooke, J. (1996). *Marketing Tourism, Hospitality, and Leisure in Europe*. International Thomson Business Press.

Lundberg, D.E, (1990) *The Tourist Business*, 6th edn. Van Nostrand Rheinhold, New York.

Seaton, A.V. (1996). Tourism and relative deprivation: the counter revolutionary pressures of tourism in Cuba. In *Proceedings of the 'Tourism and Culture: Towards the 21st Century' Conference*, eds M. Robinson, N. Evans and P. Callaghan. Centre for Travel and Tourism/Business Education Publishers, Sunderland, UK.

Sharpley, R. (1994). *Tourism, Tourists and Societies*, 2nd edn. Elm Publications, Huntington, UK.

Steward, J. (1996). Tourism place: images of late imperial Austria. In *Proceedings of the 'Tourism and Culture: Towards the 21st Century' Conference*, eds M. Robinson, N. Evans and P. Callaghan. Centre for Travel and Tourism/Business Education Publishers, Sunderland, UK, pp. 203–215.

CASE STUDY 2: The international spa and health wellness market

We have seen that spas played a significant role in the historical development of tourism. While their popularity has declined in countries such as the UK, it is still a very large market worldwide, and some spas are enjoying a renaissance. The World Geothermal Congress of 2010 emphasized the important role of balneology in modern tourism development, and the Congress of 2015 especially focused on Eastern Europe.

THE DEVELOPMENT OF THE SPA MARKET

The history of the spa market goes back a long way, but the growth of the popular spa began in the 1990s. A report published in 1996 by Deloitte-Touche estimated that every year there were some 160 million visits paid to spa resorts in Europe, the USA and Japan alone. The same document suggested that there were over 2000 spa resorts in Japan, nearly 450 in Italy, and 250–300 in each of the USA and Germany.

Deloitte-Touche's research indicates that the proportion of spa visits in a country's overall population was probably highest in Germany and Japan. However, length of stay for Japanese visitors was one of the lowest in the world at around one to two nights, while French visitors were the highest at over 20 nights.

In the same year, the Economist Intelligence Unit published a report on European spas (Cockerell, 1996). This contained a number of interesting statistics, including the following.

- In Germany, spa towns received between 40 and 45 per cent of domestic and international tourist trips, and accounted for around half of all visits to European spas. Spa visiting in Germany was popular with both sexes, and all age and income groups. It was also linked to social tourism and the health service in Germany.
- While German people often also travelled abroad in search of spa treatment, most Italians and French tended to stay at home and use domestic spa resorts.
- The market in France was split between traditional thermal spa resorts and the more modern thalassotherapy complexes. Provision for the former was usually subsidized while that for the latter was almost wholly commercial.
- The motivation for thermal spas was largely medical whereas that for thalassotherapy was not.
- The thalassotherapy market was also younger than the market for thermal spas.
- In 1994, it was estimated that the European international health holiday market involved around 1.7 million tourists, around 1 per cent of all tourism demand in Europe.

The growing popularity of thalassotherapy is illustrated by the creation of new centres, in recent years, in countries including Cyprus, Morocco, St Lucia, Venezuela, Indonesia and Japan.

The increased concern with health and beauty is linked to a growth in new types of resort, including:

- pelotherapy (mud treatment) and heliotherapy (sun treatment) in Israel
- seaweed alyotherapy in Ireland.

To ensure their future, spas are seeking to diversify their offer to attract wider market segments. Some thermal establishments have opened up to day visitors, while others have established other health facilities such as outdoor jogging tracks. Many resorts have sought to become leading venues for major sporting or cultural activities and events. They are also developing better leisure shopping attractions. They are aiming to make themselves attractive to more market segments by offering something for everyone.

THE CONSUMER

There are differences between consumers who choose to go on a spa holiday and those who choose to go for a day spa experience. Market research in the UK (Mintel, 2005) showed that it is women from the 18 to 24-year-old age group who are most likely to express an interest in going on a spa holiday. Evidence suggests that older consumers (over 45s) have little or no interest in going to a spa complex. The rise in day spas has also attracted a new audience with women from higher socioeconomic groups showing a particular interest in this type of experience (Mintel, 2005).

THE SPA MARKET TODAY

The spa market has now become international in nature with consumers travelling to spas as a total holiday, but a larger percentage of the business is part of a total holiday package. This desire to include a spa as part of a hotel complex is a relatively new trend that has fuelled international hotel development across the world. The focus on in-house spas in hotels has brought dividends to a number of hotel groups across the world. The Mandarin Oriental Hotels in London, Miami and New York, for example, have been voted the best in town according to a survey of 17,000 *Condé Nast Traveller* readers in the USA and the UK (Caterer-online.com, accessed 5 April 2005).

The development of spas has also led to the growth of certain resorts on an international basis. Examples of some of these resorts are shown in Exhibit 2.1.

Exhibit 2.1 Examples of worldwide spas

Name of spa	Location
Banyan Tree Spa	Seychelles
Chiva-Som International Health Resort	Thailand
Les Sources de Caudalie	France
Mandara Spa	JW Marriott Phuket Resort and Spa, Thailand
Mandara Spa	The Datai, Malaysia
Mandara Spa	One and Only Ocean Club, Bahamas
Shambhala Spa	Parrot Cay, Turks and Caicos Islands
Six Senses Spa	Soneva Fushi Resort and Spa, Maldives
Spa Village	Pangkor Laut Resort, Malaysia
Willow Stream Spa	The Fairmont Banff Springs, Canada

Source: Condé Nast Traveller (2002)

There has been a growth in spa operators specializing in spa experiences. Some examples of these in the UK are shown in Exhibit 2.2 – competition is quite tough in the UK market, with specialist tour operators competing head-on with mainstream operations.

Exhibit 2.2 Examples of spa operators, UK 2010

Spa operator	Type of business	Countries offered
Caribtours	Tailor-made holidays including spa escapes	Caribbean
Champneys Health Resort	One of the world's largest destination spa groups	UK, India, Switzerland
Erna Low	Promotes spas worldwide (in addition to skiing holidays)	Hungary, Malta, Spain, Switzerland, Cyprus, Portugal, Germany, Austria, Italy, UK, South Africa, India
Healing Hotels of the World	Holistic health and wellbeing	Worldwide
Thermalia	Health and wellbeing holidays	Europe, Sri Lanka, South Africa, Jordan, Cyprus, Slovakia, etc.
Wahanda	Health, beauty, wellbeing website	UK and Europe
Wellbeing Escapes	Spa travel company	Worldwide; Thailand most popular
Luxury operators	Visits to spas as part of a package	
International Travel Connections Ltd		Worldwide
La Joie de Vivre Travel		Tropical locations
Mainstream operators	Visits to spas as part of a package	
First Choice Holidays		Worldwide
TUI UK		Worldwide

Source: Mintel (2005, 2011)

COUNTRIES THAT HAVE DEVELOPED SPA/WELLBEING TOURISM

France was traditionally a country that developed the spa business across the country with different spa and wellbeing destinations. There has been a more recent development of alternative spa destinations which has helped countries to boost their tourist revenues. Exhibit 2.3 outlines some examples of these destinations, and demonstrates that it is important for the national government of a potential spa and wellbeing country to actively promote the destination and become involved in developments and standards.

THE FUTURE OF THE SPA INDUSTRY

Mintel (2005) identified six main trends that are likely to occur in this market. These can be summarized as:

Exhibit 2.3 Countries that have developed spa/wellbeing tourism

Country	Type of spa business	Comment
Austria	Wellness tourism; range of treatments including innovative ideas such as beer baths; bathing treatments; alpine treatments	Sponsored by the Austrian National Secretary for Tourism
Hungary	Historical bathhouses, hot springs and spas; cultural establishments, thermal waters	Government-sponsored development (launched in 2001, the Széchenyi Plan)
Japan	Wellness tourism based on hot springs; long history of spa tourism going back to AD 552	Development of wellness hotels, thalassotherapy centres
Thailand	Spa centres date back 2500 years using local herbs; Thai healing famous	Many spa brand operators; Thai government formed the Federation of Thai Spas in 2004

Source: Mintel (2005)

- emergence of global spa brands – e.g. Banyan Tree
- expanding target markets – e.g. families, males and older consumers
- spa combination holiday – e.g. golf for the man, spa treatments for the woman
- growth in medical spas – e.g. in Central Europe
- increase in quality standards – e.g. standards set by the European Spas Association (ESPA)
- standardization of training – e.g. the development of diplomas in spa therapies.

Additionally Mintel (2011) reinforced the moves towards branding and medical tourism while highlighting additional trends as follows:

- traveller spa facilities – cruise ships, tourist trains (India and China) and long-haul airlines offer spa-related services
- fish therapy – Asian fish pedicure spas
- express spa treatments – treatments of 30 minutes or less, especially in the United States
- spa pods – small spa treatment areas in UK high street department stores
- boot-camp spas – week-long intensive workout courses for the 'cash rich, time poor'
- cryotherapy – specialist spas offering whole-body, low-temperature chambers.

It is predicted that the increase in obesity levels will fuel the growth of spa and wellbeing tourism across the world. Consumers will become particularly interested in the benefits offered by traditional water spas, and budget airlines will enable consumers to reach different destinations on a more regular basis.

DISCUSSION POINTS AND ESSAY QUESTIONS

1. What are the main opportunities and threats that will affect the future growth of the European spa market?
2. Apart from the desire to improve his or her health, what other factors might motivate a tourist to visit a spa?

REFERENCES

Cockerell, N. (1996). Spas and health resorts in Europe. *EIU Travel & Tourism Analyst* 1, 53–77.
Condé Nast Traveller (2002). Online spa guide. www.cntraveller.com
Mintel (2005). *Spa Holidays – UK*. January. Mintel.
Mintel (2011). *Spa Holidays – UK*. October. Mintel.

Main concepts in consumer behaviour, including models of consumer behaviour adapted for tourism

The purpose of consumer behaviour models is to attempt to present a simplified version of the relationships between the different factors that influence consumer behaviour. Various models have been developed to describe consumer behaviour with the intention of trying to control behaviour patterns. However, the models fall short of these objectives, and at best give the reader an appreciation of interactive factors that influence behaviour patterns. It is possible to review only some of the general consumer behaviour models here.

One of the earliest models of consumer behaviour was proposed by Andreason (1965), and is shown in Figure 3.1. The model recognizes the importance of information in the consumer decision-making process. It also emphasizes the importance of consumer attitudes, although it fails to consider attitudes in relation to repeat purchase behaviour.

A second model, which concentrates on the buying decision for a new product, was proposed by Nicosia (1966). This model is shown in Figure 3.2. It concentrates on the organization's attempts to communicate with the consumer, and the consumer's pre-disposition to act in a certain way. These two features are referred to as Field One. The second stage involves the consumer in a search evaluation process which is influenced by attitudes. This stage is referred to as Field Two. The actual purchase process is referred to as Field Three, and the post-purchase feedback process is Field Four. This model has been criticized by commentators because it was not empirically tested and because many of the variables were not defined (Zaltman, Pinson and Angelman, 1973).

The most frequently quoted of all consumer behaviour models is the Howard–Sheth model of buyer behaviour which was developed in 1969. This model is shown in Figure 3.3. It highlights the importance of inputs to the consumer buying process and suggests ways in which the consumer orders these inputs before making a final decision.

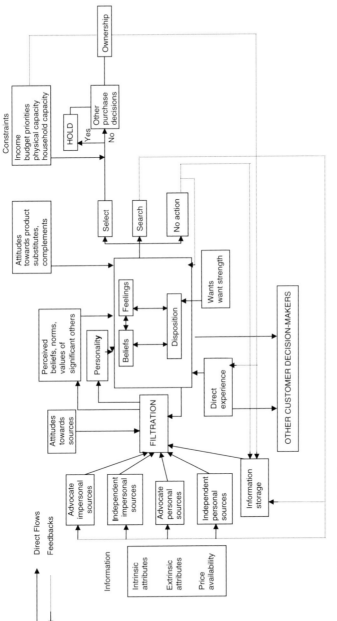

Figure 3.1 Andreason model of consumer behaviour

Source: adapted from Andreason (1965)

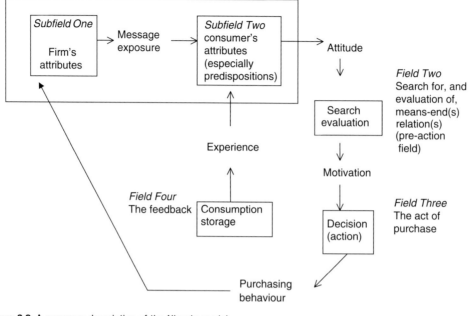

Figure 3.2 A summary description of the Nicosia model

Source: adapted from Nicosia (1966)

The Howard–Sheth model does have limitations, and does not explain all buyer behaviour. However, it was a comprehensive theory of buyer behaviour that was developed as a result of empirical research (Horton, 1984).

More recent research on consumer behaviour concentrates on the exchange processes and attempts to look at the marketer's perspective on the process. One example of such an approach is shown in Figure 3.4. This model was developed by Solomon (1996). He also suggested that consumer behaviour involves many different actors. The purchaser and user of a product may not be the same person. Other individuals may also influence the buying process, such as children when a family chooses a particular holiday. Organizations may also be involved in the buying process, for example a company looking to purchase conference packages.

The models considered so far are useful in academic research. Foxall and Goldsmith (1994) suggest that these models mean little in the absence of a general understanding of how consumers act. They describe consumer behaviour as a sequence of problem-solving stages:

- the development and perception of a want or need
- pre-purchase planning and decision-making
- the purchase act itself
- post-purchase behaviour, which may lead to repeat buying, repeat sales and disposal of the product after consumption.

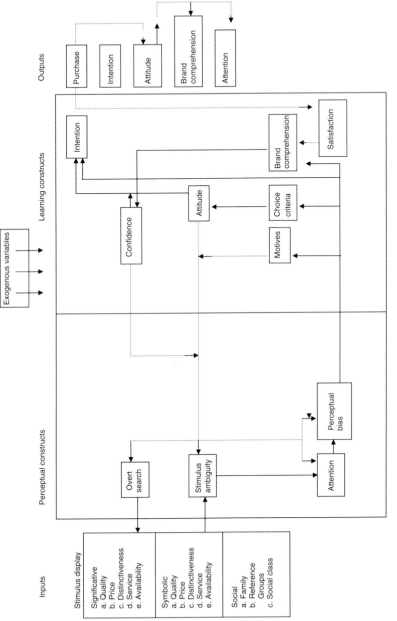

Figure 3.3 The Howard–Sheth Model of buyer behaviour

Source: adapted from Howard and Sheth (1969)

	CONSUMER'S PERSPECTIVE	MARKETER'S PERSPECTIVE
PRE-PURCHASE ISSUES	How does a consumer decide that he/she needs a product? What are the best sources of information to learn more about alternative choices?	How are consumer attitudes toward products formed and/or changed? What cues do consumers use to infer which products are superior to others?
PURCHASE ISSUES	Is acquiring a product stressful or pleasant experience? What does the purchase say about the consumer?	How do situational factors, such as time pressure or store displays, affect the consumer's purchase decision?
POST-PURCHASE ISSUES	Does the product provide pleasure or perform its intended function? How is the product eventually disposed of, and what are the environmental consequences of this act?	What determines whether a consumer will be satisfied with a product and whether he/she will buy it again? Does this person tell others about his/her experiences with the product and affect their purchase decisions?

Figure 3.4 Some issues that arise during stages in the consumption process

Source: adapted from Solomon (1996)

Much of marketing activity, they suggest, concentrates on adapting product offerings to particular circumstances of target segment needs and wants. It is also common to stimulate an already existing want through advertising and sales promotion, rather than creating wants.

The definitions and models that have been presented so far are from general marketing theory. Tourism, by its very nature, is a service rather than a product, which may have a considerable effect on consumer behaviour. Services have been defined by Kotler and Armstrong (2004) as 'Any activity or benefit that one party can offer to another that is essentially intangible and does not result in the ownership of anything. Its production may or may not be tied to a physical product.'

The intangible nature of the service offering has a considerable effect on the consumer during the decision-making process involved with purchase. This, coupled with the high-spend aspect of tourism, means that tourism for the consumer is a high-risk decision-making process. Therefore the consumer will be highly interested and involved in the purchase decision. This was recognized by Seaton *et al.* (1994):

> They involve committing large sums of money to something which cannot be seen or evaluated before purchase. The opportunity cost of a failed holiday is irreversible. If a holiday goes wrong that is it for another year. Most people do not have the additional vacation time or money to make good the holiday that went wrong.

There is a philosophical question as to whether service marketing is substantially different from product marketing (Horner and Swarbrooke, 1996). It is clear, however, that tourism products have many distinctive features which mean that consumer behaviour will be fundamentally different. To cope with these differences, academics have developed definitions and models of consumer behaviour specifically for tourism. These range from more general definitions to more detailed models.

Middleton and Clarke (2001) present an adapted model of consumer behaviour for tourism which is termed the stimulus–response model of buyer behaviour. The model is shown in Figure 3.5 and is based on four interactive components, with the central component identified as 'buyer characteristics and decision process'.

The model separates out motivators and determinants in consumer buying behaviour and also emphasizes the important effects that an organization can have on the consumer buying process by the use of communication channels.

Other models that attempt to explain consumer buying behaviour in tourism have been advanced. Wahab, Crampton and Rothfield (1976) suggest a linear model of the decision-making process in tourism. This is shown in Figure 3.6.

Mathieson and Wall (1982) suggest a linear five-stage model of travel buying behaviour, which is shown in Figure 3.7.

Gilbert (1991) suggests a model for consumer decision-making in tourism, which is shown in Figure 3.8. This model suggests that there are two levels of factors that have an effect on the consumer. The first level of influences is close to the person, and includes psychological influences such as perception and learning. The second level of influences includes those that have been developed during the socialization process, and include reference groups and family influences.

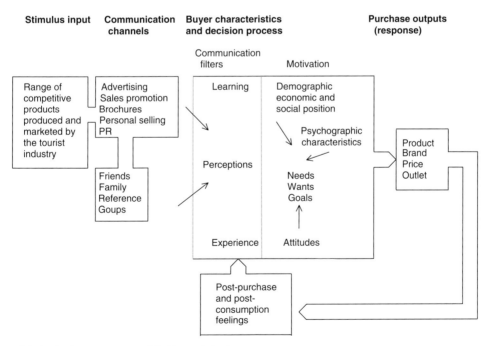

Figure 3.5 A stimulus–response model of buyer behaviour

Source: adapted from Middleton and Clarke (2001)

Initial framework → Conceptual alternatives → Fact gathering → Definition of assumptions → Design of stimulus → Forecast of consequences → Cost benefits of alternatives → Decision → Outcome

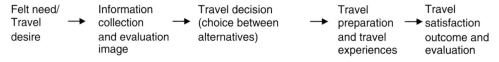

Figure 3.6 A linear model of the tourism decision-making process

Source: adapted from Wahab *et al*. (1976)

Felt need/ Travel desire → Information collection and evaluation image → Travel decision (choice between alternatives) → Travel preparation and travel experiences → Travel satisfaction outcome and evaluation

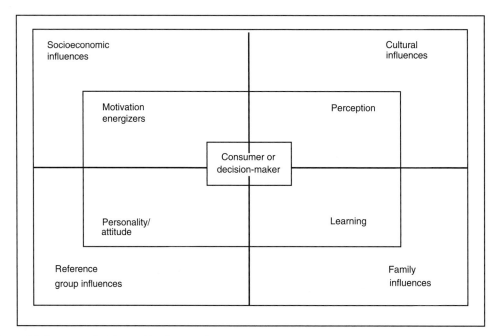

Figure 3.7 Travel-buying behaviour

Source: adapted from Mathieson and Wall (1982)

Figure 3.8 Consumer decision-making framework

Source: adapted from Gilbert (1991)

All these models that have been adapted for tourism offer some insights into the consumer behaviour process involved during the purchase and post-purchase decision stages. The problem with the models is that little empirical research has been conducted to test them against actual consumer behaviour. This is an area that requires further detailed research.

Since the previous edition of this book, research has continued on this vital area. A recent review of all research conducted on the topic from 2000–12 was published in 2014 (Cohen, Prayag and Moital, 2014). This paper, which gives an excellent overview of the literature, suggests that there are nine key concepts underpinning the area: decision-making, values, motivations, self-concept and personality, expectations, attitudes, perceptions, satisfaction, and trust and loyalty. The paper also suggests that there are three important influences on tourism behaviour: technology, Generation Y, and a rise in concern for ethical consumption. The final part of the article suggest areas that warrant further research, including joint decision-making, under-researched segments, cross-cultural issues in emerging markets, emotions, and consumer misbehavior (Cohen *et al.*, 2014). For a full review of the most recent literature on this topic, please refer to this comprehensive article. We will return to these issues later in the book when we consider models of consumer behaviour in tourism in more depth, along with new trends such as green tourism and e-tourism.

Summary

Most consumer behaviour models in tourism seem to be linear and rather simplistic when compared with general consumer behaviour models. Yet, as Figure 3.9 illustrates, the diverse characteristics of tourism mean that consumer behaviour in tourism inevitably will be very complex. The inadequacy of models of tourist behaviour is a subject that we return to in Chapter 6.

Discussion points and essay questions

1. The purchase of a holiday does not result in the consumer owning any physical product. Discuss the effect of this on consumer behaviour.
2. Evaluate the reasons for a consumer choosing to buy a composite tourism product rather than the individual components.
3. The media can have a major influence on consumer choice in tourism. Evaluate the ways in which a tour operator can use this feature to boost sales.

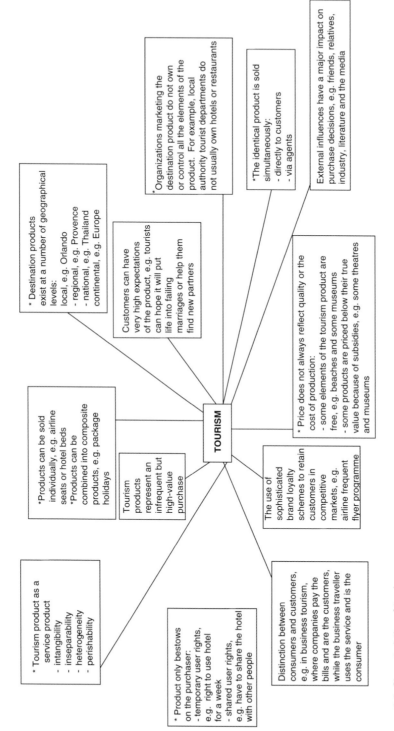

Figure 3.9 Characteristics of tourism

Exercise

Design a small-scale consumer panel that could be used to evaluate the reasons for consumers choosing a particular tourism product.

References

Andreason, A.R. (1965). Attitudes and consumer behaviour: a decision model. In *New Research in Marketing*, ed. L. Preston. Institute of Business and Economic Research, University of California.

Cohen, S.A., Prayag, G. and Moital, M. (2014). Consumer behavior in tourism: concepts, influences and opportunities. *Current issues in Tourism* 17 (10), 872–909.

Foxall, G.R. and Goldsmith, R.E. (1994). *Consumer Psychology for Marketing*. Routledge, London and New York.

Gilbert, D.C. (1991). An examination of the consumer decision process related to tourism. In *Progress in Tourism, Recreation and Hospitality Management*, Vol. 3, ed. C. Cooper. Belhaven Press, London.

Horner, S. and Swarbrooke, J. (1996). *Marketing Tourism, Hospitality, and Leisure in Europe*. International Thomson Business Press.

Horton, R.L. (1984). *Buyer Behaviour. A Decision Making Approach*. Charles E. Merrill, New York.

Howard, J.A. and Sheth, J.N. (1969). *The Theory of Buyer Behaviour*. John Wiley and Sons, New York.

Kotler, P. and Armstrong, G. (2004). *Marketing Management: Analysis Planning, Implementation*, 4th European edn. Pearson Education, Upper Saddle River, NJ.

Mathieson, A. and Wall, G. (1982). *Tourism: Economic, Physical and Social Impacts*. Longman, London.

Middleton, V.T.C. and Clarke, J. (2001). *Marketing for Travel and Tourism*, 3rd edn. Butterworth-Heinemann, Oxford.

Nicosia, F.M. (1966). *Consumer Decision Processes*. Prentice Hall, Upper Saddle River, NJ.

Seaton, A.V., Jenkins, C.L., Wood, R.C., Dieke, P.V.C., Bennett, M.M, MacLellan, L.R. and Smith, R. (eds) (1994). *Tourism: The State of the Art*. John Wiley and Sons, New York.

Solomon, M.R. (1996). *Consumer Behaviour*, 3rd edn. Prentice Hall, Upper Saddle River, NJ.

Wahab, S., Crampton, L.J. and Rothfield, L.M. (1976). *Tourism Marketing – A Destination Orientated Programme for the Marketing of International Tourism*. Tourism International Press, London.

Zaltman, G., Pinson, C.A. and Angelman, R. (1973). *Methodology and Consumer Research*. Holt, Rinehart and Winston, New York.

CASE STUDY 3: Las Vegas, Nevada, USA

INTRODUCTION

Las Vegas is situated in Nevada on the western side of the USA. It is 4000 kilometres from New York City, 450 kilometres from Los Angeles and 900 kilometres from San Francisco. The city is visited by approximately 41 million visitors each year, and has over 151,000 hotel and motel rooms spread throughout the metropolitan area.

Major projects planned for Las Vegas since the turn of the millennium include developments by Trump International in early 2007 and the MGM Mirage Project CityCenter, a mixed-use urban complex of leisure, accommodation and retail space which opened in 2009.

Las Vegas is unsurpassed as a resort because of its impressive range of entertainment, casinos, dining, nightlife and host of other attractions. It has become known as the city that never sleeps, offering the visitor a unique, one-stop, multidimensional vacation.

THE HISTORY AND DEVELOPMENT OF LAS VEGAS

Las Vegas, Spanish for 'The Meadows', was well known as being an oasis-like valley that attracted Spanish travellers on their way to Los Angeles during the gold rush. John C. Fremont led an overland expedition west and camped in Las Vegas Springs on 13 May 1944.

Nevada was the first US state to legalize gambling. This led to the position today where more than 43 per cent of the state general fund is provided by gambling tax revenue. Legalized gambling suffered a brief lull in 1910 when a strict anti-gambling law became effective in Nevada. Legalized gambling returned to Nevada during the Great Depression. The first major resort growth of Las Vegas was completed by Tommy Hull when he built the El Rancho Vegas Hotel-Casino in 1941. The success of this hotel-casino fuelled the massive expansion boom which occurred in the late 1940s when construction of several hotel-casinos and a two-way highway from Las Vegas to Los Angeles took place. One of the earliest resorts was the Flamingo Hotel, which was built by mobster Benjamin 'Bugsy' Siegel who was murdered by an unknown gunman.

The resort was developed extensively during the 1950s. The Desert Inn opened in 1950, and the Sands Hotel in 1952. Other resorts that opened in the 1950s were the Hacienda, the Tropicana and the Stardust hotels. The Moulin Rouge Hotel-Casino opened in 1953 to accommodate the growing black population.

The city realized as far back as 1950 that a way to fill hotel rooms during the slack periods in the year was to encourage the convention business. A 90,000 square foot exhibition hall, the Las Vegas Convention Center, was opened in April 1959. The Las Vegas Convention and Visitors Authority (LVCVA), which is supported mainly by room tax revenue, now attracts more than 2 million convention delegates every year.

Las Vegas has always been at the forefront of gambling and entertainment technology. The resort was one of the first to have multiple slot machines in the 1960s.

Video machines were introduced in the 1970s and computerized slot machines were soon to follow.

Las Vegas developed the concept of the mega-resort when it lost exclusive rights to gambling casinos because gaming was legalized in Atlantic City, New Jersey in 1976. The first of these mega-resorts was the Circus Circus Hotel-Casino, which incorporated an entertainment park, hotel and casino.

Other mega-resorts that have been developed include The Mirage hotel-casino (1989), The Excalibur (1990), The Treasure Island (1993) and the MGM Grand Hotel and Theme Park (1993). These mega-resorts involve huge investment plans. The MGM Grand Hotel and Theme Park, for example, cost $1 billion to build, with its elaborate hotel, casino, theatres arena and theme park.

The city has also been keen to encourage leisure shopping. The multi-million dollar project 'The Fremont Street Experience' was opened in 1995. This shopping centre was designed by the Jerde Partnership to create a lively urban centre which incorporates light, sound and entertainment. A brief summary of the history of Las Vegas is shown in Exhibit 3.1.

Exhibit 3.1 The history of Las Vegas

1892	Discovered by Spanish explorers
1911	The city of Las Vegas is incorporated
1931	Hoover Dam construction begins
1941	El Rancho Vegas opens
1946	Bugsy Siegel opens Flamingo Hotel
1959	Las Vegas Convention Center opens
1975	Nevada gaming revenues reach $1 billion
1989	Mirage opens – 3039 rooms
1990	Excalibur opens – 4032 rooms
1991	Construction of MGM Grand Hotel and Theme Park begins
1993	Grand Slam Canyon Adventure Dome opens
1993	Treasure Island opens – 2900 rooms
1993	Luxor Hotel opens – 2526 rooms
1993	MGM Grand Hotel and Theme Park opens – 5005 rooms
1994	Work begins on the Fremont Street Experience
1994	Boomtown opens a 300-room hotel-casino
1994	The first non-stop charter service from Europe begins from Cologne, Germany
1994	The Fiesta, the first hotel-casino in North Las Vegas, opens
1995	Clark County population is estimated at more than 1 million residents
1995	Visitor Center Hoover Dam opens
1995	Announcement of construction of $420 million Paris Casino Resort
1996	The Orleans Hotel and Casino opens
1997	The New York-New York Hotel and Casino opens on 3 January – more than 100,000 people a day visit the new resort during its first days of operation

1997	Sheldon Adelson breaks ground in April to build the 3000-suite, $1.8 billion Venetian Resort Hotel Casino on the grounds of the original Sands Hotel
1997	The Aladdin Hotel closes on 25 November making way for a $1.5 billion resort hotel and shopping complex
1997	Harrah's Entertainment Inc. buys Showboat Inc. in a $1.154 billion deal
1997	The Frontier Hotel, owned by the Elardi family, is sold to Phil Ruffin, a Kansas industrialist, for $165 million
1998	Starwood Hotels & Resorts buys the ITT Corporation for $14.5 billion; the purchase includes the acquisition of Caesars Palace and the Desert Inn
1998	Northwest Airlines inaugurates non-stop service on 1 June from Tokyo to Las Vegas; Japan Airlines inaugurates non-stop service on 2 October; Korean Airlines starts three non-stop charter flights from Seoul to Las Vegas in August
1998	The Bellagio, billed as the most expensive hotel in the world ($1.7 billion), opens on 15 October
1998	A 66-year-old Las Vegas resident hits a $27.58 million progressive Megabucks jackpot on 15 November at the Palace Station Hotel Casino
1998	Annual gross gaming revenue in Nevada hits the $8.1 billion mark, while the number of visitors to Las Vegas totals 30.6 million people
1999	Harrah's Entertainment Inc. purchases the Rio All-Suite Hotel and Casino for $888 million on 1 January
1999	MGM Grand Inc. buys Primadonna Resorts, taking 100 per cent ownership of the New York-New York Hotel and Casino and Whiskey Pete's, Buffalo Bill's and Primm Valley Resort and Casino in Primm
1999	Mandalay Bay opens on 2 March with 3300 rooms, as does the Four Seasons Hotel with 424 rooms
1999	Phase one of the Venetian Resort Hotel Casino opens on 3 May with 3036 suites
1999	Circus Circus Enterprises changes its name to Mandalay Resort Group
1999	Paris Las Vegas opens on 1 September
2000	A $3 billion deal closes selling Caesars World Inc., including Caesars Palace, to Park Place Entertainment
2000	The Resort at Summerlin changes its name to The Regent Las Vegas
2000	MGM Grand Inc. announces the purchase of Mirage Resorts Inc. in the largest corporate buyout in gaming history
2000	The new Aladdin Resort and Casino opens in August on the Strip
2000	The Desert Inn is bought by casino/hotel entrepreneur Steve Wynn, who implodes it to make way for construction of Wynn Las Vegas, a 2700-room, $2.7 billion property
2000	The MGM Grand Hotel and Casino satellite registration/hotel check-in facility at McCarran Airport opens, the first facility of its kind in North America
2001	Clark County's population reaches 1,498,274, while Las Vegas gets to 506,111
2001	Station Casinos opens the Green Valley Ranch Resort and Spa, a $300 million dollar property in Henderson
2001	The three-millionth marriage certificate is recorded in Clark County on 9 February
2003	Clark County's population reaches 1,641,529; Las Vegas' grows to 535,395

2003	In April, Caesars Palace opens the Colosseum, a $95 million contemporary replica of its namesake in Rome and home to Caesars Palace's newest resident performer, Celine Dion
2003	The Stratosphere releases plans for its latest thrill ride, a teeter-totter-like device situated nearly 900 feet above Las Vegas Boulevard, aptly called X Scream
2003	Las Vegas Premium Outlets open in downtown Las Vegas
2003	The Fashion Show mall completes a $1 billion expansion, including a towering outdoor multimedia platform called The Cloud
2003	Mandalay Bay opens new 1120-suite tower, THEhotel
2004	Harrah's Entertainment purchases Binion's Horseshoe
2004	The Strip dims its lights for President Ronald Reagan's passing; other dignitaries to receive such a remembrance upon their passing have included President John F. Kennedy, Rat Pack members Sammy Davis Jr, Frank Sinatra and Dean Martin, and George Burns
2004	The Las Vegas Monorail, a $654 million mass transit system, opens to the public
2004	Las Vegas Sands releases new details about its planned $1.6 billion Palazzo casino resort on the Strip
2005	Las Vegas celebrates its Centennial year throughout 2005, beginning with the New Year's fireworks display; its 100th birthday on 15 May was celebrated with the world's largest birthday cake and a re-creation of the 1905 land auction that started the Las Vegas community as we know it today
2005	Wynn, Las Vegas, the destination's newest mega-resort, opens on 28 April
2005	MGM Mirage announces Project CityCenter, an 'urban metropolis' with 4000 hotel rooms and 1650 condominium units, at nearly $5bn the largest privately funded project in the USA
2006	Nevada celebrates 75 years of legalized gaming
2006	McCarran Airport ranked fifth busiest passenger airport according to Airports Council International North America's annual traffic rankings
2006	Nevada's restaurant industry growing more quickly than in any other US state
2007	MGM Mirage CityCenter offers first residences for purchase
2007	Tropicana Resort and Casino celebrates 50 years on Las Vegas Strip
2007	Las Vegas Springs Preserve opens: 180-acre cultural and historic attraction considered the 'birthplace' of Las Vegas, features museums and galleries
2007	Las Vegas joins New York City, San Francisco and Los Angeles as the only cities with restaurants and hotels featured in the Michelin Guide 2008
2008	Caesars Palace raises its table game limit to the highest in Las Vegas, while in the Colosseum Bette Midler becomes the new resident headliner, replacing Celine Dion after a five-year run
2009	CityCenter starts recruiting for its 12,000 jobs
2009	Las Vegas Convention Center celebrates Fiftieth Anniversary
2009	British Airways starts daily non-stop flights to/from Heathrow
2012	McCarran International opens a new Terminal 3 building for domestic flights
2013	Las Vegas Global Business District unveiled for the Convention Center
2014	'What happens here stays here' marketing campaign celebrates 10 years
2014	Las Vegas hosts Red Bull Air Races for the first time

Source: LVCVA.com

LAS VEGAS TODAY

Las Vegas has become America's top resort destination, offering visitors an unparalleled range of hotels, casinos and entertainment. The climate is very warm, particularly in the months of April to September. Las Vegas averages 294 days of sunshine per year and the average daily rainfall is very low. The dazzling strip offers a wide range of entertainment, and the Fremont Street Experience provides an exciting shopping experience. Las Vegas has its own international airport – McCarran International Airport – where an average of more than 750 scheduled and charter flights arrive every day. Las Vegas has abundant nightlife and offers superstars, five major production shows, and Broadway musicals all year round. The city also has the extravagant strip casinos where visitors marvel at the glittering array of buildings and lights.

Hotels and motels in Las Vegas

The city has approximately 150,544 hotel/motel rooms (in 2014) which appeal to a wide cross-section of visitors, whether they are holidaymakers, convention visitors or business travellers. The city has accommodation ranging from multi-suite accommodation, which is bigger than an average home, to low-budget, one-room hotel accommodation. Many Las Vegas hotels offer a wide range of added-value services, including multilingual staff, gaming lessons for the novice gambler, entertainments, golf courses, travel and entertainment reservation desks, and tour attraction desks. Las Vegas has fifteen of the twenty-five largest hotels in the world and has specialized in the development of mega-resorts, which incorporate hotels, leisure facilities, casinos and attractions. Large hotels include The Venetian, MGM Grand, Wynn, Luxor, Bellagio, The Mirage, Circus Circus, Bally's and Caesars Palace.

A full range of restaurants offering a wide range of cuisines is also available in Las Vegas.

Casinos in Las Vegas

Gambling is one of the major attractions of Las Vegas. The city offers non-stop gaming in a variety of casinos. The gambler can take part in poker, craps, baccarat, blackjack, roulette and slot machines on a 24-hour basis. The resorts also offer classes in gambling for those visitors who are unfamiliar with the games. The range of casinos in Las Vegas is shown in Exhibit 3.2.

The city also hosts year-round gaming tournaments which have their own rules, entry fees and promotional packages that may include a two- or three-day stay, dining specials, parties and banquets. Most tournaments are open to the public and take place at casinos or resorts.

Exhibit 3.2 Casinos in Las Vegas (2014)

Aliante Casino Hotel and Spa	JW Marriott Las Vegas Resort Spa and Golf
Aria at CityCenter	Las Vegas Club Casino
Arizona Charlie's Boulder	LINQ Hotel and Casino
Arizona Charlie's Decatur	Longhorn Casino
Bally's Las Vegas	Lucky Club Hotel and Casino
Barley's Casino	Luxor Las Vegas
Bellagio	Mandalay Bay
Best Western Plus Casino Royale	Mardi Gras Hotel and Casino
Bighorn Casino	MGM Grand Hotel/Casino
Binion's Gambling Hall and Hotel	Main Street Station
Boulder Station Hotel and Casino	The Mirage
Buffalo Bill's	Monte Carlo Hotel and Casino
Caesars Palace	M Resort
California	New York-New York Hotel and Casino
Cannery Casino and Hotel	Oasis at Gold Spike
Circus Circus Hotel/Casino/Theme Park	The Orleans Hotel and Casino
Club Fortune Casino	O'Sheas Las Vegas
Cosmopolitan	Palace Station
The Cromwell	Palazzo
Day's Inn Town Hall Casino	Palms Casino Resort
D Las Vegas	Paris Las Vegas
Eastside Cannery Casino Hotel	Planet Hollywood
El Cortez	Plaza
Eldorado Casino	Poker Palace
Ellis Island Casino	Primm Valley Resort and Casino
Encore at Wynn Las Vegas	Red Rock Casino Resort and Spa
Excalibur	Rio
Fiesta Henderson	Sams Town
Fiesta Rancho	Santa Fe Station
Flamingo	Searchlight Nugget Casino
Four Queens	Siegal Slots and Suites
Fremont	Silver Nugget Casino
Golden Coast	Silver Sevens Hotel and Casino
Golden Gate Hotel and Casino	Silverton Hotel and Casino Lodge
Golden Nugget Hotel and Casino	Skyline Restaurant and Casino
Gold Strike Hotel and Gambling Hall	South Point
Green Valley Ranch Resort and Spa	Stratosphere
Hard Rock Hotel and Casino	Suncoast
Harrah's Las Vegas Casino Hotel	Sunset Station
Hooters	Texas Station
Jerry's Nugget	Treasure Island
Jokers Wild	Tropicana Las Vegas

Tuscany Suites and Casino	Westin Las Vegas Hotel and Casino
Venetian	Whiskey Pete's
Westgate Las Vegas Resort and Casino	Wynn Las Vegas

Source: LVCVA.com

Las Vegas shows

Las Vegas offers visitors a range of spectacular shows in many of the resorts and hotels in the city. The range of shows on offer in the 2015 season is shown in Exhibit 3.3. There are also adult shows, comedy shows and magic shows.

Exhibit 3.3 A sample of shows in Las Vegas, 2015

- Absinthe – Spiegeltent at Caesars Palace
- B-A Tribute to the Beatles – Saxe Theatre, Planet Hollywood
- Blue Man Group – Venetian Las Vegas
- Carrot Top – Atrium Showroom Luxor Hotel
- Celine Dion – Colosseum at Caesars Palace
- Chippendales – Rio in Las Vegas
- Cirque de Soleil Mystere – Mystere Theatre, Treasure Island
- Cirque du Soleil O – O Theatre Bellagio
- David Copperfield – Hollywood Theatre, MGM Grand
- Elvis-Experience – Westgate Las Vegas
- Evil Dead the Musical – V Theatre Miracle Mile, Planet Hollywood
- Fantasy – Atrium Showroom, Luxor Hotel
- KA-Cirque Du Soleil – MGM Grand, Las Vegas
- Menopause the Musical – Harrah's Hotel
- Michael Jackson Live – Stratosphere Las Vegas
- Million Dollar Quartet – Harrah's Showroom, Harrah's Hotel
- Mystère-Cirque Du Soleil – Treasure Island, Las Vegas
- Olivia Newton-John – Flamingo Showroom, Flamingo Hotel and Casino
- 'O' – Cirque Du Soleil – Bellagio Las Vegas
- Penn & Teller – Rio Las Vegas
- Rita Rudner – Main Showroom Harrah's
- Rock of Ages – Rock of Ages Theatre, Venetian
- Steve Wynn's Show Stoppers – Encore Theatre, Wynn Las Vegas
- Superstars on Stage – V Theatre at Planet Hollywood
- Terry Fator – Terry Fator Theatre, Mirage
- Thunder from Down Under – Excalibur Hotel and Casino
- Tony n' Tina's Wedding – Windows at Bally's

- V The Ultimate Variety – V Theatre Planet Hollywood
- Vegas the Show – Saxe Theatre, Planet Hollywood Resort and Casino
- X Rocks – Rio Crown Theatre
- Zumanity – Cirque Du Soleil – New York/New York Hotel and Casino

Source: LVCVA.com

Recreation in Las Vegas

A full range of recreation facilities are available for visitors to Las Vegas. The weather encourages sport on a year-round basis. Most Las Vegas resorts have swimming pools and many also have health clubs and, increasingly, spa facilities. Championship golf courses and a host of tennis facilities are available.

Attractions and sightseeing in Las Vegas

The hotels and casinos of Las Vegas offer a varied range of attractions; the latest range is shown in Exhibit 3.4.

Exhibit 3.4 The range of family attractions available in Las Vegas hotels and casinos, 2014

- Adventuredome at Circus Circus Hotel-Casino
- Dolphin Habitat at The Mirage Hotel – 2.5 million gallon pool with dolphins
- Fremont Street Experience – 12.5 million lights and 550,000 watts of sound in a canopy transforms five blocks of Downtown into a light-and-music show
- Gondola ride at the Venetian – which also houses Madame Tussauds Las Vegas
- Hershey's Chocolate World at New York-New York hotel-casino
- High Roller – 550-foot-tall observation wheel
- Shark Reef at Mandalay Bay Hotel-Casino – one of the world's largest aquariums
- Stratosphere Tower – the tallest free-standing observation tower in the USA – Sky Jump and Big Shot Ride
- Titanic: The Artifact Exhibition at Luxor Hotel – includes real artifacts from the ship along with a replica of the Titanic's staircase

Source: LVCVA.com

It is also possible for visitors to Las Vegas to visit areas of outstanding beauty in the surrounding area. There are scenic destinations such as the Great Basin National Park in Northern Nevada, the Grand Canyon in Arizona, Death Valley in California, and Bryce Canyon and Zion National Park in Utah. Visitors can travel to these areas by car, bus or plane.

Getting married in Las Vegas

Las Vegas has become known as the wedding capital of the world. There are more than 50 wedding chapels in the city, and more than 115,000 couples obtain wedding licences every year in Las Vegas. There is no waiting period and blood tests are not required for weddings in Las Vegas, which explains the reason for its popularity. There are many organizations that can organize any style of wedding for visitors, ranging from a black-tie affair to exchanging vows on a motorcycle at a chapel's drive-up window. The more exotic types of wedding ceremony include getting married in a hot-air balloon, or being married by an Elvis Presley impersonator. The Excalibur Hotel can provide medieval costumes for a ceremony which is reminiscent of Merry Old England. The Tropicana has a thatched-roof bungalow in a Polynesian setting, which is also offered for wedding ceremonies.

THE LAS VEGAS CONVENTION AND VISITORS AUTHORITY

The LVCVA was created in 1995 by the Nevada Legislature to manage the operations of the Las Vegas Convention Center and to promote southern Nevada throughout the world as a convention location.

The LVCVA has been very successful and there has been remarkable growth of visitors coming to Las Vegas because it is an excellent resort location. The Las Vegas Convention Center opened in 1959 with 90,000 square feet of space. The Center is now one of the largest meeting facilities in the USA, with more than 1.6 million square feet of usable space available.

The LVCVA also operates The Cashman Center with 100,000 square feet of meeting and exhibition space, a 10,000-seat baseball stadium, and a 2000-seat theatre.

The twelve members of the LVCVA board of directors have overseen the growth of Las Vegas as a business, conference and resort destination. They have a set policy to increase the number of visitors to Las Vegas and Clark County each year. The LVCVA board of directors has representatives from Clark County, the City of Las Vegas, North Las Vegas, Henderson, Boulder City and Mesquite, as well as from the hotel/motel industry and the business and financial communities. The LVCVA board can use their combined knowledge and experience to help Las Vegas maintain its leadership in the tourism and convention business.

VISITORS TO LAS VEGAS

Growth has shown a steady rise over the past decade (Exhibit 3.5), with tourist numbers of over 41 million in 2014. The volume of visitors to Las Vegas is fairly evenly spread throughout the year.

The spend by visitors to Las Vegas is also growing steadily, with visitors spending $33.7 billion in the Las Vegas area during 2004. The average visitor spend depends on the reason for the visit. Trade show delegates and convention visitors spend more than the average leisure visitor. This shows the importance of trade conventions and

Exhibit 3.5 Visitor volumes to Las Vegas, 1986–2014

Year	Visitor volume	Room inventory
1986	15,196,284	56,494
1988	17,199,808	61,394
1990	20,954,420	73,730
1992	21,886,865	76,523
1994	28,214,362	88,560
1996	29,636,361	99,072
1998	30,605,128	109,365
2000	35,849,691	124,270
2002	35,071,504	126,787
2004	37,388,781	131,503
2006	38,914,889	132,605
2008	37,481,552	140,529
2010	37,355,436	148,935
2012	39,727,022	150,481
2014	41,126,512	150,544

Source: LVCVA (2014)

delegates for the Las Vegas economy; where 5.2 million delegates attended 22,000 conventions and business meetings in 2014.

The LVCVA has been trying to encourage the growth of the convention and trade show market in Las Vegas. The success of this activity can be seen when the growth figures for this type of business are considered. The figures for the 1986–2014 period are shown in Exhibit 3.6, and show an explosion of convention visitors in the early part of this century, though it should be noted that in 2001 the LVCVA extended its methodology to try to capture all business visitor numbers from both trade conventions and smaller business related meetings.

The demographic profile of visitors to Las Vegas is shown in Exhibit 3.7. It can be seen that there is an approximately equal split of male and female visitors, and a large proportion of visitors to Las Vegas are from the USA itself. International visitors post-millennium typically represent 18 per cent of all visitors, which is a fairly constant figure.

The LVCVA undertakes an annual visitor profile study which reveals some interesting information about the behaviour of visitors when they are in Las Vegas. The highlights of this survey for 2014 are shown in Exhibit 3.8. It can be seen that there is high repeat purchase behaviour among visitors to Las Vegas, with over 80 per cent of visitors returning during the 2004–14 period. Tourists represent a high percentage of visitors to Las Vegas, but business and convention visitors are also an important part of the market, particularly as they have a higher per capita spend on average. Arrival by air represents an important part of the market, although arrival by other methods of transport, such as car or bus, is equally important. This will be explored in more detail later. Room occupancy is predominantly in pairs, although single and triple occupancy

Exhibit 3.6 Growth in convention attendance in Las Vegas, 1986–2014

Year	Number of conventions	Attendance
1986	564	1,519,421
1988	681	1,702,158
1990	1,011	1,742,194
1992	2,199	1,969,435
1994	2,662	2,684,171
1996	3,827	3,305,507
1998	3,999	3,301,705
2000	3,722	3,853,363
2002*	23,031	5,105,450
2004	22,286	5,724,864
2006	23,825	6,307,961
2008	22,454	5,899,725
2010	18,004	4,473,134
2012	21,615	4,944,014
2014	22,103	5,169,054

* LVCVA methodology changed to include all business meeting data therefore representing all business related visitors.

Source: LVCVA (2014)

Exhibit 3.7 Las Vegas visitor demographics

Visitor type	1994	2004	2010	2012	2014
Male (per cent)	50	52	50	51	49
Female (per cent)	50	48	50	49	51
Mean age (years)	47.1	49	49.2	44.8	45.2
Retired (per cent)	26	26	27	19	20
Married (per cent)	66	73	79	75	80
US resident (per cent)	86	87	82	83	81
International (per cent)	14	18	18	17	19

Source: LVCVA (2014)

are also important. Single occupancy is particularly important in the business and convention market.

Visitors to Las Vegas often come on multiple visits during any one year and short stays are more common than longer vacations. Visitors with children represent a small part of the market, probably explained by the high incidence of gambling in the resort, which is not always appealing to families. Large numbers of visitors to Las Vegas do participate in some gambling during their visit, and often spend a large proportion of the day in this activity. A smaller proportion of visitors also gamble outside Las Vegas.

Exhibit 3.8 Las Vegas visitor profile highlights 2004–14

Trait	2004	2010	2012	2014
First vs repeat (per cent)				
First-time visitor	19	18	16	19
Repeat visitor	81	82	84	81
Purpose of current visit (per cent)				
Vacation/pleasure/gambling	67	76	76	77
Business/convention	16	17	16	15
Other	17	7	8	8
Transportation (per cent)				
Air	47	41	43	42
Ground (auto/bus/RV)	53	59	57	58
Room occupants (per cent)				
One	11	13	13	11
Two	74	77	71	73
Three	8	6	7	8
Four or more	7	5	9	8
Other trip characteristics				
Number of visits in past year	1.8	1.7	1.6	1.6
Adults in party	2.6	2.4	2.4	2.4
Nights stayed	3.6	3.6	3.3	3.2
Visitors with children (per cent)	10	7	11	10
Expenditures per visitor ($)				
Food and drink (per trip)	238.8	256.82	265.11	281.88
Transportation (per trip)	64.64	62.87	57.77	68.83
Shopping (per trip)	124.39	122.8	149.29	149.77
Shows (per trip)	47.21	49.28	42.89	47.56
Sightseeing (per trip)	8.01	7.21	9.63	14.49
Hotel/motel room (per night)	86.22	79.64	93.13	86.55
Gambling behaviour				
Gambled while in Las Vegas (per cent)	87	80	72	71
Daily hours gambled	3.3	2.9	2.6	2.6
Gambling budget ($)	544.93	466.20	484.70	530.11
Origin (per cent)				
Eastern states	10	6	7	7
Southern states	13	11	11	12
Midwestern states	7	12	11	9
Western states	48	54	54	53
California	31	30	31	33

Trait	2004	2010	2012	2014
Origin (per cent)				
Arizona	6	7	6	6
Foreign	13	18	17	19
Ethnicity (per cent)				
White	80	86	75	77
African American	6	5	5	4
Asian/Asian American	7	3	9	10
Hispanic/Latino	7	6	8	8
Other	0	1	3	1

Source: LVCVA (2014)

A large proportion of visitors to Las Vegas come from the Western states of America and California (79 per cent in 2004 rising to 86 per cent in 2014). This helps explain the importance of road transport to the city. A smaller percentage of visitors come from abroad (13 per cent in 2004 rising to an average of 18 per cent in recent years). The large majority of visitors have a White ethnic origin, though in recent years Asian and Hispanic visitor numbers have been rising. There has been a steady growth in visitor arrivals by air over a ten-year period, especially by passengers travelling on scheduled airlines, as opposed to charter airlines where there has been a small decline. The growth of arrivals by scheduled airline can be explained by the fact that business and convention visitors are growing in numbers. Convention attendees are much more likely to use scheduled airlines than charter airlines.

The reasons for visiting Las Vegas have also been researched by the LVCVA. The results of this are shown in Exhibit 3.9.

Exhibit 3.9 Reasons for visiting Las Vegas (2014)

Visitor type	First time (per cent)	Repeat (per cent)
Vacation/pleasure	69	42
Convention/corporate meeting	5	10
Friends/relatives	8	11
Other business	2	6
To gamble	4	14
Special event	3	7
Wedding	5	3
Passing through	3	5
Other	1	1

Source: LVCVA (2014)

Tourists come to Las Vegas for a variety of reasons. One of the primary motivations is vacation and pleasure, which is available in the resort's casinos and hotels. Las Vegas also offers the tourist unparalleled entertainment opportunities, including shows, eating experiences and attractions.

One issue for hospitality operators in Las Vegas has been the balance between gambling and other activities, particularly when they have been trying to encourage children to visit their operations. Tourists have also been encouraged to visit Las Vegas by the impressive range of golf courses that have been developed around the fringes of the city.

It is also becoming popular among foreign visitors to combine a visit to Las Vegas with a more extensive tour of other parts of the USA.

THE LAS VEGAS VISITOR PROFILE SURVEY

The Las Vegas Visitor Profile Survey is conducted on an ongoing basis so that an assessment of the Las Vegas visitor and trends in visitor behaviour is shown over time. The survey involves personal interviews with a sample of visitors near to hotel-casinos and motels (3600 during 2014). Statistically significant differences in the behaviour, attitudes and opinions of visitors from year to year are highlighted in the annual report.

A summary of results from the 2014 survey is shown in Exhibit 3.10.

Exhibit 3.10 Summary of the 2014 Las Vegas Visitor Profile Survey

	Data
Demographic profile (per cent)	
Married	80
Employed	64
Retired	20
White	77
40 years or older	57
From Western USA	53
Household income of $40,000 or more	85
Reasons for visiting (per cent)	
For vacation or pleasure	77
Attendance at convention or trade show	15
Other	8
Trip characteristics and expenditures	
Visitors travelling in party of two (per cent)	67
Average party size (persons)	2.4
Visitors in party with a member under 21 (per cent)	10
Average length of stay in Las Vegas (nights, days)	3.2, 4.2
Visitors stayed in a hotel (per cent)	94
Gaming behaviour and budgets	
Visitors who said they gambled while in Las Vegas (per cent)	71
Average gambling budget ($)	530.11

Demographic profile (per cent)	Data
Entertainment (per cent)	
Visitors attending a show during their stay	65
Visitors who came just to gamble	2

Sample size: 3600 personal interviews.

Source: Las Vegas Visitor Profile (2014)

This survey shows that a high percentage of visitors to Las Vegas were white, married and over 40 years old. A high percentage of visitors came for vacation or pleasure, although attendance at conferences was also important. A large proportion of visitors stayed in hotels, and gambled regularly while they were in Las Vegas, although gambling as a reason to visit is declining over time.

PROFILE OF INTERNATIONAL TRAVELLERS TO LAS VEGAS

Las Vegas has managed to attract international visitors to the city and is now the sixth most popular city within the USA for overseas visitors (2013–14), surpassed by New York (first), Miami (second), Los Angeles (third), Orlando (fourth) and San Francisco (fifth). However, Las Vegas is ranked only sixteenth in the United States as the international airport of entry (2014).

The principal source of international travel statistics for the USA and Las Vegas is the US Department of Commerce's International Trade Administration (ITA), which conducts an ongoing survey of international travellers to the USA. The National Travel & Tourism Office (NTTO) within the ITA is now responsible for reporting international visitor statistics in the USA. The origin of visitors arriving by air is shown in Exhibit 3.11.

Exhibit 3.11 Origins of visitors to the United States, 2014

Traveller residence	International arrivals	Percentage
United Kingdom	3,972,655.00	11.5
Japan	3,579,363.00	10.4
Brazil	2,263,865.00	6.6
People's Republic of China	2,188,387.00	6.4
Germany	1,968,536.00	5.7
France	1,624,604.00	4.7
South Korea	1,449,538.00	4.2
Australia	1,276,124.00	3.7
India	961,790.00	2.8
Italy	934,066.00	2.7
Colombia	881,219.00	2.6
Spain	700,084.00	2.0
Argentina	684,727.00	2.0

Traveller residence	International arrivals	Percentage
Venezuela	615,975.00	1.8
Netherlands	615,856.00	1.8
Sweden	543,336.00	1.6
Switzerland	486,506.00	1.4
Taiwan	413,048.00	1.2
Ireland	395,331.00	1.1
Israel	355,466.00	1.0
Russia	343,310.00	1.0
Ecuador	335,275.00	1.0
Norway	310,204.00	0.9
Denmark	305,331.00	0.9
Belgium	280,121.00	0.8
Saudi Arabia	275,770.00	0.8
Dominican Republic	271,724.00	0.8
New Zealand	260,601.00	0.8
Chile	248,512.00	0.7
Peru	246,438.00	0.7

Source: OTTI (2014)

There are differences between travellers from different countries in terms of the types of activities they take part in during their stay in Las Vegas and their average daily expenditure. Gambling and shopping are the top leisure activities for all overseas visitors to Las Vegas. Visitors from countries such as Australia, Republic of China, Taiwan, Switzerland and Germany are particularly interested in casinos and gambling. The Japanese, an important segment of all overseas visitors, are particularly heavy spenders in Las Vegas.

One challenge that the LVCVA will face in the future is how to attract an increasing number of overseas visitors, particularly in the quieter periods of the year. The hotels, resorts and casinos will have to decide on their particular target market and design their products and services accordingly.

CONCLUSION

Las Vegas has developed as the entertainment capital of the USA. It has evolved from its early development as a gambling centre into a wider leisure and entertainment base as gambling restrictions were lifted in other areas of the USA. Las Vegas attracts visitors from the USA, and also a growing number of overseas visitors who book either independently or as part of package holidays. An important part of the development of Las Vegas as a destination has been the growth of the city as an ideal location for trade fairs, conferences and conventions. The city has ambitious plans for the growth of this business into the next century.

However, it also performs the role of the place to go to do things you can't do at home – or don't want to do at home for fear of what neighbours and friends might think. Hence the well known saying 'what happens in Vegas stays in Vegas'.

DISCUSSION POINTS AND ESSAY QUESTIONS

1. Las Vegas has been developed as a place to visit for gambling. Discuss the opportunities and threats that this could bring to the city in its quest to attract new market segments to Las Vegas.
2. Las Vegas has become the wedding capital of the world. Discuss the reasons for this market development. Outline the opportunities that this development brings to Las Vegas and the wider business community.

REFERENCES

LVCVA (2014). *Las Vegas Visitor Profile Study*. Las Vegas Convention and Visitors Authority. Note: All LVCVA.com data taken from website for last full year of data (2014).

OTTI (n.d.). Monthly Tourism Statistics. US Office of Travel & Tourism Industries, Washington, DC. http://travel.trade.gov/research/monthly/arrivals/

The purchase-decision process

In this part, we look at the factors that influence tourists to purchase a particular tourism product. Part 3 goes on to consider the ways in which we can model how these factors are translated into the final purchase decision.

The factors influencing tourists' purchasing decisions are divided into:

- **motivators** – those factors that motivate a tourist to wish to purchase a particular product
- **determinants** – those factors that determine to what extent tourists are able to purchase the products they desire.

However, before we move on to the two chapters that cover these issues, perhaps we should begin with a few words about the tourism product itself.

- The product is **complex and multi-layered** in that:
    - it has both tangible elements (hotel beds, food etc.) and intangible elements (service delivery)
    - it can range from a simple one-night stay in a hotel or a day trip to a theme park to a tailor-made eight-week round-the-world itinerary.
- The tourist buys an **overall experience** rather than a clearly defined product. The experience has several clear phases:
    - the anticipation phase before the trip commences
    - the consumption phase during the trip
    - the memory phase after the trip has ended.
- The tourist is **part of the production process** in tourism, which means that their:
    - attitudes, mood, and expectations affect their evaluation of their tourist experience rather than just the quality of the product they are offered by the industry
    - behaviour directly impacts on the experience of their fellow tourists with whom they share a resort, aircraft or hotel.

- The tourist experience is heavily **influenced by external factors**, which are beyond the control of the tourist or the company that sells them a product. These external influences include weather, strikes, war and disease outbreaks.

In this part of the book, we restrict ourselves to a consideration of one type of tourist product, the package holiday. This is the most complex tourism product and is the one that distinctly separates tourism products from those of other industries such as hospitality and transport.

Out of necessity, we will have to generalize about the subject and about the motivators and determinants that affect tourists. But we must recognize that, as Ryan (1997) says: 'The context, meanings, and experiences of tourism can vary from holiday to holiday, from tourist to tourist. To talk of the "tourist experience" seems to imply a homogeneity which, in reality, is not always present.'

4

Motivators

Introduction

A wide range of factors motivate consumers to buy tourism products. In this chapter we examine the motivators that encourage tourists to make particular purchase decisions. We begin by outlining the range of motivators that are thought to influence tourists, then discuss how motivators vary between different types of tourism product and different groups of people.

It is important to recognize that there is still a dearth of detailed, reliable research on this subject, across the whole breadth of tourism. Some of the comments in this chapter therefore represent subjective observations on the part of the authors. However, in most cases many other academics and practitioners would concur with these observations.

The number and range of motivators

Motivating factors in tourism can be split into two groups:

- those that motivate a person to take a holiday
- those that motivate a person to take a particular holiday to a specific destination at a particular time.

There are many potential motivators that could relate to either or both of these factors. Furthermore, there are a number of potential 'variations on a theme' for each individual motivator, and myriad ways in which they can be combined.

No widely recognized way exists of categorizing the main motivating factors in tourism. Some of the major ones are outlined in Figure 4.1.

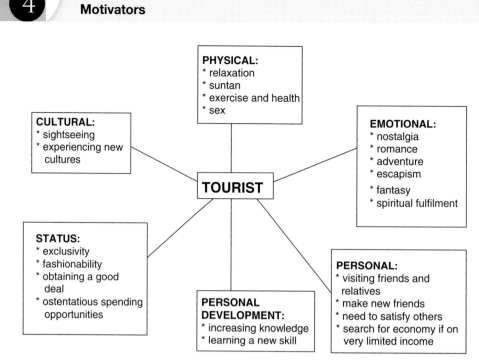

Figure 4.1 A typology of motivators in tourism

However, there are other ways of classifying motivators in tourism and the wider field of leisure. We now go on to outline some of these.

The leisure motivation scale

In 1983, Beard and Raghob developed a model called the leisure motivation scale, which seeks to clarify motivators into four types, based on the work of Maslow (1943). The four types are as follows.

- The **intellectual** component, which assesses the extent to which individuals are motivated to engage in leisure activities involving mental activities such as learning, exploring, discovery, thought or imagery.
- The **social** component, which assesses the extent to which individuals engage in leisure activities for social reasons. This component includes two basic needs – the need for friendship and interpersonal relationships, and the need for the esteem of others.
- The **competence-mastery** component, which assesses the extent to which individuals engage in leisure activities in order to achieve, master, challenge and compete. The activities are usually physical in nature.
- The **stimulus-avoidance** component, which assesses the desire to escape and get away from over-stimulating life situations. For some individuals it is the need to avoid social contact, to seek solitude and calm conditions; for others it is the need to rest and unwind.

We have to recognize, first, that the motivators which make people wish to take a holiday are not universally present. Some people appear to have little or no desire to take a holiday, for whatever reason.

Motivators and the individual tourist

Every tourist is different, and so are the factors that motivate them. The main factors that determine individual tourists' motivations are likely to be as follows.

- Their **personality**, in other words, are they:
  - gregarious or a loner?
  - adventurous or cautious?
  - confident or timid?
- Their lifestyle, which provides the context for their purchase decision. The motivations are likely to be different for people who are very concerned with being fashionable, or are preoccupied with their health, or live alone and want to make new friends, or enjoy partying.
- Their past experience as a tourist with particular types of holiday, both positive and negative.
- Their past life – most notably nostalgia. This could include where they spent their honeymoon, or military battles in which they have taken part.
- Their perceptions of their own strengths and weaknesses, whether these relate to their wealth or their skills.
- How they wish to be viewed by other people.

We must also recognize that motivators change over time for each individual in response to changes in their personal circumstances. These circumstances might include:

- having a child, or meeting a new partner
- an increase or reduction in income
- worsening health
- changing expectations or experiences as a tourist.

Multiple motivations

No tourist is likely to be influenced by just one motivator. They are more likely to be affected by a number of motivators at any one time.

Office workers staring out of their office windows in suburban London today may be motivated by a desire to take any holiday, anywhere, to escape the monotony of their daily working life. However, they may have a number of other motivators that would influence the type of holiday they would like to take. They may, for example, want to:

- escape a wet spell at home, enjoy some sun and get a suntan
- take some physical exercise as a contrast to their sedentary lifestyle and to improve their health
- pursue a hobby, whether it be surfing or eating Italian food
- widen their circle of friends or find a new partner
- see a particular church or museum
- relax.

Most people's holidays represent a compromise between their multiple motivators. Either one motivation becomes dominant, or a holiday is purchased which ensures all of the motivators can be at least partly satisfied.

Shared motivators

We rarely take holidays alone, but who we take them with has an influence over the factors that influence our decisions.

Imagine a woman who is married and the mother of two young children, a member of a women's football team and a churchgoer. Her motivations may be different depending on which group she is intending to holiday with. If she is taking a trip with her children, then meeting their needs and keeping them happy may be her main motivation. On the other hand, she and her husband may be taking a trip on their own, to celebrate their wedding anniversary, in which case romance may be the main motivator. When she takes a trip to play football with her team, it may be seen as escapism or a chance to indulge her passion for playing football. Finally, with her fellow churchgoers she may be seeking spiritual fulfilment from a trip.

It is rare for every member of a holiday party to share exactly the same motivators. Differences in this respect undoubtedly account for much of the stressful side of holiday-making.

Many trips represent a compromise among those in a group of people travelling together, whereby:

- the views of a dominant member may prevail
- each member will go their own way for at least part of the time
- the group will stay together but each member will be allowed to choose what they will all do on one or two days.

Expressed and real motivators

We do not always express our true motivations.

- We might not feel our motivations will be seen by others as acceptable. It can be difficult to admit that you are only going on holiday to party and enjoy casual sex. It is far easier to talk about a more general desire to relax, unwind and 'have a good time'.

- We may not always recognize our motivations – they may be subconscious or unconscious.
- We might recognize that our motivations are apparently conflicting. For example, we may want to relax by dancing and partying all night!
- We may be aware of contradictions between our motivating factors and our actual behaviour. We may claim to want to improve our French when we go to France and meet French people. Then, because of our circumstances and budget, and perhaps due to fear, we might book a stay in an English-owned villa, in a village in the Dordogne where there seem to be few French people and everyone speaks English. This could be the result of an unfortunate chain of events – or the outcome of the triumph of a subconscious motivator not to be humiliated in public, on holiday, because of our current lack of ability to speak French.

Perhaps we can best describe the points made above through a mini-case study of a hypothetical family, the Browns.

THE BROWN FAMILY

In 2000, Mr and Mrs Brown married and took their honeymoon on the French Riviera. Both were keen sailors and chose this destination because they wanted to be able to go sailing together every day. They were besotted with each other, and every evening they sought the most romantic places they could for late candlelit dinners. Dancing and having sex were high on their list of priorities and they did not care if they never spoke to another person during the whole of their holiday. Both were young and adventurous and took part in a range of other activities such as rock-climbing and ballooning. Mrs Brown would have also liked to look around the art museums but her husband was not interested, so she gave in because she did not want her husband to be unhappy.

By 2015 things have changed. The Browns now have two young daughters, and their relationship has deteriorated. Mr Brown is still obsessed with sailing but Mrs Brown has given it up. This year they are on holiday with friends at an old farmhouse on a Greek island. They say this is because they have not seen these friends for many years. However, their real motive is to minimize the need for them to have to talk to each other, and to give them an opportunity to share the childcare and go off separately from time to time. The whole holiday has been planned around keeping the children happy, for they know that if the children are miserable, everyone in the group will have an awful holiday. Mrs Brown secretly hopes to meet a new lover on the beach while her husband is out sailing. Mr Brown wants to sail to help him relax. However, one evening they go together, at their friends' suggestion, for a candlelit dinner in a romantic restaurant overlooking the harbour. The evening is a disaster – there is an icy atmosphere and they barely speak to each other.

Mrs Brown spends much of her time taking part in her new interest of horse-riding, which she took up following last year's holiday in Majorca, when she tried riding for the first time. Mrs Brown chose the farmhouse because it has a swimming pool to keep the children happy, and all modern conveniences in the kitchen to minimize the work involved in preparing meals and doing the dishes. This matters a lot because, these days, Mr Brown rarely helps out in the kitchen. Before coming away they told their neighbours they were taking a holiday to relax. The truth is that it was a last attempt to see if they could rescue their ailing marriage.

This mini-case study illustrates some of the points made above, and also shows the close link that exists between motivators and determinants. The latter subject will be taken up in Chapter 5, but let us now return to the question of motivators.

Motivators and different market segments

Not only are motivators different for each individual tourist, but perhaps they also vary between different market segments. The tourism industry seems convinced that segments are based on demographic criteria, assuming that:

- young people want to party, relax, drink heavily, have sex, dance and make lots of new friends
- elderly people have a preference for sedate activities such as bowls and bingo, and to be obsessed by nostalgia
- parents are preoccupied with the need to keep their children happy, and also want to escape from their parental responsibilities from time to time to spend time together.

There has been some research to test the motivating factors for different demographic groups. In 1996, Kaynak et al. published a study of Irish travellers' perceptions of salient attributes that led to their travel preferences regarding major foreign holiday destinations. This study found significant differences between tourists of different ages, genders, educational attainment, income and marital status. Young people preferred vacations that gave opportunities for activity-based holidays, while older travellers sought restful destinations with sightseeing opportunities. The more highly educated respondents showed a preference for destinations that offered opportunities for nature-based or cultural activities. On the other hand, those people with a lower level of educational attainment stressed the importance of a vacation where they could try new and unfamiliar activities that were very different from their everyday life. Those on lower incomes saw their holiday as a chance to get away from the monotony of everyday life and indulge in activities that built up their self-confidence. Higher-income earners wanted an intellectually stimulating holiday with excitement, and the chance to increase their knowledge of the destination area.

Motivators and gender

One aspect of demographics which the tourism industry seems to believe determines personal motivators is gender. Different products such as golf trips or shopping trips seem to be based solely on a desire to match the perceived motivators of men and women. However, when we look at a range of personal motivators, there is some evidence to suggest that there is, in fact, relatively little difference between the sexes.

Research quoted by Ryan (1995) noted that, for 14 motivators, in three cases there were significant differences in the weighting given to them by men and women. Women placed rather more value on trying to use a holiday to:

- avoid daily hustle and bustle
- relax physically
- relax emotionally.

National and cultural differences

As yet, relatively little research appears to have been done on national and cultural differences in relation to motivators. This is surprising at a time when more and more tourism organizations are seeking to sell their products to people in other countries.

We know that in some instances there are great similarities between groups of countries in terms of motivators. People in northern European countries and the northern states of the USA are often motivated by the desire to develop a suntan. However, in hot countries such as India and Saudi Arabia, the intention is to take trips to the cooler hilly areas to escape the intense heat at lower altitudes.

Some motivators are universal, such as nostalgia and romance, and the desire to see sights, although actual behaviour will be influenced by the nationality and culture of the tourist.

Many people around the world seek some form of spiritual fulfilment. However, the desire for such fulfilment and the wish to embark on a pilgrimage to gain it is more common generally among Muslims than Christians.

Motivators and different types of tourism product

Marketers clearly try to link the products they develop to the factors that motivate their target markets. Conventional wisdom certainly seems to indicate a belief that some motivators are closely associated with different types of tourism product. This is perhaps best illustrated in the visitor attractions sector. Figure 4.2 suggests some possible links between motivators and different types of visitor attraction.

Theme park	- excitement - risk and adventure - escapism - status if it has the best 'white-knuckle ride'
Museum	- learn something new - nostalgia - status if internationally famous
Art gallery	- aesthetic pleasure - relaxation - pursue special interest in art - status, if seeing world famous paintings
Leisure shopping complex	- escapism - search for a bargain - status, if buying designer label product
Golf course	- exercise - make new friends - status, if it is a prestigious course

Figure 4.2 Major motivators and different types of visitor attractions

We can see that there are some different motivators for different types of products, but there are also common ones such as status. Most of us are interested in status, but its meaning varies from one type of attraction to another.

It is also important to recognize that the motivators listed in Figure 4.2 are highly generalized. They ignore the fact that attractions serve many markets which each have their own different motivators. Young people at a theme park may want excitement for themselves, but grandparents may go there with their grandchildren to please them. Families may search out the gentler rides, while parents may want the nostalgic pleasure of revisiting a park they visited as children.

Motivators and the timing of purchase decisions

Motivators can also vary depending on when the decision to purchase a holiday is made. A last-minute booking may reflect a desire to obtain a discounted bargain or a wish to surprise a partner, or be a response to stress at work. Alternatively, a vacation booked many months in advance may be a result of a desire to:

- visit a famous annual event where early booking is essential to secure accommodation and flights
- enjoy the pleasure of looking forward in anticipation to the holiday.

Conclusions

It appears that the issue of motivation is highly complex and depends on a range of factors, including:

- the personality and lifestyle of the potential tourists
- their past experiences
- who they are planning to take a vacation with
- their demographic characteristics
- how far in advance they book their trip.

It will become clear that there are great similarities between motivators and determinants. There is a thin line, a grey area, between our desires and the factors that determine our actual behaviour.

REALITY TELEVISION SHOWS, TOURIST BEHAVIOUR AND TOURISM ORGANISATIONS

One phenomenon we have seen in a number of countries in recent years is 'reality' television shows based around tourism organisations and tourist behaviour. We will illustrate this through UK-based examples. There are several main types of programme.

- Hotel based – where cameras go behind the scenes to see what happens and show incidents in the lives of both staff and guests. An early example in the UK was 'Hotel', set in the Britannia Adelphi hotel in Liverpool, broadcast in 1997. It showed examples of poor service and lost tempers amongst staff, and after the first show was broadcast the owners claimed that it misrepresented the hotel – but they must have anticipated that bad things make more watchable TV than good things. In recent years there have been a string of programmes looking behind the scenes of luxury hotels, such as the Savoy in London and the Burj-al-Arab in Dubai. Here the focus is on how the rich live and the high level of personal service they demand.
- Airline based – where viewers get to see interactions between staff and passengers around the check-in function. These tend to be a little repetitive, revolving around lost passports, drunken passengers, missed flights, delayed flights and lost baggage. In the UK there have been several different series featuring the charter airline EasyJet. Again, both customers and staff often look bad in the scenarios

that play out. In addition, there have been international spin off series, including one in the USA which focused on the budget airline Southwest. There have also been shows that are less 'fly-on-the-wall' and more showcases giving a very positive view of the company portrayed; recent UK examples have focused on Virgin Atlantic and British Airways.

- Airport based – where the cameras show what happens behind the scenes at an airport. These tend to be informative, but also feature vignettes around passengers and their problems. In 2015 UK TV had programmes about both Gatwick and Stansted airports that were more informational, and were gentle and undramatic. A rather more edgy show aired at the same time about Bangkok airport, where a major element of the show focused on the personalities of the staff, some of whom were 'larger-than-life' characters.
- Cruise ship based – where again viewers get to see behind the scenes, largely from the point of view of the staff. One such show was 'The Cruise', which featured one of the ship's entertainers, Jane McDonald, who became a TV presenter and recording artist as a result of her appearance on the show.
- Resort-based – where the focus is on the behaviour of tourists, which is normally bad behaviour. There are a number of series looking at hedonistic tourists, called 'What happens in X', utilising a phrase originally associated with Las Vegas. There have been versions of this show covering Sunny Beach in Bulgaria and Kavos in Greece. The coverage is sensationalized and designed to shock and titillate. Other resort-based shows have focused on the 'reps', the tour operator's staff who work in the destinations. Other programmes have portrayed the problems associated with tourism in destinations including the 'Costa del Crime'.

All these shows – and those listed above are just a selection – are voyeuristic to some extent, but staff and customers are clearly willing to participate in them. To what extent they reflect reality is debatable: it is likely that both will behave differently when cameras are present.

Some staff members have become minor celebrities as a result of participating in these programmes, and TV companies have made significant sums from what is, after all, cheap-to-produce television.

It is a struggle to understand why companies would wish to participate. Given that the best television is based on crises and lost tempers, the camera focuses on showing what happens when things go wrong. Half an hour of watching things going wrong could lead potential customers to believe that the quality of service is not all it should be.

There are two other kinds of 'reality' TV programmes about tourism that we are increasingly seeing on our screens.

'Coach Trip' is a show where strangers are put together on a bus and taken on a trip around Europe, experiencing a variety of activities and interacting with each other. At regular intervals people are voted off the trip by their fellow travellers. This pseudo-sociological kind of show has been replicated in other contexts, for example:

- putting very different families together in a large villa and seeing what happens
- getting families to try each other's preferred holidays – of course, the researchers choose types of holiday they know the other family will hate.

In these cases, conflict and the machinations between participants are the highlights of the show.

The second type of programme is those based on investigative journalism, where journalists investigate particular issues. There are serious 'heavy news' programmes about everything from airport security to exposés of sex tourism in destinations hosting mega-events such as the World Cup and the Olympics. There are also edgy programmes where a 'celebrity' presenter sets out to explore an issue. A current example on UK television is 'Stacey Dooley Investigates', in which a young woman looks at issues ranging from the working and living conditions of hotel workers in Mexico to the sale of drugs in coastal resorts in Bulgaria. These have been criticized as sensationalist, but they perhaps reach an audience that would not watch more serious investigative journalism programmes. Finally, there are what we can term 'consumer protection' programmes, where the aim is to support customers fighting against unjust treatment by tourism organisations and organisations in other industries. These injustices could be unfair extra charges, a holiday ruined by building work at a hotel, or food poisoning on a cruise ship. The programmes set out to obtain redress for the aggrieved traveller – and to entertain the wider audience at the same time.

There seems little reason to believe that these types of programme will not continue to increase. They are cheap to make, and audiences watch them.

Discussion points

1. Why do you think there has been a growth in this kind of programming in the UK in recent years?
2. Why might a company agree to participate in these shows?

Discussion points and essay questions

1. Examine the ways in which an individual's personality may affect their motivators in relation to taking a holiday.
2. Discuss the view that consumers from different demographic market segments will be motivated by a different set of factors.
3. Compare and contrast the likely motivators of people taking a 'sun, sea, sand and sex' holiday to a Greek island as against those on an upmarket cruise around the Caribbean.

Exercise

Design and implement a questionnaire survey of a small number of adults to try to ascertain the main motivating factors influencing their choice of holiday. Then produce a critical evaluation of your survey to highlight and account for its weaknesses.

References

Beard, J. and Raghob, M.G. (1983). Measuring leisure motivation. *Journal of Leisure Research* 15 (3), 219–228.

Kaynak, E., Kucukemiroglu, O., Kara, A. and Tevfik, D. (1996). Holiday destinations: modelling vacationers' preferences. *Journal of Vacation Marketing* 2 (4), 299–314.

Maslow, A.H. (1943). A theory of human motivation. *Psychological Review* 50 (4), 370–396.

Ryan, C. (1995). Learning about tourists from conversations: the over 55s in Majorca? *Tourism Management* 16 (3), 207–215.

Ryan, C. (ed.) (1997). *The Tourist Experience: A New Introduction*. Cassell, London.

CASE STUDY 4: Adventure tourism in New Zealand

INTRODUCTION – WHAT IS ADVENTURE TOURISM?

There is growing consumer interest in adventurous pursuits as part of a holiday. But what is adventure tourism? Swarbrooke *et al.* (2003) suggest there is no single characteristic that sums up the nature of 'adventure'. They do, however, identify certain characteristics or qualities that are associated with adventure tourism, and these are shown in Exhibit 4.1.

Exhibit 4.1 Core characteristics of adventure tourism

- Uncertain outcomes
- Danger and risk
- Challenge
- Anticipated rewards
- Novelty
- Stimulation and excitement
- Escapism and separation
- Exploration and discovery
- Absorption and focus
- Contrasting emotions

Source: Swarbrooke *et al.* (2003); Mintel (2011)

They also identified the themes that have been influential in the historical development of adventure tourism, and these are shown in Exhibit 4.2.

Exhibit 4.2 Themes in the historical development of adventure tourism

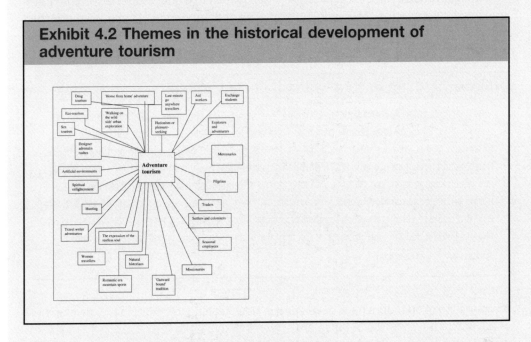

It is well recognized that adventure travellers are not one uniform group. Adventure travellers may be older people who want to experience new things, backpackers who want holidays that are different, or a new group of consumers who see adventure as an exciting alternative to the more traditional holiday (Mintel, 2001b).

The different types of adventure travel have also been identified by Mintel (2001b) and these are shown in Exhibit 4.3. Adventure travel incorporates a wide range of different experiences and activities, and appeals to a wide cross-section of market segments.

Exhibit 4.3 Different types of adventure travel

- **Destination driven** – the consumer picks a particular country or region to explore
- **Vehicle** – the travel is based around the means of transport, e.g. boat or off-road vehicle
- **Non-vehicle** – the travel is based around walking or running
- **Activity-driven** – e.g. camping, hiking, cycling, scuba diving, snorkeling
- **Family** – the family goes as a unit for an adventurous experience
- **Multi-activity** – the travel package incorporates a number of activities
- **Extreme activity** – extreme sports are the basis of the travel
- **Ethical** – the travel involves some element of sustainability
- **Prestige** – the travel involves status-building

Source: Mintel (2001b)

ADVENTURE TOURISM IN NEW ZEALAND

New Zealand has become recognized as a destination that encourages adventure travel in many different forms. The wide open spaces and temperate climate have provided the country with an opportunity to exploit this type of tourism. Exhibit 4.4 shows that the country is aiming actively to develop this type of tourism experience.

Exhibit 4.4 Adventure tourism in New Zealand

New Zealand's landscape and temperate climate lend themselves to outdoor activities. The country is renowned for its range of adventure pastimes – the best known being bungee jumping, jetboat riding, rafting and skiing. But adventure means different things to different people, and the best aspect of the New Zealand adventure scene is that it provides activities rated from 'soft' to 'extreme' – from hiking and waterskiing to mountain climbing and caving. The adventure tourism industry makes the most of having a country surrounded by sea, criss-crossed by rivers and lakes, covered in native bush and with a central spine of spectacular snow-capped mountains. There's something for everyone who enjoys the outdoor lifestyle and the special sense of freedom the relatively sparsely populated land provides.

Source: www.newzealand.com

A wide range of operators have developed in New Zealand to underpin the development of adventure travel. Some of these are shown in Exhibit 4.5.

Exhibit 4.5 More adventures than time

Being a creative bunch, New Zealand adventure operators are always adding new activities, and new dimensions to the available activities. The best source of information on these is from www.newzealand.com, where thousands of operators are listed. Where available, the websites of the official professional bodies associated with or related to these pastimes are listed below.

Abseiling/rappelling

Bungee

Canoeing/kayaking (www.rivers.org.nz)

Canyoning

Caving (www.massey.ac.nz)

Diving (http://nzu.org.nz)

Fly by wire

Gliding (www.gliding.co.nz)

Hang gliding (www.nzhgpa.org.nz)

Heli-hiking

Heli-skiing

Horse riding

Hot air ballooning

Hunting

Jet boating

Off road driving (www.nzfwda.org.nz)

Orienteering (www.nzorienteering.org.nz)

Parapenting

Parasailing

Rafting (www.internationalrafting.com; www.slalomnz.org.nz)

Rock climbing (www.climb.co.nz)

Sailing/boating (www.msa.govt.nz; www.cbes.org.nz; www.nzmarine.com; www.yachtingnz.org.nz)

Skiing (www.newzealand.com/uk/skiing)

Sky diving

Snowboarding

Snowshoeing

Surfing (www.slsnz.org.nz)

Motorcycle tours	Water-skiing
Mountain climbing (www.mountainsafety.org.nz)	Windsurfing
Mountain biking (https://alpineclub.org.nz;	Ziplining
www.climb.co.nz; www.nzmga.co.nz)	Zorbing
	(www.newzealand.com/uk/plan/business/zorb-new-
	zealand)

Source: www.newzealand.com

The country has also developed adventure experiences which are possible because of the wide open spaces that are available in the country. One example of this is the Great New Zealand Trek, which it is possible to complete on foot, bike or horseback. Details of this trek are shown in Exhibit 4.6.

Exhibit 4.6 The Great New Zealand Trek

Travel the length of New Zealand on horse, mountain bike or foot in The Great New Zealand Trek. This is a unique way for people to travel the country in 12-week-long stages of around 250 kilometres.

The first stage started from Cape Reinga to Kohukohu in Northland from 11–19 March 2006, and raised $22,048.13 for the MS Society in Wellington. Stage 2 continued from the Hokianga in 2007, finishing at the bottom of the Pouto Peninsular. 2014 saw stage 9 being the first stage in the South Island, and the stages will continue until participants reach Bluff in Southland in 2018.

Participants choose their mode of transport and travel between 30 and 45 kilometres per day for six days with a rest day halfway.

The Great New Zealand Trek is supported by a crew of 80 people and will offer luxuries from professional caterers, massage, luggage, transport, hot showers, movies, bar and café, to entertainment such as a talent quest, mechanical bull, karaoke and slave auctions.

The week lets participants experience the outdoors while meeting like-minded people from around the world.

The 'open route' system will ensure the enjoyment and safety of participants. Instead of controlling the pace with a lead and end rider, the track, which is off-road wherever possible, will be marked with red ribbons and marshals will be positioned along the way, allowing people to travel as quickly or slowly as they wish.

'After all, it is a holiday', says event organizer Stephen Old, who organized the inaugural Great New Zealand Horse Ride in 1996 attracting 483 riders, making it the largest horse ride of its kind in the world. Since organizing his last Great New Zealand Horse Ride in 2000, he has worked in the film industry as Horse Coordinator for *The Lord of the Rings trilogy* and *The Last Samurai* followed by stunt work on *King Arthur* in Ireland.

'The Great New Zealand Trek is a very unique experience that I believe will grow into a Kiwi icon, capturing the interest of people from all walks of life', says Old.

The Great New Zealand Trek raises funds for the Multiple Sclerosis Society of New Zealand. Old sold the Trek to a charitable trust in 2013.

Source: www.newzealand.com

Certain areas of New Zealand promote themselves as particularly suitable for adventure travel. Queenstown, for example, advertises itself as a town where tourists can undertake a wide range of adventurous activities (Exhibit 4.7). It is interesting that this web page also gives hints for booking a range of accommodation, and links to the web pages of other companies that operate adventurous activities in the area. This allows travellers to put together their own holiday package.

Exhibit 4.7 Queenstown – the active capital

All of our South Island trips have at least one free day in Queenstown because there is so much to do here! This glamorous town is nestled on the shores of Lake Wakatipu beneath the majestic Remarkables mountain range. Today this premier visitor destination is known as the 'adrenaline capital of the world', but Queenstown originally got its name because 'it was fit for Queen Victoria'.

Queenstown has more than its share of breathtaking scenery and a diverse range of attractions, but it's the 'cruisy' locals whom international visitors find most enchanting. We located our main office in Queenstown because our staff enjoy the outdoor lifestyle so much – but we're not the only ones who like it here. In 1998 Queenstown was again voted 'Friendliest Foreign City' in a poll of 37,000 readers of *Conde Nast Traveler,* a top US publication. In the same publication, we were positioned as the 14th best city in the world (the only New Zealand destination to rank in the top 20) alongside others such as Vienna, London, Paris and Hong Kong. In the winter, Queenstown transforms into a popular ski resort to rival its glamorous sister city Aspen, Colorado.

Queenstown has repeatedly won accolades year after year. In 2014 Queenstown was named Australasia's Leading Destination at the World Travel Awards, and as New Zealand's number one destination in the 2014 Travellers' Choice Awards by TripAdvisor.

Its scenic environs has also achieved global awareness through successful films such as *The Lord of the Rings* trilogy.

For adrenaline junkies who live for the next rush, Queenstown is the perfect place to spend a few days bungee jumping, white-water rafting, jet boating, or trying whatever the newest craze happens to be. Others who prefer a more relaxed pace can take one of the many scenic walks, join a wine tasting tour, ride up the gondola, or relax by a warm fire at one of the local pubs. There are also plenty of bars and clubs to choose from if you'd like to go out for a night on the town.

Your guides can help you plan your free day in Queenstown when you arrive and even make bookings for you, but we'll try to cover some of the many activities, walks, tours and trips available here. Don't worry, most tours can be booked when you get to town and there are lots of 'combo' packages available if you can't choose just one! There's enough to keep even the most active person busy, and it's the perfect place to just sip a latte at an outdoor cafe and do some world-class people watching.

Hiking

Although there's plenty of opportunity to, you don't have to spend money to have a good time in Queenstown. There are about a dozen well marked hikes in town that you can explore on your own, and many more just a short taxi ride away (and hitchhike back like we locals do). Ask your guide for a map or pick one up at the Department of Conservation (DOC) office when you get into town. Our favourite is up to Ben Lomond for amazing views of the lake, town and surrounding mountains. Start at the Fernhill roundabout just past the youth hostel, and take One Mile Creek Track up to Lomond Crescent via Skyline Road, then Bobs Peak at Skyline Chalet. The last hour up to the summit is pretty steep, but worth the climb (Moderate, 3 hours to Saddle one way; a quick ride back down, and you can take the gondola one or both ways. For an easier hike, take the Sunshine Bay walking track that starts/finishes about 1 km past the Fernhill roundabout on Glenorchy Road (Easy, 1 hour return). Or stroll along the lakefront in Queenstown Gardens and learn to play frisbee golf (Easy, 15 to 45 minutes).

Mountain biking

You can often borrow one of our bikes or rent a mountain bike in town to explore some of the famous single tracks in the area. Charge down Skipper's Canyon if you dare, or ride up to Moke Lake with a picnic on a nice day. For a gentler ride, try the Frankton track or the Sunshine Bay track.

Bungee jumping

Queenstown is the home of bungee jumping. A.J. Hackett created the very first commercially available jump, the Kawarau bridge, which is still in use today. Since that first site in 1988, bungee jumping has become a worldwide phenomenon and there are now numerous sites to choose from in town.

Jet boating

Jet boating is also very popular for a real-life rollercoaster ride. Just imagine what you can do in a very powerful, highly maneuverable craft that only requires 2 inches of water! The most famous ride is through the dramatic Shotover Canyon where you'll skim across the river inches away from the cliff face. There's a multitude of jet boating trips available in and around Queenstown.

Whitewater rafting

Many people choose to go rafting while in Queenstown, and once again there are lots of rivers (Class II–V) and operators to choose from, ranging from novice-friendly to experienced paddlers only. Depending on the time of year and river, you could enjoy a scenic helicopter ride to the put-in.

Skydiving

Want something even more extreme? How about flying to high altitude over stunning scenery. As the anticipation builds, the countdown begins, your tandem instructor gives the signal – and together you make 'the Ultimate Jump'. Free fall at awesome speeds of up to 200 kph. The speed, the sensation of flying and the sheer excitement make skydiving an adrenaline rush that cannot be equalized.

Golf

Arguably New Zealand's most scenic golf course, Kelvin Heights was opened in 1975 and is located on a peninsula overlooking Lake Wakatipu, close to picturesque Queenstown. The magnificent setting ensures that this is a course much sought out by local and overseas golfers. The sheer beauty of the surroundings makes it a delightful course to play in any season. The snowcapped peaks of the nearby mountains, together with the ever-changing colours of the lake will ensure a round you'll long remember and cherish. Millbrook, away from town is a very prestigious 'Country Club' resort and world-class golf course.

Fishing

If you want fresh fish for dinner, it's not far from your plate. New Zealand has some of the best trout and salmon fishing in the world, and Queenstown is a renowned fishery and popular base for anglers in the South Island. From a few hours fishing from a boat charter on Lake Wakatipu with an experienced guide to helicopter-accessed fly fishing in a remote area for the more experienced fishermen, there are options for every level of angler. Or bring your own rod and try your luck in some of the numerous lakes and rivers around Queenstown.

Wine tasting

The Queenstown and Central Otago wine region is the fastest growing wine region in New Zealand. This area is renowned for its Pinot Noir and has won more gold medals for this variety than any other New Zealand Region. This region is also achieving recognition for quality Chardonnay, Riesling, Pinot Gris and Sauvignon Blanc varieties. Wine tours of the vineyards in the area are available and there's a new tasting room overlooking Lake Hayes featuring the best of the bunch.

Other things to do

High-country horses – spend an hour, two hours or a whole day in the saddle, soaking up the stunning scenery in nearby Glenorchy.

Accommodation

Blue Peaks Apartments & Lodge – quality visitor accommodation and true Southern hospitality – we stay here on our trips.

A Line Hotel and Aurum Apartments – very nice, centrally located – another place we sometimes stay.

Heritage Hotel – very nice, located on Lake Wakatipu.

Thomas's Hotel – on the Waterfront – Queenstown's closest lakeside accommodation, right in the heart of town. Four floors of accommodation – with rooms ranging from standard or budget (twins, doubles, triples) to multishare rooms, all with en suites.

Colonial Village Motel and Apartment Accommodation – Queenstown motel accommodation offering character, charm and stunning views.

A few great examples of some of the 'boutique' accommodations to be found around Queenstown

The Stone House – located in the heart of Queenstown, New Zealand's spectacular adventure playground, The Stone House offers exclusive and intimate boutique accommodation combining personalized old-world charm and modern comforts.

The Dairy Guesthouse – provides luxury bed and breakfast accommodation in Queenstown, New Zealand. Experience fine lodging in the heart of Queenstown.

Brown's Boutique Hotel – designed along traditional European lines, this small intimate hotel is only three minutes' walk to the centre of town and features stunning views of the Remarkables mountain range from every room.

Source: www.queenstownnz.co.nz

CONCLUSIONS

New Zealand has become an important destination for a wide range of adventure based holidays due to the geography and climate of the country, both of which are eminently suitable for this type of development.

DISCUSSION POINTS AND ESSAY QUESTIONS

1. Discuss the reasons for a growth of interest in adventure-based holidays.
2. Find an example of one travel company that operates in New Zealand. Discuss the ways in which this company has advertised to potential customers, and suggest an improvement that you would make to their campaign.
3. Critically analyse the natural and human-made factors that are necessary for the development of adventure travel in a region or country.
4. Evaluate the types of people who are likely to favour an adventure-based holiday. Explore how you would promote a destination to these types of people.

REFERENCES

Mintel (2001b). *All-Inclusive Holidays*. June. Mintel.

Swarbrooke, J., Beard, C., Leckie, S. and Pomfret, G. (2003). *Adventure Tourism – The New Frontier*. Butterworth-Heinemann, Oxford.

Determinants

Types of determinants

There are two types of determinants:

- factors that determine **whether** or not someone will be able to take a holiday
- factors that determine the **type** of trip, if the first set of determinants allow a holiday to be taken.

In this chapter we are generally considering the latter set of factors. The type of trip taken can encompass a huge range of variables, including:

- the destination
- when the trip will be taken
- the mode of travel
- the duration
- who will comprise the holiday party or group
- the type of accommodation
- the activities undertaken during the holiday
- how much will be spent on the trip.

We can further subdivide determinants into those that are:

- **personal** to the tourist
- **external** to the tourist.

These two types of factors are illustrated in Figures 5.1 and 5.2, respectively. Both are generalized pictures, but they serve to illustrate the variety of determinants that exist. Some of these determinants might preclude an individual from taking any trip. Health

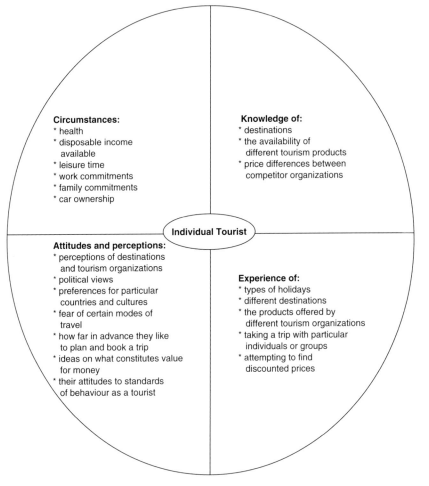

Figure 5.1 Personal determinants of tourist behaviour

problems could be the best example of this phenomenon. Others will simply affect the type of trip which is taken.

It is clear that the determinants listed in Figure 5.1 will not carry equal weight with all tourists at all times. Different individuals will perceive certain determinants to be more important than others, based on their attitudes, personalities, principles, fears and past experiences. Even for the same individual, the weighting given to each determinant will vary over time with changes in age, family situation and experience as a tourist. Personal determinants that are shared by a large proportion of the population may represent a market opportunity for the tourist industry.

As economies grow in the Pacific Rim, and European and American companies fight to compete in world markets, there are pressures on leisure time. Managers feel they need to be at work for as much of the time as possible. This has been one reason for the growth in intense, short-duration forms of vacation such as themed weekend

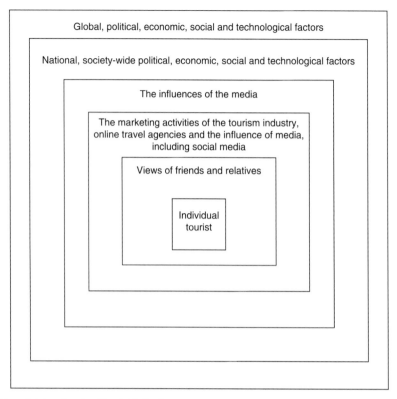

Figure 5.2 External determinants of tourist behaviour

breaks. These meet the needs of tourists looking for a short break from work that will stimulate them.

At the same time, many airlines have seized on the determinant that can stop some people taking any form of foreign holiday – the fear of flying. This determinant clearly reduces their potential market. Therefore they have begun to offer courses to help people overcome their fear of flying.

It is clear from these two brief examples that the tourism industry can exploit certain determinants, or seek to influence them, for its own benefit.

Perhaps the best example of the industry influencing and exploiting a determinant is the issue of price. Many tourists like to feel they have found a holiday at a discounted price. There is potentially considerable status value in being seen to have 'negotiated' a good deal for a tourism product. Therefore the industry emphasizes the bargain dimension in its selling through banner headlines in travel agencies and offers such as 'free child places', '20 per cent off' and 'free insurance'.

The factors in Figure 5.2 can be broken down into subfactors, as the following examples demonstrate.

- Political factors:
    - government legislation and policy

- immigration restrictions and visa requirements
- civil disorder and terrorism
- nature of the political system
- taxation policy, e.g. airport taxes
- tourist taxes.
- The media:
  - travel media, e.g. holiday features on television, in newspapers and guidebooks
  - non-travel media, e.g. news programmes and wildlife programmes on television
  - social media, which are perhaps becoming the most important of all today (discussed in more detail in Chapter 17).
- Tourism organization marketing:
  - foreign destinations' advertising campaigns
  - tour operators' brochures
  - online travel agencies' offers and promotions.

The extent to which tourists' behaviour is determined by their own personal determinants or external determinants varies according to personality and lifestyle. Extrovert people may be more inclined to take account of external determinants, such as the views of their many friends and relatives. Introverts may rely more on their own experiences. Well educated people who regularly watch news programmes and take an interest in worldwide social or environmental issues might be influenced by external factors such as the human rights record of a particular country's government. Those who either do not worry about such things, or do not even know of the situation in that country, might not even consider this factor.

It is also important to note that most determinants can be either facilitators or constraints upon tourists who wish to turn their motivations and desires into reality. For instance, high disposable income will be a facilitator, while limited and low disposable income would be a constraint. Likewise, a guidebook that paints a rosy picture of a resort would be likely to persuade a potential tourist to visit it, in contrast to a negative portrayal which would normally have the opposite effect.

Determinants of group travel

In the case of group travel, whether it be a family or a party of friends, the issue of determinants is particularly complex. Each individual has his or her own determinants, but a group has a set of determinants of its own. Each individual's determinants must be satisfied in a way that keeps the group as a whole content. This means compromise on the part of every group member.

Alternatively, a strong group member may impose his or her own determinants, such as a fear of flying, on every other group member. The others might have preferred to fly to their holiday destination, but find themselves taking a ferry instead to meet the needs of the dominant group member.

The myth of rational decision-making

Tourists do not make wholly rational decisions based on perfect information. They may be ignorant of many of the determinants listed in Figures 5.1 and 5.2. Alternatively, they may be well aware of the determinants but choose to ignore them. For example, a young couple with two small children and stressful jobs may know they cannot afford a holiday, but they feel so desperate for a break from the daily routine that they decide to take a trip anyway. This is not rational behaviour, although to anyone in their situation it is wholly understandable. As in other aspects of life, pressure and emotion often overwhelm logic.

The role of unforeseen circumstances and opportunism

Following on from the issue of rational decision-making are the twin matters of unforeseen circumstances and opportunism. Plans based on a tourist's current situation may become obsolete overnight owing to unforeseen changes in their personal circumstances. An obvious example relates to the tourist's health, where a decision to take a skiing holiday based on good previous experiences of such holidays would need to be rethought if the prospective tourist broke a leg.

Unforeseen circumstances can have a positive effect on tourist behaviour. A family may have decided they can't afford to take a trip from the UK to France this year. Then the value of the pound against the euro rises dramatically – as it did in 2015, from 1.2 to as much as 1.4 – and newspapers start offering cheap ferry tickets. This persuades the family to change their minds and take a short trip to northern France.

The last-minute discounted purchase phenomenon

The concept of determinants is geared to the idea of a relatively long period spent by the tourist planning the vacation, gathering information and evaluating alternatives. However, a growing phenomenon of the tourist industry is the last-minute purchase decision. Here the determinant is a desire to escape at short notice and a willingness to accept a less-than-ideal product if the price is low enough. In any event, vacation planning times have been reducing in recent years, for a number of reasons, including a growth in supply – for many destinations, tourists no longer need to fear that if they leave their decision-making too late there will be no flights or hotel rooms left. At the same time, the global economic crisis has reduced consumer confidence, so people want to be sure they will still have a job before they commit to spending a lot of money on a vacation.

The role of the tourism industry

The tourism industry plays a major role in influencing the determinants of tourist behaviour. For example, it:

- develops products specifically to match the determinants of some tourist behaviour, e.g. offering packages designed for tourists who have particular health problems such as mobility difficulties
- provides information to prospective tourists on everything from health problems to visa requirements, destination climate data to the destination's cultural attractions
- designs its promotional messages to fit the key determinants of the behaviour of different groups of tourists, e.g. emphasis on discount deals for those with limited income or those who like to search for bargains; reassurance about the safety of a destination; or selling the resort to families as having good facilities for children.

A key role is played in this respect by the travel agent, who is the intermediary between producers in the tourism industry and their clients. As Ryan (1997) says: 'The information provided becomes part of the information that determines a holiday-maker's expectations. The travel agent possesses the means to create the antecedents of success or failure of the holiday.'

Poor or inappropriate advice from an agent that leads to the tourist having an unsatisfactory holiday may well determine their future behaviour. It might make them:

- avoid using the same agent in the future
- decide not to buy the products from the same tourism organization again
- give a negative view of their holiday destination to friends and relatives.

Of course the rise of ICT means that the travel agent is now more likely these days to be an online agent rather than a retail outlet in the high street. This can make complaining more difficult, but it has also given much more choice to consumers.

Time lapses and determinants

Many tourists probably make purchasing decisions under the influence of determinants, or perceptions of determinants, that are outdated. They might have perceptions of destinations and tourism organizations that are no longer accurate.

For example, someone might still have an image of a quiet unspoilt Greek island as it was 20 years ago when they last visited it. This may persuade them to make a return trip to the island, which is now highly developed and crowded. Or a business traveller may avoid booking with an airline because of its reputation gained a few years ago for being unreliable and having old aircraft. However, in the intervening period this problem might have been eliminated by the purchase of new aircraft.

Tourism organizations must be aware of these time lapses and outdated determinants of tourist behaviour when planning their marketing activities.

One-off bad experiences as determinants of tourism behaviour

The industry should not underestimate the impact of one-off bad experiences as determinants of future tourist behaviour. For example, a delayed flight, or a failure of the airline to deliver a pre-ordered special diet meal, or the loss of baggage on one flight, could result in tourists:

- boycotting the airline in future
- giving negative views about the airline to friends and relatives.

Conclusions

The determinants of tourist behaviour are complex and diverse. They include personal determinants, which are different for each tourist. There are also external determinants, which will be interpreted in different ways by individual tourists. Finally, we have also seen that the issue of determinants is linked to other matters, such as the actions of the tourism industry, the idea of rational decision-making, last-minute purchases and the composition of holiday parties.

In Chapter 6 we will see how motivators and determinants combine in the purchase-decision process.

Discussion points and essay questions

1. Describe the ways in which personal circumstances such as health, family commitments and work commitments could influence the type of trip taken by tourists.
2. Discuss the range of media that might influence tourist behaviour and the ways in which they might affect purchase decisions.
3. Explore the reasons why tourists' perceptions may not accurately reflect the main determinants that are, in reality, affecting them at a particular time.

Exercise

Carry out a survey among a small group of your friends/colleagues/fellow students to try and identify which of the determinants in Figures 5.1 and 5.2 were the most influential when they last booked a holiday. Then produce a report outlining your results and noting any difficulties you experienced in collecting and interpreting the data.

References

Ryan, C. (ed.) (1997). *The Tourist Experience: A New Introduction*. Cassell, London.

CASE STUDY 5: PGL adventure holidays

INTRODUCTION

PGL Travel Limited is the leading British company providing adventure-based school trips and holidays for young people. The adventure experiences are designed around holiday centres which the company has bought or leased, and developed. Young people go to PGL without their parents, and it is often the first time they have been away from their family for any length of time. The holidays incorporate a selection of outdoor and indoor activities, and accommodation can range from tents to dormitories. The company has also developed substantial business in the schools adventure market, and offers family holidays through the summer.

BACKGROUND

The company takes its name from the initials of the man who started it in the 1950s – Peter Gordon Lawrence. The idea for the company came to Peter when he went on holiday to Austria in 1955 and sailed down the Danube in a folding canvas canoe. In 1957 he started to organize canoe camping trips for young adults down the River Wye. Peter led the groups himself, and called his new venture PGL Voyages. He expanded the business to Wales and the Brecon Beacons National Park.

In the 1960s and 1970s the PGL experience was based on canoeing, sailing and pony trekking, with accommodation in tents. During the early years the company developed holidays for school groups, and expanded these to include the Ardeche Gorge in the South of France, with permanently staffed headquarters in France as well as the UK.

The company gradually grew during the 1980s to become the leading UK provider of adventure holidays. Properties were bought and converted to permanent centres. This development included the acquisition of a mansion house in Perthshire and the flagship 250-acre estate of Boreatton Park in Shropshire.

During the 1990s PGL gradually diversified into other markets, including educational tours for schools and field study courses. There was a considerable expansion into the schools adventure market in 1991–92, when the company acquired the Quest Outdoor Adventure programme from a failed competitor and later bought out its biggest rival, 3D Education and Adventure.

Peter Lawrence, its founder, sadly died in August 2004, but left behind the solid foundation of a company that provides countless opportunities for young people to experience fun and adventure, and gain personal development.

THE COMPANY TODAY

The company now has over 55 years' experience and is recognized as Britain's leading operator of activity holidays for children and teenagers. PGL has 22 centres in the UK, Spain and France, and has recently opened two more in Australia (Exhibit 5.1). A full range of its products are described in Exhibit 5.2.

Exhibit 5.1 Summary of PGL Centres

UK Centres
Devon (North): Beam House
Devon (South): Barton Hall
Dorset: Osmington Bay
Herefordshire: Hillcrest
Isle of Wight: Little Canada; Whitecliff Bay
Lancashire: Winmarleigh Hall
Lincolnshire: Caythorpe Court
Scotland (Highlands): Dalguise
Shropshire: Boreatton Park
Surrey: Marchants Hill
Sussex: Windmill Hill
Wales: Llwyn Filly; Tregoyd House
Wiltshire: Liddington

Spanish Centre:
La Fosca

Source: www.pgl.co.uk

French Centres
Château du Tertre
Château de Grande Romaine
Le Pré Catelan
Domaine de Segries
Lou Valagran
Mimosa

Ski resort countries
Andorra
Austria
Czech Republic
France
Italy
Spain
USA

Exhibit 5.2 PGL product range

PGL School Trips (Primary Schools)
We'll inspire, motivate and challenge your pupils to raise aspirations, build their confidence and support their achievement. Each day brings a new adventure and the chance to try something new with the encouragement of their friends.

Bring them back more inspired and eager to learn – even walking a little taller!

Bringing out the best in young people is what we do best and with PGL, you can be sure you'll get the very best support for a great school trip. With us, everything is included – the activities, equipment, accommodation and food. Your dedicated 'Groupie' will be on hand to support you and your group and they'll run lively entertainment sessions in the evenings so you can relax after a busy day.

Special Themes – Outdoor Education, French Language and Culture

PGL School Trips (Secondary Schools)
Bring your students outdoors with PGL and see what a difference a day makes.

We take learning outside to challenge, engage and inspire your students, helping them reach further and achieve more. A PGL experience is one they'll never forget.

We know how to bring out the best in your students and we'll give all the support you need for a successful school trip that will help develop engaged, motivated students, eager to learn.

It's great value too. With us, everything is included; all activities, equipment, accommodation and food. You'll also get a dedicated 'Groupie' to look after you throughout your stay – they'll run evening entertainment sessions each evening so you can relax after an active day.

PGL School Trips (Secondary Schools)

Choose from our activity centres in the UK, France or Spain and take them on an unforgettable learning outside the classroom adventure that will make a real difference.

Special Themes – Outdoor Education, French Language and Culture, Sports Weekends, Skiing and Snowboarding, Field Studies, Maths, Science and Computing

PGL Group Residential Weekends

For thousands of young people, a PGL adventure is more than just a weekend away.

Our centres offer an exhilarating mix of adventure activities for groups of 7 to 17 year olds, designed to inspire, motivate and bring out the best in young people.

For many, it's the start of an amazing new journey.

Our residential activity centres are well equipped to accommodate groups of all sizes, whether you're looking to bring a small group or organize a regional gathering – we'll give you all the support you need.

Group Themes – Brownies and Guides, Cubs and Scouts, Brigades and Cadets, Youth Groups, Sports Clubs, Faith Groups

PGL Adventure Holidays (7–17 year olds)

Since 1957, over 8,000,000 children and parents have discovered what makes PGL, the UK's no.1 for children's 'summer camp' activity breaks. Our all-inclusive residential holidays offer children bags of fun activities, new friends and freedom to express themselves but in a safe, supportive environment with first class care. Residential breaks start from only £99pp and birthday parties from just £16pp and we have centres nationwide.

Special Themes – Multi-Activity Holidays, Action and Adventure, Creative Kids, Love to Learn, Overseas

PGL Family Holidays

If your family enjoys experiencing new things, meeting like-minded families and having a great time together, then you'll love our holidays. You'll see your children's confidence grow – and your own – as you take part in family team activities by day, and enjoy sociable evenings relaxing together by night. We have over 50 years' experience in running activity holidays and creating special memories that last a lifetime.

Special Themes – UK Multi-Activity holidays, 'More Adventurous' in UK and France

PGL International Students

We're the UK's largest and most trusted provider of outdoor education and residential courses for the under 18's and we have a large number of our own, purpose-built centres across the UK.

Your clients will use English on an informal basis as they participate in outdoor adventure activities with young English people on their holidays.

They'll visit cultural and historical sites close to our centres – and have the chance to interact in English of course.

And they can choose to study in a formal setting with daily English Language tuition in small classes run by CELTA qualified staff.

Special Themes – English Language Programme, Adventure Activity, Tailor-Made English Experience, French Language Adventure and Culture

Source: www.pgl.co.uk

The company offers a full range of activities, including archery, raft building, motor sports, abseiling, canoeing, orienteering, assault courses, sailing, windsurfing, climbing and others (Exhibit 5.3).

Exhibit 5.3 Full range of activities offered across the PGL Centres

Abseiling	Aeroball	All aboard
Aquafun	Archery	Beach walk
Bikeability	Blokarting	BMX
Bodyboarding	Bouldering Wall	Canoeing
Cat Walk	Challenge course	Circus Skills
Climbing	Coastal walk	Crate Challenge
Dragon Boats	Dry Slope Skiing	Eco Trail
Fencing	First Aid	Forest Trail
Giant Swing	High Ropes course	Hiking
History Trail	Jacob's Ladder	Kayaking
Keelboat sailing	Kite Flying	Low Level ropes
Matrix	Mountain Biking	Nature Trail
Orienteering	Powerfan	Problem Solving
Quad Biking	Raft Building	Rifle Shooting
Sensory Trail	Sequoia Scramble	Sports Games
Street Surfing	Survivor	Team Challenge
Team Games	Trapeze	Tree Climb
Treetop Study Trail	Tunnel Trail	Vertical Challenge

Source: PGL website (2015)

All holidays include care and tuition by well trained staff, use of specialist equipment and clothing, evening entertainments and full-board accommodation.

The adventure centres and activities require the professional help of head office staff. The company's Alton Court head office complex includes over 100,000 cubic feet of warehouse capacity for storing all the specialist equipment required.

PGL Travel Limited is recognized by major activity organizations including the Council for Learning Outside the Classroom, Royal Yachting Association, Institute of Outdoor Learning and the British Canoe Union.

CUSTOMERS OF PGL TRAVEL LIMITED

The holidays are designed for young people aged 7–17 years inclusive. Customers can choose a range of holidays designed for different age ranges. The young people who go to PGL are often experiencing time spent away from their families for the first time. This means that the safety and security of the young people is a major priority for the company, and these aspects are stressed in the promotional literature for the holidays.

The young people who go on a PGL holiday gain many experiences from their time at the centre. They may be away from home for the first time and are learning about leading a more independent life. They may be looking for excitement and adventure in a range of different activities; and for new friends and new experiences. Some comments made by young people who have been on PGL holidays are shown in Exhibit 5.4.

Exhibit 5.4 Comments by young people (and their parents) after a PGL holiday

'The staff laughed and smiled 24 hours a day!'

'The first thing Anthony said as he got off the coach was: "Sorry I didn't send you a postcard, but I was having too much fun to stop and write it!"'

'If your brother or sister is driving you up the wall, go to PGL – and get away from it all!'

'Non-stop fun, from start to finish!'

'Going away on her own wasn't a problem – everyone was so friendly she settled in straight away'

'PGL is a great "kids only" holiday where you can meet millions of new friends'

'Not a minute went by when I was not having fun. Watch out – I'll be back!'

'When Matthew met us at the end of his holiday he was wearing a wall-to-wall grin!'

'Jonathan returned from his holiday over a fortnight ago and is still talking about it – that sums up the experience!'

'I'm completely gobsmacked! I loved it and I want to come back!'

'Yet again, PGL has succeeded in giving my teenagers an excellent week!'

'Buckets and spades have obviously been replaced by adventure and activities!'

'Congratulations on a very professional organization. Please give all your staff my thanks'

'It's the ultimate fun experience – why can't it be next summer already?'

Source: www.pgl.co.uk

The customers for PGL holidays are largely from the ABC1 socioeconomic groups. They are professional people who read the quality newspapers and have a relatively high standard of living. They live in a good standard of owner-occupied accommodation and often own more than one car.

PROMOTION OF PGL HOLIDAYS

The promotional strategy of PGL has helped to sustain the company as the market leader in the activity holidays market. A loyal following of party leaders and children has been built up through an emphasis on quality, safety and value for money, all of which are highlighted in the promotional literature.

PGL focuses on six methods in its communication mix:

- direct mail
- personal selling

- advertising
- public relations
- word of mouth
- the internet.

The mix of communication methods used is amended according to the product and the effectiveness of each tool relative to the market. Advertising, for example, is more effective for marketing holidays aimed at the individual unaccompanied child.

The promotional mix for PGL is shown in Exhibit 5.5.

Exhibit 5.5 Promotional mix

Direct mail – direct mail is the most cost-effective marketing tool for PGL's needs – it enables us to accurately target our customers and assess quantitatively the success of different campaigns. Underlying all PGL direct mail activity is the central database which encompasses all existing clients and enquirers plus details of potential customers. Specialist mailing lists are also purchased from external suppliers. Items mailed include brochures, newsletters and videos for use at home or parents' evenings.

Advertising – advertising features in varying degrees in most of PGL's campaigns depending upon the overall marketing mix for each product. It is mainly used in conjunction with individual holidays for children and teenagers. PGL adverts appear in the quality Sunday newspapers and supplements, educational supplements and children's publications, to name but a few, and are often timed to coincide with brochure launches and special offer mailings.

Public relations – PR activities include press releases, advertorials in newspapers and magazines, newsletters and the provision of holidays for competitions. Journalists are also encouraged to send their children on PGL holidays and report on their experiences. PGL tries to work closely with the communities surrounding our centres, supporting local fetes, sporting events etc. Similar opportunities also exist for supporting school fetes, sports days and newsletters and PGL has sponsored a number of achievement awards at school prize-giving ceremonies.

Word of mouth (social media) – word of mouth is the most powerful promotional tool and PGL actively encourages positive word of mouth by rewarding existing clients when they introduce a new group or individual to PGL. It regularly updates 'recent Tweets' on its website, giving reviews, and also posts captioned photos of group activities. This is reinforced by a comprehensive Facebook site showing reviews, videos and photos of participating groups and schools. There is also a PGL YouTube channel with information and promotional videos, linked through from its Facebook pages.

Internet – apart from its webpages with links to online brochures, the website is also used as a teacher/tour leader resource guide, providing not only general product-related information but also information linked to risk assessments, codes of practice and educational benefits that help groups to prepare for trips. Additionally the website promotes free 'familiarization trips' for international agents attending Alphe educational conferences.

Source: www.pgl.co.uk

CONCLUSIONS

PGL Travel has been developing its product to meet the growing interest in holidays for young people wanting to experience quality time away from their families and the increasing demand for adventure-based school trips. They offer well run and secure holiday centres staffed by experts in their field. This gives parents the security of knowing that their children will be looked after in an appropriate environment. For the children, PGL offers exciting adventures and new experiences. Many of the children who go on a PGL holiday can't wait to get back for their next one!

PGL has been able to adapt its offerings over the decades and improve its support and resources for teachers and group leaders. Being part of the Educational Division of HolidayBreak, itself a subsidiary of the 'oldest tour operators in the world', Cox and Kings Ltd of India, it is no longer a single company pioneering activity holidays to families and small groups; it has become a key provider of educational activity holidays as part of a major global educational travel group.

DISCUSSION POINTS

1. Evaluate the role of safety in the choice of outdoor pursuits made by parents and organizations for children.
2. 'Buckets and spades have been replaced by adventure and activities.' Explain the reasons for this change in the types of holidays young people are demanding.
3. PGL has sometimes been linked to the phrase 'parents get lost'. What positives or negatives would you consider come from using this phrase in the company's promotional activities?

Models of the purchase decision-making process

Introduction

Having considered the motivators and determinants of tourist behaviour in Chapters 4 and 5, it is now time for us to look at the purchase decision-making process as a whole. Before that, we need to spend a little time looking at the characteristics of the product that tourists purchase. Tourism products are complex because they exist at two different levels:

- the package holiday, which is a combination of the products of individual sectors including accommodation, transport, destinations and visitor attractions
- the products of these individual sectors which can be sold as stand-alone products, such as an air ticket or a theme park visit as part of a day trip.

In this chapter we focus on the former, as it is the product which distinguishes the tourism industry from other industries such as transport and the hotel industry.

Tourism products and services

Tourism products are largely services. Marketing theorists have attempted to define services in relation to their intangibility and the fact that purchase of a service never results in the ownership of anything. They have attempted to clarify the differences between products and services by stating the characteristics of services as follows.

- **Intangibility** – services are intangible in that they cannot be seen, tasted or smelled before purchase. Tourism companies have tried to overcome this problem by offering consumers videos of holiday locations to make the experience seem more 'real'. The use of advanced technologies such as virtual reality is also predicted to overcome this problem. Despite these advances, consumers still have to take considerable risks when choosing their tourism product because of its intangible nature.

- **Inseparability** – services have the characteristic of overlap between the production and performance of the service, and the consumption of it. A service in its purest sense has the provider and customer face to face. This influences consumer buying behaviour and means that consumers may change their behaviour patterns according to their experiences.
- **Heterogeneity** – it is very difficult for a tourism provider to give the same level of service at every consumption time. The mood that the consumer is in will also affect their appraisal of the service. It will never be the same twice. This means it is very difficult for a consumer to judge the potential quality of experience they will gain when they purchase a tourism product. It also means that it is dangerous for them, when considering a repeat purchase, to rely on past experiences. What was a happy experience in the past may turn out to be the complete opposite next time. The consumer may have changed and have different perceptions and expectations. Similarly, the service may have changed over time.
- **Lack of ownership** – the consumer has access to the activity or facility only when he or she buys the service. The consumer never owns anything at the end of the transaction. Service often leads to feelings of satisfaction rather than the ownership of a tangible item. This means that the purchase of a service will have a considerable emotional significance for the consumer.

Convenience versus shopping goods

The characteristics of services are only one aspect of tourism products. General marketing theorists have also separated out convenience and shopping goods as having different characteristics (Middleton and Clarke, 2001). A convenience good is a manufactured item which typically has a low price and is bought frequently. A shopping good typically has a high price and is bought less frequently. Shopping goods generally satisfy higher-order needs in Maslow's hierarchy of needs. Howard and Sheth (1969) noted that the purchase of convenience-type goods involves the consumer in routine problem-solving behaviour, whereas the purchase of shopping goods involves the consumer in extensive problem-solving.

The spectrum of buyer behaviour for these two types of goods or services is explored in more depth in Figure 6.1. This figure shows that the characteristics of services which fit into the shopping products category have a considerable effect on consumers' buying behaviour. From this it can be seen that a much more complex set of issues is involved in the purchase process for tourism products than for fast-moving consumer goods. The process involves the consumer in a more difficult set of decisions, a lengthier decision time and a higher level of commitment. Middleton and Clarke (2001) suggest that this results in lower brand loyalty and the expectation of a more limited distribution chain.

Convenience products	Shopping products
Mainly low unit value/price	Mainly high unit value/price
Mainly perceived necessitates	Mainly non-essential

$$\longleftrightarrow$$
$$\longleftrightarrow$$

Low problem-solving	High problem-solving
Low information search	High information search
Low customer commitment	High customer commitment
High purchase frequency	Low purchase frequency
High brand loyalty	Low brand loyalty
High-speed decision process	Low-speed decision process
High rapidity of consumption	Low rapidity of consumption
Extensive distribution expected	Limited distribution expected

Spectrum of products associated with the spectrum of buyer behaviour

Convenience products	Shopping products

Urban bus transport	Holidays
Commuter train transport	Hotel accommodation
Bank services	Air transport
Post office services	Private education
Take away foods	Motor cars
Washing powder	Freezers
Cigarettes	Carpets
Branded chocolate bar	Furniture

Figure 6.1 Spectrum of buyer behaviour characteristics – goods or services

Source: adapted from Middleton and Clarke (2001)

Let us now consider some of the other complexities in consumer behaviour involved in the purchase of tourism products. These complexities are shown in Figure 6.2 and are summarized below.

High involvement in purchase decision and high consumer commitment

The behaviour of consumers when they are purchasing tourism products and services demonstrates a high involvement in the process and high levels of commitment because of the nature of the products and services. This means that the behaviour patterns during purchase are not routine and every purchase occasion will show different approaches. The consumer will be actively involved in the buying process and will 'shop around' before coming to a decision. Therefore the decision process will take longer.

Consumers will also change their behaviour patterns according to the type of holiday to be taken, their motives for the particular purchase occasion and their position in the family life cycle.

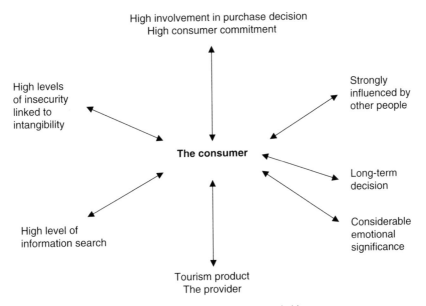

Figure 6.2 The complexity of consumer behaviour in tourism: the demand side

High levels of insecurity linked to intangibility

The intangible nature of tourism products and services means that consumers can often have high levels of insecurity during purchase. They cannot try out the product or service before purchase and will therefore be looking for reassurance about their choices. This will mean that their behaviour patterns will be complex and will probably involve many people and agencies. Traditionally, this meant that an individual might take advice from friends, family, travel agents and television holiday programmes, for example, before making a choice of annual holiday. However, in recent years consumer-generated media such as TripAdvisor and online fora such as that offered by Lonely Planet have become perhaps the most important tool tourists use to try and reduce the risks inherent in buying an intangible product.

Considerable emotional significance

The purchase of a holiday will be a major event in an individual's life. It is the holiday that is going to let the individual escape from the work environment and grey skies to renew his or her flagging spirits. The choice of holiday may also affect other close members of the family, and compromises might have to be made during the decision-making process. The consumer might also be considering other substitute products and services in place of a holiday. They might, for example, be thinking about the purchase of other major items, such as a car or home, rather than spending money on a holiday. This type of decision has particular emotional significance for individuals and their close associates.

Strongly influenced by other people

Individuals are likely to be strongly influenced by other people during the decision-making process for tourism products. If we take an example of individuals choosing a holiday product, they are likely to be influenced by other members of their family and by members of other reference groups. This makes their behaviour patterns very complex and difficult to study. The people who influence their decision will also change their views over time. The rise of consumer-generated media also means that today the people who most influence the tourist may well be total strangers, rather than friends or family.

Long-term decisions

Despite the growth in the last-minute holiday bargain, most decisions that individuals make about tourism products are made a long way in advance. This means that individuals might be in a completely different frame of mind when they make their purchase decision from when they actually go on holiday. It also means that individuals will be trying to predict what they want to do in the future. This means that the decision itself may have an immediate effect on them. We all know the hope and anticipation felt when, in the depths of winter, we book a holiday in sunny climes!

High level of information search

We have already seen that the choice of tourism products usually has considerable emotional significance for the individual. This will mean that individuals will usually carry out an extensive information search before making their final choice. This will involve consultation with individuals, groups, organizations and media reports before a decision is made. This process of research and reflection means that behaviour patterns are very complex.

From the above, we can see that the purchase of tourism products and services does not involve the consumer in routine behaviour patterns. This is completely different from their behaviour patterns when they are purchasing fast-moving consumer goods, which is more mechanized and predictable.

The tourist decision-making process

The decision to purchase a tourism product is the outcome of a complex process. This is the result of a number of factors, which we consider in this chapter, relating to consumers and to the external influences that act upon them.

However, it is also true that the diverse and interdependent characteristics of many tourism products make the purchase decision in tourism a complex phenomenon in its

* Which destination (country, region, resort) ?

* Which mode of travel (scheduled air, charter air, ferry, rail, coach, car, bus) ?

* Which type of accommodation (serviced or non-serviced) ?

* How long will the holiday be (days / weeks) ?

* At which time of the year will the holiday be taken
  (season, month, specific date) ?

* Package holiday or independent travel ?

* Which tour operator (if package holiday) ?

Figure 6.3 Decisions involved in choosing a holiday

own right. This fact can be illustrated by thinking about the range of decisions a tourist has to make when choosing a holiday. These can be seen in Figure 6.3.

There are myriad factors that affect the holiday purchase decision, some of which are illustrated in Figure 6.4. Clearly these relate strongly to the motivators and determinants outlined in Chapters 4 and 5.

While Figure 6.4 is only a selection of the relevant factors, it does give a good idea of both the number and scope of such factors.

It is also important to recognize that the complexity of tourist decision-making is heightened by the fact that choosing their holiday is not the final decision tourists have to make. Once on holiday, they have to make a further set of decisions about what to do when they arrive at their destination. They have to decide how to spend each day in terms of excursions and leisure activities as well as where to eat and drink, and so on. Each of these apparently simple decisions is the result of a complex decision-making process.

Models of purchase decision-making in tourism

We have already considered models of consumer behaviour for tourism in Chapter 3. Cooper et al. (2005) have identified three stages in the development of general consumer behaviour theory in relation to purchase behaviour, as follows.

* The early empiricist phase, covering the years between 1930 and the late 1940s, was dominated by empirical commercial research, and the industry attempted to identify the effects of distribution advertising and promotion decisions.
* The motivational research phase of the 1950s placed a greater emphasis on in-depth interviews, focus groups as a perception test, and other projective

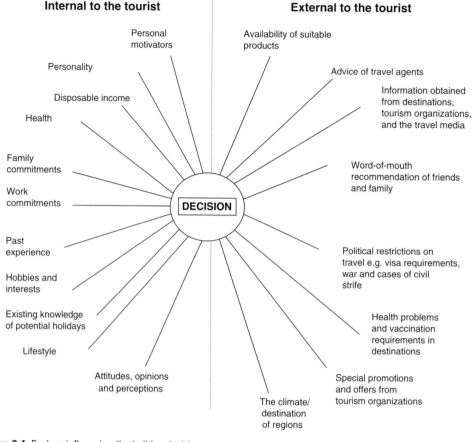

Figure 6.4 Factors influencing the holiday decision

Source: adapted from Horner and Swarbrooke (1996)

techniques. There was a great deal of activity directed at uncovering real motives for action which were perceived to lie in the deeper recesses of the consumer's mind.

- The formative phase from the 1960s provided the first general consumer behaviour textbook (Engel, Kollat and Blackwell, 1968); other influential books (such as Howard and Sheth, 1969) followed soon after.

However, early interest in consumer behaviour tended to focus on manufacturing industries, and later on general service industries. It was only in the 1970s that academics began to develop purchase-decision models in tourism. It is important to recognize that these purchase-decision models were being developed simultaneously with the work of writers such as Cohen (1972, 1979) and Plog (1977) on the related subject of tourist typologies.

In Chapter 3 we considered models such as those developed by Wahab, Crompton and Rothfield (1976) and Mathieson and Wall (1982). These models all seem to see the decision as a linear process, and no distinctions are made about which factors might weigh more heavily than others when decisions are being made.

In 1987, Moutinho published a vacation tourist behaviour model which differed from most previous models in two respects:

- it recognized that there are three distinctly **different stages** in the decision-making process:
  - pre-decision stage and decision process
  - post-purchase evaluation
  - future decision-making.

(the model recognized that the latter stage would feed back to the first through a loop in the system)

- it explicitly noted that purchase decisions are a result of three **behavioural concepts:**
  - motivation
  - cognition
  - learning.

There are many other models, although this brief section has highlighted the most widely discussed 'classical' models.

A critique of purchase-decision models in tourism

Most of the models we have discussed so far have some common weaknesses that:

- limit their value in explaining the complex way in which purchase decisions are made in tourism
- make it difficult for tourism marketers to make use of them when developing their marketing strategies.

The main weaknesses are as follows.

- In general they are based on little or no empirical research, and there is little evidence that they represent the reality of how decisions are actually made.
- A large number of the best known models are now at least 15 years old. This is a significant weakness in an industry where consumer behaviour is believed to be constantly evolving. Thus most of the major models pre-date recent developments in tourist behaviour, including:
  - the rapid rise of the internet as a means of purchasing airline tickets and hotel beds
  - the impact of 'no-frills' budget airlines

- the rise of the all-inclusive resort holiday
- the growth of direct marketing
- the increasing popularity of last-minute spontaneous purchases of tourism products
- the growing influence of consumer-generated media on tourist behaviour.
- Most of the models developed to date have originated from work carried out by academics in North America, Australia and Northern Europe. Few, therefore, reflect the nature of consumer behaviour in the main emerging markets of South East Asia and Eastern Europe.

Another major criticism is that these models tend to view tourists as a homogeneous group. Clearly this is not the case. Every tourist is different, and it is possible to segment tourists on the basis of a range of factors that will influence their own individual process of making a purchase decision. Some of these factors have been explored in Chapters 4 and 5, and include, for example:

- whether tourists are travelling alone or if they are members of a family group or party
- how experienced tourists are and their past experiences as tourists
- their personality – e.g. some tourists make spontaneous last-minute decisions about their holiday plans while others might enjoy spending months planning their trip.

Many models also fail to recognize the impact that motivators and determinants have on the purchase decision. Some motivators and determinants may be so powerful that they totally dominate the purchase decision, to the exclusion of all other factors. These could be as diverse as an obsessive hobby such as steam railways or rock climbing, or a health problem.

The majority of models also presume a high degree of rationality in the decision-making process, which is not always evident. Rational decision-making in tourism is limited by both the imperfect information available to most tourists, and the fact that many consumers will be influenced by their own opinions and prejudices, which may be irrational.

Most models also seem to assume that purchase behaviour and the process of making a decision remains constant regardless of the nature of the holiday being purchased. This is questionable, as the following contrasting examples show.

- The purchase of a 28-night tailor-made round-the-world package by a couple, valued at £5000, which includes stopovers with pre-booked airport transfers and accommodation in Dubai, Hong Kong, Tahiti, Sydney, Los Angeles and New York. A range of alternative airline offers have to be studied and bookings made to ensure seats on all the relevant flights. Pre-planning is also required in terms of pre-trip vaccinations. The consumer has a definite start and finish date for the tour, dictated by available annual leave from his or her job, so there is no flexibility about departure and return dates.

- The purchase of a heavily discounted last-minute 14-night holiday by young students who simply want the cheapest summer sun holiday available. The destination is irrelevant and departure dates are fairly flexible, as the tourists have seven weeks off college in which to take the two-week-long trip. However, they can't make a decision until they have found out whether or not they will be required to re-sit any examinations. Once they know they are able to travel, they want to be on the beach, as soon as possible.

Clearly, in these cases the nature of the purchase decision and the effort put into making it will vary significantly. Similar differences would exist if we were to examine other types of holidays.

Purchase decision-making and marketing in tourism

Marketing professionals in tourism are increasingly aware of the need to understand how their consumers make their decisions to purchase a particular product. Currently, the research conducted by tourism organizations about consumer behaviour is beginning to tackle this subject seriously. It would therefore be fortuitous if the academic models could be used by marketers.

An appreciation of how consumers make decisions helps marketers develop their marketing plans in relation to, for example:

- when to attempt to influence consumers, e.g. focusing marketing activities on the time when most consumers are making decisions to buy a particular product
- the choice of advertising media based on which media the majority of consumers use to gain information about tourism products
- the selection of appropriate distribution channels or marketing intermediaries.

Therefore we have to ask ourselves if the models are reliable enough to be used in this way. Perhaps not – as noted above, many of the models are at least 15 years old.

We mentioned the review of all the research on the topic that has been published by Cohen et al. (2014) in Chapter 3. It is important to highlight the areas where recent research has been focused. These include:

- **decision-making** – how do individuals make decisions when purchasing a holiday?
- **values** – what personal and shared values influence decision-making?
- **motivations** – what motivates consumers to behave in a certain way and choose particular products?
- **self-concept and personality** – what features of an individual's view of themselves and their personality affect their tourism behaviour?
- **expectations** – how does an individual's expectations of tourism products and services affect their behaviour?

- **attitudes** – how do a person's attitudes affect their purchasing behaviour?
- **perceptions** – how do a person's perceptions affect their purchasing behaviour?
- **satisfaction** – what influences tourist satisfaction? (It is interesting that the authors found the most research being published in this area.)
- **trust and loyalty** – how are trust and loyalty built up, and what are their features? How can organizations build trust and loyalty?

Marketing professionals who want to see if they can put these models into practice to guide their activities need to see if there is any link between them and the technique of market segmentation. For, in a sense, these techniques represent an attempt to explain purchase decisions by reference to various characteristics of the tourist. In other words, segmentation splits the population into subgroups who share the same purchase characteristics. It suggests that the decision of everyone in the subgroup is determined primarily by one set of influences. These influences, in classical marketing theory, are divided into four criteria:

- **demographic** – age, sex, race, stage in the family life-cycle
- **geographical** – where the tourist lives
- **psychographic** – the tourist's personality and lifestyle
- **behaviouristic** – the relationship of the tourist to the product, e.g. the benefits they expect to receive from the purchase; whether they are first-time purchasers or regular purchasers of the product.

Tourism marketing traditionally relies heavily on segmentation, yet of these four sets of characteristics, only the psychographic plays a significant role in current purchase-decision models in tourism. Yet marketers are also aware of the limitations of the four segmentation criteria outlined above. It is widely recognized that purchase behaviour is a result of the combination of two or more of these criteria, not just one.

   The models do not help us to identify or predict the behaviour of individual tourists. It is very difficult to operationalize such general models at a time when marketing is increasingly a matter of targeting individual tourists, using computer databases. Nevertheless, there seems little doubt that, despite their weaknesses, these models have a role to play in tourism marketing.

Conclusions

We have looked at the process by which tourists make their purchase decision to buy a vacation, and how this process has been modelled by academics. These models appear to have some significant weaknesses in terms of describing, let alone explaining, the process by which tourists decide to buy a holiday. This chapter also briefly highlights the potential links that exist between purchase-decision models and market segmentation techniques. Our last thought on this subject must be that we still have a long way to go before we understand how tourists choose their vacations. Research is continuing and being published on the topic at a rapid rate and on a whole series of interconnected issues. There is still room for further research on other areas, including group and individual decision-making; under-researched market segments such as disabled, gay and lesbian tourists, and migrant workers; cross-cultural issues in emerging markets; emotions; and consumer misbehaviour (Cohen *et al.*, 2014). The fact that tourism decision-making is emotional, and often is not based on the rational decision-making to which many of the models of consumer behaviour relate, means that the emotional aspect of tourism needs to be researched in much more depth, using qualitative rather than quantitative methods of research.

Discussion points and essay questions

1. Outline the factors that make the study of purchase decision-making in tourism such a complex activity.
2. Evaluate the main strengths and weaknesses of one model of consumer behaviour, as ways of explaining how tourists make purchase decisions.
3. Discuss the problems that marketing professionals might experience in trying to put into practice the models of purchase-decision behaviour outlined in this chapter.

Exercise

Think about the most recent holiday you purchased and produce a simple model to illustrate the process you followed to make the decision, and the factors that you took into account. Then ask a group of friends, fellow students or colleagues to do the same, independently, without talking to each other. Compare the models and identify and try to explain the similarities and differences. Finally, note the difficulties experienced in carrying out this task. What do they tell you about the problems of studying purchase-decision behaviour?

References

Cohen, E. (1972). Towards a sociology of international tourism. *Social Research* 39, 64–82.

Cohen, E. (1979). A phenomenology of tourist experience. *Sociology* 13, 179–201.

Cohen, S.A., Prayag, G. and Moital, M. (2014). Consumer behaviour in tourism: concepts, influences and opportunities. *Current Issues in Tourism* 17 (10), 872–909.

Cooper, C.P., Wanhill, S., Fletcher, J., Gilbert, D. and Fyall, A. (2005). *Tourism: Principles and Practice*. Pearson, Harlow, UK.

Engel, J.F., Kollat, D.J. and Blackwell, R.D. (1968). *Consumer Behaviour*. Holt, Rinehart and Winston, New York.

Horner, S. and Swarbrooke, J. (1996). *Marketing Tourism, Hospitality, and Leisure in Europe*. International Thomson Business Press.

Howard, J.A. and Sheth, J.N. (1969). *The Theory of Buyer Behaviour*. John Wiley and Sons, New York.

Mathieson, A. and Wall, G. (1982). *Tourism: Economic, Physical and Social Impacts*. Longman, London.

Middleton, V.T.C. and Clarke, J. (2001). *Marketing for Travel and Tourism*, 3rd edn. Butterworth-Heinemann, Oxford.

Moutinho, L. (1987). Consumer behaviour in tourism. *European Journal of Marketing* 21 (10), 3–44.

Plog, S. (1977). Why destination areas rise and fall in popularity. In *Domestic and International Tourism*, ed. E. Kelly. Institute of Certified Travel Agents, Wellesley, MA.

Wahab, S., Crampon, L.J. and Rothfield, L.M (1976). *Tourism Marketing*, Tourism International Press, London.

CASE STUDY 6: Gay and lesbian tourism in Australia

A DEFINITION OF GAY AND LESBIAN TOURISM

The growth of marketing to gay and lesbian tourists can be attributed to the wider acceptance of diversity by society, and acceptance of gay and lesbian consumers in general (Adams, 1993). Stuber (2002) argues that gays and lesbians now fit into a market segment because they can be measured, are accessible through a variety of communication methods, show fairly homogeneous consumer behaviour, and are stable as a group. He also states that it is well recognized in the industry that the strategic marketing of tourism products and services to gays and lesbians will be a profitable undertaking that can bring about success for a wide variety of organizations involved in the tourism process. These tourism organizations include destination marketers (e.g. New York, Key West and San Francisco in the USA, Brighton and Blackpool in the UK) and events organizers (e.g. the Mardi Gras in Sydney; and the Sydney Olympics 2000, where gay and lesbian tourists were encouraged by tour operators such as Olivia, the US-based lesbian-focused package holiday company). In the wider tourist market, the lesbian, gay, bisexual and transgender (LGBT) market is seen as an increasingly important niche (Mintel 2015). In Australia the sector is also known as lesbian, gay, bisexual, transgender and queer (LGBTQ) or lesbian, gay, bisexual, transgender and intersex (LGBTI).

GAY AND LESBIAN TOURISM IN AUSTRALIA

Australia now markets itself as a destination for groups of travellers who have special needs. This includes backpackers and singles, the over-fifties, families, and gay and lesbian travellers. The country promotes its perfect climate, dazzling beaches, great restaurants, vibrant communities, friendly atmosphere, and festivals and dance parties as being particularly attractive to gay and lesbian travellers (www.australia.com).

The fact that Australia has a population drawn from many ethnic, religious and cultural groups could partly explain why the population often accepts that being 'different' is acceptable. All areas of Australia promote themselves as being suitable for gay and lesbian travellers to visit. Sydney is considered to be the gay and lesbian capital of Australia, with a wide range of hotels, clubs, restaurants and shopping outlets that are targeted at the gay and lesbian traveller. The details of Sydney as a gay and lesbian venue are explored in the official website of Tourism Australia (www.australia.com) and we can see an extract from these web pages in Exhibit 6.1.

Exhibit 6.1 Sydney, New South Wales – a gay and lesbian view

Sydney – According to Gore Vidal (and he should know) 'San Francisco thinks it's the city that Sydney is'. There are few doubts now that Sydney is one of the great gay and lesbian destinations in the world. Perhaps it's the long warm summer, perhaps it's the history as a penal colony, perhaps it's because Sydney just loves to party so much, but whatever the reason, the lesbian and gay communities have made their mark on Sydney and stamped it as a world centre for tolerance, diversity, flamboyance and a damn good time.

Sydney has the biggest gay and lesbian population in Australia and it shows. From building sites to restaurants, bars to beaches, shops to hospitals, there does not seem an area or industry without a significant gay or lesbian presence.

February is the time when all this comes to the fore with the Sydney Gay and Lesbian Mardi Gras, the biggest celebration of gay and lesbian pride, culture and arts in the world, where the number of spectators for the parade each year is bigger than for any other event. The national prime-time television coverage never fails to win its time slot. The three-week-long Festival is amongst the biggest gay and lesbian arts festivals anywhere and the party is one of the largest of its kind in the world: 10,000 participants, 144 floats in 2014 with 2000 volunteers helping to make the event special for the hundreds of thousands of spectators.

Throughout the rest of the year the gay and lesbian population does not hibernate. The bars, clubs and venues thrive. There are more dance parties throughout the year, more celebrations, art activities, community events and fireworks.

Gay and lesbian activities are centred in Oxford Street in Darlinghurst and King Street in Newtown. Cafes, bars, cinemas and shops catering to the market abound in these areas. However, increasingly lesbians and gay men are not confining themselves to these 'ghettos'. Leichhardt has long been a recognized as a 'dyke' centre. Marrickville, Bondi, Elizabeth Bay, Bronte, Surry Hills and Redfern are suburbs with a strong gay presence.

In central Sydney it would be harder to find accommodation that is *not* lesbian or gay friendly, than accommodation that is. Virtually all the major central hotels are used to and welcome the influx of gay and lesbian tourists around Mardi Gras and are happy to receive them all year round. Smaller hotels in the areas of Darlinghurst and Surry Hills depend on the lesbian and gay market and are well versed in the ways of catering for the community.

Keeping up to date with the stream of venues and events in Sydney is easy. Pick up any of the free community publications for the latest information:

- *Sydney Star Observer*, a 36-year-old tabloid and online magazine aimed at the LGBTI community
- *Q Magazine*, a Melbourne-based gay lifestyle magazine
- *Sydney Morning Herald*

Eating out – Eating out is one of the things Sydneysiders do best. Considering the range and quality of restaurants and cafes, it is little surprise Sydney home kitchens are some of the most under-used in the world. For gay and lesbian travellers there is no need to seek out queer-specific eating places. Anyone is hard pushed to go to a restaurant without finding a 'family member'.

Shopping – Gay and lesbian-specific shopping is mainly focused on Oxford Street and in Newtown again.

- Aussie Boys is a two-storey store for lesbians and gay men with a strong emphasis on party clothes, from stylish shirts to shorts. However, everything from underwear to sunglasses is available along with a few souvenirs and gorgeous little items for friends and family back home.
- Sax Fetish offers off-the-peg leatherwear and accoutrements, everything from your polished chrome codpiece to leather briefcases. Harnesses, masques, crops, paddles, jackets, shorts, bras . . . teddy bears. Sax produce most of their own goods themselves but also have other suppliers.
- The Bookshop Darlinghurst offers the best selection of gay and lesbian titles in Australia and possibly beyond. If they don't have it, they'll order it specifically for you. Great place to discover more about the growing staple of Australian gay and lesbian writers. Staff are friendly, and informed. They give good lit. Open til 9.00 pm, great for late evening browsing.
- In operation since 1974, The Feminist Bookshop offers 'books for a changing world'. Great selection of works that often cannot be found elsewhere along with cards, posters, T-shirts and gifts.
- The Toolshed offers a large selection of adult toys and magazines, clothing and swimwear. Many dance parties sell tickets through these shops.

Health and well being – When shopping and partying get too much, it's time to relax, unwind, or work out. An example of a gym is City Gym, Crown Street, East Sydney (www.citygym.com.au).

Gay Games – Every four years since 1982, the Gay Games are held somewhere in the world. It is a vast gathering of people participating in sport and cultural activities, with more competitors than the Olympic Games. The Gay Games are founded on the principles of participation, inclusion and personal best. Anyone can enter regardless of sexuality or ability. The Games are a marvellous time of friendship, support, celebration and sporting achievement. Staged by the Federation of Gay Games, which aims to represent the LBGT perspective to sport and culture.

Community support – Sydney has a full and active network of support and community groups. These are a few of the key ones:

- Sydney Gay and Lesbian Mardi Gras (www.mardigras.org.au)
- Gay and Lesbian Counselling Services
- Gender Centre – transgender support (www.gendercentre.org.au)

Source: Tourism Australia, www.australia.com

A full listing for all the major destinations is also given for the following cities on the destination webpage:

- Victoria – Melbourne
- Canberra

- Western Australia – Perth
- Tasmania – Hobart
- Northern Territory – Darwin
- Queensland
- Brisbane and Gold Coast.

Exhibit 6.2 GALTA – Gay and Lesbian Tourism Australia

What is GALTA?

A national network of tourism professionals dedicated to the welfare and satisfaction of all gay and lesbian travellers within and to Australia. GALTA – Gay and Lesbian Tourism Australia Ltd is a nonprofit organization operated by a team of elected individuals who work with federal, state and regional tourism bodies, corporations, businesses and individuals to develop and grow the gay and lesbian market and increase awareness of gay and lesbian travellers and their needs.

Why does GALTA exist?

GALTA recognizes the needs of two distinct groups. One is gay and lesbian travellers seeking quality tourism-related services that provide a genuine interest in them, and welcome them. The other is businesses that wish to make their products or services available to these travellers.

What does GALTA do?

GALTA represents members by forming close alliances with local, state and national tourism bodies, assisting members in attracting a qualified niche market. Through newsletters, symposiums/workshops, trade shows, fair days, regional networking functions/dinners and its website, GALTA provides members with a wide distribution network and exposure to gay and lesbian travellers around Australia. GALTA also enjoys a successful close working relationship with the International Gay & Lesbian Travel Association (IGLTA, www.iglta.org).

Where is GALTA?

GALTA members are located across Australia, from major capital cities to rural and coastal destinations. Members represent major hotels and resorts, airlines, tourism organizations, accommodation providers, restaurants/cafes, travel services, individuals and media, all of whom are dedicated to the professional development and growth of the gay and lesbian tourism niche market to, from and within Australia.

When does GALTA work?

GALTA recognizes the importance of gay and lesbian cultural festivals and pride events around the country and maintains a regular presence at these events. It also recognizes the needs of lesbians and gays who travel all year round to capital cities and other destinations for both work and pleasure.

Source: www.galta.com.au

THE MARDI GRAS IN SYDNEY

Sydney Gay and Lesbian Mardi Gras is probably the world's greatest celebration of gay and lesbian culture, art, fun and community. It started off as a small protest march and has become a large festival that happens every year in February, which draws visitors from across the world. The festivities begin at the festival once it goes dark, and there is a week of dance, parties, films, sports, art and debates. The festival is also accompanied by a shopping spree with stores donating to Australia's largest HIV/AIDS charity – the Bobby Goldsmith Foundation. There is a wide spectrum of music and entertainment, and drag queens jostle for attention in the crowd.

The parade features floats, marketing groups and events. The Mardi Gras Party at Fox Studio, which has shows, costumes and dancing all night, is a major event. The festival encourages gay and lesbian travellers to visit Sydney in February, but also acts as a magnet for all tourists to visit the city to take part in the spectacular event.

GALTA – GAY AND LESBIAN TOURISM AUSTRALIA

GALTA has been established to deliver a service to all gay and lesbian visitors to Australia. Details of GALTA are shown in Exhibit 6.2.

CONCLUSIONS

Australia has been very focused in establishing a well recognized gay and lesbian tourism business. It has taken a strategic view of this development using well balanced management principles and practices, so that gay and lesbian travellers can be accommodated alongside other visitors to Australia. The Mardi Gras festival in Sydney has proved a particular magnet for gay and lesbian visitors.

There is, however, one word of caution from GALTA: while this case study highlights how the development of a niche market can drive tourism growth, once a must-see on the LGBT international traveller's wish list, it seems Australia is losing ground to other global destinations with a notable absence on recent holiday wish-lists of the most gay-friendly places to visit. From Lonely Planet's "Most Gay-friendly Nations" to the *Huffington Post*'s "Top LGBT hot-spots" Sydney and Australia do not feature in 2015. As GALTA President John Stringer puts it: "Sadly, Australia is viewed as one of the least progressive [in regard to LGBT equality] and this isn't helping to attract international LGBT visitors."

DISCUSSION POINTS AND ESSAY QUESTIONS

1. Evaluate the reasons for Australia being particularly committed to the growth of gay and lesbian tourism.
2. Discuss the importance of festivals such as the Mardi Gras festival Sydney for the development of gay and lesbian tourism.
3. Discuss the ways in which a country or city can balance the development of gay and lesbian tourism with other forms of tourism development.
4. Assess the nature and importance of having a well-developed tourism infrastructure to underpin the development of gay and lesbian tourism.

REFERENCES

Adams, M. (1993). The gay nineties. *Inventive* September, 58–62.

Mintel (2015) *Travel and Tourism – Hawaii Report*. May. Mintel.

Stuber, M. (2002). Tourism marketing aimed at gay men and lesbians: a business perspective. In *Gay Tourism: Culture, Identity and Sex*, eds S. Clift, M. Luongo and C. Callister. Continuum, London and New York.

Typologies of tourist behaviour

In Part 2 we looked at how individual tourists make their purchasing decisions. It is now time to look at ways in which academics and marketers have sought to group tourists together on the basis of shared characteristics. This has resulted in typologies of tourists and methods of segmentation. Part 3 considers both of these.

These typologies are important for a number of reasons. They:

- represent an attempt to increase our knowledge of consumer behaviour in tourism
- can help marketers make important decisions on product development, pricing, promotional media and distribution channels
- may form the basis of market segmentation techniques
- potentially could help to predict future trends in tourist behaviour.

In Chapter 7 we consider both the typologies academics have produced and the application to tourism of classical segmentation techniques.

Typologies of tourist behaviour and segmentation of the tourism market

For over three decades, academics have sought to produce meaningful typologies of tourists and their behaviour. At the same time, practitioners have tried to apply and adapt classical market segmentation techniques to the tourism industry. In this chapter we consider both of these approaches separately, although clearly there are links between them.

Academic typologies

The most fundamental debate, perhaps, is that about whether people are tourists or travellers. Although the term 'tourist' dates back two centuries, it has entered popular usage only in recent decades. Sharpley suggested that the terms 'tourist' and 'traveller' were used interchangeably to describe 'a person who was touring' (Sharpley, 1994).

However, nowadays the two words mean different things. There is the idea that a tourist is someone who buys a package from a tour operator, while a traveller is a person who makes their own independent arrangements for their vacation. The idea has grown up that the latter type of behaviour is somehow superior to, or better than, the former. Therefore many people who buy tourist packages want to still see themselves as travellers (Horner and Swarbrooke, 1996).

As Sharpley noted, the term 'traveller'

> is usually applied to someone who is travelling/touring for an extended period of time, particularly backpacking on a limited budget. It contains a spirit of freedom, adventure, and individuality.
>
> The word tourist, on the other hand, is frequently used in a rather derogatory sense to describe those who participate in mass produced, package tourism.

> (Sharpley, 1994)

Boorstin illustrated that the debate over this issue is full of subjective judgements when he wrote about the 'lost art of travel' in the following terms:

> The traveller, then, was working at something; the tourist was a pleasure seeker. The traveller was active; he went strenuously in search of people, of adventure, of experience. The tourist is passive; he expects interesting things to happen to him . . . he expects everything to be done to him and for him.

(Boorstin, 1992)

As the quote shows, this debate is not new, but it has come back into focus in recent years as status-conscious tourists have sought to differentiate themselves from other tourists and their experiences. As Sharpley (1994) noted, 'disliking and trying to avoid other tourists at the same time as trying to convince oneself that one is not a tourist is, in fact, all part of being a tourist'.

Culler (1981) put it succinctly when he wrote that 'all tourists can always find someone more touristy than themselves to sneer at'.

The tourism industry has, in recent years, recognized the implications of this whole debate and has begun to emphasize more and more the 'non-touristy', 'unspoilt' nature of destinations. It has also sought to massage the egos of customers by convincing them that the product they are buying means they are travellers, not tourists.

Having discussed this general issue about the classification of tourists, it is now time for us to turn our attention to a consideration of some well known academic typologies of tourists. As tourism has become a more complex issue, researchers have tried to classify tourists into groups that share similar behaviour. It is interesting to look at these typologies in chronological order to see if we can identify any trends in the classification of tourists.

Cohen (1972)

The influential sociologist Erik Cohen identified four types of tourists in 1972.

- The **organized mass tourist** buys a package holiday to a popular destination and mainly prefers to travel around with a large group of other tourists, following an inflexible, predetermined itinerary. In general such tourists tend not to stray far from the beach or their hotel.
- The **individual mass tourist** buys a looser package that allows more freedom, such as a fly–drive holiday. Individual mass tourists are more likely than organized mass tourists to look for the occasional novel experience. However, they still tend to stay on the beaten track and rely on the formal tourist industry.
- The **explorer** makes his or her own travel arrangements and sets out, consciously, to avoid contact with other tourists. Explorers set out to meet local people, but they will expect a certain level of comfort and security.
- The **drifter** tries to become accepted, albeit temporarily, as part of the local community. Drifters have no planned itinerary and choose destinations and

accommodation on a whim. As far as possible, drifters shun all contact with the formal tourism industry.

Cohen described the former two types of tourist as institutionalized tourists, and the latter two as non-institutionalized. The latter are the pioneers who explore new destinations; the institutionalized travellers then follow later when it has become less adventurous and more comfortable to travel there because of the development of a tourist industry and infrastructure. Sharpley (1994) quotes Goa in India as an example of this phenomenon.

Richard Sharpley criticizes Cohen's typology on the grounds that the institutionalized and non-institutionalized types are not entirely distinct from each other. He argues that even 'explorers' make use of specialist guidebooks to choose their transport routes and accommodation.

Plog (1977)

In 1977 Plog sought to directly link personality traits with tourist behaviour, and divided people into psychocentrics and allocentrics. He argued that the former were less adventurous, inward-looking people. They tend to prefer the familiar and have a preference for resorts that are already popular. Allocentrics, on the other hand, are outward-looking people who like to take risks and seek more adventurous holidays. Plog believed such people would prefer exotic destinations and individual travel. Between these two extremes, Plog suggested a number of intermediate categories such as near-psychocentrics, mid-centrics and near-allocentrics. He suggested that psychocentric American tourists would holiday at Coney Island while allocentrics take their vacation in Africa, for example.

Sharpley quite rightly criticizes this idea of linking types of tourists with specific destinations. He wrote: 'Destinations change and develop over time; as a resort is discovered and attracts growing numbers of visitors, it will evolve from an allocentric to a psychocentric destination' (Sharpley, 1994).

Perreault, Dorden and Dorden (1979)

Based on a survey of 2000 householders, these authors produced a five-group classification of tourists:

- **budget travellers**, who had medium incomes but sought low-cost vacations
- **adventurous tourists**, who were well educated and affluent and showed a preference for adventurous holidays
- **homebody tourists**, who were cautious people who took holidays but did not discuss their vacation with other people, and spent relatively little time planning it
- **vacationers**, who were a small group who spent a lot of time thinking about their next holiday and tended to be active people in lower-paid jobs
- **moderates**, who had a high predisposition to travel but were not interested in weekend breaks or sports.

Cohen (1979)

In 1979 Cohen suggested a five-group classification of tourists, based on the type of experience they were seeking:

- the **recreational tourist**, for whom the emphasis is on physical recreation
- the **diversionary tourist**, who seeks ways of forgetting their everyday life at home
- the **experiential tourist**, who looks for authentic experiences
- the **experimental tourist**, whose main desire is to be in contact with local people
- the **existential tourist**, who wants to become totally immersed in the culture and lifestyles of the vacation destination.

Sharpley (1994) noted that this classification was not 'based on any empirical research: it is a mechanical categorisation'. Cohen's typologies have served as a starting point for many new conceptual redefinitions. Yannakis and Gibson (1992), for example, tried to test Cohen's model and added more tourist types, including sun lover, action seeker, escapist and sport lover, in addition to Cohen's drifter, explorer, individual and mass tourist.

Westvlaams Ekonomisch Studiebureau (1986)

A survey of 3000 Belgians produced the following typology, which identified seven types of tourists:

- **active sea lovers**, who want to take a holiday by the sea, with a beach close by
- **contact-minded** holiday-makers, who value making new friends on holiday and being hospitably received by local people
- **nature viewers**, who want to be well received by the host population while enjoying very beautiful landscapes
- **rest-seekers**, who want a chance to relax and rest while on holiday
- **discoverers**, who like cultural holidays and some adventure, but also like to meet new people
- **family-oriented sun and sea lovers**, the largest group, who like to do things together as a family and seek 'child-friendly' activities
- **traditionalists**, who value safety and security and try to avoid surprises by sticking with familiar destinations and types of holiday.

Dalen (1989)

A Norwegian survey of 3000 individuals led to a four-group classification.

- **Modern materialists** want to get a tan to impress people when they get home. They like partying and are more concerned with drink than food. Hedonism is their main motivation.

- **Modern idealists** also seek excitement and entertainment, but want to be more intellectual than the modern materialists. They do not, however, want mass tourism or fixed itineraries.
- **Traditional idealists** demand quality, culture, heritage, famous places, peace and security.
- **Traditional materialists** always look for special offers and low prices, and have a strong concern with personal security.

Gallup and American Express (1989)

American Express commissioned a survey of 6500 people in the USA, the UK, West Germany and Japan, which resulted in the following five-type classification:

- **adventurers**, who are independent and confident and like to try new activities
- **worriers**, who worry about the stress of travel and their safety and security while on holiday
- **dreamers**, who are fascinated by the idea of travel, and read and talk a lot about their travel experiences and different destinations
- **economisers**, who simply see travel as a routine opportunity for relaxation rather than as a special part of their life, and want to enjoy holidays at the lowest possible price
- **indulgers**, who want to be pampered when they are on holiday.

Smith (1989)

Smith identified seven types of tourists:

- **explorers** are a small group who travel almost as anthropologists
- **elite tourists** are experienced frequent travellers who like expensive, tailor-made tours
- **off-beat tourists** aim to get away from other tourists
- **unusual tourists** make side trips from organized tours to experience local culture
- **incipient mass tourists** travel to established destinations where tourism is not yet totally dominant
- **mass tourists** expect the same things they are used to at home
- **charter tourists** have little or no interest in the destination itself, provided the holiday gives them the entertainment and standards of food and accommodation they expect.

Wood and House (1991)

The debate about sustainable tourism has, in recent years, led to some moralistic and judgmental approaches to the classification of tourists. For example, there is the idea of the 'good tourist', put forward by Wood and House in 1991. Such tourists behave in a responsible manner towards the environment and the host community in their holiday destination. It is argued that all tourists can aspire to join this group if they modify their behaviour in particular ways. Horner and Swarbrooke (1996) have suggested that, for tourism organizations, 'this group may represent a potentially lucrative niche market, which must be sold products it can feel good about buying'.

Wickens (2002)

Relatively few writers have attempted to produce typologies of tourists visiting a particular destination. One recent exception is that produced by Wickens in relation to a resort on the Chalkidiki peninsula in Greece. She based her research on Cohen's typology of 1972, and produced a five-group typology.

- **Cultural heritage tourists** are interested in the natural beauty, history and culture of Greece. They long to experience the 'traditional Greek village life' portrayed in the holiday brochures. They use the seaside resort as a base from which to tour the attractions in the region. This group tends to be made up of family groups and older holiday-makers.
- **Ravers** are attracted by the nightlife and the cheapness and availability of alcohol. They also enjoy the sun and the beach. They tend to swim and sunbathe in the day, and go clubbing at night. These are mostly young males.
- **'Shirley Valentines'** are women on holiday with other women who hope for romance and sexual encounters with Greek men. For these women, their holiday represents an opportunity to get away from their everyday life of domesticity.
- **'Heliolatrous'** tourists are sun-worshippers whose main aim is to get a tan. They spend much of their holiday in the open air.
- **'Lord Byrons'** tend to return year after year to the same destination, and even the same hotel or accommodation unit. They are in love with Greece, particularly its perceived relaxed, laid-back lifestyle. They want to be treated as a guest, not as a tourist. They are after nostalgia and lament the impact of mass tourism on their favourite destination.

Urry (2002)

Urry, in the UK at least, popularized the term the 'post-tourist' in the early 1990s, which had earlier been mentioned by writers such as Feifer (1985). These tourists are a product of the so-called 'postmodern' age. They recognize that there is no such thing as an authentic tourism product or experience, and accept pseudo events for what they are. To post-tourists, tourism is just a game and they feel free to move between different types of holiday. Today they may take an eco-tourism trip to Belize, while next year they may lie on a beach in Benidorm.

As Feifer (1985) stated, the post-tourist is conscious of being a tourist, an outsider, 'not a time traveller when he goes somewhere historic; not an instant noble savage when he stays on a tropical beach; not an invisible observer when he visits a native compound'.

If such a tourist is now a reality, as Sharpley suggested in 1994:

> For the post-tourist, then, the traveller/tourist dichotomy is irrelevant. The traveller has matured and evolved into an individual who experiences and enjoys all kinds of tourism, who takes each at face value and who is in control at all times. In effect, the post-tourist renders tourist typologies meaningless!

Wickens, 2002

In more recent years there has been a tendency to try and subdivide the groups, arguably accompanied by the development of niche markets in the marketing arena. Wickens demonstrated that, in the Greek context, Cohen's 'individual mass tourist' group could be divided into a number of smaller subcategories. This idea has also been researched in relation to backpackers, where Cohen's 'drifters' group could be subdivided into a number of distinct subcategories (Brenner and Fricke, 2007).

Uriely *et al.*, 2002; Uriely, 2005

The emergence of smaller groups in the typology literature was researched by Uriely in Israel, who suggests that backpackers seek different tourist experiences and therefore fall into well-defined subgroups. The researcher did mention, however, that although this approach represents a more realistic picture of the complexity of tourism behaviour, it could also lead to a failure to capture the overriding features of the tourism phenomenon (Uriely, 2005).

Pearce, 2008

This researcher adopts a more supply side approach and suggests that leisure tourists could be divided according to the way they purchased their travel products. He suggests that there are three distinct categories – package, independent and customized – where the package tourists purchase ready-made products; the independent tourist tends to behave in a spontaneous way; and the customized tourist purchases tailor-made products that are not normally included in standard packages.

We have just looked at a brief selection of typologies that have been produced over the past 35 or so years. Many others have been omitted because of limitations of space. However, we have tried to offer a range of influential and less well known typologies from authors of different nationalities. It is now time to see if we can identify some common threads in those we have discussed.

A comparison of typologies

Most of the typologies attempt to group tourists together on the basis of their preference for particular vacation experiences in terms of:

- destinations
- activities while on holiday
- independent travel versus package holidays.

Some recognize that tourists' motivations are tempered in reality by the determinants that contribute to their choice of vacation, such as disposable income.

A number of influential early typologies were not based on empirical research; but many of the more recent typologies – Perreault, Dorden and Dorden, Dalen, American Express, for example – have arisen out of empirical studies. In 1987 Plog attempted to produce a typology of typologies. He wrote:

> researchers may actually come up with fairly similar dimensions but may label them differently. As it turns out, there possibly are a very limited number of psychographic/personality dimensions . . . These dimensions may be more clearly defined, or combined in various ways, but they are covered by about eight broad categories.

> (Plog, 1987)

These categories are (Plog, 1987):

- venturesomeness
- pleasure-seeking
- impassivity
- self-confidence
- playfulness
- masculinity
- intellectualism
- people orientation.

A critique of typologies

Not surprisingly, the attempts to classify tourists which we have discussed, and others, have attracted criticism on a number of fronts.

- 'Broad-brush' typologies based on simplistic stereotypes cannot hope to encompass the complex patterns of behaviour we see in the real world.
- Almost all the typologies do not allow for the fact that individual consumers can

move between types in response to the impact of different determinants over time, including changes in health, income, leisure time, and family and work commitments.

- They also tend not to recognize that many holiday-makers do not have autonomy over their choice of holiday destination and vacation activities. The decision is often the result of a compromise between the tourist and the other members of the holiday party, whether they are friends or relatives. Therefore what someone does on holiday may not reflect their true desires or personality.
- Many of the most influential typologies are at least ten years old and therefore cannot represent the many changes in consumer behaviour that have taken place in recent years. They often pre-date newer developments such as mass long-haul holiday markets, budget cruises and the internet, for example. Research is still ongoing, however, on this increasingly complex issue.
- There is still a bias towards Europe and the USA in the vast majority of typologies. Far less has been published on the types of tourists found in Asia, Africa and the Middle East, for example, which might yield very different results.
- On the other hand, some typologies are generally used as if they can be applied to people in all countries. They appear to ignore national and cultural differences, which surely weakens their validity.
- Researchers have sometimes attempted to develop generally applicable typologies from surveys with small samples, which are, at best, questionable.
- Many typologies are descriptive and, as such, do not greatly help us to increase our understanding of tourist behaviour.
- They often ignore the fact that people may mature as tourists as they become more experienced as travellers. As Lowyck, Van Langenhave and Bollaert (1992) argue, it must be debatable 'whether it makes sense at all to divide people into different types without taking into account their full life spans'.
- Too many typologies ignore the gap between professed preferences and actual behaviour, which is an important phenomenon in the tourism market. The gap can be caused by a number of factors, including social conventions, ego, and even self-delusion.
- There are also methodological criticisms of the typologies. For example, some commentators argue that some researchers have allowed their own value judgements to influence their work.
- There are still many gaps in the typology literature. For example, little has been written about the business tourist.

These criticisms are not intended to decry the idea of typologies, but rather to illustrate how difficult it is to develop convincing typologies. Perhaps it also proves that there will never be one typology that reflects the behaviour of all tourists. Instead, we may need as many typologies as there are tourism products, tourism markets, countries and cultures.

Examples of typologies used in ecotourism/nature-based tourism

Weaver, 2001

This researcher considers the nature-based tourist or ecotourist and suggests that there are two categories within this group:

- the 'hard' ecotourist who is environmentally conscious, often travels in groups and engages in specialized activities
- the 'soft' ecotourist who likes to experience short-term nature-based experiences as part of a longer holiday experience.

Strasdas, 2006

This researcher divides nature-based tourists into six different categories according to their commitment to ecology. The categories suggested are as follows:

- committed nature tourists
- interested nature tourists
- casual nature tourists
- nature tourists with specific cultural interests
- sports/adventure tourists
- hunting/fishing tourists.

Arnegger, Woltering and Job, 2010

These researchers suggest a product-based typology for nature-based tourism and put forward a new conceptual framework in a two-dimensional matrix. They suggest four basic travel motivations:

- nature conservation
- nature experience
- sports/adventure
- hedonistic.

They also suggest four different types of tourist products:

- independent
- *à la carte*
- customized
- standardized.

This results in a typology of 16 different types. They also suggest that this could help managers create more sustainable forms of tourism, but that more empirical testing is required to explore the conceptual model. So the question this leaves is whether typologies of increasing complexity are of any relevance to practical marketing operations?

Marketing applications of typologies

Notwithstanding their considerable limitations, these typologies, while not developed with marketing in mind, have a potential role to play in tourism marketing. This could clearly contribute to decisions over product development, price and distribution.

However, their main role could well be in the field of promotion, particularly in the design of the messages that tourism organizations attach to their products for different groups of potential customers. For example:

- 'travellers' want to be convinced that the holiday they may buy is not the type of 'package' bought by 'tourists'
- Perreault et al.'s 'budget travellers' need to be told that their prospective holiday package represents good value for money
- Plog's 'allocentrics' need to have the adventurous aspect of a product highlighted for them
- Dalen's 'traditional idealists' must be persuaded that their desired destination is safe
- Strasdas' 'casual nature tourist' may just want an add-on excursion to their holiday experience to make them feel good.

On the other hand, practitioners would find it difficult to do these things, as current methodologies would make it very difficult and expensive for them to identify each of these groups and target different messages to different groups.

So we will move on to consider the ways in which organizations classify tourists that tend to focus on quantifiable variables and are devised specifically to make marketing more effective.

Market segmentation

Market segmentation has been well defined by Dibb et al. (2005) as:

> The process of dividing a total market into groups of people with relatively similar product needs, for the purpose of designing a marketing mix that precisely matches the needs of individuals in a segment.

This clearly illustrates the fact that market segmentation is a form of consumer classification designed specifically to serve the marketing function. This is one difference between segmentation and the typologies discussed above, which were developed largely by academics who generally were not concerned with their potential role in marketing. The second key difference is that whereas the typologies have been devised specifically in relation to tourism, segmentation is a concept derived from general marketing across all industries.

Classical segmentation criteria and their applications in tourism

There are five classical ways of segmenting markets; in other words, the consumer population can be subdivided, on the basis of five different criteria, into groups that share similar characteristics as buyers. We will now discuss each of these in turn, in terms of their use in the tourism industry.

Geographical segmentation

This method categorizes market groups on the basis of geographical factors, and is widely used in tourism, as the following examples illustrate.

- Theme park markets are often described in terms of catchment areas, expressed in geographical terms. In other words, Disneyland Paris is said to have an international catchment area and Alton Towers a national market, while most others in the UK have a regional catchment area.
- Tour operators consider where their clients live when deciding which departure airports to offer flights from.
- Airlines develop their routes on the basis of geographical patterns of demand.
- An assumption is made that people from cool northern climates will often show a preference for warmer southern climates when selecting their holiday destinations.
- Urban dwellers often desire to visit rural locations for leisure, as a contrast with their everyday environment.

Socioeconomic segmentation

This technique seeks to subdivide markets on the basis of socioeconomic variables. In the UK this is really another term for socioeconomic class, as the British approach to socioeconomic segmentation is based largely on the JICNAR classification. This splits society into six groups, based on occupation, represented by the letters A, B, C^1, C^2, D and E. While this is an apparently crude approach to segmentation, it is widely used, with tourism organizations describing their markets in terms of classes A and B, or C^2D. For example, the case of the UK theme park market is an example of the latter, with museums and opera performances being typical of the former.

Demographic segmentation

This form of segmentation, based on subdividing the population on the basis of demographic factors, has proved particularly popular in tourism, as the following examples illustrate.

Stage in Family Life-Cycle	Likely Preferences and Needs of Consumers
Child	Stimulation. Other Children to play with. Parental guidance and support.
Teenagers	New experiences. Excitement. Status. More independence from parents. Opportunities for active participation. Social interaction with other teenagers.
Young adult	New experiences. Freedom of action. Opportunities for active participation. Social interaction with other young adults.
Young couple	New experiences. Romance.
Young couple with baby	Facilities for babies. Economy. Ease of access for pushchairs and prams.
Growing families	Economy, eg. a family ticket. Something for all the family to do.
'Empty nesters'	Chance to learn something new. Passive rather than active participant most of the time.
Elderly	Watching rather than doing. Economy. Company of other older people. Easy accessibility for people with mobility problems.

Figure 7.1 The family life cycle and visitor attractions

Source: adapted from Swarbrooke (2001)

- Age – some tour operators, notably Saga and Club 18–30 in the UK, segment their potential market purely in terms of age.
- Gender – many weekend break packages and conference partner programmes base their market on gendered stereotypes. For instance, golf is usually seen as a male activity while it is argued that women will prefer shopping.
- Religion – this is clearly at the heart of the pilgrimage market.

One demographic factor that has always been heavily used in tourism is the idea of family status. The assumption is that a consumer's behaviour is determined by where they are in the family life cycle. Figure 7.1 illustrates how this model might be used in relation to the market for visitor attractions.

This family life-cycle model is based on the approach used by the tourism industry. However, there are other forms of the life-cycle model. The approach is also used by tour operators, including:

- holidays for teenagers who are holidaying separately from their parents and wanting independence and an active holiday, for example PGL in the UK (see Case Study 5)

- so-called family holidays where free child places are offered to make holidays more affordable for growing families
- products which have been traditionally aimed at 'empty nesters' to take advantage of their disposable income and leisure time, such as cruises and painting holidays.

Other demographic factors, such as language, have also been used by tourism organizations. Destination marketing agencies have to produce literature in the different languages spoken by their key markets, for instance.

Two criteria that have rarely been used are race and nationality. The former is very sensitive but perhaps it will become increasingly utilized as Europe becomes more of a multicultural society. Already race is a very relevant criterion in the USA, with the rise of the African American market. At the same time, the rise of transnational companies in tourism, such as Accor and TUI, may make national differences an ever more important way of segmenting the market for an organization's product.

The three methods we have discussed so far are rather crude, but they are relatively easy to measure. The next approach is more sophisticated, but is also more difficult to identify and measure.

Psychographic segmentation

This technique is based on the idea that people's lifestyles, attitudes, opinions and personalities determine their behaviour as consumers. This is a more modern approach than the other three we have considered, and it has already begun to influence a wide range of industries, including clothing, food, drink, perfume and cars. It is also beginning to be seen in tourism, as the following examples show.

- Health farms and spas target their marketing at consumers who aspire to lead a healthy lifestyle.
- People who are environmentally aware and whose lifestyle is influenced by environmental concerns are a good target market for conservation holidays.
- Hedonistic sun, sand, sea and sex holidays are usually targeted at extrovert people.
- People who seek thrills are the target market for bungee-jumping or 'white-knuckle rides' at theme parks.

This method of segmentation is the most modern, and it is the most fashionable with marketers at the moment.

Behaviouristic segmentation

This technique groups consumers according to their relationship with a particular product. The range of variations in this approach is illustrated in Figure 7.2. This diagram is clearly selective but it shows both the number of approaches and the links between them.

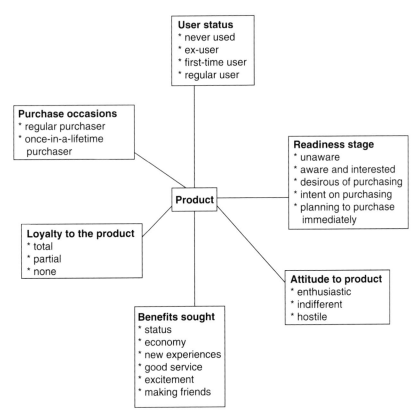

Figure 7.2 Different forms of behaviouristic segmentation

Behaviouristic segmentation is used widely in tourism as we can see from the following examples.

- Airlines' frequent flyer programmes (FFPs) are aimed at regular users to increase loyalty to the product and make people more enthusiastic purchasers of it.
- Hotels and airlines stress the quality of their service.
- Budget tour operators, airlines and hotel chains promote services to consumers whose main 'benefit sought' is economy.

A critique of the classical methods of segmentation

There are three major criticisms of the application of the classical segmentation techniques to tourism, as follows.

- Some of the techniques are dated and have not kept pace with changes in society; for example, the traditional family life cycle looks increasingly inappropriate with the rise of divorce and single-parent families, non-related group households, and couples who choose not to have children.

- Some techniques fail to recognize that tourist behaviour changes over time in response to changes in the circumstances of each tourist. Therefore they will move between segments from time to time as their income grows, their health deteriorates, or they start using the internet to obtain tourist information.
- Much of the market research in tourism is too poor and unreliable to allow us to implement any of these methods accurately.

In general, therefore, all we can do, perhaps, is segment general behaviour or motivations rather than individual people. Marketers must then try to identify and target who is in their particular segment at a specific time when they are seeking to sell a certain product.

Tourism-specific methods of segmentation

While the five classical methods come from general marketing, some tourism academics and practitioners have sought to suggest other techniques that are especially relevant to tourism. For example, Middleton and Clarke (2001) suggest six ways of segmenting markets in travel and tourism:

- purpose of travel
- buyer needs, motivations and benefits sought
- buyer and user characteristics
- demographic, economic and geographical characteristics
- psychographic characteristics
- price.

While four of these are similar to the classical methods, they are worded differently. More fundamentally, Middleton and Clarke add two others – purpose of travel and price.

   Other authors have suggested different methods of segmentation for individual sectors within tourism. Swarbrooke (2001) has suggested three extra criteria in relation to the visitor attraction market:

- visitor party composition, including individual, family group or groups of friends
- visit type and purpose, such as educational trips and corporate hospitality
- method of travel to attractions, for instance, private car or public transport.

Likewise, Shaw (1999) offered a range of appropriate ways of segmenting the airline market, including:

- journey purpose – business, holiday, visiting friends or relatives
- length of journey – short-haul or long-haul traveller.

Shaw believed that these were important criteria in determining the kinds of product a consumer would wish to purchase.

The special case of business tourism

Business tourism is unusual in terms of segmentation in that the market can be segmented into two types of buyer or user:

- the business traveller, who is the consumer of the product, the user of the service, but who usually does not pay the bill
- their employer, who is the customer, the purchaser who pays the bill.

Tourists' response to perceived and real threats: a new approach to typologies and segmentation

In the early years of the twenty-first century, the global tourism industry has been rocked by a series of major threats that have fundamentally affected tourist behaviour, including:

- the events of 11 September 2001 (9/11) in the USA, and also the terrorist attacks that have specifically targeted tourists since 2002 in countries such as Egypt, Kenya and Indonesia
- health scares including SARS and Asian flu
- natural disasters such as the tsunami in South East Asia and hurricanes in the Caribbean and the USA.

As yet, little research has been done on this subject but if such phenomena are going to be a major issue for tourism in the future, we need to understand more about how different types of tourists react to these threats, which is as much to do with their attitudes as it is to do with the reality of the threat.

Taking terrorism as an example, we can already see potential typologies/methods of association, as any terrorist attack or threat seems to elicit the following responses from different types of people:

- stop travelling anywhere altogether
- still travel but avoid certain types of transport
- still travel but avoid certain types of destination
- go ahead with their plans to visit destinations even if there is a perceived terrorist threat, but avoid places that are seen as high risk, such as Western-owned hotel chains or tourist bars
- go ahead with their travel plans to visit places with a perceived threat and make no concessions to the fear of terrorism

- after a terrorist attack, decide to visit the place that has been attacked as a show of 'solidarity' with its residents
- after a terrorist attack, decide to visit destinations that are attacked because of a belief that terrorists never strike twice in the same place
- after a terrorist attack, decide to visit the destination because in the immediate post-attack period prices will be very low.

It would be interesting to do more research on this approach to typologies/segmentation in the future.

This distinction becomes important when one considers airline FFPs, for example. Traditionally the employer (customer) has paid the bill, but it has been the business traveller (consumer) who has enjoyed the benefits of the FFP, such as free flights for partners. Now airlines are realizing that it is the customers who really need to be wooed and are trying to appeal to them with discounted fares.

Marketing applications and segmentation in tourism

We noted earlier that segmentation is designed to serve the need of marketers. It is not surprising, therefore, that writers such as Middleton and Clarke (2001) believe that 'Market segmentation and product formulation are mirror images if they are correctly matched.'

Indeed, segmentation is designed to help with all four Ps of the marketing mix – product, price, place and promotion. This link is discussed in more detail in Chapter 11, so at this stage we simply need to make two brief points.

First, successful marketing is not based on one method of segmentation alone; instead it makes use of a blend of different techniques that will be different on every occasion. We might link personality with geographical place of residence, or we might focus on benefits sought in relation to different demographic factors. A combination of socioeconomic, geographical and demographic factors underpins the use of the ACORN residential neighbourhood classification system in tourism marketing.

Secondly, tourism organizations have to deal with what Middleton and Clarke (2001) have called 'multiple segments'. For example, they say that hotels serve at least five segments – corporate/business clients, group tours, independent vacationers, weekend/midweek package clients, and conference delegates: 'most (tourism) businesses deal with not one but several segments'.

Conclusions

While we have considered the so-called academic typologies separately from segmentation techniques, there are clearly links between them. According to Horner and Swarbrooke (1996):

The typology of Plog (1977) is based firmly on the principles of psychographic segmentation in that it is based on the personality of the tourist ... Concepts such as the 'post-tourist' are closely linked to another element of psychographic segmentation, namely lifestyles. For the post-tourist, tourism is just another aspect of their post-modern lifestyle.

We have seen how difficult it is to produce convincing typologies and segmentation methods, and how all the existing approaches have attracted criticism.

It is important to continually update both the typologies and our approaches to segmentation in order to reflect changes in society and consumer behaviour. Finally, perhaps, we should not focus on how academics or marketers see tourist behaviour, but rather try to find out how tourists themselves evaluate their own behaviour. It is, after all, consumers' perceptions that shape their real behaviour.

Discussion points and essay questions

1. Discuss the potential application of the following typologies of tourists' behaviour to the marketing of tourism products:
   (a) Cohen (1972)
   (b) Plog (1977)
   (c) Dalen (1989)
   (d) Weaver (2001).
2. Evaluate the concept of the 'post-tourist' and examine its potential impact on the tourism market.
3. Discuss the extent to which the typology published by Cohen in 1972 is still relevant today in the light of changes in consumer behaviour and tourism markets.
4. Develop your own typology of tourists for a destination of your choice, like that produced by Wickens (2002) for a resort in the Chalkidiki region of Greece.

Exercise

Write a report examining the application of the five classical methods of market segmentation to one of the following markets:

- mass package tours
- scheduled airlines
- theme parks
- country house hotels
- cruises
- health spas.

Suggest which method or methods are most relevant, and which combination of methods would be most appropriate.

References

Arnegger, J., Woltering, M. and Job, H. (2010). Toward a product-based typology for nature-based tourism: a conceptual framework. *Journal of Sustainable Tourism* 18 (7), 915–928.

Boorstin, D. (1992). *The Image: A Guide to Pseudo-Events in America*. Vintage Books, New York.

Brenner, L. and Fricke, J. (2007). The evolution of backpacker destinations: the case of Zipolyte, Mexico. *International Journal of Tourism Research* 9 (3), 217–230.

Cohen, E. (1972). Towards a sociology of international tourism. *Social Research* 39, 64–82.

Cohen, E. (1979). A phenomenology of tourist experience. *Sociology* 13 (10), 179–201.

Culler, J. (1981). Semiotics of tourism. *American Journal of Semiotics* 1 (1/2), 127–140.

Dalen, E. (1989). Research into values and consumer trends in Norway. *Tourism Management* 10 (3), 183–186.

Dibb, S., Simkin, L., Pride, W.M. and Ferrell, O.C. (2005). *Marketing Concepts and Strategies*, 5th European edn. Houghton-Mifflin, Boston, MA.

Feifer, M. (1985). *Going Places*. Macmillan, London.

Gallup and American Express (1989). Unique four national travel study reveals traveller types. News release. American Express.

Horner, S. and Swarbrooke, J. (1996). *Marketing Tourism, Hospitality, and Leisure in Europe*. International Thomson Business Press.

Lowyck, E., Van Langenhave, L. and Bollaert, L. (1992). Typologies of tourist roles. In *Choice and Demand in Tourism*, eds P. Johnson and B. Thomas. Mansell, London.

Middleton, V.T.C. and Clarke, J. (2001). *Marketing for Travel and Tourism*, 3rd edn. Butterworth-Heinemann, Oxford.

Pearce, D. (2008). A needs–functions model of tourism distribution. *Annals of Tourism Research* 35 (1), 148–168.

Perreault, W.D., Dorden, D.K. and Dorden, W.R. (1979). A psychological classification of vacation life-styles. *Journal of Leisure Research* 9 (1), 208–224.

Plog, S. (1977). Why destination areas rise and fall in popularity. In *Domestic and International Tourism*, ed. E. Kelly. Institute of Certified Travel Agents, Wellesley, MA.

Plog, S. (1987). Understanding psychographics in tourism research. In *Travel, Tourism, and Hospitality Research: A Handbook for Managers and Researchers*, eds J.R.B. Ritchie and C.R. Goeldner. John Wiley and Sons, New York.

Seaton, A.V., Jenkins, C.L., Wood, R.C., Dieke, P.V.C., Bennett, M.M., MacLellan, L.R. and Smith, R. (eds) (1994). *Tourism: The State of the Art*. John Wiley and Sons, New York.

Sharpley, R. (1994). *Tourism, Tourists and Societies*, 2nd edn. Elm Publications, Huntington, UK.

Shaw, S. (1999). *Airline Marketing and Management*, 4th edn. Ashgate, Farnham, UK.

Smith, V. (ed.) (1989). *Hosts and Guests: The Anthropology of Tourism*, 2nd edn. University of Pennsylvania Press, Philadelphia, PA.

Strasdas, W. (2006). The global market for nature-based tourism. In *Natural Heritage, Ecotourism and Sustainable Development*, eds H. Job and J. Li. Lassleben, Kallmünz, Germany, pp. 55–64.

Swarbrooke, J.S. (2001). *The Development and Management of Visitor Attractions*, 2nd edn. Butterworth-Heinemann, Oxford.

Uriely, N. (2005). The tourist experience: conceptual developments. *Annals of Tourism Research* 32 (1), 199–216.

Uriely, N., Yonay, Y. and Simchai, D. (2002). Backpacking experiences: a type and form analysis. *Annals of Tourism Research* 32 (1), 199–216.

Urry, J. (2002). *The Tourist Gaze: Leisure and Travel in Contemporary Society*, 2nd edn. Sage, Thousand Oaks, CA.

Weaver, D.B. (2001). Ecotourism as mass tourism: contradiction or reality? *Cornell Hotel and Restaurant Administration Quarterly* 42 (2), 104–112.

Westvlaams Ekonomisch Studiebureau, Afdeling Toerislisch Underzoeu (1986). *Toerishische gedragingen en attitudes van de Belgen in 1985*. Reeks Vakontieanderzaeken, Brussels.

Wickens, E. (2002). The sacred and the profane: a tourist typology. *Annals of Tourism Research* 29 (3), 834–851.

Wood, K. and House, S. (1991). *The Good Tourist: A Worldwide Guide for the Green Traveller*. Mandarin, New York.

Yannakis, A. and Gibson, H. (1992). Roles tourists play. *Annals of Tourism Research* 19 (2), 287–303.

CASE STUDY 7.1: Irhal.com: the leading travel information source for Muslims

by Saskia Faulk

Since 2010, Muslim travellers have a leading online information source: Irhal.com. Outbound travellers from the Middle East and Muslim travellers everywhere can find specific information about *masjid* (mosque) locations, halal-friendly restaurant and hotel ratings, and time-zone-adjusted prayer times in 85 cities worldwide. Muslims define halal using the Arabic word 'permissible' according to the teachings of the Koran. There are also maps, health-and-safety information, child-centred activities, shopping listings, and other more general information needed by travellers based on extensive, up-to-the-minute research. Irhal.com also has a Facebook wall, where people post interesting discussions about travel and more general news items.

The founder of Irhal.com, Dubai-based Irfan Ahmad, shared his experiences with us in an interview in December 2010.

> **Question:** What inspired you to launch a website?
>
> **Irfan Ahmad:** The story of Irhal.com is a long journey. It began in 1980. I was walking towards Harvard Square in Cambridge, Massachusetts, and saw a sign on a shop window which said, 'Please go away . . .'. I was intrigued. Why would anyone ask customers to go away? I walked closer. 'Please go away . . . often!' read the sign. How appropriate for a travel agency!
>
> Fast forward to April 2010. I launch a travel website – www.Irhal.com. 'Irhal' is an Arabic word that means 'go away'. The window sign of that Cambridge travel agency is the inspiration for the name. But why did I launch a travel website? Another flashback. In 1998, after selling advertising space in international newspapers and magazines for more than 10 years, I took the plunge into the online world. I convinced Yahoo! to let me sell online advertising for them in the Middle East. Advertisers and ad agencies did not want to change. They understood quarter-page and full-page ads. Pixels and swfs and gifs were gibberish to them. But I persisted. The online advertising market grew. Gold diggers came. Funded by venture capitalists, smart young entrepreneurs set up websites. They talked big. They partied big. And they blew away their money. And then

it happened. One of the most respected online sites in the Middle East – ameinfo.com – was bought for $29 million. I had seen the site grow. I knew the two Danes who ran it. I had struggled alongside them to sell online advertising. And I was happy that the internet had finally come of age in the Middle East. And I was proud of their success. And I said to myself, 'I can do this, too!' So, in the summer of 2007, the seed for Irhal.com was planted.

Question: Why did you choose to start a site that focuses on travel?

Irfan Ahmad: The internet has changed the way we travel. And the way we plan it. Airlines and hotels have realized that travel decisions are being made online. And they are advertising online to influence travellers. Some of my biggest clients are from the travel sector. Besides, living in Dubai – which is a world of perpetual summer – makes you yearn for rain and snow and the crunching of autumn leaves under your feet. So, a travel website was born.

Question: What differentiates Irhal.com from other travel sites?

Irfan Ahmad: Irhal.com is an informational website. It aims to provide destination guides to travellers from the Middle East. Its goal is to become an indispensable source of information for outbound travellers from the region. Irhal.com is not aimed at being a Travelocity or Expedia, which caters to the transactional needs of travellers. We're not about booking hotels and airline tickets. We simply want to be a guide; a source of travel inspiration for those seeking ideas on where to go. For those who have already made up their mind about where they wish to go, we want to be their resource for telling them about places to visit in the city, where to get food and where to shop. And of course, we also inform them about their religious needs.

All travel sites provide touristic information. We are no different insofar as tourist information is concerned. Where we stand out is in providing information on prayer timings, halal restaurants and mosque locations. And other bits and pieces of information that would intrigue Muslim travellers and bring them back to Irhal.com repeatedly.

Question: What are some religious issues specific to Muslims that affect their travel preferences?

Irfan Ahmad: Every Muslim is supposed to pray five times a day. Each prayer lasts for about five to ten minutes and has to be offered in specific time bands spread throughout the day. The *Fajr* or Morning Prayer can be offered when dawn breaks: about 90 minutes before the sun rises, and has to be completed before sunrise. *Zuhr* prayers are offered at midday and have a two-hour time band, while *Asr* prayers start after *Zuhr* time ends and can be offered until just before sunset. After sunset is the time for *Maghrib* prayers. This also has an approximately 90-minute time band. About 90 minutes after *Maghrib* is time for the last prayer of the day: *Isha*.

Prayer timings vary based on the time of year as well as the latitude and longitude where a person is located. For Muslim travellers visiting a city for less than two weeks it is advisable to join the *Zuhr* and *Asr* prayers and the *Maghrib* and *Isha* prayers in two separate prayer sessions. When travelling, Muslims need to pray only three times a day instead of the obligatory five.

Ramadan is an important holy month each year. In 2010 it started in mid-August and ended in mid-September. The Muslim calendar is a lunar calendar and each month starts with the sighting of a new moon. Since the lunar calendar is 11 days shorter than the Gregorian calendar (the one generally used today), Ramadan begins a little earlier each year. In 2011, it will begin in the first week of August. And over a 30-year cycle a Muslim will experience Ramadan in every season.

Another important aspect of a Muslim traveller is dietary needs. Practising Muslims do not eat pork or drink alcohol. While Muslims eat beef, mutton and chicken, these have to be slaughtered in the Islamic way to be classified as halal. Instead of killing an animal or bird by stunning, its neck has to be cut to allow the blood to flow out – similar to the kosher method used by Jews. Practising Muslims prefer to eat in restaurants that offer halal meat.

Question: What are some things hotels and restaurants can do to accommodate Muslim travellers?

Irfan Ahmad: Since prayers, as I just described, are part of a person's daily routine, it is important that hotels offer facilities for the convenience of Muslim travellers. Offering something as simple as a prayer rug is a great way to make a Muslim feel at home. As prayers are offered while facing the *Qiblah* (the direction of Makkah, Saudi Arabia), hotels in many Muslim countries have a small sticker on the ceiling or bedside table in all guest rooms indicating the direction of Makkah.

While a Muslim can offer prayers alone in a hotel room, it is preferable to pray with others in a prayer room or mosque. Some hotels make arrangements for this by designating a room for prayers. Nearby washroom facilities are also necessary since it is important to wash one's face, hands and feet before praying.

Regarding dietary needs, food prepared for Muslims should not be mixed with pork or anything that has come into contact with pork products. For example, the frying pan or grill used for making omelettes in the morning should not be also used for frying bacon or ham. No alcohol should be used in the preparation of meals.

Irhal.com lists several halal restaurants in each city for the convenience of practising Muslims. Many hotels have started offering halal meals to their guests – particularly during the month of Ramadan when Muslims fast from sunrise to sunset.

Question: Can you describe the visitors to Irhal.com?

Irfan Ahmad: In October 2010, Irhal.com was visited by more than 150,000 unique visitors who viewed over 1 million pages of the site. The majority of the visitors viewed our Arabic section. Our audience profile consists mainly of people from Saudi Arabia and the UAE. Other Gulf countries, such as Kuwait, Qatar, Bahrain and Oman along with Lebanon, Syria, Jordan and Egypt, account for 90 per cent of the traffic on the site.

While we have not done any survey of the Irhal.com visitor yet (we are planning to do this in early 2011) we know that the visitors are mainly high-net-worth Arabs. The English section of the site is visited by both Arabs and expats in the Middle East. There is usually some difference in the travel patterns of the English and Arabic site visitor.

Question: Do you know about the travel choices of visitors to your website?

Irfan Ahmad: An analysis of the most popular destinations in each section shows that 11 out of the top 25 cities visited in the Arabic section are in Muslim countries, while in the English section only five cities are in Muslim countries.

Recent headlines proclaiming bans on face veils and minarets, and the announcement by the German Chancellor that Muslims in Germany should integrate and observe Christian values, have not had any significant impact on the attitude of Irhal.com visitors. Both Europe and the United States continue to be destinations of choice. During the holy month of Ramadan, Makkah became the most popular destination as Muslims make an effort to visit the city; subsequently, Chicago seems to have overtaken it to become a popular destination.

Dubai is a popular destination among Arabs and among expats living in the region, and its popularity among the visitors of Irhal.com reflects this.

Question: To what degree does religion play a role in travel choices among your visitors?

Irfan Ahmad: If religion were the dominant factor for selecting a destination, cities in Muslim countries would have been more popular on Irhal.com. Kuala Lumpur – which gained in significance after 9/11, as there was a shift in travel away from the US and Europe towards the Far East – is ranked No. 28 among Arabs and is not even in the top 50 destinations on the English section of Irhal.com. Malaysia is trying to woo travellers from the Middle East, and in 2009 almost 400,000 people from the Middle East visited Malaysia – but this number pales in significance compared with the fact that 24 million tourists visited Malaysia in 2009.

Travellers from the Middle East are looking for destinations that can offer them respite from the scorching temperatures in the region, and are also searching for family adventure. They usually take short breaks in neighbouring countries, but three- to four-week vacations during the summer. During these long vacations they need their halal food and other religious conveniences, and that is why hotels around the world are beginning to offer special facilities for the Muslim traveller. In fact, segregated swimming pools and female-only spa facilities are coming up, and women – who traditionally did not enjoy sea/beach vacations – are being pampered with offers meeting their religious proclivities. Muslim women should dress modestly and not reveal too much of their body to men. Swimming pools or private beaches where no men are allowed and where outsiders cannot peep in comply with the requirements and help them enjoy without any worries.

DISCUSSION POINTS AND ESSAY QUESTIONS

1. Go to the Irhal.com's section 'Top Destinations' (Irhal.com/Top-Destinations.html) and select a city of your choice that is not in the Middle East. Analyse the information that is provided and determine, based on a quick comparison with a city in the Middle East, to what degree your city of choice offers Muslim-friendly options. What differences can you see between your city and a Middle-Eastern one in terms of tourism offerings interesting for, or particularly compatible with, Muslim travellers?

2. Get together in small groups and find out about each other's travel preferences and restrictions, based on religion or values. Use some of the following questions to discover how these preferences and restrictions play a role in your choice of type of holiday, destination, or choice of restaurant.
   - Do you have any special requirements or strong preferences relevant to restaurants, hotels or airlines based on your religion or values, for example regarding prayer facilities or a destination sought after for pilgrimage?
   - Do you have any restrictions relevant to restaurants, hotels or airlines due to your religion or values, for example regarding meat, seafood or alcohol?
   - What are the main times of year for travel according to religious or traditional festivals/holidays, such as Lent or Ramadan, and the preferences travellers might have at those times?

   Summarize your group's findings in an informal five-minute presentation.
3. Read the *Muslim Visitor's Guide* from Tourism Western Australia (a state government agency) to get an idea about how a regional tourism authority attempts to make Muslim tourists and students feel at home. Do a quick search online to determine if your city/region offers specialized information like this for Muslim or other travel groups. If so, how do the guides compare? Link to the Muslim visitor's guide: www.australia.com/en-sg/news/muslim-friendly-australian-holiday-ideas.html

---

CASE STUDY 7.2: Segmenting the leisure shopping market

Leisure shopping – buying things for pleasure rather than out of necessity, and enjoying the actual process of shopping – is a major element of the tourism market today. For some destinations it is the core of their tourism product, and many tourists now spend more on retailing than they do on their flight or accommodation.

However, like all markets the leisure shopping market is not a homogeneous one; it can be divided into different segments on the basis of different criteria. Let us now examine some of these criteria.

First, there is the issue of how far tourists are willing to travel for leisure shopping. This may vary from a few kilometres to thousands of kilometres. The distance travelled will, of course, also have an impact on the duration of the trip.

We could also segment the market on the basis of either ability to spend or willingness to spend – which are not the same thing. This segment could range from those willing to spend thousands of US dollars or euros on a trip to those unable or unwilling to spend more than a few dollars or euros. For some, window-shopping may be as important a part of the experience as actually buying something.

As with all types of tourism, the leisure shopping market may also be divided into domestic, inbound and outbound segments. Leisure shopping can also be segmented in terms of its seasonality, built around events such as sale periods or Christmas shopping, or even specially organized shopping festivals.

It is also perhaps important to distinguish between trips where retailing is the main purpose of the trip and a general vacation where shopping will be undertaken on just one or two days. We can also segment this market on the basis of who is taking the trip – a person on their own, a couple, a family or a group of friends. In the UK, for example, groups of women friends may well take a shopping trip together.

It is also interesting to split the market based on the kinds of outlets people prefer to visit, including:

- major shopping malls
- small independent shops
- factory outlets and warehouses that sell products directly from the manufacturers
- traditional markets or *souks*.

Some people will shop in all such outlets, while others will have particular preferences.

It is also interesting to see if we can divide the market into segments based on the products people like to buy. In other words, people may prefer to buy branded designer goods through to traditional local products. At the same time, we also have people who are only really interested in particular types of product, which might include clothing, jewellery, CDs and DVDs, or food and drink. And while most people like to buy new products, some really enjoy buying second-hand items from shops and flea markets.

Many people would argue that the market can be easily segmented by gender; in other words, women like leisure shopping more than men. However, while there may be some truth underpinning this view, it is far too stereotypical given that many men enjoy shopping and some women hate it.

In tourist destinations, there is also always the distinction between those who are shopping for themselves and those who are buying for others.

There are also some ethically questionable or unethical forms of leisure shopping, including people who:

- shop for profit – buy things with the express intention of taking them home to sell
- exceed the legal limit on purchasing certain goods such as alcohol or tobacco, to the point where they are engaging in 'smuggling'
- buy illegal souvenirs, for example ancient artefacts or items made from endangered animals.

Having looked at the different ways of segmenting, we will now briefly look at the role leisure shopping plays in tourist destinations, illustrated through Exhibit 7.1.

As leisure tourism has grown, so too have the sources of advice available for tourists concerning leisure shopping opportunities in destinations. There are now specialist guidebooks on leisure shopping in particular cities, often also giving advice on where to stay and eat. Most of these guides are 'mainstream', but often include details of quirky and unusual retail outlets as well. More 'traditional' guidebooks to destinations as a whole, such as those published by Fodor, Frommer, Lonely Planet, Time Out and so on, offer a lot of advice about where to shop.

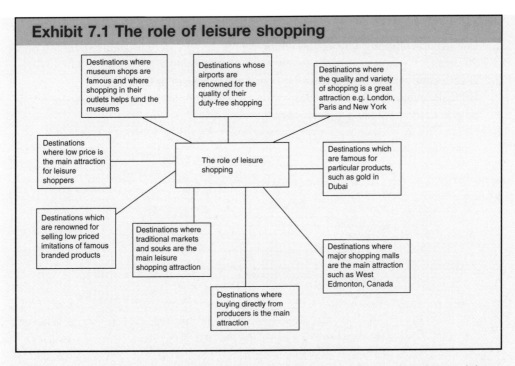

Exhibit 7.1 The role of leisure shopping

- Destinations where museum shops are famous and where shopping in their outlets helps fund the museums
- Destinations whose airports are renowned for the quality of their duty-free shopping
- Destinations where the quality and variety of shopping is a great attraction e.g. London, Paris and New York
- Destinations where low price is the main attraction for leisure shoppers
- The role of leisure shopping
- Destinations which are famous for particular products, such as gold in Dubai
- Destinations which are renowned for selling low priced imitations of famous branded products
- Destinations where traditional markets and souks are the main leisure shopping attraction
- Destinations where major shopping malls are the main attraction such as West Edmonton, Canada
- Destinations where buying directly from producers is the main attraction

Travel features in magazines and newspapers also tend to focus attention on leisure shopping. Destinations often organize special shopping festivals in the off-peak season to boost demand, including examples in Dubai and Hong Kong.

In many cities, tourists can now take organized shopping tours. For example, in New York tours are available to food shops and clothing shops, as well as trips to out-of-town shopping complexes such as Woodbury Common Premium Outlets. Leisure shopping malls have almost developed into mini-destinations in their own right. Multi-development complexes and food courts in many countries have become day-trip destinations.

Leisure shopping is a global phenomenon, but it is particularly well established in the US domestic market, and is also a major factor influencing the destination choice of many outbound tourists from recently developed countries in Asia, for example. It is also a major activity for tourists from former communist countries, for whom leisure shopping is a relatively new experience.

CONCLUSIONS

In the past 20 years, leisure shopping has grown dramatically worldwide and is now a major component of the global tourism market. However, it is a very diverse market which has yet to be thoroughly researched. It seems likely to continue to grow and become an even more important phenomenon for tourist destinations.

DISCUSSION POINTS AND ESSAY QUESTIONS

1. Discuss the reasons why leisure shopping has grown so dramatically over the past 20 years.
2. Discuss the ethical issues raised by certain aspects of leisure shopping.
3. Critically evaluate the suggestion made by some commentators that leisure shopping is fundamentally a female market.

Tourism demand and markets

Having looked at the theoretical dimension of tourist behaviour in Parts 2 and 3, we now turn our attention to the current facts and figures relating to tourism demand and markets worldwide.

In four chapters we will explore:

- the global pattern of tourism demand
- national differences in demand in relation to domestic, outbound and inbound tourist flow
- the nature of demand in different market segments
- the markets for different sectors of tourism.

CHAPTER 8

The global pattern of tourism demand

Introduction

In this chapter we consider the patterns of tourism demand, divided by global regions. We start our analysis by considering the factors that influence tourism demand, and continue by considering some of these key factors in more detail. These include the economic position of the regions or countries, the degree of urbanization and the overall quality of life. The chapter will finish with an analysis of tourism demand for regions of the world and we will draw comparisons between the different regions.

Factors that influence tourism demand

The factors that influence the levels of global tourism were explored by the World Tourism Organization (WTO) in 1995. These factors are shown in Figure 8.1.

Tourism arrivals and receipts

There was a growth of international tourist arrivals from 565 million in 1995 to 636.6 million in 1998, and the WTO has predicted this will grow to 101.56 billion by 2020 (UNWTO, 2005). The WTO has also explored the influences and determinants that affect the choices individuals make when choosing a tourism product. These are shown in Figure 8.2.

It can be seen from Figures 8.1 and 8.2 that many issues have an effect on levels of tourism demand. Demographic and social changes affect the patterns of tourism demand. One example of this is the ageing demographic profile in Europe, which is having an effect on the development of tourism products specifically aimed at third age sections of the population. Consumer knowledge of available tourism products also influences tourism demand. This is particularly important in developed countries,

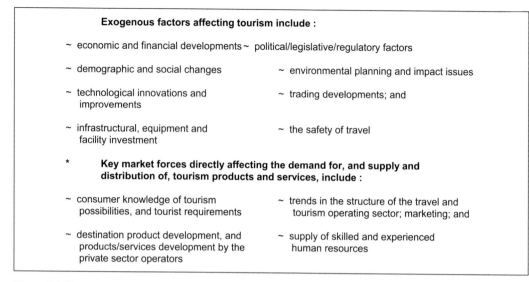

Exogenous factors affecting tourism include :

~ economic and financial developments ~ political/legislative/regulatory factors

~ demographic and social changes   ~ environmental planning and impact issues

~ technological innovations and   ~ trading developments; and
  improvements

~ infrastructural, equipment and   ~ the safety of travel
  facility investment

*   **Key market forces directly affecting the demand for, and supply and
      distribution of, tourism products and services, include :**

~ consumer knowledge of tourism   ~ trends in the structure of the travel and
  possibilities, and tourist requirements   tourism operating sector; marketing; and

~ destination product development, and   ~ supply of skilled and experienced
  products/services development by the   human resources
  private sector operators

Figure 8.1 Factors shaping the development of tourism

Source: WTO (1995)

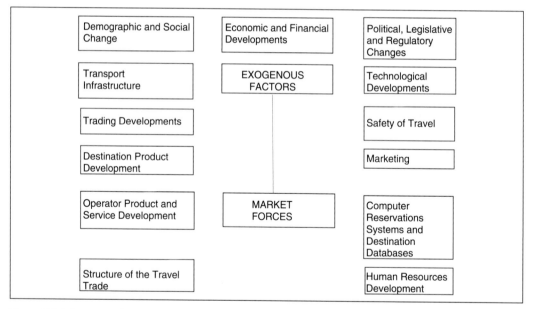

Figure 8.2 Influences and determinants

Source: WTO (1995)

where individuals will generally be eager to learn about the opportunities for travel, particularly where political or economic factors have affected their decisions in the past.
The growth of television programmes and specialist magazines on tourism has been
a reflection of the growing interest in tourism. These programmes have also fuelled

tourism demand, as has the growth and development of tourism companies offering more choice to consumers. The development of large aircraft, most recently the A380 which can travel long distances and carry large numbers of passengers, has helped in the development of new long-haul destinations. The use of the internet for both information searching and booking tourism products has been perhaps the most important factor in the growth of international travel.

The reduction in prices of tourism holidays has also increased the demand for tourism products. The development of good value-for-money holiday packages by UK package holiday operators, for example, has been the main reason for the large numbers of British people travelling overseas on holiday packages, resulting in strong outbound tourism from the UK. However, as we saw in the recent economic crisis in the UK, economic conditions can temporarily reverse this trend.

Key determining factors influencing tourism demand

We now consider some of the factors that influence tourism demand in more detail.

The economic position of the region or country has a direct effect on the levels of tourism demand. There are various ways of measuring economic activity of individual countries or regions. It can be anticipated that the world's biggest economies will provide a large proportion of tourism demand. It is interesting to look at the gross domestic product (GDP) per capita for different regions of the world, and a summary of these is shown in Table 8.1 for Europe and Table 8.2 for major countries of the world.

Income distributions have changed in different areas of the world owing to three major factors – economic reasons, demographic reasons and policy considerations (Euromonitor, 2004). Tables 8.1 and 8.2 show changes in income distribution over the past few years, and it can be seen these have been much more pronounced in some

Table 8.1 Gross domestic product (GDP), total, $US per capita

Country	2011	2012	2013	2014
France	37350.34	37273.28	37606.78	38857.98
Greece	26675.36	25462.37	25666.50	26015.63
Hungary	22523.83	22494.00	23336.25	24473.94
Ireland	44909.15	45209.74	45642.09	47795.93
Italy	35494.45	35054.24	34836.43	35067.21
Luxembourg	91283.68	91754.18	90723.66	93261.17
Netherlands	46388.50	46386.97	46749.31	47634.76
Poland	22065.23	22869.07	23697.58	24510.33
Portugal	26932.42	27000.51	27509.23	28316.71
Slovak Republic	25067.37	25724.84	26498.54	27584.45
Slovenia	28491.97	28455.38	28864.40	29923.37
Sweden	43709.27	43869.26	44646.27	45113.05
United Kingdom	36534.36	37383.19	38255.60	39215.64

Source: OECD (2015b)

Table 8.2 Gross domestic product (GDP), total, $US per capita

Country	2010	2011	2012	2013	2014
Australia	42253.18	43801.57	43675.72	44706.35	44612.17
Austria	41815.90	44045.1	44892.24	45092.88	46151.10
Belgium	39345.62	41206.04	41675.24	41863.94	42986.51
Brazil	14178.50	15065.36			
Canada	40055.26	41567.44	42283.47	43038.07	44057.24
Chile	18172.59	20188.53	21108.32	21888.04	22253.77
China (People's Republic of)	9031.01	10016.63	10917.47	11874.38	
Colombia	10786.51	11586.87	12125.33	12695.07	
Czech Republic	26940.78	28602.62	28635.61	28962.64	30366.37
Denmark	41812.08	43318.51	43564.52	43797.23	44835.19
Estonia	21056.27	23535.54	24688.8	25780.3	26312.21
Euro area (18 countries)	36006.71	37384.08	37493.74	37713.78	38752.49
European Union (28 countries)	33168.84	34482.59	34794.41	35210.73	36174.49
Finland	38296.16	40251.14	40209.11	39869.11	39765.36
France	35896.08	37350.34	37273.28	37606.78	38857.98
Germany	39562.82	42089.46	42730.19	43108.31	44788.34
Greece	28900.82	26675.36	25462.37	25666.5	26015.63
Hungary	21477.60	22523.83	22494.00	23336.25	24473.94
Iceland	38662.87	39619.94	40606.01	42035.81	43648.24
Indonesia	8488.71	8906.89	9432.724	10022.58	
Ireland	42904.37	44909.15	45209.74	45642.09	47795.93
Israel	28773.18	30193.01	31647.69	32504.72	33086.09
Italy	34395.68	35494.45	35054.24	34836.43	35067.21
Japan	33747.64	34312.11	35600.73	36224.94	36485.40
Korea	30465.25	31327.15	32021.74	33089.08	34355.90
Latvia	17639.77	19966.82	21349.16	22956.26	23281.40
Lithuania	20052.38	22530.31	24083.67	25714.68	26646.75
Luxembourg	84109.85	91283.68	91754.18	90723.66	93261.17
Mexico	15139.41	16366.30	16808.21	16891.09	17710.06
Netherlands	44752.11	46388.50	46386.97	46749.31	47634.76
New Zealand	30942.11	32220.52	32860.66	34989.24	36401.46
Norway	58775.40	62737.80	66357.73	65635.29	64873.79
OECD – Europe	33926.94	35314.05	35575.90	35947.96	36818.78
OECD – Total	35046.36	36338.94	37139.22	37891.90	38898.08
Poland	20501.86	22065.23	22869.07	23697.58	24510.33
Portugal	26924.42	26932.42	27000.51	27509.23	28316.71
Russia	20497.95	22569.81	24084.96	25365.64	
Saudi Arabia	45291.62	49229.77	52015.93	53712.82	
Slovak Republic	24258.77	25067.37	25724.84	26498.54	27584.45
Slovenia	27560.52	28491.97	28455.38	28864.40	29923.37
South Africa	11623.17	12143.91	12555.49	12890.54	
Spain	32360.51	32678.45	32774.36	33111.45	33720.17
Sweden	41727.29	43709.27	43869.26	44646.27	45113.05
Switzerland	51120.53	54550.69	55915.51	56939.69	57743.83
Turkey	16001.4	17692.27	18001.84	18599.27	19053.76
United Kingdom	35924.21	36534.36	37383.19	38255.6	39215.64
United States	48307.10	49731.54	51434.70	52985.48	54639.92

Source: OECD (2015a)

countries than others. We will now give a brief overview of the changes that have occurred across the world.

Asia Pacific

There are extreme variations between different areas of the Asia Pacific region. Income is distributed across the region according to regional dimensions, education levels, ethnic groups and the division of urban and rural areas. Japan, Hong Kong and Singapore have the highest GDP per capita of the whole region. There are very big differences within countries according to the concentration of urban areas. In China, for example, there are huge divergences between the prosperous coastal regions and the relatively poor interior.

Africa and the Middle East

The income inequality between households in the Middle Eastern and African countries is relatively low. Gender inequality is high, however, with economic share of the income being on average less than a fifth of that of men's average in the Arab countries, for example (Euromonitor, 2004).

South Africa has an uneven distribution of household income and this difference can largely be explained by race, with white-headed households having higher average incomes compared with black-headed households.

Western Europe

There has been rising inequality of incomes in Western Europe, starting during the 1990s. This developed as a result of the demographic changes that the region experienced. The increase in the number of old people and smaller households has meant that the distribution of income has polarized between lower-income households and those where both partners work and have a relatively higher household income. The households with two partners, who are working, whether or not they have children, are an obvious target for the tourism industry.

Eastern Europe

There have been two patterns of income distribution that have occurred in Eastern Europe. In Central and Eastern European countries, where welfare systems have been preserved, the distribution of income has remained fairly static. In Russia, however, there has been a rising inequality in income distribution owing to a rise in earnings among professionals and the self-employed. This emerging high-income group is an obvious target for the tourism industry.

North America

The USA has experienced increasing income inequality since the late 1960s. The highly skilled professional workers at the top of their professions have experienced real wage gains, whereas at the other end of the spectrum the poor have become poorer. Increases in divorces, separations and a trend towards later marriages have also contributed to a decline in the traditional higher-income household composed of two working adults.

We have only looked at a small sample of regions of the world, but this has demonstrated that the distribution of income is undergoing significant change in certain areas of the world. It is also important to look at the distribution of income in relation to other factors, such as the following.

- Gender – this will be determined by the role of women in the total workforce of a country and the equality of incomes between the sexes.
- Education – the increase in education of a particular population will have an effect on the income distribution among the population. It is argued that a more unusual tertiary education system, for instance, will lead in the longer term to a fairer distribution of income from the privileged few.
- Age – there are major differences between countries and regions regarding the distribution of income among older people. Generally, elderly people living alone and elderly couples constitute a large proportion of households with low incomes. It is important to remember, however, that there are also an increasing number of affluent one-person and two-person households that can be targeted with tourism products.

We can also consider figures for disposable income for a range of countries to give us some clues as to the countries that will generate tourism spend.

It can be seen from Table 8.3 that there has been a significant growth in the purchasing power of the average household in a number of countries over the past decade. Hong Kong and the United Arab Emirates remain high in the table, with Singapore showing rapid growth during the same period. Many European countries have also shown growth during the same period. It is interesting to note that South Korea appears in the top 20 countries because of large growth in average household income over the past decade.

International tourism demand

The WTO has made predictions about the levels of inbound and outbound tourism that will be experienced over the next decade, and its 2005 predictions for the levels of inbound tourism are shown in Table 8.4. It can be seen from these predictions that Europe will lose market share in the amount of international tourist arrivals, with the East Asian and Pacific regions growing in importance.

Table 8.3 Disposable income (purchasing power parity, PPP) 2003 in the top 20 countries of the world (international $ per household at current prices)

Rank	Country	PPP	Percentage growth 1995–2003
1	Hong Kong (China)	69,155.5	20.7
2	United Arab Emirates	64,063.6	6.6
3	Singapore	63,789.1	57.2
4	USA	61,872.8	30.2
5	Kuwait	58,238.0	11.4
6	Taiwan	50,936.8	27.4
7	Ireland	48,238.4	50.7
8	Canada	45,569.8	25.7
9	Italy	44,642.5	16.1
10	Japan	44,544.5	13.6
11	Austria	43,830.6	19.7
12	UK	41,490.0	23.7
13	Australia	41,267.0	32.4
14	France	41,068.5	26.2
15	Norway	40,103.2	21.1
16	Belgium	39,717.4	18.9
17	Germany	37,143.4	28.0
18	Netherlands	37,143.4	28.0
19	Spain	34,857.5	11.7
20	South Korea	34,308.1	46.1

Source: adapted from Euromonitor (2004)

Table 8.4 WTO *Tourism 2020 Vision*: forecast of inbound tourism, world by regions (millions international tourist arrivals by tourist-receiving region)

Region	Base year 1995	Forecasts		Average annual growth rate (%) 1995–2000	Market share (%)	
		2010	2020		1995	2020
Total	565.4	1006	1561	4.1	100	100
Africa	20.2	47	77	5.5	3.6	5.0
Americas	108.9	190	282	3.9	19.3	18.1
East Asia and Pacific	81.4	195	397	6.5	14.4	25.4
Europe	338.4	527	717	3.0	59.8	45.9
Middle East	12.4	36	69	7.1	2.2	4.4
South Asia	4.2	11	19	6.2	0.7	1.2
Intra-regional	464.1	791	1183	3.8	82.1	75.8
Long-haul	101.3	216	378	5.4	17.9	24.2

Source: UNWTO (2005)

Table 8.5 World's top destinations 2020

Rank	Country	Base year 1995 (million)	Forecast 2020 (million)	Average annual growth rate (%) 1995–2000	Market share (%) 1995	Market share (%) 2020
1	China	20.0	130.0	7.8	3.5	8.3
2	France	60.0	106.1	2.3	10.6	6.8
3	USA	43.3	102.4	3.5	7.7	6.6
4	Spain	38.8	73.9	2.6	6.9	4.7
5	Hong Kong (China)	10.2	56.6	7.1	1.8	3.6
6	Italy	31.1	52.5	2.1	5.5	3.4
7	UK	23.5	53.8	3.4	4.2	3.4
8	Mexico	20.2	48.9	3.6	3.6	3.1
9	Russian Federation	9.3	48.0	6.8	1.6	3.1
10	Czech Republic	16.5	44.0	4.0	2.9	2.8
	Total (1–10)	272.9	716.2			

Source: UNWTO (2005)

The predictions for the world's top destinations by 2020 are shown in Table 8.5. It can be seen that countries such as China, Hong Kong and the Russian Federation move into the top 10. Other countries that are predicted to grow in popularity include Asian destinations such as Thailand and Singapore, along with South Africa (UNWTO, 2005).

New and existing tourism destinations are beginning to grow in importance, and the growth in the popularity of long-haul travel will continue to fuel these developments.

Tourism departures and expenditures

The major industrialized countries will remain the leaders in the countries that are producers of tourists who go abroad. Table 8.6 shows the predictions for 2020 of the world's top outbound countries.

It can be seen that there are two important newcomers to the list, which tourism marketers will have to think very hard about in their planning for future business. These two new countries are China entering at fourth place, and Russia entering at tenth place.

The latest data from the WTO support these earlier predictions. A summary of international tourism trends is shown in Figure 8.3.

Conclusions

We have considered the factors that affect world tourism demand figures. Inbound and outbound tourism are predicted to grow in importance over the next decade. Outbound tourism is predicted to grow rapidly from countries within the Asian regions. The Asian, African and Middle Eastern outbound markets are in their introductory or

Table 8.6 World's top outbound countries 2020

Rank	Country	Base year 1995 (million)	Forecast 2020 (million)	Average annual growth rate (%) 1995–2000	Market share (%) 1995	Market share (%) 2020
1	Germany	75	153	2.9	13.3	9.8
2	Japan	23	142	7.5	4.1	9.1
3	USA	63	123	2.7	11.1	7.9
4	China	5	100	12.8	0.9	6.4
5	UK	42	95	3.3	7.4	6.1
6	France	21	55	3.9	3.7	3.5
7	Netherlands	22	46	3.0	3.8	2.9
8	Italy	16	35	3.1	2.9	2.3
9	Canada	19	31	2.0	3.4	2.0
10	Russian Federation	12	31	4.0	2.1	2.0
	Total (1–10)	298	811			

Source: UNWTO (2005)

- International tourist arrivals increased by 4.3 per cent in 2014, reaching a total of 1133 million after topping the 1 billion mark in 2012.
- The Americas recorded the strongest growth with an 8 per cent increase in international arrivals, followed by Asia and the Pacific and the Middle East (both +5 per cent). In Europe arrivals grew by 3 per cent, while in Africa they were up by 2 per cent.
- France, the United States, Spain and China continue to top the rankings by both international arrivals and receipts. Mexico re-entered the top 10 arrivals at position 10. By receipts China and the United Kingdom both moved up two places, to 3 and 7, respectively.
- China, the world's top tourism source market, has contributed its exceptional pace of growth, increasing expenditure abroad by 27 per cent in 2014 to reach a total of US$165 billion.
- Forecasts prepared by WTO in January 2015 point to a 3–4 per cent growth in international tourist arrivals in 2015 – in line with the *Tourism Towards 2030* long-term forecast of 3.3 per cent a year.
- By WTO region, prospects for 2015 are strongest for Asia and the Pacific and the Americas (both +4 to 5 per cent), followed by Europe (+3–4 per cent), the Middle East (+2–5 per cent) and Africa (+3–5 per cent).

Figure 8.3 International Tourism Trends in 2014

Source: UNWTO (2015)

growth stages and there will be great potential for developments from these regions in the future.

The nature of demand may alter as increasing numbers of outbound tourists travel from these regions. Increasing interest in beach holidays and environmental issues are examples of trends that are predicted for outbound tourists from Japan and Asia in general.

In Chapter 9 we will turn our attention to national differences in tourism demand.

Discussion points and essay questions

1. Explain the reasons for the development in levels of inbound and outbound tourism from East Asia and the Pacific regions of the world.
2. Explore the relationship between consumer knowledge of tourism opportunities and demand for tourism products. Discuss the ways in which a consumer can gain knowledge about tourism opportunities.
3. Evaluate the reasons for Japanese tourists showing a growing interest in beach-type rather than city-based holidays.

Exercise

Design and conduct a small-scale survey of tourists to discover their interest in visiting the East Asia and Pacific area of the world. Do they envisage any problems involved in visiting areas such as these?

References

Euromonitor (2004). *World Income Distribution*. Euromonitor International, London.

OECD (2015a). *Household Disposable Income Data*. Organization for Economic Co-operation and Development, Paris.

OECD (2015b). *Gross Domestic Product (GDP) Data*. Organization for Economic Co-operation and Development, Paris.

UNWTO (2005). *Tourism 2020 Vision*, Vols 1–4. World Tourism Organization, Madrid.

UNWTO (2015). *2030 Vision*. World Tourism Organization, Madrid.

WTO (1995). *Global Tourism Forecasts to the Year 2000 and Beyond*, Vol. 1. World Tourism Organization, Madrid.

CASE STUDY 8: Taiwan: the emergence of a new major outbound tourism market

Taiwan has a population of around 23 million and its economy has grown in recent years at an average rate of nearly 9 per cent per annum.

In the early 1990s the Taiwanese government sought actively to encourage its population to take holidays abroad, both to promote the country's image abroad and to help with international relations for the country, which has an unusual existence owing to its lack of recognition by the People's Republic of China.

Travel restrictions have been relaxed and increased disposable income has stimulated the growth of outbound tourism from Taiwan. The number of Taiwanese tourists travelling abroad has grown dramatically from 1.6 million in 1988 to a little under 7.5 million in 2002, rising to 12.2 million in 2013.

Of the tourists who took international trips in 2013, 88 per cent visited other Asian destinations, with 42 per cent going to mainland China and 18 per cent to Japan, a rising Taiwanese destination with Taiwanese visitor numbers doubling since 2009. The major Western destination was the USA, with under half a million Taiwanese visitors, representing 3 per cent of outbound travel in 2013.

A few Asian destinations account for the overriding majority of Taiwanese tourist destinations. Hong Kong/Macau, Korea and Thailand were key destinations.

Being from a recently developed country, Taiwanese tourists were relatively inexperienced travellers tending to travel on highly organized group tours; however, recent numbers show an increasing confidence and appetite for international travel, especially within South East Asia.

Similarly for the Taiwanese inbound market in recent years, Taiwan's international appeal as a destination has been growing rapidly from 3.9 million visitors in 2009 rising to 7.4 million in 2013. Taiwanese visitor sources closely reflect outbound destinations, with 89 per cent coming from East Asian countries. China and Hong Kong represents 53 per cent of the market with some 3.9 million visitors arriving in 2013, while Japan was the next biggest source, making up just less than 19 per cent of the market. As with outbound tourism, the USA represented the biggest non-Asian source with 384,000 visitors, just over 5 per cent of the Taiwanese tourism market.

The recent growth in both outbound and inbound tourism looks set to continue, representing a maturing of the Taiwanese market and its position within its region, especially in a change in attitude towards its neighbour the People's Republic of China.

DISCUSSION POINT

Discuss how changes in the relationship between the governments of Taiwan and the People's Republic of China in the future may affect tourism flows between the two countries.

ACKNOWLEDGEMENT

The data for this case study are from UNWTO (2015a, b).

REFERENCES

UNWTO (2015a). Taiwan (Province of China): country-specific: arrivals of non-resident visitors at national borders, by country of residence 2009–2013. 04.2015. *Tourism Statistics* (2), 9.
UNWTO (2015b). Taiwan (Province of China): country-specific: outbound tourism 2009–2013. 05.2015. *Tourism Statistics* (2), 9.

National differences: domestic, outbound and inbound

Introduction

In Chapter 8 we looked at the pattern of world demand divided by regions of the world. It has been shown that certain areas of the world, such as the Asia Pacific region, are growing rapidly in their levels of tourism. In this chapter we consider the differences between individual countries in more depth. We start by considering the outbound and inbound tourism figures for a range of countries, and then we consider individual countries in more depth. This will enable us to look at particular issues related to tourism demand on a country-by-country basis. The chapter concludes with a discussion on the similarities and differences between individual countries in relation to their tourism figures.

Inbound and outbound tourism receipts

Table 9.1 illustrates inbound tourism numbers for the main regions of the world with forecasts up to 2030.

On the basis of these data, a number of points can be made.

- The number of international tourist arrivals worldwide is expected to increase by an average of 3.3 per cent over the period 2010–30, and international tourist arrivals worldwide are expected to reach 1.4 billion by 2020 and 1.8 billion by 2030.
- International tourist arrivals in the emerging economies of Asia, Latin America, Central and Eastern Europe, Eastern Mediterranean Europe, the Middle East and Africa will grow at double the rate of the advanced economies.
- The global market share of Asia and the Pacific, the Middle East and Africa will grow, and as a result there will be a decline in Europe and the Americas. This

Table 9.1 Forecast of tourist arrivals in millions by region

Region	Actual		Forecast		
	1980	1995	2010	2020	2030
Total	277	528	940	1,360	1,809
Africa	7.2	18.9	50.3	85	134
Americas	62.3	109.0	149.7	199	248
Asia/Pacific	22.8	82.0	204.0	355	535
Europe	177.3	304.1	475.3	620	744
Middle East	7.1	13.7	60.9	101	149
South Asia	2.2	4.2	11.1	21	36

Market share (%)

Region				2010	2030
Africa				5.3	7.4
Americas				15.9	13.7
Asia/Pacific				21.7	29.6
Europe				50.6	41.1
Middle East				6.5	8.2
South Asia				1.2	2.0

Average annual growth rate (%)

Region	Actual	Overall forecast		Forecasts	
	1980–95	1995–2010		2010–20	2020–30
Total	4.4	3.9		3.8	2.9
Africa	6.7	6.7		5.4	4.6
Americas	3.8	2.1		2.9	2.2
Asia/Pacific	8.9	6.3		5.7	4.2
Europe	3.7	3.0		2.7	1.8
Middle East	4.5	10.5		5.2	4.0
South Asia	4.3	6.6		6.8	5.3

Source: UNWTO (2015b)

is a result of the mature destinations in North America, Northern Europe and Western Europe (UNWTO, 2015b).

Let us now turn our attention to considering individual countries in more detail.

The USA

The USA is one of the most important countries in the world in relation to inbound and outbound tourism receipts. The market for outbound tourism from the USA is thought to have great potential for growth as, for a developed country, relatively few US citizens currently take international vacations. At the same time, inbound tourism looks

Table 9.2 Tourism statistics: USA				
Inbound arrivals	2010	2012	2013	2014
Tourists (overnight visitors)	60,010	66,657	69,995	74,757
Outbound statistics	2014			
US resident outbound market	68.2 million			
Top five destination countries visited by US citizens	Number of visitors (millions)			
Mexico	25.9			
Canada	11.5			
UK	2.8			
Dominican Republic	2.7			
France	2.1			
Main purpose of visit	Percentage of visitors			
Vacation/holiday	51			
Visiting friends and relatives	27			
Business	11			
Convention	3			
Other	8			

Source: adapted from UNWTO (2015a); US Department of Commerce, National Travel and Tourism Office (NTTO) (2015)

set to rise due to the fact that the country contains many of the icons of world tourism including New York, Hollywood and the Grand Canyon.

International travel has not been appealing to Americans in the past, and historically fewer than 20 per cent of Americans owned a passport in the 1990s (Euromonitor, 2004). However, economic growth and competitive prices fuelled the growth in tourism over the period 1990–95. There was a growth in outbound tourism during 1993 despite the fact that there were unfavourable currency values. The growth in inbound tourism grew slowly over the period 1990–95 because of the welldeveloped market and problems with the economy in some adjoining countries such as Mexico.

The overall volumes of inbound and outbound tourism in the USA for the period 2010–14 are shown in Table 9.2.

The market for inbound tourism into North America, which represents two-thirds of international arrivals in the Americas region, grew in 2014 largely due to the surge in visitors from Mexico, which is a reversal of previous trends. The USA is now second in the league table in terms of tourism arrivals, behind France, and still holds the number one position in terms of tourism receipts, totalling US$177.2 billion in 2014 (UNWTO, 2015). It can be seen that there has been a growth in outbound tourism, with vacation/holiday travel and visiting friends and relatives being the main reasons for travel. Mexico and Canada are the most visited countries by US tourists; the top overseas

Table 9.3 Tourism statistics: Germany				
Inbound arrivals	*2010*	*2012*	*2013*	*2014*
Tourists (overnight visitors)	26,875	30,407	31,545	33,005
Top markets (thousands)	*2012*			
Netherlands	4,200			
Switzerland	2,500			
United States	2,300			
United Kingdom	2,200			
Italy	1,600			
	2008	*2009*	*2010*	
Outbound departures (million)	86	86	86	

Source: UNWTO (2015a); OECD (2014)

markets are the UK, France, Italy, Germany, Spain, China, India, the Philippines and the Netherlands (US Department of Commerce, 2015)

Germany

Germany is an important country in relation to both inbound and outbound tourism receipts. In terms of the latter, Germany is perhaps the most important market for outbound tourism in the world in terms of its propensity to travel per head of population. Table 9.3 shows the predictions for both inbound and outbound tourism for Germany over the next decade.

The following points can be made about the state of tourism in Germany.

- Tourism is one of the most important economic activities in Germany, although outbound tourism far exceeds inbound tourism.
- Inbound tourism is predicted to rise steadily over the next decade, with the most arrivals still originating in Europe. The countries of Central and Eastern Europe will play a major part in this growth.
- Japan is an important Asian market for the German tourism industry.
- Outbound tourism will continue to rise steadily over the next decade and will remain high, provided there is no downturn in the economy.

Japan

The appreciating value of the yen has historically encouraged overseas travel by the Japanese, whilst the high cost of living has had a negative effect on the numbers of incoming visitors. Declining visitor numbers have also been accompanied by a reduction in spending by foreign tourists. The market for inbound and outbound tourism for Japan is shown in Table 9.4.

Table 9.4 Tourism statistics: Japan						
Inbound arrivals	2010		2012	2013	2014	
Tourists (overnight visitors)	8,611		8,358	10,364	13,413	
Top markets (thousands)	2012					
Korea	2,044					
Chinese Tapei	1,467					
China	1,430					
United States	717					
Hong Kong, China	462					
	2008	2009	2010	2011	2012	
Outbound departures (thousands)	15,989	15,446	16,637	16,994	18,490	

Source: UNWTO (2015a); OECD (2014)

The following points can be made with reference to the inbound and outbound tourism for Japan.

- Outbound tourism significantly exceeds inbound tourism, but inbound tourism will continue to grow in Japan with the majority of the growth coming from the East Asia and Pacific regions.
- Outbound tourism is predicted to grow over the next decade, although a slight decline has been experienced from time to time due to adverse economic conditions.

However, a major question mark hangs over Japan because of its demographic situation, with a high proportion of elderly people and a relatively small and declining indigenous working-age population. This could significantly affect the outbound market.

The UK

The UK is an important tourism market in both outbound and inbound terms. The inbound and outbound tourism figures are shown in Table 9.5.

The following points can be made in relation to the inbound and outbound tourism statistics for the UK.

- The outbound travel market fell dramatically in 2008–10 due to the economic crisis but was recovering a little by 2011–12. Later data is likely to show that the outbound market has come back strongly in 2014–15 due to a strengthening economy and the improved exchange rate of sterling against the euro.
- Inbound tourism has grown steadily over the past five years and is quite strong.
- Arrivals from Europe continue to grow, but arrivals from the USA have remained static over the past five years. New markets such as China, the Middle East and Russia continue to be a focus for tourism market development.

Table 9.5 Tourism statistics: the UK

Inbound arrivals	2010		2012	2013	2014
Tourists (overnight visitors)	28,296		29,282	31,064	32,613
Top markets (thousands)	2012				
France	3,787				
Germany	2,967				
Ireland	2,840				
Netherlands	2,453				
Spain	1,735				
	2008	2009	2010	2011	2012
Outbound departures (thousands)	69,011	58,614	55,582	56,836	56,538

Source: UNWTO (2015a); OECD (2014)

Table 9.6 Tourism statistics: France

Inbound arrivals	2010		2012	2013	2014
Tourists (overnight visitors)	77,648		81,980	83,633	83,700
Top markets (thousands)	2012				
Germany	12,226				
UK	12,205				
Belgium	10,436				
Italy	8,025				
Netherlands	6,355				
	2008	2009	2010	2011	2012
Outbound departures (thousands)	30,960	30,646	29,973	31,153	29,775

Source: UNWTO (2015a); OECD (2014)

France

France has always been a major destination for foreign tourists, largely owing to the range of scenery and attractions that the country can offer the foreign visitor. France also has an excellent climate for tourism, ranging from the sunny Mediterranean in the south to the snowy French Alps. This has led to the development of tourism in both the summer and winter months. Revenue from inbound tourism more than doubled during the 1990s despite the worldwide recession and a strong French currency.

France did, however, experience problems in its tourism market during 1995, when there was a sharp decline in the size of foreign receipts from tourism as well as the number of visitors going to France because of a combination of political and economic factors. Since that time, tourism revenue has continued to grow in the country.

Table 9.6 gives an overview of the inbound and outbound tourism statistics for France.

We can make the following points about French tourism.

- There has been a steady state in the market of outbound tourism from France, despite the many holiday opportunities that France offers to the French, and the state of the economy. However, outbound tourism per head of population remains low compared with Germany and the UK.
- The French have easy access to bordering European countries such as Spain, Switzerland, Italy and Germany. Despite this, a large proportion of the French still prefer to remain at home for their holidays.
- Inbound tourism that originates from Europe continues to rise with the reliance on the main bordering European countries such as Germany, the UK and Belgium.

Spain

Spain is a major European holiday destination. It offers a wide range of scenery and an excellent climate, which has allowed the country to develop substantial tourism receipts, particularly in the package holiday business. Outbound tourism for Spain is shown in Table 9.7.

The following issues can be highlighted.

- Spain has experienced a steady increase in arrivals during the past decade. There are increasing numbers of tourists from Eastern Europe, including Russia, visiting Spain. The European market constitutes the majority of the inbound tourism business for Spain with a large majority originating from the UK and Germany.
- Outbound tourism showed a slight overall increase during the period 2008–11 but there was already a decline in 2012 as the economic crisis began to affect outbound tourism.

Table 9.7 Tourism statistics: Spain

Inbound arrivals	2010		2012	2013	2014
Tourists (overnight visitors)	52,677		57,464	60,675	64,995
Top markets (thousands)	2012				
UK	13,654				
Germany	9,336				
France	8,969				
Italy	3,572				
Netherlands	2,549				
	2008	2009	2010	2011	2012
Outbound departures (thousands)	11,229	12,017	12,397	13,347	12,185

Source: UNWTO (2015a); OECD (2014)

- The market for outgoing tourism from Spain is still a young market that offers substantial potential for growth. The Spanish like to go to other European countries, and France is the most popular destination. Other cheaper destinations such as Turkey, Tunisia and Morocco are also becoming popular with Spaniards.
- Spain has developed its tourism offering over recent decades, with a new emphasis on cultural tourism, sports tourism (including golf and water sports) and conference business.

Newly emerging tourism-generating countries

We have already considered the increasing importance of countries that are experiencing a dynamic growth of the outbound market. Two countries that are at a dynamic stage of their development are India and China. Many destinations are experiencing a strong increase in visitor numbers from these two countries, and this trend seems set to continue and intensify.

Other countries experiencing a strong growth in outbound travel during the past decade are Singapore and Hong Kong (part of China, but with its own specific pattern of demand), with Thailand and Indonesia beginning to emerge as important growth areas. China is also expected to show considerable growth in outbound tourism statistics. Table 9.8 summarizes the tourism statistics for the country and shows the rapid growth in outbound tourism that has occurred over the past few years.

The two most important points about China are as follows.

- There was an enormous increase in outbound tourism 2008–12 caused by economic growth and government policies.
- Inbound tourism has been pretty static, and both outbound and inbound flows are low for a country of China's size.

Table 9.8 Tourism statistics: China					
Inbound arrivals	*2010*		*2012*	*2013*	*2014*
Tourists (overnight visitors)	55,665		57,725	55,686	55,622
Favourite destinations					
Asia The Pacific Increasingly Europe					
	2008	*2009*	*2010*	*2011*	*2012*
Outbound departures (thousands)	45,844	47,656	57,387	70,250	83,183

Source: UNWTO (2015a); OECD (2014)

National differences in tourism markets

Figure 9.1 illustrates the relative scale of domestic, inbound and outbound tourism in ten selected countries. The allocation of 'high', 'medium' and 'low' takes into account the geographical size of the country and its resident population, for example.

A deeper investigation of the factors behind these differences shows that:

- there are many different factors that account for different scales of domestic, inbound and outbound tourism
- even where the scale of the market is relatively similar, the markets themselves can be very different.

Let us now illustrate this by considering each country in turn.

Australia

Australia, as a developed economy where people have relatively high amounts of leisure time, has a reasonably highly developed domestic tourism market. Its inbound market has traditionally been related to in-migration from Europe but has now grown to include leisure tourists from Asia and Europeans who do not have relations in the country.

However, its geographical isolation ensures that it will never be a mass-market destination for people from other continents. A large proportion of Australians travel abroad for holidays, reflecting both Australia's geographical isolation, which creates a desire to see other places, and the availability of time and disposable income. However, its isolation influences the market in that the major outbound segment is young people who travel abroad for one month up to a year. If you live thousands of miles from most potential destinations, a short trip hardly seems worthwhile. The young people and their parents often see a journey to Asia, Europe or North America as completing their education and opening their eyes to the wider world. It could thus be seen as the modern version of the 'Grand Tour'.

Country	Domestic	Inbound	Outbound
Australia	Medium	Medium	High
Dominican Republic	Low	High	Low
France	High	High	Medium
Germany	Medium	Low	High
Japan	Medium	Low	Low
Netherlands	Medium	Medium	High
Nigeria	Medium	Low	Low
Russia	Medium	Low	Medium
Spain	High	High	Medium
USA	High	Medium	Low

Figure 9.1 Suggested relative levels of domestic, inbound and outbound tourism in ten selected countries

The Dominican Republic

The Dominican Republic, on the other hand, is a poor, developing country with low levels of domestic and outbound tourism as a result. However, it has become a major destination in recent years for:

- Europeans looking for inexpensive, all-inclusive, sun, sand and sea holidays in an exotic location
- gamblers from Caribbean countries and South America who come to play the casinos.

In the latter case the local language, Spanish, is the visitors' *lingua franca* so there is no language problem.

France

France is the world's top tourist destination because of:

- its generally attractive climate
- its diversity of attractions, from the culture and romance of Paris to the chic of the Riviera, from the friendly villages of Brittany to the vineyards of Burgundy, from the beaches of the west coast to the Alpine ski resorts
- government investment in the tourism product from the 1960s such as new resorts on the Languedoc-Rousillon coast
- its strong image for food and wine
- its accommodation establishments and restaurants offer relatively good value (outside Paris!)
- effective marketing of the product by the government.

These factors also help to explain the country's high level of domestic tourism and the medium level of outbound tourism. However, there are other reasons. A high proportion of French people own a second home in their own country, which encourages them to take domestic trips. Furthermore, while it could be seen as an issue of 'chicken-and-egg', the outbound tourism sector is not highly developed, which means foreign holidays remain quite expensive for French people. Language problems further constrain people's ability to take holidays abroad.

Germany

Conversely, in Germany outbound tourism is very high, reflecting both the highly developed state of the economy and the statutory holiday entitlement enjoyed by employees, together with a lack of domestic attractions. The climate is not good for summer sun holidays and there is a lack of stylish coastal resorts and attractive cities. The same reasons also explain the medium level of domestic tourism and the low inbound demand. For foreign tourists Germany is an expensive destination, again reflecting the highly developed state of its economy.

Japan

Japan, perhaps surprisingly in view of the stereotypes of the Japanese tourist, in reality generates relatively low levels of outbound demand. This is largely the result of the high cost of living in Japan and the long hours worked there. Indeed, the Japanese government is so worried about the latter fact that it is now encouraging citizens to take more holidays. The main segment that does travel from Japan is young women travelling together, the so-called 'office ladies', and other segments rarely found elsewhere, such as the 'working soldiers'. As a developed economy, Japan has medium levels of domestic tourism but receives only a low level of inbound tourism. This may be due to its high cost of living, language difficulties, or its isolation from traditional tourist trip-generating countries. With the help of Asian tourist markets, which are actually closer to Japan in some cases, it might become more widely visited in the future.

The Netherlands

As an affluent country, the Netherlands generates large numbers of outbound tourist trips. Outbound tourism is also stimulated by the small size and lack of diversity of the Netherlands itself, which limits domestic tourism opportunities. The highly unbalanced nature of the Netherlands and its flat terrain leads Dutch people to seek foreign destinations that are more rural and hilly. They are major players in the camping and caravanning and eco-tourism markets. The lack of diversity and hills also reduces inbound tourism to the Netherlands, which is restricted to the city of Amsterdam and the bulb fields in spring.

Nigeria

As a developing country with a large population, Nigeria has a medium level of domestic tourism, largely related to visiting friends and relatives. Its relatively low level of economic development also resists outbound tourism, although there is an annual outflow of Muslim pilgrims to Mecca and an inflow of business tourists. Because of its unstable political history and poor infrastructure, it attracts relatively few tourists.

Russia

Domestic tourism in Russia is at the medium level, reflecting the well-developed domestic tourism industry that grew up under Communism. Subsidized social tourism at Black Sea resorts created a large domestic market but this has shrunk since the end of Communism. Domestic tourism is probably lower than it was ten years ago because of the reduction in subsidies and the drastic reduction in the living standards of most

Russians. Inbound tourism was always low because of political restrictions on such tourism, but it is now being constrained by political instability, crime and the weakening of the transport infrastructure. Outbound tourism is growing but is still restricted to small wealthy elite. However, this small market is high-spending and is very attractive, as shopping tourists and second home-owners travel to a variety of destinations from Benidorm to Cyprus, Dubai to New York.

Spain

Spain has a welldeveloped domestic tourism market based on the variety of attractions in the industry, both in the countryside and on the coast. Family-owned second homes in the country also stimulate domestic tourism as does the large-scale provision of social tourism schemes in the country. The breadth of attractions also account for the high level of inbound tourism, albeit most of it gravitating to the coast. In recent years the emphasis has switched to other aspects of the country, notably the cities. This began in 1992 with the Olympics in Barcelona, Madrid being designated as the European City of Culture, and Expo '92 in Seville. Spanish outbound tourism is still only at a medium level but is growing, particularly among young people who are travelling abroad for education and culture in ever greater numbers.

The USA

Finally, we turn to the USA, where domestic tourism is high owing to the:

- range of attractions available and diversity of its landscapes
- welldeveloped transport infrastructure
- highly developed tourism industry, which is a world leader in theme parks, for example.

The same reasons attract a growing number of inbound tourists from Europe and Asia, as well as from Canada. At the same time, outbound tourism from the USA is lower than one might expect, partly because of the attractions of holidaying at home.

However, the lack of outbound trips taken by American tourists also reflects other factors, such as:

- their general lack of skills in speaking foreign languages
- their fear of terrorist attacks
- the fact that many people in the USA are too poor to afford the cost of travelling outside the USA.

We can see therefore that the scale of domestic inbound and outbound tourism reflects a range of different factors – some general and some specific to particular countries.

Domestic tourism

Traditionally we focus on international tourism, but in most countries the greatest volume of tourism is actually domestic. In countries with large populations, such as China and India, domestic tourism greatly outnumbers inbound and outbound tourism. The larger and more diverse a country, the more likely it is to have high levels of domestic tourism, particularly where many people cannot afford international travel.

Conclusions

The economic situation perhaps remains the most important factor affecting tourism demand worldwide. Domestic and outbound tourism demand tends to fall in countries facing recessions, yet a recession in destination countries can lower prices which can actually attract tourists to these countries. However, the current Eurozone crisis and ongoing economic troubles in Europe have not always had the effect one might have expected because there are other powerful factors at work, not least the fact that in some Northern European countries many people now see a foreign vacation as a necessity, not a luxury.

Differences in the geography of countries can provide clues about likely differences in outbound tourist behaviour. The French, for example, have a beautiful country with a favourable climate and well developed infrastructure for tourism. They also have considerable variations in geographical and climatic conditions, so it is possible to ski and worship the sun in beautiful surroundings at different times of the year. These factors have encouraged the French to stay at home for holidays, which has meant that figures for outbound tourism are lower than for other industrialized countries. Perhaps one of the reasons the Dutch outbound market is so large is that the Netherlands is a flat country with little landscape or climate diversity.

The UK, in comparison, has experienced a long-term trend of high outbound tourism figures. Many factors have contributed to this, not least the poor summer weather that the UK traditionally experiences. However, the market has also been driven by the existence of highly efficient tour operators and budget airlines giving UK residents enormous choice and reasonable prices. International travel is also still a source of status in the UK market. The most important influence on the growth of outbound travel, however, has been the development of package holiday companies in the UK over a long period. This has made the package holiday to sunny climes accessible to people from all social backgrounds.

Discussion points and essay questions

1. 'The development of inbound tourism by a country is much more dependent on natural features than marketing activity' (Horner and Swarbrooke, 1996). Discuss this statement with reference to individual countries.

2. Discuss the importance of the fully inclusive tour or package holiday in the development of international tourism, and discuss how this is changing and might change in the future.
3. Explore the reasons why affluent industrialized countries have different levels of inbound and outbound tourism.

Exercise

Select a country that is experiencing a growth in inbound and outbound tourism. Quantify the growth figures over the past ten years and suggest reasons for this trend.

References

Horner, S. and Swarbrooke, J. (1996). *Marketing Tourism, Hospitality, and Leisure in Europe*. International Thomson Business Press.

OECD (2014). *Tourism Trends and Policies*. Organization for Economic Co-operation and Development, Paris.

UNWTO (2015). *UNTWO Tourism Highlight 2015 edition*. World Tourism Organisation, Madrid.

UNWTO (2015b). *2030 Vision*. World Tourism Organization, Madrid.

US Department of Commerce (NTTO) (2015). http://travel.trade.gov/

CASE STUDY 9: The segmentation of the outbound Japanese market

Japanese tourists are one of the classical stereotypes of the tourism world. Yet it is still a market that is little understood by many businesses wishing to attract Japanese tourists.

There has been a steady growth in outbound tourism from Japan over the past 20 years. Details of this growth are shown in Exhibit 9.1. The reasons for the growth in outbound tourism from Japan have been attributed to a number of factors that are explored in Exhibit 9.2.

Exhibit 9.1 Trends in number of Japanese travelling abroad 1980–2014

Year	Outbound travellers (millions)
1980	3.91
1982	4.09
1984	4.66
1986	5.52
1988	8.43
1990	11.00

Year	Outbound travellers (millions)
1992	11.79
1994	13.58
1996	16.69
1998	15.81
2000	17.82
2002	16.52
2004	16.83
2006	17.53
2008	15.99
2010	16.64
2012	18.49
2014	16.9

Source: Japanese Tourism Marketing Co., www.tourism.jp/en/

Exhibit 9.2 Reasons for the growth in outbound tourism from Japan

- Steady population growth since 1980 up to 2008 with bulges in the 35–40 and 60–66* age groups, though the overall population has now entered a period of steady decline.
- Japanese propensity for hard work has fuelled income growth.
- Increased demand to go abroad.
- Increased air capacity.
- Increased business travel.
- Increased interest in Asia as a tourism destination.

*The ageing of this 'baby boomer' group may have future impact on Japanese outbound travel, especially for more expensive long-haul destinations.

The destinations of Japanese outbound tourists are shown in Exhibit 9.3 and an example of the purpose, motivation and barriers for travel in Exhibit 9.4.

For those accustomed to the Western European and North American markets, the Japanese market has very different characteristics based on Japanese culture.

Dace (1995) was one of the first authors to suggest different categories of Japanese tourists, as follows.

- **Working soldiers:** male managers in the 30–50 age group who have difficulty in finding time for a vacation because of their work commitments. They appear to want to enjoy 'meaningful experiences rather than just visual tours' (Beecham, quoted in Dace, 1995). They are also enthusiastic, discerning shoppers.
- **Silver greys:** 50–60-year-olds who have been influenced by growing up in the era of post-war austerity in Japan. They live frugal lives but when on vacation they like

Exhibit 9.3 Japanese outbound travel by top 12 leading destinations, 2013

	2009	2011	2013	2013 market share (%)
Total	20,419,033	22,271,221	23,109,792	
USA	2,918,268	3,249,569	3,730,287	16.14
China	3,317,459	3,658,169	2,877,533	12.45
Korea, Republic of	3,053,311	3,289,051	2,747,750	11.89
Thailand	982,607	1,103,073	1,515,718	6.56
Taiwan	975,832	1,242,652	1,381,142	5.98
Guam	825,129	824,005	893,118	3.86
Singapore	489,987	656,417	832,845	3.60
Germany	537,984	642,542	711,529	3.08
France	697,000	612,259	682,384	2.95
Hong Kong	779,600	787,220	607,877	2.63
Viet Nam	356,700	481,500	604,050	2.61
Malaysia	395,746	386,974	513,076	2.22

Source: Japan Tourism Marketing Co. Tourism Statistics

Exhibit 9.4 Japanese outbound travel – purpose and reasons 2011

Purpose	Trips Number (million)	per cent	Travel arrangements (per cent)		
			Package	Group	Individual
Holiday	12.1	71.2	61	2	36
Business	1.9	11.1	0	4	93
Visiting friends and family	1.0	6	n/a	n/a	n/a

Top motivations to travel (2011)	Rank	Factors hindering travel (2011)
Nature and scenery	1	Language problems
Historical sights	2	Security concerns
Local cuisine	3	High costs
Shopping	4	Foreign food
Relaxation	5	Not interested
Experiencing different culture	6	Health concerns

Source: Japan Tourism Marketing Co. Tourism Statistics

to 'let themselves go'. However, they want the familiar when on holiday, including Japanese food and guides who speak their language.

- **Full mooners:** mature married couples who prefer to take single-centre holidays and are very quality-conscious.

- **Technical visits** and **work-related study tours**: Japanese companies use work-related study tours as a way of recruiting and rewarding staff. Most such tourists are men and many such trips are combined with leisure pursuits such as golf.
- **Student travel**: school, college and university students take, generally, short-duration trips, most popular in February. They tend to book flights and accommodation-only packages.
- **Young affluent** (*Shinginsi*): 20–30-year-olds who have grown up in a period of affluence in Japan. They like to flaunt their money and are independently minded. They rarely take packaged vacations and are major participants in the short-break and activity holiday markets.
- **Office ladies**: unmarried women in their early twenties. They have high disposable income and they tend to be living at home with their parents. They like Western countries and enjoy visiting capital cities, such as Paris and London, and shopping. They like organized tours, although there is a trend towards more independent travel.
- **Honeymooners**: defined by the fact that they go overseas for their honeymoon. This is true for as many as 95 per cent of Japanese couples (Beecham, quoted in Dace, 1995) who choose Asian destinations, European cities or places in the USA.

The Japanese market does have a controversial dimension in terms of:

- the demand of some Japanese tourists that their destinations should offer Japanese food, service, guides, and so on. This can alienate some local communities, as has been seen on the Queensland coast in Australia, for example
- Japanese male tourists are a significant proportion of the sex tourism market in many Asian destinations.

It can be seen that the USA is the major tourist destination for Japanese tourists, Hawaii being the top wish-list destination to visit (Japanese Tourism Marketing, 2012). A large proportion of tourist trips are for leisure purposes, with business travel being of secondary importance. However, whilst Japanese outbound travellers are fairly evenly balanced by gender (55 per cent male to 45 per cent female), this does hide two particular groups of travellers. Males of working age tend to travel on business, whereas twenty-something females tend to travel internationally more than their male counterparts. An emerging issue for inbound destinations is that the 50+ female market is declining both in size and in ability to afford non-Asian travel, which could have a market impact in the future, especially for European destinations.

Research has been conducted to investigate the special nature of Japanese tourists on the basis of their cultural identity. Ahmed and Krohn (1993) considered the special characteristics that Japanese tourists require, as a result of their cultural identity, when visiting the USA. These characteristics are shown in Exhibit 9.5.

Exhibit 9.5 Special characteristics of Japanese culture that influence tourist behaviour

- Belongingness (e.g. travelling with other/s)
- Family influence (e.g. purchasing gifts for family)
- Empathy (e.g. not expressing true personal feelings)
- Dependency (e.g. being loyal and devoted)
- Hierarchical acknowledgement (e.g. behaving in relation to social status)
- Propensity to save (e.g. saving to overcome insecurity)
- The concept of *kinen* (e.g. collecting evidence of travel to show others)
- Tourist photography (e.g. the importance of photography)
- Passivity (e.g. avoidance of physical activity)
- Risk avoidance (e.g. avoiding adventurous pursuits)

Source: Ahmed and Krohn (1993)

DISCUSSION POINTS AND ESSAY QUESTIONS

1. Discuss the reasons for the growth in the outbound Japanese tourist market in the past 20 years.
2. Explore the motivations of the different market segments of Japanese tourists.
3. Critically analyse the consumer behaviour of one market segment of outbound Japanese tourists. Explore what this will mean for destination marketers.
4. Evaluate the different activities that the typical Japanese leisure tourist will engage in during their holiday experiences. Discuss what your findings will mean for destination marketers who are trying to attract Japanese tourists.
5. Discuss the reasons for the Japanese outbound tourist shift from European and long-haul destinations to Asian and short-haul destinations over the past 10 years.
6. What are the implications for the international tourism markets of the ageing of the 'baby boomers'?

REFERENCES

Ahmed, Z. and Krohn, F.B. (1993). Understanding the unique consumer behaviour of Japanese tourists. *Journal of Travel and Tourism Marketing* 1 (3), 73–86.

Dace, R. (1995). Japanese tourism: how a knowledge of Japanese buyer behaviour and culture can be of assistance to British hoteliers in seeking to develop this valuable market. *Journal of Vacation Marketing* 1 (3), 281–288.

Japan Tourism Marketing Co. Tourism Statistics: Country-specific: Outbound tourism 2009–13. www.tourism.jp/en/statistics

Japan Tourism Marketing Co. Tourism Statistics: Country-specific: Outbound tourism 1995–2013. www.tourism.jp/en/statistics

Japan Tourism Marketing Co. Tourism Statistics: Country-specific: Basic indicators (Compendium) 2009–13. www.tourism.jp/en/statistics

10 CHAPTER

The nature of demand in different segments of the tourism market

Until now, we have tended to focus on the traditional vacation as the core tourism product and the conventional holidaymaker as the tourist. However, we know that the tourism market is very diverse and the product is far from homogeneous. Therefore in this chapter we will look at the nature of demand in a number of the different segments of the tourism market. This is not an attempt to produce a comprehensive typology of market segments in tourism, rather to illustrate the diversity of market segments in tourism, each of which has its own demand characteristics:

- family market
- hedonistic tourists
- backpacker market
- visiting friends and relatives (VFR)
- excursionists or day-trippers
- educational tourists
- religious tourists
- 'snowbird' market
- ethnic minority tourists
- tourists with disabilities
- social tourism
- short-break market.

The family market

Families come in many different shapes and sizes. In the USA and Northern Europe, the family most usually means a 'nuclear family' with either one or two parents and one to three children. In Southern Europe, the Middle East and many Asian countries, 'extended' families may have a higher number of children and may include other relatives in the holiday party and/or in the purchase decisions.

In this section we will focus upon the nuclear family of Northern Europe. This segment represents the core market for many tour operators and types of products, including camping and caravanning trips, self-catering holidays and theme parks.

The core determinant in the family market is the existence of children. Many families choose holidays that meet the needs of their children, which will vary depending on their age.

- **Babies.** Here the need is to choose a holiday where the baby's safety and comfort will be the primary concern. This could mean avoiding countries with poor hygiene standards and choosing airlines and hotels that offer special services for babies, such as free baby food.
- **Infants**, from two to five years old, where a short journey to the destination can be a priority as children may get bored on long journeys. Safety in this case may mean ensuring that young children who are keen to practise walking cannot get into danger on balconies or near swimming pools.
- **Early school-age children**, from around five to twelve years old, often want to play with children of a similar age and may be content with the simple pleasures of play areas and swimming pools.
- **Teenagers**, aged from thirteen to eighteen, will usually want to be independent and enjoy more adult activities.

The point eventually comes when the young person wants to take a holiday separately from their parents. This could take the form of:

- an educational trip organized by their school
- an organized children's camp such as BUNAC or Camp America
- an activity-based trip such as a PGL canoeing holiday in the UK or a farm-based vacation, for example, the Gîtes d'Enfants in France
- a single-sex holiday with a group of friends.

On the other hand, many children may continue into early adult life to take at least some holidays with their parents, particularly if they cannot afford a holiday because they are on a low income. In many European countries this group has perhaps grown in recent years due to the impact of the economic crisis on young people.

The number of children in a family also has an impact on demand. Families with several children may need to look for an economically priced holiday owing to the high cost of raising children. This explains why they are a major component of the market for camping and caravanning holidays, for example.

The preference of many families for self-catering holidays is partly explained by the desire to minimize holiday costs. However, it is also a result of the desire of some families not to be bound by the formality and etiquette involved in staying in a hotel and eating at particular times. Children tend not to fit well into such rigid regimes and self-catering has the advantage of being less regimented.

At the same time, other families show a preference for all-inclusive resorts because they know that once they have paid the upfront price they will incur no further costs.

The tourism industry works hard to attract the lucrative family market, particularly through discounts for children and free child places. However, often such offers are of little value to single-parent families, as they are usually based on the stereotypical nuclear family of two adults and several children. Thus the industry is failing fully to come to terms with a rapidly growing variation in the traditional family market.

Hedonistic tourists

A very different market is that of the hedonistic tourist, the pleasure-seeker. This market is traditionally associated with younger people and brand names such as Club 18–30 in the UK and the infamous 'spring break' market in the USA. It is a development of the original four s's concept of sun, sand, sea and sex tourism, with perhaps the addition of a fifth 's', sangria, to represent the consumption of alcohol.

Increasingly the hedonistic tourist in recent years has also driven the growth of a distinctive style of nightlife and partying in destinations such as Ibiza. For hedonistic tourists the main motivator is the desire for physical pleasure and social life. At the same time there is a fashion dimension, with different resorts coming in and out of fashion depending on the perceived quality of the local nightlife. There is also a hierarchy in terms of cost and sophistication, with new entrants such as Sunny Beach in Bulgaria developing a reputation for low-cost party tourism.

The hedonistic tourist's day often looks very different from that of the family on holiday. They tend to wake late and then spend their time round the swimming pool or on the beach. They will then usually go out partying and not get to bed until the following morning.

Hedonistic tourists often travel in single-sex groups of friends and prefer the freedom and economy offered by simple self-catering accommodation. This phenomenon of hedonistic tourism is particularly associated with Northern Europe and has been criticized on two main grounds:

- the heavy drinking can lead to fights and problematic relations with the local host community – the so-called 'lager lout' phenomenon
- the fear that much of the casual sex on such holidays is unprotected and therefore carries the risk of spreading HIV or AIDS.

However, we should note that hedonistic tourism is not a new phenomenon in tourism. It is well known that Romans visited spas for largely hedonistic reasons, and in the late nineteenth and early twentieth centuries young men travelled to Paris to gamble and visit brothels. The only difference, really, is that modern hedonistic tourism is a mass market and the tourism industry promotes this form of tourism overtly, as in the Club 18–30 advertising campaigns of the mid-1990s onwards.

There are some forms of 'hedonistic' tourism, on the other hand, which are either illicit or illegal, notably the phenomenon of sex tourism in destinations such as Bangkok and the Philippines. Increasingly children are being drawn into this activity. The key difference, of course, from the hedonistic tourism discussed above is that in this case payment may be involved and one of the partners may well be an unwilling participant. The main sex tourism client tends to be male and older than the 'sun, sea, sand, sex and sangria' tourist. They can be of any nationality, but this market appears to be well developed in Japan and Northern Europe. An increasing number of governments are seeking to clamp down on this kind of behaviour, although with varying degrees of success. These governments' actions demonstrate that, in this case, the old marketing cliché 'the customer is always right' is wrong!

The backpacker market

Another form of tourism that traditionally has been associated with the younger market is backpacking, whereby tourists use a rucksack or backpack rather than a suitcase to carry all they need for their trip. The term has come to signify more than simply the type of luggage used by this type of tourist. It also implies:

*   independent rather than packaged travel
*   a desire to keep expenditure to a minimum
*   a tendency to try to get off the beaten tourist track
*   a trip that might extend beyond the usual one-to-two-week duration of a normal holiday.

The latter point is very important because it is linked to the fact that most backpackers were traditionally students, who have long vacations. Or it can involve people taking a year out from education before they begin college, or taking a year out after completing a college course, the so-called 'gap year' market. It is therefore a form of travel based on the idea of spending a longer period over a vacation than is the norm for most people.

Backpacking is a truly international market that is popular with young people from every developed country, particularly the USA, the UK, the Netherlands, Germany, Australia and Japan. It could be argued that this is an early example of the truly global tourist, for the behaviour of backpackers tends to be similar regardless of their nationality. This is partly because backpacking has its own parallel travel media consisting of guides such as the 'Lonely Planet' and 'Rough Guide', series and backpackers are able to share experiences and advice through social media. These tourists read the same guides and therefore often stay in the same accommodation and visit the same attractions.

Backpacking is very popular currently in long-haul destinations such as South East Asia and South America. Within Europe there is the wellknown phenomenon of the 'inter-railer', backpackers who travel across Europe by rail, utilizing discounted rail-fare packages offered to young people.

Backpacking is likely to grow as the numbers of students around the world grow. However, it is unlikely to become popular with other groups in society because there seems no prospect of most people in employment gaining much more paid holiday.

In the 2007 edition we said 'however, it could begin to appeal more to early retired people who have the time and want to be a little more adventurous in their holiday-making activities'. Interestingly, in the intervening years we have actually seen the growth of 'gap-year' backpacking trips by middle-aged adults taking career breaks or early retirement.

Visiting friends and relatives

The VFR market is one for which there is little reliable data. Because such people do not stay in commercial accommodation and are usually domestic tourists, they are rarely recorded by tourism statisticians. While this market is of no real interest to the accommodation sector, it is very important for the visitor attraction market. Friends and relatives usually feel obliged to take their visitors out during their stay, which brings business for local attractions.

For some people, particularly those on lower incomes, VFR can be an inexpensive alternative to a normal holiday. The VFR market clearly involves a strong social motivation or it can be driven by a sense of family duty. It may also be related to more formal occasions such as weddings and funerals.

Students tend to be heavily involved in the VFR market in two main ways:

- they make many new friends at college, who they may visit during their vacation and/or after their course has ended
- they are visited by their parents and feel obliged to show them around the area.

Although most VFR tourism is domestic, there is an international dimension. This is particularly the case in relation to people whose relatives have emigrated to another country. Some notable tourist flows as a result of this phenomenon are:

- Turkish workers travelling home from Germany to Turkey, and their relatives visiting them in Turkey
- relatives travelling between the UK and India or Pakistan
- British people travelling to visit relatives in Australia and New Zealand
- tourist flows between North African countries and France.

Visiting friends and family, notably the latter, is particularly highly developed in Middle Eastern and Asian countries, where the extended family is the norm.

The huge influxes, taking place at the time of writing, of migrants to Europe from troubled countries such as Syria will in turn lead to a rise in VFR flows between those countries and Europe.

In Europe the VFR market is also being driven upwards by the huge increase in second home purchases by British people and other Northern Europeans. They are then inviting their friends and relatives to join them at their second homes for their holidays. Also we have more people retiring to a foreign country and, again, inviting their friends and relatives to visit them. In the early days of second home ownership and overseas retirement by Northern Europeans, the main impact was seen in countries such as France, Spain and Cyprus. However, in recent years the phenomenon has spread beyond Europe to embrace places as diverse as Florida and Thailand.

Excursionists and day-trippers

The day-tripper or excursionist is generally a domestic tourist and is the core market for most visitor attractions, many seaside resorts and some rural areas.

In general, excursionists do not wish to travel too far, given that they have only one day or less available for their leisure activities. This often results in the day-trip market for an attraction being limited to those who live within one and a half hours' driving time, although in larger countries such as the USA excursionists may be willing to travel further than this for a day-trip. While the duration of a trip is generally the whole day, it could be as short as three to four hours.

Some day-trips require preplanning and booking, but the majority do not. They can therefore be a spontaneous decision. Day-trippers have a spare day and will decide in the morning where to go. Their decision may well be influenced by the weather. If it is sunny a theme park trip might be selected, while rain could well result in the selection of an indoor attraction such as a museum.

The day-trip market is largely a car-based market, although coach excursions also play a significant role in the market. Day-trippers are also major consumers of food and drink services and tend to make considerable use of leisure shopping facilities.

While day-trips are normally domestic, they can be international, for example shopping trips by Britons to France or Malaysian people to Singapore. At the same time, there has been a growth in longer-distance trips.

Educational tourists

There has been a massive growth in the broad field of educational tourism in recent years. This has been fuelled by both the growth in higher and further education worldwide and the desire of many older tourists to learn something new during their annual vacation.

Travelling for education is not a new phenomenon. In the UK in the seventeenth and eighteenth centuries, the sons of the aristocracy undertook the 'Grand Tour' to complete their education. Since the 1980s, in Europe, there has also been a growth in school student exchange schemes.

Educational tourism today has a number of dimensions.

- Student exchanges between universities where students may travel for periods ranging from two or three months to a year. In some cases, in Europe, these have been subsidized by European Union initiatives such as the ERASMUS programme.
- Young people attending language classes in a foreign country, which can last from a week to several months. Part of these courses may be trips to see local attractions, and students may well live with local families for the duration of their course.
- Themed holidays, where tourists travel with like-minded people to pursue a common interest which could be archaeology, a foreign culture, painting or cooking.
- Students from Asia whose parents have decided they should receive at least part of their higher education in Europe, North America or Australasia because they believe this will enhance their career opportunities.

In the first two cases and the latter, the consumer (i.e. the tourist) may not be the actual customer who makes the decision or pays the bill. In these cases, the customer might be the college or the parents.

Religious tourists

Religious tourism is one of the oldest forms of tourism. It is unique, perhaps, in that it is driven by a sense of duty and obligation rather than a search for pleasure and leisure.

The Hajj pilgrimage by Muslims to Mecca in Saudi Arabia is undoubtedly the greatest single flow of religious tourists in the world today. It is estimated that in 1996, around 200,000 Muslims made this pilgrimage from Indonesia alone. The BBC reported in 2014 that some 1,400,000 pilgrims visited Mecca. Every able-bodied Muslim with the financial means is expected to make this pilgrimage at least once during their lifetime. The Hajj takes place during a set period each year, namely the twelfth month of the Islamic calendar. However, there are pilgrimages that can take place at any time of the year, such as Umroh.

The Christian pilgrimage phenomenon inspired classic literature such as Chaucer's *Canterbury Tales*. However, it is now much less important than it once was owing to the decline in the number of active worshippers, particularly in Europe. However, there are still pilgrimages to Rome, Jerusalem, Santiago de Compostela and Lourdes. In recent years the St Jacques route to Santiago seems to have experienced a growth in popularity.

Pilgrimages and visits to holy sites are also a major motivator of religious tourism trips for Hindus and members of other religions.

In general, the phenomenon of the pilgrimage is a highly restricted market, being available only to believers in a particular faith. However, the traditional infrastructure of religious tourism has also become an attraction for non-religious tourists, most notably visiting cathedrals and churches.

At the same time, owing to the growing pressures of life, many nonbelievers are taking short trips to religious establishments for relaxation and spiritual enlightenment. For instance, men (only) can visit Orthodox Greek monasteries at Mount Athos in Greece for a short period, free of charge, provided they abide by the regime of the monastery.

The 'snowbird' market

The first international mass tourism market was based on the summer sun holiday, where Northern Europeans travelled to Southern Europe in the summer to get a suntan. One of the latest major growth markets in the USA and Northern Europe is also inspired by climatic motivators. In the USA this involves 'snowbirds' from the cold, snowy northern states of the USA travelling to southern states such as Florida and California for their mild winter climate. In Northern Europe it involves people travelling to Southern European destinations to escape the winter climate at home.

On both continents this phenomenon has two interrelated characteristics:

- the trips are of long duration, from four weeks to four months
- they are normally taken by retired people who have the time to take such a long vacation.

The motivations of older people to take such trips are not so much related to the desire to get a suntan, but rather by a wish to:

- escape the cold weather in their own state/country
- reduce their expenditure on heating at home
- improve their health, given that they may suffer from illnesses such as arthritis which may be exacerbated by the damp, cold weather in their home state/country
- make new friends and have a less lonely life than they might in their own community.

It remains to be seen whether the 'pensions crisis' in many European countries, highlighted in the recent European financial crisis, will dampen this market, in Europe at least.

Ethnic minority tourists

Many countries contain ethnic minority communities, many of whom may have been in the country for generations. Often people in these communities will have maintained contact with their original country, and will have their own patterns of tourism and tourism infrastructure.

In many developed countries, few people from ethnic minorities are regular purchasers of the products of the mainstream tourism industry. Few customers of the major UK tour operators, for example, come from the Asian, Afro-Caribbean or Chinese communities.

However, that is not to say that many people from ethnic minority groups are not making leisure trips, as we saw in the section on VFR tourists. In some cases, though, lack of disposable income in ethnic minority groups, which suffer above-average rates of unemployment, is probably a factor in the low take-up of holidays offered by tour operators.

In recent years we have seen similar phenomena in other countries that have welcomed substantial numbers of immigrants. For instance we have large-scale tourist flows of Turkish in-migrants travelling back to their country of origin from their new home country of Germany. At the same time, the major growth of in-migration from Asian countries to Australia has likewise created new tourist flows between these areas of the world. In the USA, a country where the vast majority of the population have in-migrated over the past 150 years, patterns of travel between the new home and the previous country of residence or origin have been well established for many years.

However, in the USA in recent years we have seen the rise within the African American community of a distinctive and separate tourism infrastructure of travel agents and vacation organizers. This parallel market relates to both leisure and business tourism. In the latter case there is, for instance, an organization of African American convention organizers. This may reflect the maturing of a market, or a reaction against what may be seen as the failure of the mainstream tourism industry to meet the needs of this particular market.

Tourists with disabilities and health problems

One of the most controversial areas within tourism is the issue of tourists with disabilities and their opportunities to take tourist trips. In many cases tourists with disabilities are denied equal access to tourist products.

However, we need to recognize that there are many kinds of disability and degrees of disability, including:

* mobility problems, ranging from elderly people who may have difficulty climbing stairs to people who are confined to a wheelchair
* sight difficulties, ranging from minor impairment to a complete lack of vision
* hearing difficulties, ranging from minor impairment to complete hearing loss.

These are the most widely recognized disabilities and health issues that affect travel, but there are many others. These include those who require daily dialysis, those who are severely obese, and those with dietary constraints such as needing gluten-free foods.

Clearly, the needs of such tourists may dictate every aspect of their holiday choice and may even determine whether they are able to take a holiday at all. The situation is further complicated if their condition is such that they need someone to accompany them, for this person may not be easy to find, and will normally have to pay as much as the traveller with disabilities.

The situation for travellers with disabilities varies from country to country, being more sympathetic in the USA and Scandinavia than in most other countries. An American person with mobility issues wishing to travel to Scandinavia, for example, should be able to do so with relatively few problems. However, a Zambian traveller with the same problem wishing to visit South America may find it an impossible dream.

Social tourism

Social tourism is a largely European phenomenon that is based on the idea that tourism is a social right of the citizen and/or that tourism brings social benefits to the individual, so that some form of subsidy or state support is justified.

In the current climate of deregulation, privatization and reduced public expenditure in Europe, social tourism is under threat. Nevertheless, it is still significant in countries such as Germany, France and Spain. It takes a number of forms, including:

- subsidized visits to health spas for people with particular illnesses in France
- the state- and employer-supported Chèques Vacances scheme in France, which helps workers on lower incomes to be able to afford to take a holiday
- non-profit-making holiday centres owned and operated by trade unions or voluntary sector organizations in a wide range of European countries, notably in Germany, France or Spain.

Social tourism reached its peak, perhaps, in the former Soviet Union, where it encompassed every worker and was the core of the Soviet domestic tourism industry. It also had an international dimension within the old Eastern bloc nations, where tourists used subsidized resort facilities and accommodation in other Eastern European countries.

The short-break market

The growth of the five-day week with a full two-day weekend, and the rise of car ownership and faster aircraft, have helped stimulate the development of the short weekend break market since the 1960s in the developed world. It is also now a growing phenomenon in the newly developing economies of Asia. In most cases, the short break is an additional holiday rather than a substitute for the main annual holiday.

Short breaks exist in a number of forms, including:

- romantic weekends for a couple in a city such as Rome or Paris, or for an American couple in an old New England inn
- shopping trips, for example a group of women friends in the UK going to London, or a party of Russian tourists flying to Paris to buy luxury goods, or a visit to Indonesia by a group of Singaporean tourists who want to buy authentic craft products
- visiting friends and relatives
- health resorts or health spa breaks, designed to relieve stress or improve the health of the tourist
- special interest and activity breaks, such as fishing trips, painting, horse-riding or golf
- breaks built around a special event, whether it be a theatre performance or a football match
- unwinding, relaxing breaks in country house hotels in the UK or Gîtes d'Interludes in France, for example
- visits to arts and cultural festivals both domestically and internationally, such as Glastonbury in the UK or the Verona Opera Festival.

While not comprehensive, this list of types of breaks illustrates that they are both domestic and international. One of the fastest-growing sectors in tourism is the international city-break market. Furthermore, tourists are prepared to travel further and further for a short break. In 2014–15, breaks of four and five nights were being offered by UK tour operators to New York, Montreal, Dubai, Cape Town or even Hong Kong.

Although it is difficult to generalize, short breaks tend to be either:

- planned and booked well in advance to heighten the sense of anticipation
- purchased at the last minute as a reaction to stress or a particularly difficult week at work, or as a spontaneous celebration of a happy event or good news.

In the developed world, the short break is likely to grow in importance as work pressures arising from the competitive situation in all industries increase.

This market will continue to benefit from developments in ICT that provide consumers with more choice whilst enriching their experience once in the destination through a wide range of apps for mobile devices. This is important as most short breaks tend to be to city destinations and tourists want to get the maximum value from their short time in a new place. ICT helps them achieve this.

Conclusions

We have seen that there are a number of different submarkets within tourism, some of which are interrelated. For example, the VFR phenomenon is a submarket, but is often also a form of short-break market. Furthermore, it is a significant element of the day-trip market when VFR tourists are taken to visitor attractions by their hosts. It would be possible to identify a number of other such submarkets.

For tourism marketers it is important to realize that the tourism market is not a homogeneous whole, but rather a collection of overlapping submarkets each with its own characteristics.

Discussion points and essay questions

1. Discuss the likely problems that might arise from the presence in a resort of both hedonistic tourists and families at the same time.
2. Evaluate which sectors of tourism benefit most *and* least from *both* VFR tourists and backpackers.
3. Explore the possible motivators and determinants of a day-trip to an art gallery *and* a beach resort *and* a craft workshop.

Exercise

Make contact with a local or national group which represents people with any type of disability or health problem. Ask them what difficulties their members experience, as a result of their disability, when they are choosing and taking a holiday. Finally, suggest what the tourism industry could do to make it easier and more enjoyable for their members to take a holiday.

CASE STUDY 10.1: The inbound market to the Republic of Cyprus

The Republic of Cyprus, which joined the European Union in 2004, has become one of Europe's leading tourist destinations over the past 20 years or so. After the Turkish invasion of 1974, which left some of this leading resort under Turkish occupation, the Republic of Cyprus had to restructure its tourism industry and develop new resort areas and attractions. Its success in this rebuilding after 1974 is clearly demonstrated by the fact that in 2005 it attracted 2.5 million visitors and has held this number steadily over the past decade.

In this case study we discuss the inbound tourism market industry, trends and key issues. Let us start by looking at the volume of inbound tourism. All data used comes from the Statistical Service, Ministry of Finance, and Republic of Cyprus unless otherwise stated.

In 2005, Cyprus received 2,470,057 international tourist arrivals, a figure that has remained fairly consistent over the following 10 years (Exhibit 10.1.1).

Exhibit 10.1.1 Arrivals by region and by nation 2006–2014

Country of usual residence	Year				
	2014	2012	2010	2008	2006
All countries	**2,441,239**	**2,464,908**	**2,172,998**	**2,403,750**	**2,400,924**
Europe (EU)	2,251,554	2,315,866	2,017,588	2,267,501	2,273,688
Other European	805,384	622,245	351,738	302,146	222,195
Africa	10,965	11,132	11,115	12,336	11,446
America	19,856	25,087	31,366	27,784	26,353
Total North America	19,169	24,318	29,767	26,744	25,430
Total South and Central America	686	769	1,599	1,039	922
Asia incl. ex-USSR Asian states	148,436	100,464	97,699	83,650	76,011
Gulf countries	26,060	17,338	19,914	24,366	16,733
Oceania	10,226	12,247	14,183	12,200	12,759
Not stated	200	111	1,044	276	664
Top 15 inbound source nations (at 2014)	*2014*	*2012*	*2010*	*2008*	*2006*
1 United Kingdom	871,523	959,463	996,046	1,242,655	1,360,136
2 Russia	636,766	474,426	223,861	180,926	114,763
3 Sweden	106,666	117,286	109,746	124,948	94,028
4 Greece	100,955	132,990	127,667	133,015	126,768
5 Germany	86,397	144,407	139,190	132,058	152,808
6 Israel	68,822	39,420	37,876	32,034	34,197
7 Norway	56,746	69,410	63,347	63,470	50,664
8 Switzerland	48,947	46,853	41,744	38,603	41,559
9 Ukraine	41,093	19,482	11,766	8,847	6,374
10 Lebanon	32,687	25,658	20,664	14,192	11,442
11 Denmark	30,554	31,763	30,335	38,216	30,802
12 France	29,166	35,955	28,749	36,099	37,779
13 Poland	29,063	30,981	18,439	20,358	13,707
14 Belgium	26,131	25,930	24,125	26,368	24,267
15 Finland	23,921	29,216	32,886	32,333	30,333

Source: Statistical Service, Ministry of Finance, Republic of Cyprus, 2015

Exhibit 10.1.2 Changes in arrivals, top 20 inbound destinations

Destination	2014	2013	Percentage change from 2013	Arrivals change from 2013
Russia	636,766	608,581	4.63	28,185
Israel	68,822	43,656	57.65	25,166
Switzerland	48,947	41,708	17.36	7,239
Ukraine	41,093	34,027	20.77	7,066
Austria	23,665	16,804	40.83	6,861
Lebanon	32,687	25,835	26.52	6,852
Poland	29,063	24,878	16.82	4,185
Romania	18,161	14,808	22.64	3,353
United Arab Emirates	16,722	14,606	14.49	2,116
France	29,166	27,156	7.40	2,010
Netherlands	22,218	20,244	9.75	1,974
Denmark	30,554	30,014	1.80	540
Belgium	26,131	28,813	−9.31	−2,682
Greece	100,955	104,955	−3.81	−4,000
Finland	23,921	28,383	−15.72	−4,462
United States	15,847	21,930	−27.74	−6,083
Norway	56,746	65,739	−13.68	−8,993
Sweden	106,666	117,961	−9.58	−11,295
Germany	86,397	98,933	−12.67	−12,536
United Kingdom	871,523	891,233	−2.21	−19,710

Source: Statistical Service, Ministry of Finance, Republic of Cyprus, 2015

Cyprus also attracts tourists from outside Europe and the Eastern Mediterranean (e.g. from Israel and the United Arab Emirates). Many international arrivals are likely to be people with friends and relatives in Cyprus (e.g. from the United States, Australia and Greece).

Tourist arrivals in Cyprus (shown in Exhibit 10.1.2) tend, as in most countries, to fluctuate year on year, however there are some key underlying trends around these individual fluctuations. Particular decreases and increases in visitors from different countries, especially over the past 10 years or so, could be a result of a number of factors as diverse as:

- economic recession in the generating country
- economic conditions within the host country – Cypriot banking crisis
- security issues around the Mediterranean and Middle East
- opening of new airline routes
- marketing efforts of the Cyprus Tourism Organisation and tour operators in these particular countries.

In recent years, Cyprus has tried to market itself, with some success, as a winter tourism destination. However, as Exhibit 10.1.3 shows, the overwhelming majority of tourists arrive in the spring and summer quarters, although German and Greek arrivals are slightly more spread across the whole year.

Exhibit 10.1.3 2014 Quarterly arrivals (actual and percentage)

Top six arrival countries of residence	Cypriot quarterly arrivals 2014 (actual)				
	Q1	Q2	Q3	Q4	Total
United Kingdom	59,603	291,411	372,527	147,976	871,517
Russia	17,056	238,816	318,173	62,714	636,759
Sweden	3,481	38,746	51,035	13,399	106,661
Greece	19,713	28,041	26,981	26,214	100,949
Germany	9,810	27,238	24,590	24,756	86,394
Israel	5,448	17,673	30,895	14,801	68,817

Top six arrival countries of residence	Cypriot quarterly arrivals 2014 (percentage)				
	Q1	Q2	Q3	Q4	Total
United Kingdom	7	33	43	17	100
Russia	3	38	50	10	100
Sweden	3	36	48	13	100
Greece	20	28	27	26	100
Germany	11	32	28	29	100
Israel	8	26	45	22	100

Source: Statistical Service, Ministry of Finance, Republic of Cyprus, 2015

Let us now turn our attention to international tourists' spending in Cyprus. Exhibit 10.1.4 compares spending and length of stay for March 2015 with that of March 2014. The Cyprus Statistical Service estimates that in 2014 tourist revenue was €2.082 billion (about £1.5 billion). However, there are significant differences between different countries in terms of spend per head per day, as we can see from Exhibit 10.1.4.

These significant differences could reflect, for example:

• the types of segments being attracted and their tastes in accommodation
• the numbers of people who may not be paying for accommodation because they are planning to stay in property belonging to friends or relatives during their visit – this phenomenon has grown dramatically in recent years.

However, spending per day by various nationalities also changes dramatically year by year. The typical visitor spends €69.36 per day, which is slightly up from the March 2014 figure of €69.27. The biggest day spenders are the Israelis, Russians and Germans, at €115.06, €93.38 and €81.85, respectively. The lowest daily spend, perhaps not unsurprisingly, is Greek visitors with a March 2015 daily spend of €43.71.

Exhibit 10.1.4 Cypriot arrivals' expenditure and length of stay – March 2015 compared with March 2014 – per person and per day

Country of usual residence	March 2014 Arrivals	Length of average stay (days)	Expenditure (€) Per person	Per day	March 2015 Arrivals	Length of average stay (days)	Expenditure (€) Per person	Per day
Total	77,533	10.5	728.22	69.27	97,479	9.6	667.22	69.36
United Kingdom	30,368	11.5	732.06	63.73	41,149	10.7	707.20	66.28
Russia	8,134	10.2	945.24	92.37	7,855	9.0	841.36	93.38
Sweden	2,181	11.8	970.41	82.10	1,935	10.9	678.53	62.14
Greece	7,038	11.5	475.59	41.19	10,557	9.2	400.86	43.71
Germany	6,496	9.4	755.28	80.62	7,443	9.1	744.00	81.85
Israel	2,229	4.9	455.18	93.68	4,211	3.4	385.46	115.06

Source: Statistical Service, Ministry of Finance, Republic of Cyprus, 2015`

The day rate is only one way of looking at tourist spending – another important factor is how much a visitor will spend into the tourism economy over the course of their stay. Here Exhibit 10.1.4 tells a slightly different story. Because the British visitors tend to stay longer, their overall vacation spend tends to be higher compared with the shorter stay of Israeli visitors (10.7 days as against a weekend stay of 3.4 days), meaning that in overall spend British visitors rank alongside the Russian and German visitors.

Again there are factors that will influence this situation, for example in terms of preferences for different types of vacation and accommodation, and access to privately owned, non-commercial accommodation.

The gradual decline in the number of British visitors has been replaced by an increase especially from Russia and Israel but also from other Eastern European countries such as Ukraine and Poland, along with visitors from a wider range of Middle Eastern countries such as Lebanon and the United Arab Emirates. As the regional figures in Exhibit 10.1.1 show, there has also been a doubling of Asian visitors since 2006.

From these figures we can see that Russia and other Eastern European countries, the Middle East and especially Israel, and Asia are the future key markets that will drive visitor growth in the near future. Europe is still arguably the most important marketplace – despite falling numbers, British tourists still make up the largest visitor cohort, and Germany, Sweden, Switzerland, Norway and France are all still key markets for the Cyprus inbound market.

The leading national tourism market for Cyprus is still the United Kingdom. While actual year-on-year numbers naturally vary over time and circumstance, the visitor levels for 2014 of below 900,000 (871,523) were last seen in 1997 (846,309).

The peak period for British visitor numbers was between 2000 and 2006 when numbers were always over 1.3 million visitors per year, the peak year being 2001 with a visitor level of 1,486,703.

Since 2006 UK visitor numbers have been steadily declining. At the present levels of decline in the UK market and rise in the Russian market, it would not be surprising if Russia rises to become the biggest national visitor market by 2020.

Cyprus also faces competition from newly emerging destinations in the Balkans and the Middle East. For example, tourism to the United Arab Emirates and Bulgaria grew between 2002 and 2004 by 44 and 105 per cent, respectively!

Exhibit 10.1.5 gives the visitor profile data for 2014.

Exhibit 10.1.5 Cyprus tourism profile 2014

Purpose of visit (%)

Holidays	Business	Family and friends
73.30	8.50	18.10

Type of accommodation (%)

Hotels 1–5*	Apartment villages	Friends and family	Own residence	Other
52.60	15.20	15.30	7.20	9.70

Location of stay (%)

Paphos	Paralimni	Ayia Napa	Lemesos	Larnaka	Lefkosia	Other
37.00	9.40	13.30	14.60	12.50	8.90	4.30

Number of visits (%)

First time	Two or more
49.10	50.90

Type of package (%)

Package travel	Individual travel
46.80	53.20

Age (%)

20–31 years	32–44 years	45–64 years
19.90	25.80	33.50

Gender (%)

Male	Female
46.30	53.70

Source: Statistical Service, Ministry of Finance, Republic of Cyprus, 2015

Exhibit 10.1.5 shows that:

- 73 per cent of visitors are on vacation
- over half of all visitors use hotel accommodation, with only 7.2 per cent staying in their own accommodation
- Paphos is the most popular destination for visitors, with over a third of visitors staying there

- visitors are quite evenly split between repeat visitors and first timers
- similarly, there is a nearly even split between independent and package travellers
- a third of all visitors are aged between 45 and 64.

CONCLUSIONS

The Republic of Cyprus has been highly successful at attracting international tourists in recent years. However, its historically heavy dependence on the UK market has been changing over the past decade with an increase in Eastern European, Asian and Middle Eastern markets.

Cyprus is still susceptible to regional economic and political events such as the West's relationship with Russia, its natural associations with economically troubled Greece, and its proximity to the volatile Middle East. Its own intra-island relationship with Northern Cyprus is still unresolved too.

It will take clear resolve and strategies from the Republic of Cyprus authorities to build upon its established tourism base in the face of increasing competition from Asian and Eastern European markets in a politically and economically volatile region.

DISCUSSION POINTS AND ESSAY QUESTIONS

1. In 2004 50 per cent of tourists to Cyprus came from the UK, but in 2014 UK visitors were only around a third of all visitors. Is this change a strength or a weakness for Cyprus?
2. In 2004 the Russian market was less than 4 per cent of Cypriot tourism. By 2014 this has risen to over 25 per cent of the inbound market. Discuss the likely impacts of this on Cyprus.
3. Discuss the differences between British, German and Israeli visitors from the information in Exhibit 10.1.4 on typical lengths of stay and spending patterns.
4. Discuss how seasonal the market is in Cyprus compared with other destinations, and suggest ways in which seasonality might be reduced.
5. 'Lies, damn lies and statistics.' In today's increasingly volatile and uncertain geopolitical and economic climate, how relevant is historical statistical data for informing management decisions?

EXERCISE

Visit the Cyprus Tourism Organisation website (www.visitcyprus.com) and the Statistical Service website and look at the latest data on inbound tourist arrivals, spending and revenue, length of stay, place of stay, type of accommodation, and so on. Also try to find the same data for earlier years to help you identify trends in the market.

Then, on the basis of this data, devise a five-year marketing strategy for Cyprus, with an emphasis on which national markets and market segments Cyprus should target and how it should target them.

CASE STUDY 10.2: Thomas Cook's Club 18–30

INTRODUCTION

The Club 18–30 brand is owned by Thomas Cook Group plc, London. The Club 18–30 unique holiday formula has remained more or less unchanged over the years, and provides holidays for this specific age group of customers to the liveliest resorts in the central locations of major holiday regions. The company currently offers holidays to eight destinations across the Mediterranean, and flies from a number of UK airports. It also offers a full range of accommodation, from budget to all-inclusive packages.

HISTORY OF THE DEVELOPMENT OF THE CLUB 18–30 BRAND

Club 18–30 has been in existence for over nearly 50 years, being set up in the late 1960s, and was the first holiday company in the UK to specialize in package holidays exclusively for young people, singles or couples, but specifically without families or children.

Club 18–30 was originally set up by the Horizon Group, but in the early 1980s became part of the International Leisure Group (ILG), which collapsed in 1991. The collapse of ILG forced Club 18–30 into voluntary liquidation, despite the fact that it had been a profit-making division. Five weeks after the collapse, the existing directors of Club 18–30 bought the trade name and reformed the company. This move received enormous support from the travel trade and overseas suppliers. The company was prevented from trading under the Club 18–30 name owing to Association of British Agents (ABTA) legislation; hence the re-formed company became known as The Club.

The Club witnessed enormous growth during the 1990s from a small tour operator to a top ten UK operator. ABTA granted the company permission to trade under the original branding, Club 18–30, in August 1994, and so The Club reverted back to the original name.

Thomas Cook AG is now one of the biggest European holiday companies. Some facts and figures about the company are shown in Exhibit 10.2.1. The company continues to offer a 'one-stop' holiday planning experience to its customers by using a strong portfolio of brands that it has acquired. The Club 18–30 brand is positioned in the UK market to target the young holidaymaker.

Exhibit 10.2.1 Thomas Cook Group: facts and figures, financial year 2014

- First or second (by revenue) in the European leisure industry, UK and Germany
- £8.6 billion in annual sales
- 23,672 employees
- Market capitalisation of £1.5 billion
- 88 aircraft: 11th largest airline in Europe by fleet size

- 3,084 retail outlets
- Operating in 17 countries
- Strong brands include Thomas Cook, Neckermann, Condor, Ving, Spies and Tjäreborg
- 22.3 million customers

Source: Thomas Cook Group web pages and *Annual Report and Accounts 2014*

The Flying Colours Leisure Group became the owners of the Club 18–30 brand in 1995. This group was formed in November 1995 and was backed by a £40 million deal involving a major family tour operator, Sunset Holidays, and Club 18–30 was bought. In 1998 Flying Colours was bought by Thomas Cook, which incorporated Club 18–30 into its JMC (John Mason Cook) brand portfolio. More recently Thomas Cook itself has undergone several iterations of ownership and organization, currently being known as Thomas Cook Group plc with a listing on the London Stock Exchange, where it is a member of the FTSE250 index.

THE CURRENT BUSINESS OF CLUB 18–30

Thomas Cook aims to drive ambitious growth through successful market segmentation and positioning. The success of the Club 18–30 brand shows that well targeted products using a portfolio of differentiated travel products can provide a successful business strategy in the competitive holiday market. The development of the Club 18–30 brand has been recognized as a dynamic response to the conservatism that has typified the UK market for overseas holidays. While Thomas Cook Group has been carrying out a strategy of transformation and brand unifying since October 2013, Club 18–30 is one of a small collection of stand-alone brands.

Some facts and figures are shown in Exhibit 10.2.2.

Exhibit 10.2.2 Club 18–30: facts and figures

- Club 18–30 is the market leader in overseas summer sun-based youth holidays.
- More than 100,000 passengers were carried in 1995.
- The product is highly respected in the travel trade and is available from over 6,000 travel agents.
- Regional flying from a number of airports ensures a high-profile image is maintained throughout the UK.
- Constant evaluation of resorts ensures that only the most 'happening' of places make it into the company brochure.
- Over 5,000 applications are received annually for jobs as Clubreps. Fewer than 100 new Clubreps are required.
- The company launched the idea of flexible booking in a 'pick-and-mix' approach with the launch of flexibletrips.com in 2004.

Source: Thomas Cook

THE CLUB 18–30 HOLIDAY CONCEPT

The Club 18–30 holiday formula was the first of its kind in the UK, and has remained unchanged over its years of development. The company concentrates on attracting clients in the 18–30-year-old age bracket. Club 18–30 contracts hotels and apartments in the liveliest resorts and in central locations. Club 18–30 accommodation is often used exclusively for the company's clients because it was recognized many years ago that it was preferable for the clients to have their own separate facilities and places to stay.

The holidays were originally marketed as 'a fortnight of Saturday nights' and entertainment is available 24 hours a day, seven days a week. Club 18–30 also offered its clients a range of unique excursions, and Clubreps help provide an unrivalled fun holiday experience for their clients.

The range of countries on offer in the Club 18–30 range is shown in Exhibit 10.2.3.

Exhibit 10.2.3 The Club 18–30 product range

Summer 2015

- Ibiza
- Majorca
- Bulgaria
- Cyprus
- Corfu
- Crete
- Kos
- Zante

Summer 2016

- Majorca
- Ibiza
- Bulgaria
- Cyprus
- Corfu
- Crete
- Zante

Source: Club 18–30 e-brochures

The company selected resorts in an attempt to put together a Mediterranean party scene. They chose the best resorts that stayed awake 24 hours a day, and selected accommodation near to the centre of the action.

San Antonio in Ibiza was selected because it is well known as the dance capital of Europe and the area offers blue-zone beaches. The twin fun spots of Magaluf and Palma Nova on Majorca were selected for their range of bars, lots of pubs, English food and nightclubs. Resorts on Gran Canaria and Tenerife were selected for their bars, disco bars and clubs. Resorts on the Greek Islands of Corfu, Crete and Rhodes were selected for their round-the-clock entertainment. A recent addition to the product range is Cancún in Mexico.

The beach and pool are the main focal points of daytime activity, with a suntan the priority for most clients on a Club 18–30 holiday. The main action of the holiday, however, starts after dark. The resorts which the company picks have a good variety of local colour and generally have two or three major venues or attractions close at hand.

The clients prefer to stay in self-catering or bed-and-breakfast accommodation, so the company ensures that there is a good selection of wellpriced restaurants and cafés close to the accommodation.

The Clubrep is an important aspect of the Club 18–30 holiday. He or she will be with the clients pretty well around the clock and will act as a party organizer, personally taking the clients to the best bars and nightspots. The ratio of Clubrep to clients is 1:25 – he or she acts as a social catalyst and the client's best friend. Many of the clients are travelling abroad for the first time, so the Clubrep provides a vital role in making sure the clients have an enjoyable time.

The Clubrep concept became the focus for the *Club Reps* television programme based on Faliraki, Greece, in 2002. The company hoped that this programme would dispel misconceptions about the hedonistic image of the brand. The company subsequently withdrew 'bar crawls' from the product and tried to encourage customers to engage in more upmarket pursuits such as scuba diving and paintballing.

The company is now trying to improve the image of the brand with the use of an advertising campaign that communicates the 'cool' nature of the Club 18–30 holiday. However, a quick look at the Thomas Cook website and Club 18–30 pages shows that while some of the more risqué language and imagery have gone, there is still a big emphasis on clubbing, with slogans such as 'Dive In!' and 'Grab your chance to live the club life'. The 2016 brochure strap line is 'Bring it on'. Since the introduction of the Club 18–30 concept, a number of competitors have entered the market. These are shown in Exhibit 10.2.4.

Exhibit 10.2.4 Competitors of Club 18–30 holidays in the UK

Brand	Company	Product range
2wentys	First Choice	Beach/resort holidays with sub-brands Bar
2wents Shipwrecked		Blitz and Shipwrecked
2wenties Bar Blitz		
Freestyle	Thompson	Beach/resort holidays in the Mediterranean
Scene	Thomson	Thomson's main clubbing brand
Contiki	Travel Corporation	18–35 Adventure holidays across the world
Awaken	Awakenibiza.com	A variety of clubbing package holidays in Ibiza
Cheapclubbing	EasyJet	Clubbing packages
Onthebeach	onthebeach.co.uk	Online packages
clubbingabroad	clubbingabroad.co.uk	Online packages

Source: provider websites 2015

THE CLUB 18–30 CLIENT

A summary profile of the Club 18–30 client is shown in Exhibit 10.2.5. The predominant age range is 18 to 26, with an average age of 21 to 22. Lower age limits are enforced quite stringently, but the upper limits are fairly vague. If a client feels that the holiday would be suited to them, even if they are older, then they are welcome to go on the holidays. The company has a record of customers coming back year after year, and some female clients even bring their mother with them.

Exhibit 10.2.5 The Club 18–30 client

Average age	21/22
Male:female ratio	50:50
Socioeconomic group	C1/C_2/D/E
Marital status	Single
Lifestyle	In full-time employment. Resident in parental home. Influenced by fashion, music, dance and entertainment (their spending patterns reflect this).

An 18–30 holiday is usually their first holiday abroad with friends, but without parents.

Source: Club 18–30

The male-to-female ratio is generally 50:50, but varies between 40:60 and 60:40. This is partly due to price as female clients tend to go when it is cheaper, and it is also fashionable for them to get an early suntan in May or June. Most of the clients go on a Club 18–30 holiday with a friend of the same sex. In low season, the average number of people per booking is two. In high season this rises to three or four, with groups of friends sharing apartments. Many customers go on a Club 18–30 holiday for their first holiday experience away from their parents.

THE ADVERTISING CAMPAIGN

The Saatchi & Saatchi advertising agency, London, was appointed by Club 18–30 in October 1994 to handle the advertising campaign for the brand, and has handled the campaign since then. The original campaign objectives set by Club 18–30 were to increase bookings for summer 1995, raise the awareness of the Club 18–30 brand name and accurately reflect the nature of Club 18–30 holidays to the appropriate target market.

The campaign which the advertising agency developed highlighted the fun of a Club 18–30 holiday in a 'tongue-in-cheek' way. It was designed to speak to the target market (17 to 25 year olds) via their type of media (48-sheet posters) and in their style of language.

The advertising agency designed a series of posters that incorporated controversial and suggestive statements which were designed to appeal to the target audience. Examples of the poster copy are shown in Exhibit 10.2.6.

The initial campaign spend was £250,000, which allowed the company to concentrate a month-long, medium-weight campaign around the area where there was potential

---

Exhibit 10.2.6 The 1995 Club 18–30 poster campaign – copy

'It's not all sex, sex, sex'

'Girls. Can we interest you in a package holiday?'

'It's advisable not to drink the local water. As if . . .'

'Beaver España'

'You get two weeks for being drunk and disorderly'

'Discover your erogenous zone'

'The summer of 69'

Source: Flying Colours, 1995

---

for growth. The campaign was nationwide, other than Scotland and London, and was particularly concentrated in catchment areas of regional airports such as Newcastle, Manchester, Birmingham, East Midlands, Cardiff, Belfast and Bristol. The posters were placed in major town centres where the largest population of young people in the 18–30 age range live and work. Research showed that the target group found the poster campaign humorous and appealing. The campaign also portrayed the products in a true light and consciously discouraged families, and other groups of people who would not enjoy this type of holiday, from booking a Club 18–30 holiday. The campaign commenced in January 1995 and for the 1995 season Club 18–30 enjoyed record bookings, 30 per cent higher than the previous year.

The company decided to run an amended version of the campaign in 1996. There had been criticism of the campaign and the Advertising Standards Authority (ASA) insisted on vetting the Club 18–30 campaign before it was run. The company decided to run a 48- sheet billboard campaign along the lines of the previous 'Jolly Japes' campaign, but the posters urged the reader to look for the real advertisements in magazines such as *Sky*, *Loaded* and *Company*. These magazines were chosen because they are read by the target audience. It also allowed the company to design press advertisements which were much more explicit, but similar to the first campaign.

The awareness and public relations gained from this campaign made an essentially small budget work very hard. The advertising campaign continued to make sure that the product remained at the forefront of youth culture. The brochure, which is produced on an annual basis, is a major part of this. The brochures are designed with this in mind, and there is a strong emphasis on style and fun.

Early brochure design caused comment in the trade. The brochure used 'Flo' and her 'pensioner pals' to introduce the products, and it was designed to be humorous but informative. The brochure also incorporated advertisements for other companies that sell products targeted at the same market segment.

The company was criticized for its product range and controversial advertising campaigns by some pressure groups, in the light of HIV and AIDS. The company decided to take positive action about this and although it did not consider itself as moral guardian, it thought it would be sensible to reiterate the 'safe sex' message wherever possible. Young people in the 1990s had been the first group to receive sex education advice from the government's Health Education Authority (HEA; now part of NICE). Club 18–30 recognized that young people may have sex on holiday, and for that reason, the company reacted positively to the HEA's initiative of 1991, which asked travel companies help educate young travellers in the dangers of casual sex overseas. Club 18–30 included information on safe sex and protection within every ticket wallet. The company also provided confidential supplies of condoms to clients for their Club 18–30 holiday.

The HEA sought to address the problem of drug abuse among young people in 1997. Club 18–30 responded accordingly and offered realistic advice on drugs and the laws governing their use overseas to clients before they travel.

A statement by the Club 18–30 Managing Director, Stuart Howard, in February 1996 emphasized the point:

> We believe it is important to be proactive on these issues. Everybody knows that holidays are a time of romance and excitement, and we have 30 years of experience in dealing with this. Condoms are not as reliably available in many Mediterranean resorts, as they are here. Drugs, unfortunately are widely available everywhere. Although we have no wish to set ourselves up as moral guardians, we believe that it is only responsible to take up these initiatives on our client's behalf.

Club 18–30 was one of the first tour operators to respond positively to the HEA's initiative on drugs.

More recent advertising campaigns have also been devised by Saatchi & Saatchi advertising agency.

THE FUTURE

It is predicted that the market for holidays aimed at youth will grow as disposable income continues to rise among that group. It is likely that customers will start to demand more independently designed holiday packages with an increasing emphasis on adventure-based activities.

Customers will also start to travel further afield as they become more experienced holidaymakers (e.g. Club Xtra, www.club18-30.com/club-xtra).

An increase of bookings via the internet is also becoming a feature of the market (Mintel, 2014a); Thomas Cook's online retailing grew 21 per cent in 2013, being worth more than £3 billion in sales value. In 2014 only half of its online transactions were via desktop connections, down from two-thirds, with 30 per cent being via tablets and 20 per cent via mobile phones – both increasing in usage from 2013.

CONCLUSIONS

Club 18–30 is one of the best examples of a UK brand that has aggressively targeted a particular market segment and positioned its products to suit the behaviour patterns of its clients. The company repeatedly targeted clients with effective and eye-catching advertising, which has been controversial enough to attract substantial media attention, much of it negative. The company also reacted positively to the HEA's campaigns on safe sex and drug abuse. This has meant that the company is seen to be acting positively for their clients in the face of major health concerns.

Club 18–30 now has to react to increased competition as the clubbing market niche becomes more established, and changing consumer behaviour means that some of the more controversial advertising themes have been toned down.

DISCUSSION POINTS AND ESSAY QUESTIONS

1. Discuss the ways in which Club 18–30 has been very effective in designing holidays that suit the lifestyle of its target clients.
2. Explore the dilemma for a company such as Club 18–30 when it is trying to design effective and appealing advertising campaigns without offending society at large. Discuss the ways in which Club 18–30 has overcome this potential problem.
3. 16–34-year-olds are the group most likely to undertake group holidays abroad (Mintel 2014b); they are also the most used to mobile technology and social media – what implications does this have for clubbing holiday providers and for Club 18–30 in particular?

REFERENCES

Mintel (2014a). *The Changing Face of Technology in Travel and Tourism*. August. Mintel.
Mintel (2014b). *The Consumer Experience of Group Holidays and Escorted Tours*. April. Mintel.

Consumer behaviour and markets in the different sectors of tourism

Introduction

One of the problems of writing a book on consumer behaviour in tourism is that tourism is not a single homogeneous activity or market. It is a complex web of interrelated sectors, each of which has its own characteristics in terms of consumer behaviour. In this chapter we endeavour to demonstrate the diversity of forms of consumer behaviour and markets found within tourism.

Before we go any further, we must stress that in this chapter we are concerned with the behaviour of the tourists who are the final consumers belonging to the various markets and consumer organizations. However, within the complex structure outlined in Figure 11.1, it is clear that there are other producer–customer relationships, namely those between suppliers and producers, and producers and intermediaries. This is true, for example, of the vitally important relationship between hoteliers (supplier) and tour operators (customer), and between airlines (customer) and travel agents (intermediary), both high street and online.

Most of this chapter is concerned with leisure tourism, but we should not ignore the massively important 'parallel world' of business tourism. Later in this chapter we devote some space to discussing the unique nature of consumer behaviour in business tourism.

Finally, in addition to differences between behaviour in different sectors, there are also significant differences within sectors. Towards the end of this chapter we illustrate this point through examples drawn from the tour operations and accommodation sectors.

We now look at some of the different sectors of tourism in terms of differences and similarities in relation to several key demand characteristics.

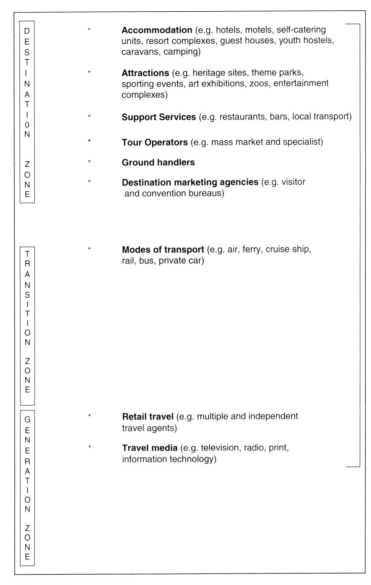

Figure 11.1 The sectors of tourism

Factors taken into account when making a purchase decision

In almost all cases, price seems to be a constant factor regardless of which sector of tourism we consider. Location is another standard factor, whether we are talking about the area of a city in which a hotel is located, the departure airport offered by tour operator or how far an attraction is from the visitor's home. We can also assume that the tourist's previous experience of an organization's services and the reputation of the organization will be relevant to purchase decisions in all sectors of tourism.

By contrast, there are also some differences, for example:

- safety is a major issue for choosing airlines in some parts of the world, or selecting a holiday destination, but would rarely be an explicit factor taken into account when choosing a hotel
- fashionability may be a major consideration when choosing a holiday destination, but is rarely so important for most people when choosing airlines or accommodation units.

Seasonality

Most sectors have peak and off-peak seasons, although these differ from one country to another. Summer in the Scandinavian market, for example, is focused on late June to the end of July; while in Mediterranean markets summer means August. In the Southern hemisphere, summer vacations mean December and January. Often peak seasons will be the same for different sectors in any particular country. School holidays will usually be the peak time of demand for tour operators, charter airlines and visitor attractions. However, for city-centre hotels and scheduled airlines, school holidays are their off-peak season because that is when business people usually take their holidays with their families.

Distance travelled to use tourism product and services

Owing to the nature of the tourism product, tourists always have to travel to the location where the tourism product or service is delivered. Until recently the shortest journey to a service was to a high-street travel agent, which could be a few hundred metres to several kilometres away for most people. However, with the rise of online travel agents, most purchases can now be made from home or office with no need to travel anywhere. But to enjoy hotels, beaches and so on the tourist still needs to travel, sometimes for many thousands of kilometres.

Frequency of purchase

We might find that in the UK, for instance, a person may purchase a number of different tourism products in a typical year:

- 12 visitor attractions (two museums, a zoo, two theme parks, two historic houses, a factory shop, an art gallery, two festivals or special events, and a waterfront development such as the Albert Dock in Liverpool)
- two inclusive tours offered by a tour operator (a summer sun two-week package and an off-peak weekend city break, although the latter is now likely to be booked independently online)
- one airline seat purchased independently, not as part of a package holiday (a flight to visit a relative in the USA)

- one hotel night purchased independently, not as part of a package holiday (hotel stopover on the way to a family wedding in another part of the country).

Methods of segmenting the market

In most sections of tourism there are some common methods of segmenting the market which appear to work well. These include:

- geographical (where consumers live)
- demographic (age, gender and family status)
- business versus leisure travellers
- frequent versus infrequent travellers
- independent tourists versus organized groups.

Alternatively, there seem to be a few approaches to segmentation that appear largely to be applicable to one sector only. For example, in the visitor attraction sector, tourists' personalities can be an important way of segmenting the market. Introvert, studious people may prefer to visit museums, while extrovert, adventurous risk-takers may form the core of the market for theme parks where 'white-knuckle rides' are the main attraction.

Price paid for the product or service

The products offered by tourism organizations vary dramatically in price. The typical range of prices for the products of different sectors is as follows:

- destinations – usually no direct fee or price is paid by the tourist to enter a destination
- retail travel – no direct price is charged to the customer although the retail travel outlet receives from the tour operator, hotel or airline a proportion of the price paid by the tourist, as commission
- visitor attractions – many are free but even the most expensive rarely charge more than £20 for admission
- restaurants – meals can vary in price, from £1 to well over £100
- accommodation – may be free (e.g. monasteries) or around £10 per night (youth hostels) at one extreme, or at the other end of the spectrum a luxury hotel or resort could charge several thousand pounds per night
- transport – coach fares can cost as little as £5–10 for several hundred kilometres, while long-distance first-class tickets by air cost thousands of pounds
- tour operators – weekend breaks, self-catering holidays and last-minute discounted holidays can cost less than £100 per person, while a fully inclusive escorted tour around the world may cost over £10,000.

Clearly the price charged also varies dramatically between countries. One night in a hotel room in a good quality hotel may cost more than £300 in London but well under £50 in Thailand. Indeed the rise of travel to less economically developed countries from highly developed countries has been partly fuelled by the lower prices so one can sleep in better hotels and enjoy better quality meals than one could in one's own country or the traveller can afford to enjoy a longer stay.

Methods of booking or reserving

In the visitor attraction sector pre-booking is rare, whereas in sectors such as airlines hardly anyone would consider not pre-booking and just turning up at an airport in the hope that a seat will be available to their chosen destination. The accommodation sector falls somewhere between these two extremes in that some people pre-book, while others wait until they arrive in a place and then walk around to find a suitable hotel. It is fair to say that in most countries the growth in supply and the opportunity to book hotels on arrival through mobile device apps is leading to a rise in people not booking in advance.

Where pre-booking is the norm, the choice is between using intermediaries or agents and booking directly with the producer. Most tour operators' products are sold via intermediaries, as are the majority of flights and ferry trips. However, the trend in all sectors seems to be towards direct booking or using online travel agents.

So, as we can see, there are both similarities and significant differences between the sectors of tourism in terms of aspects of consumer behaviour.

Special cases

The picture presented so far is much generalized, and there are three special cases which we will discuss next:

- retail travel
- destinations
- business tourism.

Retail travel (high-street travel agents)

Retail travel is a unique sector in tourism in that it does not have a product of its own. Instead it exists to provide a service – giving consumers access to the products of other tourism sectors.

Its different function in the tourism system means that it differs from the demand for other sectors in a number of respects. For example, the peak season is not when people travel but when they book their trips. In the UK, for example, this can mean the period immediately after Christmas when many people book their summer holidays.

However in recent years we have seen a trend to late and even last-minute booking which has been made easier by online travel intermediaries.

It is fair to say that traditional high-street travel agents are losing market share to online agents, although this is not the case in all countries.

Destinations

From the consumers' point of view, it is perhaps better to see the destination as a do-it-yourself (DIY) kit, rather like a 'Lego' set, rather than as a finished product. It offers tourists a range of opportunities from which they can produce their own product or experience. The choice of possible permutations is virtually limitless, subject only to constraints such as money and information, and tourists can use the destination in many different ways. This is illustrated in Figure 11.2, where we look at how different tourists might use the destination of the Greek island of Crete.

The varying ways in which different tourists will use the same destination will depend on the characteristics of these tourists, for example, their age, gender, past experience, hobbies and interests, lifestyle and personality.

Finally, as we noted earlier, destinations are unique among the sectors of tourism in that no direct charge is made for using them. It is possible for tourists to use a range of services, such as beaches, parties and free museums, without incurring any expenditure. They can also window-shop and enjoy walking around historic streets absolutely free of charge.

In recent years, tourists have been given powerful new tools to help them plan how they will use the destination and create their own unique experience. These tools include apps for smartphones and other mobile devices. Consumer-generated media have also given them access to a huge bank of reviews and opinions of other travellers that can also help them make choices.

Tourist A	Stays in a large modern resort hotel, in a quiet resort, eats in the hotel, spends most of the day sunbathing by the hotel pool and then drinking in the hotel bar at night.
Tourist B	Stays in a simple apartment complex on the coast, wakes late, sunbathes and then goes partying in the nightclubs of Aghios Nikolaos in the evening.
Tourist C	Makes their base in a small traditional pension, relaxes over long meals in local tavernas and attempts to make contact with Cretan people.
Tourist D	Uses a modern resort hotel as a base, but spends all day visiting cultural sites including the Temple at Knossos and the archaeological museum in Heraklion.
Tourist E	Stays in the cheapest accommodation they can find because they want to spend all their time and money indulging their interest in watersports such as diving and windsurfing.
Tourist F	Tours Crete by hire car, staying a few nights in each place they like the look of, has no pre-planned itinerary.
Tourist G	Takes a cruise around the Mediterranean which includes a one-day port call to Heraklion and an optional excursion to the Samarià Gorge.

Figure 11.2 Different potential uses of Crete as a destination

The parallel world of business travel

Business tourism is a very different activity from leisure tourism, and the business traveller is a fundamentally different consumer from the leisure traveller. The world of business tourism exists in parallel to that of leisure tourism. Sometimes business tourists use similar services to leisure tourists, such as hotel bedrooms and airline seats. At other times they use services that are uniquely offered to business travellers, such as convention centres. Even where they use the same hotels and airlines as leisure tourists, special provision may be made to meet business travellers' needs, such as in-bedroom computer access points in hotels and onboard fax machines on aircraft. They also have their own infrastructure of business travel agents and incentive travel organizations.

Figure 11.3 illustrates the differences between consumer behaviour in business and leisure tourism. The first item in this figure is particularly important because in recent years there has been tension in the relationship among employers (customers), business travellers (consumers) and the tourism industry, most notably airlines. Companies looking to reduce their travel budgets and arrange them more effectively have often been irritated to see airlines offering their employees who travel on business perks

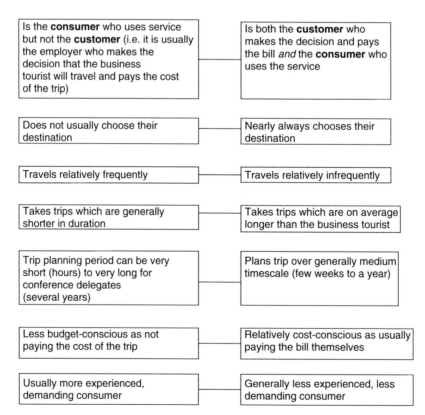

Figure 11.3 Differences in consumer behaviour between business and leisure tourists

such as Air Miles. The companies believe that as the customer who pays the bill, it is they who should receive any benefit that may be offered by airlines. Many of them would prefer lower fares instead of perks for their employees.

Taking the final element in Figure 11.3 further, the expectations of business tourists tend to be higher than those of the average leisure traveller. This may be because:

* they are more experienced travellers and therefore have a more comprehensive understanding of general standards in the tourism industry against which to judge the performance of an individual tourism organization
* they are often travelling on a higher daily budget than the average leisure traveller
* the airlines and hotel sectors have recognized the lucrative nature of the business tourist and have therefore focused their promotional efforts on impressing the business tourist, thus raising their expectations.

However, before we take this point too far, let us remember that many leisure tourists today are also business tourists in their working lives. This brings us to a further interesting point: the links that exist between business tourism and leisure tourism in terms of consumer behaviour, which include the following four examples.

* When the working day is over the business tourist becomes a leisure tourist, eating out in restaurants, drinking in bars and watching entertainment performances.
* Conference programmes often have social programmes for delegates, which will probably feature attractions aimed predominantly at leisure tourists, such as folk-lore shows and museums.
* When business tourists have finished the business they have to conduct, they may choose to stay on for a few days as a leisure tourist. This is more likely to be the case if the destination is a long way from their home or is a wellknown leisure tourism destination. They may well use this extra time to take 'add-on' trips. For instance, a trip to mainland China could be added on to a business trip to Hong Kong Island.
* Business tourists may take their partner with them; while they are working, their partner will be behaving as a leisure tourist.

Finally, we should note that in the longer term the demand for business travel may decline as the need for trips is substituted by the use of communication technologies such as video-conferencing. The market for training courses that involve students or tutors travelling to meet each other could also be reduced by the development of virtual reality simulations, which allow training to be conducted at the trainee's usual place of work. This is already playing a part in the training of surgeons in new techniques.

However, it seems likely that there will be business tourism for the foreseeable future, for as long as personal face-to-face contact is thought to be either essential or desirable.

Differences within individual sectors of tourism

In this chapter we have focused on similarities and differences in consumer behaviour between the different sectors of tourism. However, it would be wrong not to look at the differences in behaviour that can exist within the same sector. We will illustrate this point through four examples drawn from the accommodation and tour operation sectors.

Luxury hotels and budget motels

There are clearly different motivators for guests at five-star hotels than would be the case for budget motels. The luxury hotel client seeks a special experience, status and a high level of personal service. The budget motel user is motivated by a desire for a functional experience, a convenient location and economy.

Serviced and non-serviced accommodation units

Consumers who prefer to use non-serviced or self-catering accommodation for their holidays may well make this choice because they:

- have children and find self-catering more flexible than staying in hotels
- are on a limited budget and by taking food with them, or buying cheaply from local supermarkets, they should be able to enjoy a holiday in the same destination at a lower cost than would be the case if they were to stay in a hotel
- prefer to buy and cook fresh local food products rather than eat hotel meals based on imported ingredients and international menus
- could be suspicious of hygiene standards in the local hospitality industry.

Mass-market and specialist tour operators

Tourists who buy mass-market package tours and those buying the products offered by specialist operators are often seeking different benefits from their purchase. The mass-market customer may well be motivated by a desire for:

- a low-cost product
- visiting destinations that are clearly popular and have a welldeveloped infrastructure for tourists
- the company of other tourists
- a more passive, resort-based holiday.

Conversely, the tourist who buys a specialist tour operator's package may well be motivated by their wish to:

- appear to be a sophisticated consumer
- pursue a particular personal interest, whether a sport like diving or a hobby like bird-watching
- visit less popular destinations that are 'off the beaten track'
- mix with relatively few other tourists.

Long-term plans and last-minute purchases

The tour-operating field also sees significant differences in consumer behaviour in terms of when people plan and book their holidays. Some customers like to plan and book their holiday months before they travel. This might be because they fear that if they do not, they might not find the exact product or be able to arrange the itinerary they want. Therefore this type of behaviour is more commonly found among tourists who wish to take more unusual or exotic holidays, or who have definite views on which accommodation establishment they wish to use.

Other tourists prefer not to plan or book their vacation trip until very late, perhaps a few days before their departure. This could be for a number of reasons, for example:

- a belief that they may be able to take advantage of last-minute discounting by tour operators
- the excitement of making a late decision, in that one does not know one's destination until the last minute
- a late unforeseen opportunity to take time off work.

Commonly, last-minute purchase is associated with consumers who are less concerned with where they go and with specific hotels, than with price and departure dates.

Conclusions

We have seen that there are similarities and differences in demand characteristics between the different sectors of tourism. However, there are also significant differences within individual sectors of tourism.

It is important to recognize that there are differences in the structure and nature of tourism industries in different countries, so some of the points made in this chapter would vary in their application depending on the country being visited.

Discussion points and essay questions

1. Discuss the marketing implications of the differences between business tourism and leisure tourism, for airlines and hotel chains.

2. Compare and contrast the main ways of segmenting the market in the different sectors of tourism.
3. Examine the differences in consumer behaviour within an individual sector of tourism of your choice.

Exercise

Design and conduct a small survey of tourists to identify similarities and differences in the way they purchase:

- accommodation services
- package holidays
- visits to attractions.

CASE STUDY 11.1: Bikes, birds and bullets: niche tourism in South Africa

by Saskia Faulk

Hundreds of kilometres of sandy beaches, glitzy Sun City, Big Five safaris and historic homestead wineries . . . the reasons to visit South Africa are well known. Few countries can claim to have tropical rain forests, mountain terrain, deserts, savanna, temperate zones and balmy coastal regions for travellers wishing to have it all during one stay. In addition, its location deep in the Southern Hemisphere allows travellers from the north to enjoy inverted seasons: summer in December, then the mild South African winter in July while everyone back home is sweltering. In 2012, 9,188,368 tourist arrivals were recorded in South Africa, a 10.2 per cent growth year-on-year, which is much higher than the world average growth rate of 3.9 per cent. Top ten source markets for South Africa in terms of size are Zimbabwe, Lesotho, Mozambique and Swaziland. Top three international tourist arrivals were from the UK, USA, Germany and China (South Africa Tourism, 2012). Travellers who do more than scratch the shiny surface of the country learn that there are many specialized attractions and diverse regions, constituting in and of themselves good reasons to visit the country.

The Western and Eastern Cape regions, including Cape Town, have much to offer, and are the focus of this case study. Well maintained roads crisscross most of the picturesque Cape making it possible to visit different vistas comfortably by car or coach, interspersed with overnight stops in historic towns formerly known for their diamond mines. Where vines have replaced mines, today producing one-tenth of national wine output, pleasant estates offer gourmet stays. As elsewhere in the country, varied types of attractions are close by: multiple majestic waterfalls deafen at Augrabies Falls; the Kalahari Desert defies explorers to enter; the lush Orange River valley can be explored by canoe or raft excursions; and the Big Five (buffalo, elephant, leopard, lion and rhinoceros) wander a number of parks and ranches.

Yet a growing number of travellers have little interest in such a wide variety of attractions on offer: they visit the area for very specific reasons that stem from their own leisure-time interests and passions. They compose South Africa's niche tourism markets. One of the major goals of the South African tourism authorities is to encourage these small, specialized markets in addition to mass tourism. Despite their relatively small number, they constitute new growth markets, and contribute to economic development in a more diverse and local manner than mass tourism. Due to its climate, history, diversity of ecosystems and government tourism strategy, the southern tip of South Africa offers an exceptional combination of very specialized reasons to visit, several of which are illustrated below.

GREAT WHITE TOURISM

While many people may initially find it difficult to appreciate the attraction of diving with sharks, after meeting with shark enthusiasts and learning about these fascinating animals, even the most timid diver will concede it could be an interesting, even life-changing experience. Virtually all types of diving interests are catered for in many locations along South Africa's coasts, including some wellknown shark haunts. The coast off Cape Town is known worldwide as a great white shark hotspot, and at nearby 'shark alley' the world's biggest tuna stocks attract numerous other species of shark. Along this coast, shark lovers can view bull, hammerhead, mako, barracuda, blacktip, blue, giant guitar, tiger and ragged tooth sharks. While some beach authorities have installed costly shark nets with the intention of protecting swimmers and divers, the number of launch sites for diving with sharks has risen.

With the dwindling numbers of many species of shark, it is increasingly clear that they are in need of protection. The International Union for the Conservation of Nature has listed the great white shark as 'vulnerable', along with a number of other species. There is so much fear of these predators, fed by a series of scary films and rare but highly dramatized shark attacks, it seems surprising that the real victims today are sharks, not humans. Clearly diving with sharks is not only an adrenaline-pumping daredevil act, it is potentially one that contributes to the salvation of these beautiful and ancient predators, which subsequently become more valuable alive than dead. Entire towns along the coast have developed their tourism potential through shark- and whale-viewing tours. One example of this is Gansbaai (also dubbed Shark Bay), situated where the Indian and Atlantic Oceans meet on one of South Africa's southernmost tips (www.sharkwatchsa.com; Marshall, 2012). Shark-dive tourism is a growing, albeit small, niche segment seeking to view the many species of sharks that swim near the coasts of South Africa.

Most companies involved are small but have lofty aims: to offer an educational and responsible experience to tourists that protects the marine ecosystems in which they live. Preparing to go on a shark dive is often in reality an education in marine biology, with guides who devote their lives to conservation of the sharks and other marine species as well as their ecosystems. A large number of research projects are ongoing in the area, and due to the practice of tour companies allowing marine biologists to use their boats, divers may find themselves actually participating in one of these studies (Marine Dynamics Tours, 2013). In addition, companies active in this sector usually have other related areas of expertise that enrich the marine traveller's experience. The so-called marine Big Five (whales, dolphins, seals, penguins and sharks) are all present in the same coastal and ocean areas close to South Africa, and it is conceivable that a visitor aiming to see sharks could observe the other four species on an outing too, whether free-diving, cage-diving or merely boat touring.

There is no particular season for viewing sharks, but there are certain months when a particular species may be more plentiful. Diving company African Dive Adventures features a calendar on its website to help interested divers plan their trip around the species they most wish to see (www.afridive.com). The period from April to October is generally the most highly recommended for shark viewing. There is a yearly 'event' known as the Great Sardine Run in June or July, when the migratory routes of enormous schools of sardines pass close to the coast, attracting countless pelagic birds, predatory fish, dolphins and whales.

CYCLING TOURISM

Mountain biking is conquering more territory in South Africa. It is a sport that allows travellers to develop a unique relationship with their surroundings – including fauna as well as flora – for three main reasons. Firstly, because bicycles are relatively silent and non-polluting, cyclists have the opportunity to observe close-up animals that would have fled at the sound or scent of an approaching motor. A unique sense of communing with nature is possible by bicycle too, as one sees, hears and smells the surroundings more clearly than in any other vehicle. Lastly, possibly the most important reason can be appreciated by anyone who spends an inordinate amount of time seated. For active-minded travellers, it can be frustrating to be sedentary for long hours, whether on safari or a self-drive itinerary. Although no Big Five game drive will ever be available on two wheels, it is possible to explore South Africa's majestic mountains with a bit of pedal power and a sturdy mountain bike. Another interesting point is that here mountain biking is not just for tourists: South Africa has a healthy cycling culture with clubs, infrastructure and events to support it. Therefore it is highly likely that one will meet local enthusiasts on the trail as an added bonus, adding an authentic, friendly South African social experience to the other compelling arguments for biking in the country. Mountain bike trails range from easy and family-friendly to highly challenging even for wellprepared sport cyclists who have trained prior to arrival. One sample event that offers exclusive access to the South African landscape is the EAI Val de Vie Mountain Bike Challenge, held near Cape Town. The 30- and 60-kilometre route trails power through 21 picturesque farms and 30 vineyards in the Cape Winelands, many of which are not accessible for the rest of the year, when they are fenced in. The trail also passes through the Drakenstein Correctional Centre, the prison where Nelson Mandela was held, and the finish line is at an exclusive polo club. More than 1,000 'social' cyclists took part in the event last year.

Yet cycling holidays in South Africa are not just for sports fanatics: an innovative combination of mountain biking and wine tasting is on offer in the scenic Stellenbosch region. One destination management company offering carbon-negative holidays (descriptively named Bikes 'n Wines) has bike-powered tours with private tastings in up to four wineries per day in the world-renowned wine areas Constantia, Stellenbosch, Franschhoek and Paarl (www.bikesnwines.com). Along with gourmet meals and more-or-less luxurious accommodation, cyclists pedal along some of the country's most peaceful private roads winding through the vineyards and Dutch-style manor houses. Depending on the operator, itineraries can be more or less structured, designed for different fitness levels or for families with small children (who will taste different chocolates while their parents taste a handful of different wines). They can also include different categories of overnight accommodation, airport transfers, tour guides, and bike and equipment rentals.

A MOST EPHEMERAL ATTRACTION: FLOWER TOURISM

Due partly to its variety of ecosystems, South African flora is exceptionally rich in genetic diversity. Almost half its native flowers, for instance, grow in only one region of the country. One fabulous showcase for this is the Northern Cape flower route, which attracts a faithful following of plant lovers, amateur botanists, hikers and nature photographers. Even tourists with less specialized interests can be touched by the view of sculptural proteas, South Africa's national flower, dotting the scrubby landscape as far as the eye can see on one of the Cape's cliffs, framed by the stormy Atlantic and endless sky in the background. Similarly, watching the sun rise over Cape of Good Hope is a spine-tingling experience whether one is a flower-fan or not.

At South Africa's southernmost tip, the Northern and Eastern Cape regions are particularly prized by visitors with a botanical interest. From July through October, which is spring to early summertime there, travellers can witness what has been dubbed 'the Earth's greatest flower show' along the Succulent Karoo. Namakwa (also known as Namaqualand) is particularly well known in this respect, having the greatest variety worldwide of wildflowers and the richest diversity in an arid environment (www.experiencenortherncape.com). The high season for flower viewing is in July and August, but all year long nature's bounty is on view. Author and photographer Freeman Patterson called this land 'the garden of the gods', a nickname that is easily understood after the rains from a distance, whence one can see a seemingly infinite patchwork of colors: white, pale yellow, dazzling orange, with bunches of royal purple. Zooming in closer, the competing aromas, hues and textures of exquisite smaller flowers seeking sunlight among their taller cousins is a spectacle awaiting travellers who explore these wide plains on foot. In most of this area, gentle hikes interspersed with river and rockpool swims make exploring healthy as well as beautiful. Further to the north, yet within the same province, wildflowers temporarily transform a desert in the Ai-Ais Richtersveld, an immense expanse reaching up to Namibia. Unlike the rest of the Northern Cape, access to this desert is reserved for all-terrain vehicles and hardy hikers.

Botanical tourists can benefit from visiting the Namaqua National Park and a number of wildflower reserves and botanical gardens, as well as flower and rooibos tea farms.

Most international visitors are agape at seeing multicoloured daisies stretching out to the horizon that heretofore had only been seen in small bouquets at the florists, and a multitude of flowers they have never seen before – and whose very names are totally unfamiliar: *vygies*, *sporries*, *katstert* and *Pietsnot*, to name a few. Yet another botanical marvel in the area is the quiver trees, which can grow to a height of 9 metres over their 250-year lifespan. The flowers don't just attract tourists: 78 mammal, 132 reptile and 250 bird species are among the other star attractions according to the Northern Cape Tourist Board (2013). When one has seen enough flowers, travellers can explore the rock paintings that go back 10,000 years painted by indigenous bushmen (*San*), ancient inhabitants of the area. Excellent wineries, sandy beaches, waterfalls and river-rafting, and historic homesteads abound nearby too.

AVID FOR AVITOURISM

Avitourism is a specific type of nature-based travel for the serious birdwatcher seeking to observe birds in their natural habitat. Some photograph the birds, others sketch them and take notes, while the majority simply seek, identify and watch. The most serious recreational birdwatchers compile a 'life list' of birds they have seen with notes about their characteristics, behaviour and the location where they were observed. Many have travelled far and wide to observe targeted species.

According to the South Africa Tourism Authority, ornithologists have recorded more than 850 bird species in diverse habitats, with 74 species occurring nowhere else in the world. The country also boasts a robust conservation infrastructure that encourages 'birding travel' as well as a large number of breeding colonies, observation/lookout points and boardwalks, volunteer census activities, conservation centres and reintroduction programmes. A healthy number of tourism-oriented options exist also, with specialized tour operators, identified birding routes and walking trails, and there are ocean and island boat tours. Most categories of bird interests are catered to, from parrots to ostrich to penguins, with diverse habitats including grasslands, forests, wetlands, savannas, coastal and oceanic. The national tourism authority recognizes the interest of this niche on its global internet portal, and South Africa's major bird conservation organization has developed a searchable database of 'birder-friendly establishments' certified for their avitourism commitment and suitability by Birdlife South Africa (2013), including bed and breakfasts, farms, self-catering cottages and homestay options at levels of comfort ranging from camping to luxury.

TOURISM FOR THE PALATE

The exotic tastes that result from blending African, Indian, Dutch and British cuisines, to name just a few, are one uniquely South African experience. Maize-meal porridge with spicy stew, fragrant curries and Indian foods, seafood straight from the Indian and Atlantic oceans, and the South African *braai* (barbecue) featuring locally produced steaks and sausages are just some specialities for which the country is known. The famous spiced dried meats (*biltong*) have their own special allure, and more than one traveller has become addicted for life, resorting to ordering *biltong* from dedicated online businesses after returning home. Yet South Africa is also renowned for its *haute cuisine* that rivals that of the old world, with fantastic meals served in an ambiance of peerless luxury at a very competitive price (Ludman, n.d.). Ostrich carpaccio with smoked pumpkin purée, buttered poached *kingklip* and chips, coriander-crusted springbok loin . . . international flavor fusion, inventiveness and love of South African ingredients prevail here.

The Cape region of South Africa has gained a reputation for its wine over the past 400 years, as well as for its cheese and produce. The vineyards stretch around Cape Town and to the west across the Cape, totaling 260,000 acres. South Africa is the world's eighth-largest wine producer, and is slated to produce even more wine of better quality, with recent investments and replanting to the extent that most of the Cape's vineyards were planted over the past 15 years. Almost half of the plantings are red varieties such as Cabernet Sauvignon, Syrah, Pinotage and Merlot and the rest are white (mainly Chenin Blanc or 'Steen', Colombard, Sauvignon Blanc and Chardonnay (Molesworth, 2013). South African wineries are often located in scenic heritage sites, and tend to be places where the authentic Cape culture can be experienced. Seasonal menus featuring local produce expertly paired with the perfect wine are what one might expect at a Cape Winelands eatery. Some offer much more, with on-site accommodation, museums, river cruises and even game drives (Klink Wine Tourism Awards, 2013). Wine tourists tend to be between 30 and 50 years old, in higher income brackets, and in terms of wine purchases domestic tourists rank first, followed by those from the USA, the UK and Germany. More than half the visitors to Cape Town go on a vineyard tour (City of Cape Town and Kamilla SA, n.d.).

Travelers seeking a rare culinary treat head for nearby Franschhoek, the 'culinary capital' of South Africa (Ritztrade International, 2011). The name refers to the fact that the town was originally settled by French Huguenots, and possibly it is their centuries-old influence that set the standards for such haute cuisine, wines and cheeses. The Franschhoek Valley is an area of bucolic beauty surrounded by mountains and vineyards. Golf courses, tennis courts, horse-riding, cycling, paragliding and of course wine-tasting are all a short distance away, as is the world-class city of Cape Town. The historic town of Franschhoek, also referred to as a 'village', is famous for its selection of world-class restaurants, of which eight are South Africa's top-ranked, and more than 40 wineries flourish close by. In the village is also one of South Africa's best gourmet experiences and the best chef on the African continent, according to the San Pellegrino restaurant ranking (Olmstead, 2013). A family-owned Relais & Châteaux two-decades old property, Le Quartier Français, offers exquisite luxury and a spa in its small-scale cottage accommodations arranged around pools and gardens. Two restaurants presided over by multiple award-winning chef Margot Janse ensure the guests will never be hungry. Janse's stated goal is to use only African ingredients, and her influences are certainly as diverse as those influencing South African cuisine, although the cooking inspiration is resolutely modern. Guests can take lessons in chocolate-making, charcuterie, wine-tasting and blending, cooking and bread-making. They can also help make nutritious muffins for area school-children in the restaurant kitchen (Le Quartier Français, 2013).

TOWNSHIP TOURISM

Some travellers aim to immerse themselves in the living challenge of national reconciliation initiated by Nelson Mandela in his fight against apartheid by visiting now-famous townships like Soweto, or Cape Town's Khayelitsha. Short bus-tour visitors may be part of a larger market with wider interests than the usual travellers' pursuits, but there are those who are part of a niche segment seeking authentic social experiences or even voluntourists. Visitors may be curious about township life, having seen South African film productions using township locations such as *U-Carmen eKhayelitsha*, *Tsotsi*, *Izulu Lami*, *Felix*, *Sarafina!*, or even *District 9*. Some enjoy the thrill factor as an added bonus, because safety is an issue to be managed by walking in groups with the guide, being indoors before nightfall, and following other simple rules (www.khayelitshatravel. com). So-called 'slum' tourism is part of a global trend that shuns mass tourism and seeks authentic experiences portrayed as the 'other, true' face of prosperity. In terms of tourism economics, such tourists may bring benefits where they are most needed, directly at the local community level. Yet for similar reasons these tourists have been criticised as voyeurs who entertain themselves by observing the daily lives of people experiencing poverty and deprivation (Macmillan, 2011). Whatever the case, visiting a township can be a genuinely enjoyable and upbeat experience as well as a genuine learning opportunity.

On the simplest level, a township visit can last one hour or so, with the level of contact with local residents highly variable and dependent upon the philosophy of the touring operator. Several tour guide companies offer tours of Khayelitsha near Cape Town, home to 1.5 million residents and the fastest-growing township in the country. They emphasize their engaging personal contact with locals, and can arrange a night in a number of bed and breakfasts, including Cape Town's smallest hotel, lodging with local families. The guide introduces tourists to locals who often spontaneously issue invitations into their homes and some groups may be greeted by outbursts of welcoming song. More complex itineraries can encompass experiencing township food (simple, spicy and satisfying) and traditional beer and culture, heritage locations, dance shows and arts activities. Recognizing the diverse nature of such itineraries, innovative partnerships between tourism providers have developed. A wellknown example of this is SoWeToo in the formerly infamous eponymous township Soweto, South Africa's biggest, located near Johannesburg. 'So, We, Too' (as it is pronounced) is comprised of seven tourism entrepreneurs who play different starring roles in the tours: a tour service, a participatory craft collective, the prize-winning Roots Restaurant and Gallery, and other providers of enriching township experiences (www.sowetoo.co.za).

South African music boasts at least as many influences as the food, and can become similarly habit-forming once one has been exposed to it. Experiencing such music live in its home context is electrifying and touching. Township tours typically include watching a gumboot dance, which is possibly the most spectacular dance on the planet, conducted in miners' rubber boots without any orchestration. For those who seek a more immersive experience, overnight stays are arranged through hotel and bed-and-breakfast partners. Quads or bicycles are on offer for adventurous and active souls wishing to zig-zag through the typical township maze of back streets and alleyways. More risk-averse tourists can remain in their comfort zone on air-conditioned tour buses.

TRIALS AND TRIBULATIONS OF SEEKING A 'SPORTING' HUNTING HOLIDAY

Each year, millions of visitors visit South Africa's 150 national parks and reserves, among which the Kruger National Park is probably the best known. The majority leave the country with hundreds of wildlife photos. A growing number, estimated at over 6,000 hunters yearly, leave with hunting trophies as well. South Africa is the most popular hunting destination in Africa, known for its combination of rich diverse wildlife and its safe, comfortable hospitality offerings.

More than 9,000 registered private game ranches cater to the aims of hunters on territories that total more than 16 per cent of the nation's territory (Cousins, Sadler and Evans, 2008). Ranchers own more than double the amount of plains and Big Five game than that available on public lands. Such a situation contains the innate risk of 'canned hunting', the term used to describe how game and even the Big Five animals are bred in captivity for the pleasure of foreign hunters in South Africa, a reality brought to light by the media in recent years. The figures would appear to bear out such allegations: hunters exported 1,830 lion trophies from South Africa from 2001–06; and 4,062 from 2006–11, representing an increase of 122 per cent (Barkham, 2013). Investigative journalists asserted that most of these were captive-bred, and have started investigating ranches that specialize in exotic or endangered species, such as black or white rhinoceros, for hunting purposes. One journalist has termed the South African hunting tourism sector 'free-market conservation' (Borrell, 2010). The debate about privatized wildlife conservation nourished by hunting revenue continues vociferously, with no side clearly in the right or in the wrong. Hunters commonly assert that they contribute most to conservation because hunting lands could otherwise be converted to agriculture, real estate or other uses that would exclude wildlife altogether (Theroux, 2008).

Yet many hunters are looking for a real 'sporting' hunting trip where 'canned' hunting is considered dishonourable. Some appear to be more interested in the excitement of the chase rather than the actual kill, and the marketing message accent for hunting lodges is on the quality of the hospitality and educational experience as well as the friendliness and knowledge of the staff. Typically, hunters reside in traditional round thatched houses and are fed on excellent South African food (which may or may not contain game ingredients). The narrative goes that they spend much preparation time learning about animal and plant species as well as traditional hunting tactics and African stories. They also emphasize the preference to select older and male specimens for the kill, thereby weeding out already less-fit animals from the herd. Such outfitters typically supply meet-and-greet, airport firearms clearance, air and ground transfers, vehicles, the services of a professional hunter and tracker, as well as taxidermy services.

Plains game animals tend to be concentrated in the Limpopo and Eastern Cape provinces and consist mainly of gemsbok, kudu, impala, springbok, warthog, wildebeest and zebra. The Big Five animals (or Big Six if hippopotamus are included) can be legally hunted all over the country, while other countries with similar fauna, like Kenya, are more restrictive. Rates for hunting specific animals range from free of charge for a jackal to US$100 for a baboon, US$2,500 for an eland, and 'price on request' for giraffes, lions and other big game. The legal hunting season is all year, although there are certain species- and location-specific restrictions. Most hunting is undertaken between March and October, especially during the chilly months of June–August. The majority of hunters are South African, Namibian and Zimbabwean, while hunters from afar are usually Europeans and North Americans. Hunters tend to use firearms, although an increasing number of bow hunters enter South Africa, which is favoured by the climate, terrain, and there being no requirement for an import permit for bows. Two to four firearms and 200 rounds of ammunition can be imported free of charge by hunters, and a temporary firearm import permit can be issued at the airport of arrival. Handguns are permitted as hunting weapons and semi-automatic shotguns are allowed for bird shooting (South African Police Service, 2013). South Africa's Cape provinces have one trump card: unlike most other African hunting destinations, they are free of malaria so hunters can avoid necessity of taking odious malaria-preventative medications during their stay (www.africahunting.com).

EXERCISES

1. Conduct some informal research in your university regarding niche travel interests. Investigate how many students have already embarked on a holiday dedicated to their leisure-time interests and passions, and how many plan to do so. Compile a catalogue of their interests and the countries, destinations or attractions to which they are drawn. If possible, identify practical considerations for these travellers in making their decision, including air fare, transfer and accommodation costs, as well as safety or health considerations and visa requirements.
2. Have a look at some of the niche market activities described in the above case study, and visit some of the websites of tourism and hospitality companies mentioned. You will notice that, however specialized the company is, it will provide information about other diverse attractions and activities in the area. Consider the importance of having other non-niche-related activities nearby, both for these operators and their visitors.

REFERENCES

Barkham, P. (2013). 'Canned hunting': the lions bred for slaughter. *The Guardian* 3 June. www.theguardian.com/environment/2013/jun/03/canned-hunting-lions-bred-slaughter

Borrell, B. (2010). Hunters paying $150,000 to kill an endangered rhino may save the species. *Bloomberg.com* 9 December.

City of Cape Town and Kamilla SA (n.d.). *Niche Market Study*. www.capetown.gov.za/en/tourism/Documents/Niche%20Market%20StudyM_Final.pdf

Cousins, J.A., Sadler, J.P. and Evans, J. (2008). Exploring the role of private wildlife ranching as a conservation tool in South Africa: stakeholder perspectives. *Ecology and Society* 13 (2), 43. www.ecologyandsociety.org/vol13/iss2/art43/

Le Quartier Français (2013). *Cooking*. www.lqf.co.za/cooking/overview.htm

Ludman, B. (n.d.). South African cuisine. *South Africa Info*. www.southafrica.info/travel/food/food.htm#.UoPcpelwKDk

Macmillan, S. (2011). Poorism vs authenticity on township tour of Khayelitsha. *The National* 6 May. www.thenational.ae/lifestyle/travel/poorism-vs-authenticity-on-township-tour-of-khayelitsha

Marine Dynamics Tours (2013). *Great White Sharks*. www.sharkwatchsa.com/en/sharks/great-white/

Marshall, L. (2012). Is tourism good for South Africa's great white sharks? *National Geographic* 17 January. http://newswatch.nationalgeographic.com/2012/01/17/is-tourism-good-for-south-africas-great-white-sharks/

Molesworth, J. (2013). The ABCs of South Africa. *Wine Spectator* 31 July. www.winespectator.com/magazine/show/id/48567

The Northern Cape Tourism Board (2013). www.northerncape.org.za/general_information/

Olmstead, L. (2013). The best restaurant on the African continent. *Forbes* 19 March. www.forbes.com/sites/larryolmsted/2013/03/19/best-restaurant-on-the-continent/lifestyle

Ritztrade International (2011). Franschhoek-Cape Town wine region. *Cape Town.Info*. www.cape-town.info/surrounding-areas-winelands/franschhoek/

South African Police Service (2013). *Information on importation of firearms to South Africa*. www.saps.gov.za/services/flash/firearms/importation.php

South Africa Tourism (2012). *2012 Annual Report*. www.southafrica.net/research/en/page/research-reports-search/search&category=International

Theroux, L. (2008). The price of a rhino's life? $100,000. *BBC Magazine* 4 April. http://news.bbc.co.uk/2/hi/uk_news/magazine/7329425.stm

Wine Tourism South Arica (2013). Klink Wine Tourism Awards 2013: Sip, Savour, Play, Stay and Save the World. 11 October. http://winetourismsouthafrica.co.za/2013/09/30/klink-wine-tourism-awards-2013-sip-savour-play-stay-and-save-the-world/

CASE STUDY 11.2: Ragdale Hall health hydro and thermal spa

INTRODUCTION

Ragdale Hall was established in the 1970s as a business that offered customers the opportunity to experience health, beauty and fitness treatments. There have been considerable alterations made to the hall during the past 20 years. There have been additions made to the original buildings, and facilities have been regularly updated so that the latest treatments and products can always be offered to guests. Ragdale Hall is situated within easy reach of the M1 and A1, between Loughborough and Melton Mowbray in the heart of the UK's Leicestershire countryside. Guests can arrive at the hall by car or taxi from local railway stations.

Ragdale Hall is set in its own extensive landscaped gardens and combines the charm of traditional Victorian architecture with the most modern facilities, to create one of the most luxurious and relaxing health resorts in the UK.

RAGDALE HALL – THE COMPANY

Ragdale Hall has had many owners during its history. It has been operated as a restaurant and a nightclub with gambling facilities. It became a health hydro in 1972 when Slimming World purchased it. Ragdale Hall changed ownership in June 1990, when it was bought by Gary Nesbitt and Michael Isaacs, the founders of Our Price Records. These new owners have taken a personal interest in the business and have provided the finance for an extensive refurbishment and extension of the facilities.

PRODUCTS AND SERVICES ON OFFER AT RAGDALE HALL

Ragdale Hall has written a definitive guide to what a health hydro is, so that customers can understand the difference between luxury hotels with a health and leisure spa and up-market private hospitals and retreats. The criteria that have been developed are shown in Exhibit 11.2.1.

Exhibit 11.2.1 A health hydro – the criteria

- Countryside location with resort-like feel
- Provision of healthy, calorie-controlled food on a full-board basis
- Absence of alcohol (wine excepted)
- A no-smoking policy in public areas and bedrooms but provision of a small smoking room
- Provision of high-quality beauty treatments, some of which are included in overnight packages
- Large variety of exercise classes for all fitness levels provided in the inclusive rate
- Ban on pets and anyone under the age of 16
- A very high guests/staff ratio allowing the very highest standards of personal care (e.g. five-star hotel 1:1, Ragdale 2.5:1)
- Comprehensive health and beauty consultations to ensure compatibility with treatments and activities offered
- Provision of some medical/dietary advice when necessary, but to ensure safety rather than to give any treatment
- Casual dress and leisure wear in all areas at all times
- No conferences, functions or suits!
- An organization geared completely towards caring and total relaxation, from the choice of staff, type of decor, and ambience of the whole complex to the treatments and activities on offer

Source: Ragdale Hall

It can be seen from this list of criteria that the health hydro concept offers customers a very different experience from those at other types of establishment. Customer service in relaxed and pleasant surroundings is a key part of the product on offer.

Ragdale Hall has been designed to allow customers to put together their own mix of activities and treatments. Customers may choose to have an active or more leisurely time. They may want to unwind or tone up, to shed weight or to relieve their worries.

Ragdale Hall offers a full range of services, which are shown in Exhibit 11.2.2. Guests may choose to purchase a package, or may come to stay at the hall and put together their own programme of activities. These packages allow guests to purchase a range of products at one time, and still purchase a range of extra services during their stay. The extra services include body and facial treatments (incorporating Clarins, Decleor, Guinot and Kanebo products), fitness activities, and hair and beauty treatments.

Exhibit 11.2.2 The range of services on offer at Ragdale Hall

Overnight accommodation: incorporating a luxury hotel with single and double rooms and suites.

Restaurant and other catering facilities: a luxury restaurant offering meals at different calorie levels. There is also a small self-service bar and snack service facility.

Retail outlets: two shops offering a full range of beauty products, clothing and other merchandise.

Health treatments: a range of treatment rooms surrounding an impressive conservatory seating area. These include revitalizing facials, relaxing massages, aromatherapy, reflexology, thermal wraps, stress relief and detoxifying treatments.

Beauty treatments: a full range of beauty treatments available including manicure, pedicure and expert make-up. There is also a full hair service and a sun centre which offers the safest and most up-to-date tanning technology.

Exercise areas: a fully equipped gymnasium which includes the latest resistance fitness equipment, bicycles, jogging and rowing machines. There are fitness coordinators who look after customers. The Hall also has an exercise studio with fully sprung wooden floor.

Water treatments: a luxurious range of water treatments centred around two indoor pools. A steam room and luxurious new spa complex with traditional Scandinavian saunas, plunge pools, hurricane showers, whirlpool spas, flotation tanks and hydrotherapy baths complete this area.

Outdoor activities: including an outdoor swimming pool, tennis courts, etc.

Source: Ragdale Hall

All residential stays include:

- comfortable accommodation in a bedroom with en suite facilities
- breakfast served in the room, three-course buffet lunch and four-course *table d'hôte* dinner
- a full introductory tour of the Hall
- an in-depth consultation with one of the senior therapists, including advice on treatments and an individually recommended exercise programme
- a welcome reception with refreshments, allowing the opportunity to meet the Guest

Liaison Officer and Duty Manager who will ensure the break gets off to a great start

- an extensive daily programme of exercise classes to suit all fitness levels
- use of the gymnasium including induction session to cover training principles and safety
- use of the indoor and outdoor swimming pools and water exercise sessions
- unrestricted use of the whirlpool spa bath as well as separate male and female spa areas with sauna, steam and plunge-pool facilities
- unlimited use of bicycles, championship-standard tennis courts, pitch-and-putt course, croquet and boules areas
- opportunity to relax and unwind, whether in one of the relaxing lounges or outside in the beautiful gardens
- evening talks and demonstrations covering a wide range of interesting topics
- specially tailored packages to suit all needs
- weekend breaks, short or longer holidays, healthy option breaks geared around a specific objective – Focus on Fitness, Stress Buster, Slim and Shape, New You, Total Pampering.

New treatments are always being added to the list on offer. The staff at Ragdale Hall have just developed a new massage treatment called Ragdale Multi Method Massage. Two highly skilled therapists work in unison to give the customer a feeling of deep relaxation. Music and the use of aromatherapy oils are used during this type of massage. Ragdale Hall is also considering using further holistic treatments such as kinesiology.

The food is considered a very important part of the product at Ragdale Hall. Guests can choose a menu to help them lose weight, or they may choose to eat a healthy balanced diet but with more calorific content. This is particularly important when the guest is taking part in strenuous physical exercise programmes during their stay.

Ragdale Hall has a wealth of experts who can offer advice on special subjects such as:

- bodycare during pregnancy:
  - suitable treatments
  - products which help alleviate the symptoms of pregnancy
  - exercise programmes
- advice about safety in the sun:
  - the best products
  - skin care routines
- care of those forgotten extremities – the hands and feet
- alternative therapies:
  - the concept
  - the difference between each one and who they can help
- stress management:
  - including giving up smoking
  - lifestyle
  - diet
- menopause:

- treatments and activities to counteract its effects.

OTHER HEALTH RESORTS IN THE UK

There are other health resorts in the UK offering a similar range of products to Ragdale Hall, such as Champneys Henlow Grange and Stobo Castle, and hotels offering in-house spas, such as Chewton Glen in Hampshire. Customers at Ragdale Hall come from all over the UK, although a proportion come from areas within a short drive time. It is clear that customers choose the health resort they want to visit according to the range of facilities and treatments on offer and their geographical location. Once a customer has chosen their preferred health resort, they are likely to be very loyal to it and return over and over again.

THE GUESTS AT RAGDALE HALL

A summary of the types of guests who stay at Ragdale Hall is shown in Exhibit 11.2.3. It can be seen that a Ragdale Hall guest is usually female, aged 35 or over, working

---

Exhibit 11.2.3 The guests at Ragdale Hall

92 per cent of guests are female, 8 per cent are male

- Guests are generally in the age range 35–70
- Guests are usually professional or working women, usually from socioeconomic groups ABC_1
- Guests have a personal interest in health and nutrition and are generally trying to lead a healthier lifestyle
- 64–65 per cent of guests have visited Ragdale Hall before. The average number of visits per year is two to three. Lengths of stay vary, but the three-night packages and day packages are very popular
- Guests live in all areas of the UK
- Guests do come on their own, but it is more common for them to be in pairs or in small groups

Source: Ragdale Hall.

---

and from a higher socioeconomic group. The interest in health and nutrition has been growing rapidly over the past ten years. There has been intense interest in the mainstream media in the UK, and people are generally much more knowledgeable about health and nutrition than they were ten years ago. Treatments such as aromatherapy and flotation are widely recognized by people in general in the UK, whereas ten years ago these treatments were considered rather 'freaky' and unusual. This growing knowledge and education about healthy lifestyles, which has been fuelled by the government report *The Health of the Nation*, has meant that people, particularly women, are much more conscious about their general levels of health and fitness.

This growing interest has encouraged the development of the health hydro business, which offers guests the opportunity to experience health and beauty treatments and to 'chill out' from the everyday stresses and strain of modern living. The health hydro now appeals to people, especially women, from different backgrounds. It is not just the reserve of the 'health freak' or the celebrity model.

BENEFITS GUESTS RECEIVE AT RAGDALE HALL

There are a wide range of benefits which guests say that they gain from a visit to Ragdale Hall. These are shown in order of importance in Exhibit 11.2.4.

Guests leaving Ragdale Hall always express feelings of total relaxation and the desire to go back as soon as possible. It seems that the experience is often almost addictive for a large number of guests. The accompanying example testimonials, shown in Exhibit 11.2.5, illustrate this point very effectively.

Exhibit 11.2.4 Benefits guests receive from their visit to Ragdale Hall (in order of importance)

- Relief of stress
- Improvements in looks
- Becoming more healthy
- Escapism
- Losing weight
- A holiday experience
- Recovering from illness
- Getting ready for a big day (e.g. marriage or birth of a child)

Source: Ragdale Hall

Exhibit 11.2.5 Testimonials of guests

'To celebrate our 40th birthdays, my friend and I spent a week at Ragdale Hall Health Hydro last July. There we, too, learned not to feel guilty about spending time on ourselves – and about leaving behind our families, pets, jobs and so on, for the first time ever.'

'A little bit of pampering not only made me look better, but more importantly made me feel good and has helped re-establish a sense of my own worth after years of putting myself last in the pecking order. This is having a knock-on effect of making me more pleasant to live with – as my family will testify.'

'It strikes me that the hectic lifestyle many women lead, well into middle age and beyond, goes against the natural rhythm of things. Making time for ourselves to relax and feel good must go some way towards redressing the balance and can only benefit our health overall. Long live health hydros and beauty treatments.'

Source: Ragdale Hall

CONCLUSIONS

The health hydro concept has developed recently as a response to a growing interest in healthy lifestyles. Ragdale Hall has responded to this trend and offers guests the opportunity to relax and be pampered in luxurious surroundings.

DISCUSSION POINTS AND ESSAY QUESTIONS

1. Evaluate the reasons for the growth of interest in the health hydro concept. How will this develop in the future?
2. Discuss in detail the **motivators** and **determinants** for customers of Ragdale Hall.

Source: This case study has been taken from material made available by Ragdale Hall in 2006. For the most up-to-date information please refer to the website www.ragdalehall.co.uk.

CASE STUDY 11.3: easyJet: the rise of a no-frills low-cost carrier (LCC)

BACKGROUND

The European air-travel market opened up in the 1990s because of the deregulation of the industry, bringing about the establishment of a wide variety of budget airlines that offer seats at increasingly competitive prices. In Europe, air ticket prices have decreased with the increasingly competitive nature of the market, although there is still a way to go before such a fiercely discounted market as that in the USA is achieved. By 2014, 49 per cent of UK consumers chose low-cost carriers (LCC) over scheduled full-service carriers with a share of 42 per cent (Mintel, 2014).

STELIOS HAJI-IOANNOU – THE MAN AND HIS BUSINESS IDEA

Stelios Haji-Ioannou is the son of a Greek shipping tycoon. He graduated from the London School of Economics and gained a Master's degree in shipping trade and finance at the City University's Cass Business School.

After involvement with his father's shipping empire after graduation, he founded Stelmar Shipping in 1991, which was subsequently floated on the New York Stock Exchange in 2001. During his time with Stelmar he became increasingly interested in the airline business and proceeded to study the American discount airlines.

He took the ill-fated American airline company ValuJet as a model for the type of business which he thought he could develop for the European market. The ValuJet company experienced the tragic crash of one of its planes into the Florida Everglades in May 1996, and it is this, it is said, which showed that his plans for a budget airline would have to incorporate safety features.

This was particularly the case for him, because he and his father were already facing charges of manslaughter because one of Troodos Shipping's tankers, the 232,000-tonne *Haven*, had blown up in Genoa in 1991, killing six crew and polluting the Ligurian coastline.

Despite the problems of the American company ValueJet, Stelios became increasingly convinced that the idea of a discount, no-frills type of airline would work in the European market. The incident that finally convinced him of this was when he tried to fly to Corfu from London, only to find that the fare was more than the cost of a 14-day package holiday to the same place. This seemed to be a ridiculous situation which should be addressed. Stelios took Freddie Laker, and particularly Richard Branson of Virgin Airlines, as role models for his own idea. He knew that he could not survive in the airline business with just a clever idea, but needed clear business planning and management control. He had the advantage of having the opportunity for substantial financial backing from his father, and has never played down the fact that without this backing he would never have been able to establish the business. The establishment of an airline business, after all, requires considerable investment over a substantial period of time.

He finally approached his father in March 1995, armed with a comprehensive business plan, in order to obtain financial backing for the company. His father backed him with a £5 million advance, which meant that he was now in the position of being ready to set up the business that he had dreamed about and planned.

The business idea that Stelios envisaged was summarized by a statement which he made in 1995: 'Our research has shown that people in both Britain and Europe are crying out for an American-style operation which will give them instant access to really cheap, reliable and safe air travel' (Haji-Ioannou, 1995).

Stelios still owns a small shareholding in the easyJet business but has given up the role of company chairman to become a non-executive director.

DEVELOPMENT OF THE EASYJET BUSINESS

The development of the easyJet business has proceeded well since the formation of the company in 1995 (see Exhibit 11.3.1).

Exhibit 11.3.1 The development of the easyJet company

1994	Stelios Haji-Ioannou has business idea for easyJet
March 1995	£5 million investment by Loucas Haji-Ioannou. Company established and prefabricated building set up at Luton airport as company headquarters. Two aircraft leased
18 October 1995	easyJet commences selling seats. Lorraine Chase launches easyJet at Planet Hollywood, London
10 November 1995	First easyJet flight
24 November 1995	Glasgow and Edinburgh services commence
26 January 1996	Aberdeen service commences

1996	Commencement of flights to Amsterdam, Barcelona and Nice. Purchase of first aircraft
1997	Increased frequency of existing routes. Plans to expand to Nordic countries, Geneva, Madrid, Berlin and Jersey. Purchase of three aircraft; two aircraft leased
2002	Expansion to offer 89 routes from 86 European airports operating 64 aircraft
2002	Merger with Go Fly to become Europe's number one low-cost airline
2003	First Airbus A319 goes into service – flying to Geneva
2004	Berlin Schönefeld becomes easyJet's largest non-UK base
2005	Fleet expands to 100 aircraft
2007	easyJet acquires Gatwick-based GB Airways
2009	easyJet becomes pan-European: 400 routes, 175 aircraft, 27 countries
2010	easyJet has highest Civil Aviation Authority passenger numbers for second year in a row
2012	Sir Stelios Haji-Ioannou resigns as a director of easyJet plc
2013	easyJet now flies to 100 destinations from London Gatwick
2013	60 million passengers fly with easyJet in 12-month period to 31 May 2013
2014	easyJet opens its 23rd base in Europe: Hamburg

Source: easyJet

This development has depended on a simple but clever idea. The airline would offer a no-frills service between a limited set of destinations at the lowest possible price. There would be no in-flight meals and only soft drinks and peanuts would be served. The company would sell direct and cut out the travel agents' 15–20 per cent commission, and there would be no tickets or fancy staff uniforms.

The business concept was summarized by its founder in 1995, when he was talking to the press: 'If we were a restaurant, we would be McDonald's. If we were a watch-maker, we would be Swatch' (Haji-Ioannou, 1995).

Stelios decided to locate his prefabricated head office next to Luton airport, which is an hour's drive from London – the home base for the flights would be Luton, where he could get flight slots. He then leased two Boeing 737s complete with pilots. The first flights to Glasgow and Edinburgh commenced in 1995, and were quickly expanded to serve six cities including Amsterdam, Barcelona and Nice. The company increased the number of flights per day to each location, and expanded the network to other European destinations during the period 2000–06. The purchase of Go Fly in August 2002 also expanded the network further. It is interesting to note that easyJet started ten years after its biggest LCC rival, Ryanair.

THE EASYJET CONCEPT

The concept of a no-frills airline offering cut-price fares has been developed by easyJet to incorporate a number of features, shown in Exhibit 11.3.2.

Exhibit 11.3.2 The easyJet concept

Head office	Prefabricated building; paperless offices
	Located at Luton airport
Staff	Senior staff headhunted from major airlines; minimum staffing levels
	Large numbers of part-time telesales operatives paid on commission-only basis
Uniforms	Cabin crew dressed in orange polo shirts, sweatshirts and black slacks
Product	Direct sales single journeys to range of destinations; very low prices
	Tickets sold direct with no use of travel agents; ticketless system
	No food – only soft drinks and peanuts served; open seating
Company livery	Orange and white livery; telephone booking numbers emblazoned on side of
	aircraft in orange for easy recognition
Positioning	Emphasis on budget accommodation with minimum service levels

Source: easyJet

In the early days, the product concept came under criticism from commentators in the travel and tourism industry. One particularly controversial area of the business was the decision by the founder to develop a direct booking service, which cut out the travel agency commission other airlines have to add on their final ticket price. Comments concerning this came from all areas of the travel industry, including easyJet's potential competitors. One comment at this time was: 'While there is room for two low cost carriers and together we will bring down fares, easyJet is making a huge mistake by ignoring the opportunity of distribution through the travel trade' (Jenns, 1995).

There was no doubt in the trade, however, that the easyJet type of operation would be replicated in the market over time. Many analysts have predicted the growth of this type of airlines in Europe.

easyJet's mission statement is shown in Exhibit 11.3.3, and its financial performance for the period 2001–05 is shown in Exhibit 11.3.4.

Exhibit 11.3.3 easyJet's Aim

Our ambition is to be Europe's preferred short-haul carrier.

Our aim is to deliver market leading returns to our shareholders through maintaining a leading European network at primary airports, with a clear focus on making travel easy and affordable for our customers. Delivering a friendly and efficient service, at a low cost, will see us realize our vision.

Source: easyJet *Annual Report and Accounts 2014*

Exhibit 11.3.4 Summary of selected financial information for five years, 2010–14

£ million

	2014	2013	2012	2011	2010
Revenue	4527	4258	3854	3452	2973
EBITDAR*	823	711	531	468	361
Operating profit	581	497	331	269	174
Profit before taxation	581	478	317	248	154
Profit for the year	450	398	255	225	121
Non-current assets	3221	2964	2968	2731	2488
Current assets	1261	1448	1327	1738	1515
Current liabilities	(1420)	(1379)	(1264)	(1177)	(1065)
Non-current liabilities	(890)	(1016)	(1237)	(1587)	(1437)
Net assets	2172	2017	1794	1705	1501
Statement of cash flows					
Operating activities	394	616	261	424	363
Investment activities	(445)	(416)	(389)	(478)	(482)
Financing activities	(526)	197	(309)	246	233
Exchange (losses)/gains	(12)	(29)	(18)	(4)	9
Net (decrease) increase in cash	(589)	368	(455)	188	123

*Earnings before interest, taxes, depreciation, amortization, and restructuring or rent costs.

Source: easyJet Annual Report and Accounts 2014

COMPETITORS

Competitors have entered the market in recent years to challenge easyJet's hold on the market. These competitors include Ryanair, currently seen as easyJet's main competitor. Previous UK-based competitors, including Buzz, Debonair and Go, all failed to survive. There are also competitors based on the continent to contend with, including Wizz. It could be argued that Ryanair – which has been very successful in financial terms – has taken the budget airline model even further, with its use of secondary airports for instance. easyJet does not have the aggressive approach to press and public relations that has been a feature of Ryanair.

EASYJET CUSTOMERS

Stelios originally envisaged that the customers for easyJet would be leisure travellers. It is becoming apparent, however, that business travellers became a large part of the easyJet market, particularly on the short-haul day-return routes. It is clear that the company is trying to change the customer buying behaviour patterns that existed previously, for example trying to encourage the impulse purchase of airline travel, rather like the behaviour patterns more commonly associated with the purchase of fast-moving consumer goods or clothing. 'We are encouraging people to take impulse purchase decisions to fly' (Haji-Ioannou, 1995). The company encouraged this type of impulse purchasing decision by using a public relations campaign showing the price of its airline seats as being comparable with, or cheaper than, that of a pair of jeans.

The growth in passenger statistics for the airline is shown in Exhibit 11.3.5. Research carried out by easyJet has shown that many different market segments are making the decision to fly with easyJet.

Exhibit 11.3.5 Passenger statistics for easyJet

Full year	Annual total (thousand)
1995	30
1996	420
1998	1,880
2000	5,996
2002	11,400
2004	24,300
2006	32,953
2008	43,659
2010	48,754
2012	58,400
2014	64,769

Source: easyJet

The main customers for easyJet originate in the UK, although this differs according to the route. The customers originate mainly from the catchment area of the airports from which the company operates. The socioeconomic profile of the customers is mixed, but tends towards the B and C_1 socioeconomic groups. The customer is usually working in a professional job and lives in an urban area.

The town of Milton Keynes is seen by the company as being particularly representative of the type of area in which customers of the airline live. They tend to be regular travellers abroad, although this picture may change in the future. Leisure travellers are a particular target group, and the cheap fares mean they are much more likely to go abroad for a weekend, perhaps on an impulse. The one-way fares are particularly attractive to customers who do not plan their return travel date. This means that easyJet seats are particularly attractive to students and to people studying and working throughout Europe on short- or long-term contracts.

Business travellers who work for small to medium-sized enterprises (SMEs) in particular are very interested in the easyJet product, because they themselves will often be responsible for the cost of the airline ticket and will therefore be keen to keep the cost of the tickets down. easyJet has also tried to target purchases of airline tickets by larger businesses in a controversial advertising campaign that stressed the extra costs of buying their staff seats on conventional carriers.

Business travellers can now travel around the cities of Europe on a much more impulsive basis, pulling off deals and visiting suppliers and customers. The cheaper airfares will encourage them to travel more readily and with less thought.

Students who have previously been put off extensive regular travel around Europe as a result of high-priced airline tickets are now being encouraged to travel more readily by companies such as easyJet, which are offering a cheaper alternative. Students are also being poached from the rail companies because prices are now comparable. This type of behaviour is illustrated in this statement: 'I would not have been able to do this in the past because of the cost. Now it is the equivalent of a rail fare' (Barnaby Jenkins, student, aged 23, purchased a long weekend in Barcelona).

easyJet has also been attractive to professional people who had previously travelled by train for business meetings and events. This is particularly noticeable on the Scotland–England route where rail travel has been relatively expensive and slow. This type of switching behaviour pattern is shown in this statement: 'I could have gone by train but when I discovered how much it was with easyJet, I decided this was the way to go' (Open University tutor).

easyJet predicts that the type of consumer profile will continue to develop and change over time as consumer behaviour patterns and competition change.

THE FUTURE

It is clear that the deregulation of the airline industry in Europe will continue to encourage small, specialist, low-cost airlines to enter the market. This will result in changing consumer buying patterns as prices drop and competition and choice increase. The use of mobile applications has also changed business operations, whilst giving customers access to greater levels of information and interaction.

Sir Stelios Haji-Ioannou, whilst still being the major shareholder in easyJet, has left the day-to-day management of the company, and left the board in 2010. He is a shareholder in Fastjet, a young LCC airline serving the African market. His easyGroup company still owns the core brand rights to the 'easy' brand, the parameters of which were subject to a court case in 2010 between easyGroup and easyJet. easyJet holds a 50-year licence expiring in December 2060. Under the terms of the October 2010 'letter of comfort' of Sir Stelios to easyJet, restrictive conditions for his involvement in European airline activities ended in October 2015.

Interestingly, in recent years he has seen fit to criticize some of the decisions made by the current management team.

CONCLUSIONS

easyJet was one of the first airlines set up to respond to the deregulation of European airspace and in doing so, along with Ryanair, revolutionized air travel for those who live in the British Isles. Like Ryanair, in its early days it was led by a visionary entrepreneur who tried new things and took risks. Now, as a mature company, it has to adopt new business strategies and ensure that it satisfies and does not upset shareholders.

DISCUSSION POINTS AND ESSAY QUESTIONS

1. Evaluate the reasons for consumers being increasingly more willing to purchase airline seats as an impulse decision.
2. Analyse the relationship of price and consumer purchasing behaviour in the short-haul airline market.
3. Discuss why independent low-cost carriers such as easyJet and Ryanair have been able to thrive compared with low-cost or budget airlines set up by major scheduled carriers such as Debonair, Buzz and British Airways' Go, which itself was subsequently sold to easyJet.
4. Discuss the similarities and differences between Stelios' extensions of the 'easy' brand compared with Richard Branson's development of the Virgin brand.

REFERENCES

Haji-Ioannou, S. (1995). *Travel Trade Gazette*, 25 October.
Jenns, T. (1995). Comments by Chief Executive, Ryanair UK. *Travel Trade Gazette*, 1 November.
Mintel (2014). *The Consumer – Types of Flights taken in the last 12 months*. September. Mintel.

Consumer behaviour and marketing

Clearly, consumer behaviour in tourism is a subject worthy of academic study in its own right. However, it is also a matter of growing interest to tourism practitioners as organizations seek to keep ahead of changes in consumer tastes so that they can ensure they offer what the customer wants. Modern tourism marketing, we are told, must be customer-centred if it is to be successful.

In this part we briefly explore two of the most important areas in which consumer behaviour and marketing are linked:

- Chapter 12 discusses the applied side of consumer behaviour research, in other words, marketing research
- Chapter 13 covers the relationship between the marketing mix (the four Ps) and consumer behaviour in tourism. This means looking at how tourism organizations might manipulate their product, price, place and promotion to reflect the characteristics and desires of their customers.

Researching tourist behaviour: marketing research

This chapter explores the changing nature of research amongst consumers who are considering taking a holiday, are already there, or have returned from their experience. It considers both commercial and academic research, and introduces some of the ways in which organizations can conduct market research. The chapter also introduces the idea that consumers are now empowered by new ICT tools, and that organizations have already begun to use this by incorporating new research techniques.

Introduction

Marketing in tourism requires that the right products and services are presented to the consumer in the right way and at the right time. Marketing communication is also a vital way in which the tourism organization talks to the customer. The communication between provider and customer results in the exchange processes that underpin marketing activity. In order for this to be achieved, organizations require appropriate and timely marketing information so that their management decision processes in the marketing department can be reassured about their crucial marketing planning activity. It is marketing research in all its forms that provides the marketing manager with this vital information. This chapter reviews the latest trends in marketing research in the tourism sector and considers the role that these new developments play in the marketing research activity of tourism organizations. The chapter also considers the ways in which the academic community can research tourist behaviour and the links that this has to the commercial market research that is undertaken by commercial organizations.

Market research is the way in which an organization gathers information to support its marketing decisions. Marketing research is concerned with the whole marketing process, whereas market research is concerned just with the market. Marketing research was defined by ICC/ESOMAR (2008) in their *International Code on Market and*

Social Research as being involved with social and opinion research and being about the systematic gathering and interpretation of data using statistical and analytical methods of the applied social sciences in order to support management decision-making. The key developments in the market research industry in general are summarized by ESOMAR (2008/09) as follows.

- Rapid changes in client markets with clients needing to understand consumer experiences and apply this knowledge in communications, product development and innovation processes.
- Holistic research approaches combining existing techniques with innovative ones. New sources of data fusion are providing opportunities to broaden the research remit.
- Faster responses are being asked for and data quality is an issue. High quality and integrity remain a core concern for the sector.
- Different levels of maturity with a more rapid growth in emerging markets.

Researching customer satisfaction is thought to be important for two main reasons.

- There is a belief that satisfying customers will turn them into regular, repeat-purchase customers who are loyal to the brand or organization. Given that it is cheaper to keep an existing customer than to go out and find a new one, this is clearly an attractive proposition.
- If a customer is satisfied, they are likely to give positive word-of-mouth recommendations for the product they have used to friends or relatives. This can obviously help increase an organization's volume of customers.

Furthermore, increasing customer satisfaction also reduces the costs – refunds and administration, for example – of handling problems and complaints.

Marketing research in tourism

Tourism organizations need marketing research data for a number of reasons, which are detailed below.

- In strategic marketing planning, it is important for organizations to consider forecasts of tourism demand so that decisions can be made effectively and efficiently. This will determine the investment in new products and services.
- In brand management and positioning, it is important for the tourism organization to investigate what customers and potential customers think about their products and services, particularly with reference to their perception of brand quality. This will enable the organization to modify brand portfolios and work on repositioning if required.
- The process of market segmentation, where the organization uses a variety of

techniques to target customers, requires underpinning marketing research to support the decision the organization makes in this area. This research will consider demographic, geographical, psychographic and behaviouristic methods of market segmentation during the marketing research process.

- New product development often requires extensive marketing research to underpin the marketing decisions that are taken. This is particularly important as part of the feasibility study which should be undertaken before a major new investment, such as a new visitor attraction or the opening of a new hotel.
- Research is often necessary to underpin the decisions that are taken about distribution systems. This is of particular importance now with changing trends in distribution including e-marketing and use of social networking.
- The development of effective and efficient promotional campaigns also requires marketing research if they are to be effective and efficient in an increasingly complex and dynamic world. Organizations have to research the types of message that are most effective for their product or service and then communicate these images using the array of new communications channels. This includes the internet, the use of social networking sites and mobile technologies.
- Marketing research is a very important part of the customer service practices involved in relationship marketing. Ongoing customer surveys will give the marketing manager the information that is necessary to enable changes to be made to improve customer services.

Marketing research falls into three main categories in relation to the function of the research findings. The first type of marketing research has a **descriptive** function. Different techniques are used to try and describe particular situations. This could be customers' perceptions of a brand or the gathering of historical sales data to support decision-making. The second function for marketing research is the **diagnostic** function, where actions of customers and their implications are explored and explained. An example of this would be an in-depth piece of marketing research on the customer perceptions of a new marketing campaign and consideration of future changes. The final function of marketing research is the **predictive** function, where research is used to predict a likely outcome. This is critical for new product development and for allowing the organization to spot new opportunities.

Tourism organizations need marketing research information for a wide variety of uses, including the following.

- **Statistical profiles** of tourists visiting everything – a country, hotel, visitor attraction etc. This will look at the visitor profiles and assess the market segments that they fit into.
- **Statistical records** of tourists including information about where they take their holidays, how much they spend and how many trips per year they take.
- Research into **how tourists make their decisions**, which usually involves a complex decision-making process.

- Research into **who makes the purchase decision**, which is particularly important for family groups.
- Research into **when the purchase decision is made**, which is of particular importance because of the seasonality of the tourism business.
- Research into **consumer perceptions**, which is of particular importance for all types of tourism organizations.
- **Tourist or guest satisfaction** research, which is important for all tourism organizations that are trying to generate repeat business from either individual customers or groups.
- **Tourism trends** research, which will be vital for the development of new products and services in the future.
- **Product positioning** research, which provides tourism organizations with information regarding how their products and services are positioned through the eyes of consumers and in relation to their competitors.
- Research into **cultural and national differences** in tourist behaviour, which is of particular importance for tourism organizations because they have both an international workforce and international customer base.
- Research into the **links between tourist consumer behaviour and the purchase of other products and services**, which provides further in-depth analysis of consumer behaviour and allows for the development of joint promotions.

Before we consider the different approaches and methods of tourism research, we should consider some of the key issues in consumer satisfaction. These have not changed markedly since our writing in 2001, and a summary of the issues involved is shown in Figure 12.1. It can be seen from this figure that there are many complexities associated with the measurement of customer satisfaction in the tourism sector because the tourism experience is multi-faceted and involves a great deal of inter-related factors, many of which are outside the tourism providers influence. Despite this, it is still vital to try to identify both long term and short term trends and to gain an appreciation of the tourist experience at all levels, from the global perspective to the individual organizational level.

Tourism organizations have had significant problems with marketing research in the past for a number of reasons, explored in Swarbrooke and Horner (2007), which provides a fuller discussion of the factors that make marketing research in tourism more complex.

The main weaknesses of tourism marketing research are presented in Figure 12.2. The diagram shows that very often the data that is used is out of date and has focused on only a small sample. One of the issues in tourism research is to try and get a larger response rate in surveys.

Longitudinal data is that which is collected over a long period of time so that trends can be determined more clearly. A lack of longitudinal data can also be an issue, and collection techniques need to become more sophisticated so that tourists' perceptions can be examined in more depth. The tourism sector is global and thus needs comparative data across national boundaries. Much of the research data that is collected is confidential to a particular organization and is therefore not disseminated to other

- **First,** not enough empirical research has been done to give us a clear view of precisely what factors determine the level of satisfaction of customers. However, there are general issues which are clearly important to many tourists, such as reliability and value-for-money. It seems likely that we each have different criteria for judging whether or not we are satisfied, based on our experiences.

- **Second,** in our industry, satisfaction can come primarily from tangible products (food, theme park rides, museum exhibitions, hotel beds, and so on) – or from the intangible service element, or both. You can be happy with the tangible product but dissatisfied with the service element and vice-versa.

- **Third,** and following on from the last point, it is often thought that service quality is very important to tourists. Yet, many organizations today which seem successful offer little real personal service, notably 'no-frills' hotels. This shows that it is important to take a broader view of service than just face-to-face contact between staff and customers. It is also about systems that ensure customers receive the product they want, efficiently and effectively. For example, budget hotel chains are increasingly using automated check-ins which is great for customers. . . as long as they work!

- **Fourth,** satisfaction is generally considered to be about meeting customer expectations. It is, therefore, important to understand these expectations when designing products and promotional campaigns. Research seems to suggest that customers' dissatisfaction results from gaps between customer expectations and their perceptions of the product and service they receive. This is fine except that everyone's expectations and perceptions are different! Furthermore, we have to recognize that some people's expectations are not realistic. For instance, a customer whose marriage is going badly wrong may expect a luxury weekend break with their partner to cure these problems! At the same time, people may pay a bargain price but expect a product that would cost much more.

- **Fifth,** tourism organizations do not control all the factors that determine the level of customer satisfaction. Holiday satisfaction can be diminished by events outside the control of tourism organizations, from rain to strikes to traffic jams.

- **Sixth,** some people argue that satisfaction in industries like tourism is related to what are termed 'critical incidents' or moments of truth. In brief, this means that customers judge organizations on how they perform when things go wrong. The argument is that when things go to plan, no-one notices but when things go wrong, customers begin to take real notice of the organization and its service.

- **Seventh,** we need to recognize that the level of satisfaction with an organization and its products is not an absolute. For many customers, how they judge the organization and it's products will relate to their experience of similar products offered by other organizations. That is why the technique of benchmarking has achieved such popularity in recent years, where organizations try to evaluate their performance in relation to other players within the same industry.

Figure 12.1 Key issues in customer satisfaction

organizations. There is a requirement to consider the researching of motivators and determinants of consumer behaviour in much more depth, which needs new and innovative methods of research. The use of new technologies is facilitating some of these new developments. It can also be seen from Figure 12.2 that there are many complexities associated with customer satisfaction in tourism markets that organizations have to strive to analyse.

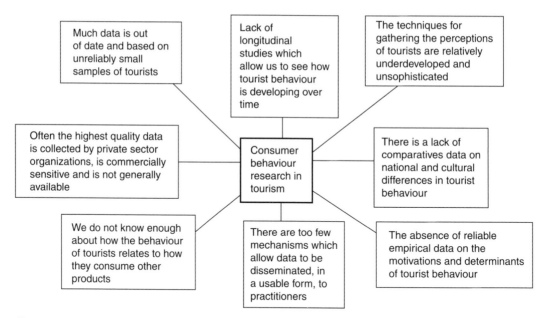

Figure 12.2 Main weaknesses in consumer behaviour research in tourism

Methods of marketing research

There are many ways of conducting marketing research in tourism. The first decision that has to be made is whether to use quantitative or qualitative methods of research.

Quantitative research

Quantitative research is where information is collected from a large population. It uses surveys or questionnaires to collect the data, which are analysed in order to give statistically valid data. A typical example of quantitative data is the surveys that destination marketing offices (DMOs) carry out to collect inbound and outbound tourism data. The questionnaires that the large hotel groups carry out are also an example of quantitative marketing research. This has the advantage of collecting a large number of responses, and the results are considered reliable and valid.

There are inherent problems associated with large-scale quantitative studies in tourism. Some of the negative aspects of this type of data collection are as follows.

- Response rates are often very low.
- The questionnaires often ask the tourist to tick boxes and thus do not explore the reasons why, or exactly what the customer is satisfied or dissatisfied with.
- Often opportunities are not taken to ask regular customers whether they think the service is getting better or worse over time.

- Certain questions can, perhaps, raise doubts in the minds of customers which may damage their image of the service.
- Many questionnaires treat satisfaction and quality as an absolute.
- Questionnaires often do not attempt to correlate key variables such as the link between satisfaction and age, gender and nationality.
- Few questionnaires try to ask customers how they would improve the product or service to increase satisfaction levels further.
- Organizations often miss the opportunity to disseminate the research findings to staff, which is a pity because this can act as a satisfier and a motivator for staff.
- Often the customer is not given the opportunity for a personal reply, although the use of the internet and social media in intelligent ways is providing opportunities for organizations in this area.

Some organizations have used commercial market research companies to improve both response rates and the quality of their customer surveys. Hilton Hotels Corporation, for example, has worked very hard with the US company Medallia to improve its guest questionnaire, improve its response rates, and make its questionnaire work across the world. An illustration of this is shown in Figure 12.3.

Qualitative research

Qualitative research, on the other hand, considers the opinions and values of others and is not number-based. This type of research is often conducted by using structured or semi-structured interviews, or in some cases uses focus groups as a way of collecting the data. Focus groups are often used when an organization is trying to elicit attitudes to and perceptions of new products and services, or brand positioning, for example. The group could be shown ideas on new advertising styles and asked for their opinions. There is a tendency to treat customers as a homogeneous mass rather than recognizing that there are different segments with their own particular needs. One way of improving the evaluation of customer satisfaction could be to run focus groups to see how well the organization is meeting the needs of different types of customers. For example, a theme park could establish separate focus groups for families and young adults, while museums could create groups for researchers, schoolteachers and families.

The use of a focus group allows individuals to develop ideas between them which they may not have been able to visualize on their own. However, focus groups can lead to bias if they are not properly constructed and administered. One problem with the use of focus groups is logistics. How do we identify potential participants and organize time-consuming group sessions when customers may be visiting for a short time and/or may be a long way from home? If it is not possible to arrange such groups *in situ*, it may be possible to arrange 'virtual focus groups' using the internet or video conferencing.

By 2000, Hilton Hotels Corporation wanted to move its mail survey online in order to capture the many benefits of internet-enabled surveying. It established the following success criteria for the new programme:

- higher response rates
- respondent-friendly surveys that were easier to complete
- cost savings
- much faster turnaround.

Solution

Hilton met with key providers of online survey solutions. Unfortunately, many failed to meet Hilton's technical or methodological standards. The Company chose Medallia to move its paper-based customer survey programme online because of:

- the strength of Medallia's proposed solution
- the capabilities of the Medallia technology platform
- Medallia's rigorous testing methodology and transition plan.

In the initial phase of the transition, Medallia conducted a parallel test of two random sub-samples of customers, administering a paper mail survey to one group and an online survey to the other. Medallia used the test results to calibrate the transition, determining such details as the optimal sampling plan and optimal sample allocation between online and mail surveys.

Results

With Medallia, Hilton not only met but exceeded all success criteria for its online programme:

- response rates doubled
- average time to complete the online survey dropped to 10 minutes, a significant improvement over the paper version
- the online surveys were respondent-friendly, with little or no need for scrolling, minimal need for mouse movement, same-page error notification, 100 per cent browser compatibility and optimal survey lengths
- item non-response declined by more than 50 per cent on average, generating much higher quality survey data
- costs declined by more than 50 per cent
- lag between survey completion and delivery of results dropped from 4–6 weeks to 24–48 hours and with such dramatic time compression the data became much more relevant, enabling Hilton to detect problems quickly and recover at-risk customers
- Medallia proved the validity of online surveying, resulting in company-wide confidence in – and acceptance of – the new methodology.

Figure 12.3 Medallia designs Hilton Hotels Corporation guest satisfaction survey

Source: www.medallia.com

As well as their value in researching the **opinions of different market segments**, focus groups can also be useful in tourism research in two other ways, as follows.

- To test ideas for **potential new products and services** to see if they will increase or decrease levels of satisfaction.

- To investigate the views of **potential markets** such as those who have never used a product or service before. The new idea can be demonstrated during the focus group and the opinions of the participants can be gauged. An example of this used recently was a piece of exploratory research on the use of mobile apps in terms of attitudes and opinions. Mobile apps can be used to aid the booking process, or act as a guide during the visit, for example.

A new method of qualitative research which has been used in tourism is the use of observation, where tourists are simply observed for their behaviour patterns. This type of research has particular ethical issues involved, especially when tourists do not realize that they are being observed. Rather than asking customers whether everything is right, it is often better to observe their behaviour, whether at check-in, at the breakfast buffet or in a museum exhibition. Observation research is a skilled concept that should be conducted by trained specialists. The use of 'mystery shopping' surveys, where an organization arranges for someone to stay or visit incognito either at their own or a competitor's facility, is an extension of the observation method of research that has been adopted by some organizations in the sector.

The use of diaries as a way of collecting information from tourists is another interesting approach to qualitative research. The tourist will collect their thoughts and perceptions every day during their holiday and the final diary will be analysed for its content. The final new approach of qualitative research is by holding informal conversations with tourists. This type of approach has been advocated by the researcher Chris Ryan (1995), who argued that 'Conversations are an excellent research methodology for revealing the confines and ambiguities involved in holiday-taking', and illustrates this with a discussion about the importance of the friendliness of the people towards the tourists:

> Free-ranging conversations are an important resource for researchers. They confirm the nature of the tourist experience, and whether the concerns identified by the researchers [involved in the project] are indeed the concerns of those questioned . . . Research that denies the opportunity for holidaymakers to speak of their own experience in their own words is itself limited.

An example of this type of approach was carried out by the authors (Horner and Swarbrooke, 2005). We interviewed a 15-year-old woman from the UK to discover her travel motivations, the idea being that she would be the future customer for tourism businesses. This piece of research, highlighted in Figure 12.4, shows how powerful this approach can be in discovering individual perceptions.

Another important issue regarding the choice of marketing research is the division between continuous and *ad hoc* research. **Continuous research** is where the researcher or organization carries out the research over the long term so that trends can be identified. This can be particularly important when a requirement is to track long-term purchase habits or to monitor how tourist behaviour changes with time and development. A recent example is the way in which tourism and hospitality organizations have

This research was carried out to consider future demand in tourism through the eyes of a young woman from Sheffield, UK. She was asked to talk about what she liked doing on holiday, her perceptions of places that she had not already been to, and her ideas on where she will travel to later in life.

Kate's most recent holiday and perceptions

Kate's most recent holiday was to Limassol in Cyprus.

- **Liked most about Limassol**: plenty of water sports, restaurants and bars.
- **Liked least about Limassol**: not enough clothes shops.
- **Most liked doing**: lying on the beach, swimming, going in the pool at the hotel, going to pubs, doing water sports.
- **Least liked doing**: going to museums (boring).
- **Least likely to do**: backpacking; learning a language (too like school).

Kate's perceptions of places she has never visited

Paris – 'At this age I don't really have the desire to go there, but I'd like to go there when I'm older. I think it's the type of place you go with your partner because it's supposed to be the city of romance (I think).'

Florida – 'I'd love to go there. From what I've heard it sounds a really fun place to go on holiday. It has Disneyland there, which I would love.'

New York – 'I'd love to go there to see all the different sights but the only thing that puts me off is everything that has gone off [Twin Towers etc.]. I definitely wouldn't want to be there on the Fourth of July.'

Venice – 'I think this kind of place is like Paris. It's not a place I'd go to with my friends. Most people that go are older and tend to go with their partner.'

Kate's future holidays

'I'll probably start taking holidays with my friends when I'm about 17 or 18, because by then I should have some money, hopefully. I'd like to go somewhere where young people go, where there's lots to do and has good nightlife, such as Ibiza. Places I'd like to visit when I'm 35 would be somewhere like Spain because I'll probably have a family by then. Places I'd go when I'm 65 would be Portugal because I've heard it's quiet, and I'll be older then. If money was no object then I'd like to go to America and Ibiza. America because there's so much to see, and Ibiza because there's apparently brilliant nightlife, nice beaches, good weather and I could get a tan. I'd like to go to a posh hotel with nice swimming pools.'

Figure 12.4 Tomorrow's tourist – Kate

Source: adapted from Horner and Swarbrooke (2005)

tried to monitor the influence of new technologies in marketing communications, such as involving Web 2.0 and social media, so that they can reflect on this in the design of their marketing communication mixes.

Ad hoc research is used for one-off occasions when the researcher or organization wants to know about situations which will influence events at a particular time. This type of research is often used in small-scale pieces of academic research such as an undergraduate dissertation. It is also often used to inform marketing decisions, such as the launch of a new product or to consider whether a new product idea is well designed and thought out. Hotel groups, for example, will carry out extensive market research before they commit to a new hotel opening, particularly when this is in a new destination, because there will have to be a detailed analysis carried out to consider cultural characteristics, market demands, and product and service demand.

There are large market research organizations that can help in the design and implementation of research. It is becoming increasingly important to consider advice from external agencies, if the budget permits, as market research techniques and approaches are becoming more complex and require knowledge about the use of new technologies that can underpin the research.

These complexities are well elucidated by ESOMAR, a world organization that tries to enable better research into markets, consumers and societies. With 5000 members in 100 countries, it aims to promote the value of market and opinion research by illuminating real issues and bringing about effective decision-making (www.esomar.org). Increasing use of the internet has meant that organizations need to think about how to conduct online research that is of good quality. This has meant that ESOMAR has had to revise its ethical, professional and legislative guidelines, and it has published a guide: 26 Questions to Assist Buyers of Online Samples for Research (ESOMAR, 2008/09). The organization also identified new areas of market research in the same year and planned to write practice guidelines to clarify best practice. This included guides to conducting research on the internet, and for contacting respondents or customers using mobile phone technology.

Long-term research into tourism trends

Destination marketing offices (DMOs) are interested in the long-term research associated with their markets in relation to their existing and emerging market segments so that they can make strategic decisions in relation to new product and service development, and design and prioritize their marketing campaigns. The DMO VisitEngland, for example, has carried out a long-term study to understand visitor satisfaction with various aspects of England as a destination. This includes the overall experience, issues of loyalty and satisfaction, the day-trip dimension, drivers of satisfaction, and the linkage of the brand to issues such as authenticity. This large-scale piece of research will impact on the future long-term tourism development strategy for the country.

One organization that assists DMOs in their research is the United Nations World Tourism Organization (UNWTO), which carries out a number of detailed pieces of research on an ongoing basis. A summary of UNWTO's mission and market research is shown in Figure 12.5. In 2008, UNWTO launched a new research initiative – 'UNWTO Future Vision: Tourism Towards 2030'. This long-term study will forecast international tourism growth up to the year 2030, identify key actual and future trends, and assess their impact on tourism development. The programme will combine industry data with the views of UNWTO members, tourism practitioners, trend experts and academics from across the world. The research will update the previous Tourism 2020

Purpose

The World Tourism Organization is the United Nations agency responsible for the promotion of responsible, sustainable and universally accessible tourism.

Priorities

- Mainstreaming tourism in the global agenda
- Improving tourism competitiveness
- Promoting sustainable tourism development
- Advancing tourism's contribution to poverty reduction and development

Tourism market trends

UNWTO provides the tourism community with up-to-date market intelligence including the latest tourism market trends, short- and long-term tourism forecasts, and knowledge on specific market segments and source markets. This includes:

- The UNWTO *World Tourism Barometer* which monitors short-term tourism trends on a regular basis and provides the sector with relevant and timely information.
- UNWTO *Tourism Highlights* provides an annual overview of international tourism data and key trends for the year. It includes the latest statistics on international tourism arrivals, international tourism receipts, a summary of tourism results by region, top tourism destinations by arrivals and receipts, outbound tourism by generating region and a ranking of top tourism spenders.
- *Tourism Towards 2030* is a long-term forecast and assessment of the development of tourism up to the first 30 years of the twenty-first century.
- Regular market research is also carried out on source markets such as India and China, and market segments such as cruise tourism and cultural tourism.

Figure 12.5 The United Nations World Tourism Organization

Source: Botterill (2012)

Vision which has been the definitive reference for the tourism industry in recent years (Botterill, 2012).

Academic research into tourist behaviour

Commercial organizations use methods of market research that they hope will bring deeper insights into consumer behaviour.

Market research in organizations provides them with a commercial advantage, and the process is often linked to a specific time in their business calendar – for example the launch of a new product or service, or the development of a new image for a destination. Academic research, on the other hand, although it can be linked to commercial organizations, tends to have the objective of simply finding out about a specific situation to continue the development of knowledge as a whole in the tourism and hospitality fields. There is a link between the two, since new methods of research are often pioneered by academics and adopted by commercial organizations if they prove to be effective. Academic organizations also on occasions conduct research on behalf of commercial organizations in the role of consultants, so in this type of activity commercial and academic research overlap.

The main issues related to academic research are the development of research questions or hypotheses on the basis of the literature review; the sampling framework where the selection of the sample respondents is derived; the methodology where the research instrument is designed, piloted then finalized; the research process where the research instrument is operationalized; and the analysis and discussion where the results of the research are analysed and conclusions drawn in relation to the previous literature review. All of these steps require an underlying knowledge and expertise and can be completed in a number of stages depending on the objectives. This book has not been designed to explore the intricacies of research design – the topic is covered well in a myriad of books about the topic – but it is important at this stage to consider a few recent examples of tourism research to explore some of the different techniques that can be adopted in relation to the objectives of the research.

Long-term academic research

Academic institutions have been engaging in long-term research to engage with the industry as a whole and to provide some of the much-needed information that the tourism industry requires. This ranges from research carried out by individuals on topics of particular interest to coordinated research programmes that influential academic institutions have developed to give them a higher profile in the educational world. Individual research initiatives include individuals such as Dimitrios Buhalis at Bournemouth University, who is leading a research programme on social media and tourism (www.buhalis.com); and Xavier Font at Leeds Metropolitan University, who is leading a research programme on e-labelling in the tourism sector (www.leedsbeckett. ac.uk/staff/dr-xavier-font).

Organizations that have developed a research centre in the field include Cornell in the USA (www.hotelschool.cornell.edu/research/chr) and The Hong Kong Polytechnic University (PolyU). PolyU is active in researching the development of tourism in Asia and has a particular interest in tourist satisfaction in the region. A large research programme was announced in March 2013 (see Figure 12.6).

Researching tourism behaviour prior to travel

Tourism researchers have had to tackle the issue that the decision to go on a holiday involves a series of complex and interrelated thought processes that can be affected by word-of-mouth communication and social media (Swarbrooke and Horner, 2007; Buhalis, 2003).

PolyU seeks to boost tourism development with Tourist Satisfaction and Tourism Service Quality Indices

The School of Hotel and Tourism Management (SHTM) of The Hong Kong Polytechnic University (PolyU) released a report on the PolyU Tourist Satisfaction Index (PolyU TSI) and the Tourism Service Quality Index (PolyU TSQI), presenting both indices for Hong Kong in the year 2014. The 2014 PolyU TSI and PolyU TSQI stood at 74.50 and 74.51, respectively, both recording year-on-year drops.

Spearheaded by Professor Haiyan Song, SHTM Associate Dean and Principal Investigator of the PolyU TSI project, the PolyU TSI measures inbound tourists' satisfaction levels across six tourism-related sectors and integrates them into an overall index. Since its launch in 2009, the PolyU TSI has served as a comprehensive system that provides authorities and industry practitioners with much-needed information for decision-making and planning. With an underlying research design resembling that of the PolyU TSI, the PolyU TSQI was launched in 2012, led by Professor Kaye Chon, Dean of the SHTM and Principal Investigator of the PolyU TSQI project. The index is a weighted average of the six tourism service quality indices, measuring overall tourism service quality.

The PolyU TSI dropped 1.46 points from 75.96 in 2013, representing the largest decline in the six years since the index was launched. At the same time, the PolyU TSQI recorded a drop of 2.79 points from 77.30 in 2013. Survey data for both indices were collected between October and November 2014, at a time when Hong Kong was affected by factors such as the slowdown of the Chinese economy and various social and political issues.

Against this backdrop, the Americas were the source market, receiving the highest TSI score, followed by Australia, New Zealand and the Pacific, Europe, Africa and the Middle East, South and Southeast Asia, Mainland China, Taiwan and Macau, and lastly Japan and Korea.

Among the six service sectors, transportation received the highest TSI score, followed by attraction, immigration, hotels, retail shops and restaurants.

The PolyU TSI evaluates service sector competitiveness not only over time, but also across international tourist destinations. It has been adopted by an increasing number of destinations, including Singapore and Macau in 2010, China's Guangdong province in 2012 and Australia in 2014. 'Although statistics show that tourists are Tadopting the PolyU TSI framework, the city managed to outperform Meizhou, Foshan, Shenzhen, Guangzhou and Macau'.

'With the PolyU TSI and the PolyU TSQI, Hong Kong is able to determine its performance and competitiveness relative to other international tourism destinations, allowing it to identify strategic areas for further development', said Professor Song.

Figure 12.6 The Hong Kong Polytechnic University research programme 2014

A piece of research carried out in 2007 attempted to analyse the different stages of holiday choice. The stages had been categorized earlier as a first stage, in which the person decided on vacation or no vacation; a second stage, where the person decided on different vacation modes (such as adventure or sightseeing); and the third stage, when the person chose the geographical location. To study this decision-making process, a survey was carried out with 2491 individuals who were visiting Spain, to explore their decision-making process. The statistical analysis of the findings showed the complexities of this multi-stage decision-making process and suggested that decisions about coastal areas preceded those associated with urban areas in the decision-making process (Nicolau and Más, 2008).

The use of questionnaires has also been used to evaluate the purchase behaviour of certain market segments. A piece of research carried out in Spain in 2009, for example, used a questionnaire to investigate the holiday decision-making process amongst women with different lifestyle and demographic profiles. Statistical analysis of the questionnaires provided interesting insights into the purchase behaviour, but it emerged that further research into women's lifestyles was required as an explanatory variable (Barlés-Arizón, Fraj-Andrés and Matute-Vallejo, 2010).

Statistically based surveys can give insights into the decision-making processes of tourists that are visiting a particular destination. The problem with this type of research is that it does not target tourists who have not visited the destination and can therefore be seen as potential visitors.

Research on the motivations of different market segments and their purchasing behaviour has also provided a focus for tourism researchers. For example, research on the tourist who likes to purchase an all-inclusive holiday shows that they attach more importance to the motivations related to convenience and relaxation, as well as safety and security in their decision-making process (Anderson, Juaneda and Sastre, 2009). Researchers can also use existing samples to construct research concerning tourist choice, for example the 2007 research (described above) to investigate Spanish tourists' buying behaviour which used a database of Spanish tourists collected by the Spanish Centre for Sociological Research (Nicolau and Más 2008).

There has been growing interest in recent years in the influence of social media and online reviews on tourists' buying behaviour, and this theme is developed further in Chapter 17. The use of online research is an interesting development in this area. One piece of research carried out in 2007 collected 168 responses from the Netherlands to an online experimental website where they were asked to respond to one of eight experimental conditions. This included their responses to both positive and negative online reviews for hotels that had been created for the research, in order to assess the impact of the reviews on the decision-making process (Vermeulen and Seegers, 2009). In this new area of research it is likely that new techniques will be used to explore tourism perceptions in more depth, and the use of experimentation is an interesting development in this area.

Researching tourism behaviour during or after travel

Research carried out in 2009 indicated that the number of research papers focusing on the tourism experience published in leading tourism-related journals had not substantially increased, and it was suggested that experience-related researched has remained under-represented in the tourism literature (Ritchie, Tung and Ritchie, 2011). However, there has been an explosion of popular books published about tourism experiences in recent times, and an increasing interest in the popular media in most countries.

The research into tourist satisfaction that has been carried out in the academic field often relies on quantitative methods and survey techniques, and often uses existing databases to provide the sample frame for the research. A piece of research carried out in the US, for example, to examine the views of risks of travel in areas where fires had previously been a problem, used a national consulting firm to provide the sample derived from National Census data. A mailback questionnaire was then used to achieve a sample response rate of 771 returned surveys, which were then analysed (Thapa *et al.*, 2013). A combination of questionnaire and interview is also often used to explore tourism experiences (Kemperman, Borgers and Timmerman, 2009).

The problem with one-off research methods is that the results give a picture only at one particular time, and do not give an ongoing picture of the tourism experience over a longer period or during the whole experience. To tackle this issue, research is often carried out over a longer time period to examine an ongoing tourism experience. One piece of research in Greece, for example, used a diary-type semi-structured questionnaire which was administered in face-to-face interviews over a long period. This piece of research gave deep insights into the tourist experience in Greek ski resorts (Vassiliadis, Prioras and Andronikidis, 2013). The use of ethnographic research has also been used to provide more detailed and accurate perceptions of the tourism experience (Bowen, 2002; Sörenson, 2003a,b). Ethnographic research is a qualitative method where participant observation and experience is part of the research process. This method of research was used by Bowie and Chang (2005) to try to evaluate tourist satisfaction. They carried out covert observation by observing participants' behaviour and also engaging with conversations with tourists as they were engaged in the tourism experience. A prolonged ethnographic study was also carried out in Cyprus during the whole of 2009 to explore rural tourist satisfaction, and this approach produced in-depth and well developed ideas for future development (Christou and Saveriades, 2010).

It is likely that longitudinal research programmes of this type will form an important knowledge base in future tourism development. Some commentators have suggested that there is an over-reliance on quantitative methods such as field studies, and there is a need for a broader research agenda in the tourism field, including the use of longitudinal studies and field experiments designed to reveal causal relationships (Tsiotsou and Ratten, 2010).

It is also predicted that the use of online research instruments will continue to develop and grow. For example, use of the online research company SurveyMonkey in both academic and commercial research programmes has been both controversial and interesting (www.surveymonkey.com). There are increasing suggestions that the data obtained from the interactive travel site TripAdvisor can be used as a vehicle for market research. The European Travel Commission, for example, signed a partnership with the company in 2013 to collaborate in market research and online activities. This collaboration will involve the sharing of market intelligence gathered from TripAdvisor with the best online travel marketing information from 33 national tourism organizations from Europe, which includes 24 EU member states. This will form a key part of the implementation of the Destination Europe initiative, which aims to develop a long-term strategy for Europe as a tourist destination (Ruggia, 2014).

There are concerns that the use of social media sites as a source of market research data may be questionable, for a number of reasons. There is a pressure to seek positive reviews, and it is not unknown for bogus feedback to be bought and sold. Secondly, the number of reviews on a particular hotel or destination may be low and therefore may not give a clear picture of the total situation. Finally, only a small percentage of the total population engage with social media, and those who do post reviews tend to be in the younger age demographics, with older, higher-spending tourists being slower to catch on to this new form of communication. This situation is, however, predicted to change over time, with more consumers beginning to engage in the social media phenomenon.

Conclusions

This chapter has tried to give the reader a flavour of the issues involved in the process of researching consumer behaviour in tourism. There is no doubt that this is an essential technique that engages the minds of both commercial managers in the field and academics who continue to research consumer behaviour in more original and engaging ways. The old techniques of research, including surveys and questionnaires, continue to be an important mechanism for the collection of data to underpin important strategic decisions in hospitality and tourism. As well as this, however, there is a move to use newer methods of research, such as focus groups, observation and social media sites. These newer methods need time to develop and mature before they can be taken seriously by both commercial companies and academics alike. All of these techniques have the ultimate goal of providing more sophisticated data about how and why consumers choose particular products and services, and how they perceive the experience once they have made the decision – in other words, giving a more sophisticated view of the motivators and determinants of tourism decision-making. This understanding can provide an organization, whether a hotel or a destination, with a competitive advantage in an increasingly competitive world.

Discussion points and essay questions

1. Explore the advantages of using social media sites as a method of market research in tourism.
2. Explore the advantages and disadvantages of using a large third-party market research organization for market research in the tourism sector.
3. Outline the approaches and types of market research that could be used by a hotel or destination considering the launch of a new product or service.
4. Critically analyse the different research techniques that can be used in academic research programmes on hospitality and tourism topics. You should consider the approach, methods and analytical techniques that could be adopted.
5. Discuss how conversations with tourists (such as the conversation with Kate in Figure 12.4) can be useful to reveal attitudes and perceptions to travel and future travel plans.

References

Anderson, W., Juaneda, C. and Sastre, F. (2009). Influences of pro-all-inclusive travel. *Tourism Review* 64 (2), 713–726.

Barlés-Arizón, M., Fraj-Andrés, E. and Matute-Vallejo, J. (2010). Identification of the profiles of women who take holiday decisions. *Tourism Review* 65 (1), 4–17.

Botterill, D. (2012). *Key Concepts in Tourism Research*. Sage, London.

Bowen, D. (2002). Research through participant observation in tourism: a creative solution to the measurement of consumer satisfaction/dissatisfaction (CS/D) among tourists. *Journal of Travel Research* 41 (1), 4–14.

Bowie, D. and Chang, J.C. (2005). Tourist satisfaction: a view from a mixed international guided package tour. *Journal of Vacation Marketing* 11 (4), 303–322.

Buhalis, D. (2003). *eTourism: Information Technology for Strategic Tourism Management*. Pearson Education, Harlow, UK.

Christou, P. and Saveriades, A. (2010). The use of ethnography to explore tourists. *TOURISMOS: An International Multidisciplinary Journal of Tourism* 5 (1), 89–100.

ESOMAR (2008/09). *World ESOMAR Review*. ESOMAR, Amsterdam, The Netherlands. www.esomar. org

Horner, S. and Swarbrooke, J. (2005). *Leisure Marketing: A Global Perspective*. Elsevier Butterworth-Heinemann, Oxford.

ICC/ESOMAR (2008). *International Code on Market and Social Research*. ICC/ESOMAR, Amsterdam, The Netherlands. www.esomar.org

ICC/ESOMAR (2015). *Code on Market Research and Social Research Data*. ICC/ESOMAR, Amsterdam, The Netherlands. https://www.esomar.org/-rev-o.pdf.publications-store/codes-guidelines.php

Kemperman, A.D.A.M., Borgers, A.W.J. and Timmerman, H.J.P. (2009). Tourism shopping behavior in a historic downtown area. *Tourism Management* 30 (2), 1159-1165.

Nicolau, J.L. and Más, F.J. (2008). Sequential choice behavior: going on vacation and choice of destination. *Tourism Management* 29 (5), 1023–1034.

Ritchie, J.R.B., Tung, V.W.S. and Ritchie, R.J.B. (2011). Tourism experience management research: emergence, evolution and future directions. *International Journal of Contemporary Hospitality Management* 23 (4), 419–438.

Ruggia, J. (2014). Fourth consecutive year of growth for Europe in 2013. *Travel Pulse* 4 March. www.travelpulse.com/news/destinations/fourth-consecutive-year-of-growth-for-europe-in-2013.html

Ryan, C. (1995). Learning about tourists from conversations: the over 55s in Majorca? *Tourism Management* 16 (3), 207–215.

SHTM (2013). PolyU seeks to boost tourism development with tourist satisfaction and tourism service quality indices. Press release 27 March. School of Hotel and Tourism Management, The Hong Kong Polytechnic University. http://hotelschool.shtm.polyu.edu.hk/wcms-common/temp/201303271946000952/news_27032013_TSI_TSQI.pdf

SHTM (2015). PolyU Released Report on 2014 Tourist Satisfaction and Tourism Service Quality Indices. Press release 6 July. School of Hotel and Tourism Management, The Hong Kong Polytechnic University. http://hotelschool.shtm.polyu.edu.hk/wcms-common/temp/201507061509220940/news_TSI_TSQI_report_20150706.pdf

Sörensen, A. (2003a). Backpacker tourism and third world development. *Annals of Tourism Research* 29 (1), 144-164.

Sörenson, A. (2003b). Backpacker ethnography. *Annals of Tourism Research* 30 (4), 847–867.

Swarbrooke, J. and Horner, S. (2007). *Consumer Behaviour in Tourism*, 2nd edn. Elsevier Butterworth-Heinemann, Oxford.

Thapa, B., Cahyanto, I., Holland, S.M. and Absher, J.D. (2013). Wildfires and tourist behaviors in Florida. *Tourism Management* 36, 284–292.

Tsiotsou, R. and Ratten, V. (2010). Future research directions in tourism marketing. *Marketing Intelligence and Planning* 28 (4), 533–544.

Vassiliadis, C.A., Prioras, C.-V. and Andronikidis, A. (2013). An analysis of visitor behaviour using time block: a study of ski destinations in Greece. *Tourism Management* 34, 61–70.

Vermeulen, I.E. and Seegers, D. (2009). Tried and tested: the impact of online hotel reviews on consumer consideration. *Tourism Management* 30 (1), 123–127.

Visit England (n.d.). Visitor Satisfaction Survey 2013–14. https://www.visitengland.com/biz/resources/insights-and-statistics/research-topics/consumer-behaviour/visitor-satisfaction

CASE STUDY 12: Discovering clients' longings: Kuoni Travel Compass®

Saskia Faulk

'Travel is the future recollection of oneself'

This maxim, perhaps restated more clearly as 'Travel makes you who you want to be', is emblazoned across Kuoni's shop-front in Lausanne, Switzerland. It is an assertion that the post-modern consumer has been understood and is co-opted to drive the company's marketing strategy. It is also a rather philosophical musing about the nature of travel and memory, and the determination of who we are – and who we want to become – being a process with which Kuoni can help us. It signals the recognition that our travel decisions are important, perhaps vital, for our identity and wellbeing. Such existential roots are further developed by the company's 'The Detourist 100' initiative.

Yet how can a travel provider truly integrate the lessons learned during its post-modern consumer research? With the introduction of its Travel Compass® in the Swiss market in 2010 (www.kuoni.com/brand-culture/customer-centricity/travel-compass), Kuoni may be as close to the answer as a company can get, and it has done so at a time when the tourism industry faces one of its biggest challenges ever: the inexorable rise of online booking giants.

With the domination of internet giants Expedia, Orbitz and others, online booking is the fastest-growing segment of the tourism market. As online offerings mushroom and become more specialized and safe, travellers realize that not only can they save lots of money, but they can also obtain real-time advice from fellow-travellers that may seem very convincing. In addition, people get an adrenaline rush when seeking low-cost or cleverly organized itineraries online: it's like a game, a hunt. People's self-esteem goes up when they find a solution to their problem and they can tell their friends how clever they are by finding a discounted rate or exclusive offer, a rare connection, or a new way to get to a given destination. The reputedly prudent Swiss are no exception to this rule, making 40 per cent of all their travel reservations using the internet, with the percentage almost doubling since 2010. Traditional travel providers have struggled to find their place in this fast-paced market, while concurrently dealing with serious external threats including economic crises, volcanic eruptions, terrorist threats and fluctuations in currency-exchange markets.

Yet consumers have different expectations for online and in-agency bookings. In the words of Thomas Stirnimann, CEO of another leading Swiss travel company (Hotelplan), online bookings are like fast food, while a gourmet food experience is what you get at the travel agency (Dao, 2010). Kuoni, in a struggle to maintain its 30 per cent of the Swiss market, has been working on both fronts: enhancing the in-store experience and consolidating its strengths on the internet. Online, the company has its global corporate portal www.kuoni.com, with the capacity to browse possibilities and brands, find a local agency and book online. In addition, in 2011 Kuoni joined the online fray by acquiring the London-based online tourist services site Gullivers Travel Associates (www.gta-travel.com), bought from its owner Travelport for US$720 million (Anon., 2011, 2013). GTA offers individual and group bookings for hotels (almost 12 million booked in 2010), flights, buses, tours and other services for clients in Asia-Pacific, Europe, the Middle East and North America. Through its business-to-business markets and consumer-based Octopus site, the booking engine was slated to transform the company into 'one of the leading global providers of online destination management services', and according to Kuoni's then CEO Peter Rothwell, helping to boost revenues by 10 per cent to $294 million. Yet Kuoni is not restricting itself to competing online, but is breaking out with an innovative bricks-and-mortar strategy with its Travel Compass® and associated store makeovers, as we shall see.

Many internet booking providers allow consumers to eliminate travel intermediaries to reduce costs, but several recent events may be changing the way travellers calculate the cost–benefit ratio of booking online. Recently a number of low-cost airlines went bankrupt, leaving passengers stranded around the world and scrambling to find flights home at their own cost. Then, ethnic and political unrest in some tourist-destination countries in northern Africa and the Middle East, as well as tsunamis, the Fukushima nuclear incident, and earthquakes demonstrated the importance of the human touch and having local ground agents who can personally track down travellers, relocate them and organize flights home. Kuoni's own exemplary reaction to such events, such as the Nairobi airport fire, drove this point home (Davis, 2013).

Another problem with online travel suppliers is that they may suffer from lack of credibility in their customers' eyes. After being seduced at first by the entire online travel purchasing process, travellers have become more sceptical, no longer knowing whether they can believe customers' reviews on sites such as TripAdvisor, or even the advice of travel bloggers. Travellers are painfully aware that it is not possible to know if a review is written by a guest or passenger, or a paid representative of a public relations agency, or even a competitor. For the moment, therefore, it is clear that a more traditional model of the travel agency still has some vital roles to play.

In response to its close observation of these changes in the market, Kuoni spent almost a decade crafting a new strategy. At the core of this was the rebranding of Kuoni's subsidiaries in Switzerland and elsewhere in order to bring people into its stores, which already benefit from prime city locations and highly trained staff. Company research also confirmed the importance of guidance and personal interaction for clients when planning a holiday. As one travel consultant put it: 'Clients don't need to go to a travel agent for travel information: in fact, they are getting *too much* information online and are often overloaded by it. What they really want to do is to have a professional simplify things for them.'

Regarding the credibility problem that online suppliers have, Kuoni has done much to deserve clients' trust, as with the pivotal role played by the company's local ground agents in recent catastrophes and crises. Yet the customer experience in-store had not been addressed until recently. From the moment clients cross the threshold, every detail of the cycle of service has been studied to offer the trust that they do not find any more on the internet. A team of welltravelled personal travel experts (PTAs) is available to talk about their experiences first-hand. If a local branch does not have an expert in an area the client is interested in, they will locate qualified people who can speak of their own experiences in the most specialized areas. In addition, PTAs attend conferences, undertake study tours and follow executive education programmes in their areas of interest. 'We simply know exactly what we're talking about. There is no online substitute for that expertise' asserts a Kuoni store-manager. There are regional experts (Maldives, Brazil, Nepal. . .), activity-area experts (safari, culture and history, adventure. . .), and specialist-area experts (cuisine, vintage trains, wine. . .) who can focus exclusively on the interests of clients, speaking on the basis of their own experiences and client preferences.

Yet with so many new travel possibilities becoming available each day, it is increasingly difficult for clients to know what they want. Consumer research has demonstrated that having a large pool of options from which to choose can be in itself a source of confusion and dissatisfaction for customers. Travel choice being such a complex process, often undertaken as a couple, a family or a group; how can travel providers help? One way, obviously, is to know – or get to know – one's clients personally in a relationship of mutual confidence, to understand their preferences and aspirations. As a Kuoni manager puts it, 'The internet can't give them that, not now and not ever, but a relationship with a Personal Travel Expert ensures that a travel insider gets to know you personally and can expertly guide you.'

As a result of its new strategy, Kuoni's flagship stores now have a real shop-front where there used to be an office behind glass. That means that anyone walking by on the busy commercial street can see employees at work inside. Yet store staff members do not have old-fashioned desks, so as not to give potential customers the impression that they are too busy to speak to clients. The atmosphere inside is very different too. This new feel to the place is more like an upscale café than a travel agent: no dusty files line the walls, no promotional stickers or plastic airplanes on desks, no postcards or garish souvenirs. Each flagship store is unique and tailored to its location.

At its flagship store in Lausanne, Kuoni manages to distil an atmosphere somewhere between a plush Istanbul lounge and an upscale Namibian safari lodge. The music is a classy, jazzy fusion of authentic tracks from a world traveller's suitcase that caresses your ears. Your eyes are rested by dimmed halogen lighting and matte taupe walls accented by the occasional bright ethnic accent, to cite but a few of the mood changers. Upon entering, a smiling, casually tailored receptionist welcomes you and asks if you know what you need, whether it is just a quick question, or you wish to meet with a PTA to discuss holiday options. If you are thinking about getting away but do not yet have a clearly-defined idea, the receptionist invites you to sit in the comfortable reading corner, dubbed the 'inspiration zone'. Delineated by a designer bookshelf in exotic wood, a personal collection of travel books (no guide books, though) vie for your attention. There you can lounge in a chair that would be at home on a spa bungalow terrace in the Maldives, and sip a cup of coffee or refreshing glass of mint tea. While you wait, you begin to get the feeling that you have already embarked on your holiday and are transported far from the busy street outside.

Based on the receptionist's intuitions after meeting you, a PTA is allocated to you, if you do not already have one. He or she arrives shortly, escorting you down a few steps towards an impressive long wooden table surrounded by upholstered chairs. Your PTA makes you feel comfortable by asking about your past travel experiences and your planning process for the next trip. If you do not have a clearly defined idea, the PTA asks if you would like to go through a discovery process together. If you agree to this, a handsome briefcase-sized box, similar in design to a traveller's trunk, is placed on the table and opened to reveal thick, richly illustrated playing cards. This is the Kuoni Travel Compass®. The same facility is possible using an iPad, for those who prefer it.

The voyage of discovery card game then begins. Your PTA explains, as he or she lays out a set of cards face up, that you should choose the Travel Compass® images that are most compatible with your holiday wishes. Laughing children are portrayed on one card; on another, sunlight filters through green leaves in a forest canopy. Yet another portrays a solitary beach and crystalline sea. Your choice of cards is set aside and another group of photo cards is selected, then another, each time with more focused questions. With the selection process of successive sets of images, you feel as if you have embarked on a short voyage of self-discovery, clarifying your vision for this trip. Upon completion of the process, your PTA examines your choices and, like a skilled fortune-teller, tells you which deductions about your holiday preferences can be made based on your card choices, confirming your preferences clearly for both of you. A discussion then ensues. Finally, your travel expert explores with you the holiday options offered by Kuoni that correspond to your profile, as well as special promotions or seasonal trips. In this way, your PTA can share some first-hand personalized advice about available possibilities, and call in another PTA for specialized input if needed. There are PTAs for almost any travel interest, no matter how esoteric. One example is wine travel, where several PTAs are experts and have an immense personal network to draw on. Because of their obvious expertise and passion for the subject, they are credible spokespeople for the travel products they sell. Other PTAs can be found at any given Kuoni store or can be contacted for a telephone or face-to-face meeting about cruise, Nordic, ecological, urban, and many other types of travel.

Of all consumer sectors, the travel industry is probably that with the most diversified offers and the most complex decision process. Travellers may be conscious of budget constraints but less cognisant of their own conscious and unconscious desires – and the holidays that correspond to them. In the past, product selection involved detailed discussion between travel agents and clients along with a strong dose of sensitivity and intuition. Because not all travel providers are equally intuitive or skilled at probing clients' desires and feelings, some travel decisions were mistakenly made, resulting in dissatisfied travellers. Worse, when travellers are not clear themselves about what they want, or cannot express their preferences clearly, travel agents risk drawing the wrong conclusions and booking the wrong kind of trip.

If you are among the estimated 50 per cent who do not precisely know where they wish to go on holiday, going through the Travel Compass® experience is a light-hearted and fun way to discreetly 'research' oneself in order to design a holiday that has the best possible fit with trips and tours available through Kuoni's massive network. Such a situation may be complicated further when you are not alone in planning the trip. For instance, setting out to travel with a friend, partner or spouse can turn the decision-making process into a conflict zone. The idea of using the Travel Compass® with expert guidance by a PTA and in the serene atmosphere of a flagship store can potentially transform this conflict into a peace-making process based on consensus. Selecting the photo cards allows travellers to uncover dreams and preferences they might not otherwise know how to express – or may not be consciously aware of – and allows partners to agree on travel fundamentals. In addition to this discovery process, the Travel Compass® takes the service provider and client through a systematic and consistent process of discovery that sets both parties at ease and forms an interesting conversation piece.

The Travel Compass® was constructed using Kuoni's internal scientific research into traveller motivations and perceptions. As the company states on its website:

> We live in increasingly complex times. People's needs are becoming more individual and differentiated, making it harder to lump them together into simple trends. As one of the leading travel companies, we have to penetrate deeper into the zeitgeist of the 21st century, continuously developing new concepts so that our travel offerings meet the needs of even the most demanding traveller.

Kuoni determined that, in order to become a truly customer-centric company, more research was needed in order to better understand its customers. Accordingly, the Market Intelligence department recruited 15,000 participants from different European countries to find out more about people's travel interests, motivation and decision-making process. Kuoni managers and travel consultants as well as statisticians, market researchers and psychologists were consulted. The analysis of the qualitative and quantitative research findings contributed to the elaboration of a workbook titled *Coast of Me – Mapping the Place of Longing* and the identification of psychographic segments based on 'longings, requirements, and expectations', or put more simply, their holiday needs. Words and images related to the different segments listed below are used by staff to identify customers' feelings, preferences and longings, which are often subconscious and difficult to articulate.

- **Seasoned exploration:** 'Immerse yourself in other cultures. Meet people. Explore the four corners of the world your own way.' Becoming an active participant and observer of culture, social interaction and individual exploration are key to understanding this segment's needs. An example of a trip that could interest this segment would be travelling on a Chinese train along a branch of the Silk Road to Lhasa, Tibet, where much exploration is done on foot.
- **Mind, body, soul:** 'Soak up some TLC. Be at ease with yourself. Pamper all your senses at luxurious retreats.' This segment is primarily inner-directed and in touch with their thoughts, feelings and physical sensations. A luxury eco-friendly spa resort with individual pool residences in Thailand could tempt this segment.
- **Reconnect:** 'Enjoy togetherness. Feel close. Intimate times in romantic places.' Experiencing travel as a couple and feeling unified with one's partner in a romantic setting are central needs for this segment. A honeymoon in a romantic safari lodge in the Masai Mara could be interesting for this segment.
- **Sociability:** 'Have fun together. Share experiences. Have a great time with good friends.' Travelling in a small group, this segment seeks to affirm friendships, belonging and shared experiences. This segment, for example, could include a reunion of old friends for a short trip to Dubai for shopping and exploring.
- **Out of the ordinary:** 'Visit cultural treasures. Experience the world's best places – and remember them forever.' This segment seeks special experiences in unique settings that are culturally different from their own. A sunset horseback trek with Bedouins near the Siwa oasis in Egypt would interest this segment.
- **Away from it all:** 'Take a time out. Recharge your batteries. Enjoy tranquility – for you to find yourself.' Internal harmony and self-exploration, stress-reduction, calm and escapism characterize this segment.
- **For the kids:** 'Play pirates. Build sandcastles. See your children's eye light up.' This segment seeks travel experiences that will benefit their parent–child bond and are centred on their children's interests and preferences. A stay at an all-inclusive beachfront resort in Mauritius featuring an activity-packed children's club and teen club could interest this segment.
- **Sun & fun:** 'Celebrate life. Flirt. Enjoy the sunny side of everything.' Social interaction, meeting new people, fun and light-heartedness are central to the travel needs of this segment, which might seek an adults-only beachfront resort in Cancun, Mexico.

Source: www.kuoni.com/brand-culture/customer-centricity/holiday-report

These categories are now used as filters on Kuoni's websites, allowing future travellers to find more easily the hotel or holiday that is most compatible with their interests. Kuoni's research department is highly active, and ongoing research is regularly published online. Very interesting and sometimes funny results of some of the latest studies on cultural differences and travel, the 'Holiday Report', are available for consultation on the website. Thanks to this extensive research, Kuoni can train staff how to communicate better with customers face-to-face. It effectively allows their travel consultants to use the company's research on the psychology of decision-making to guide clients towards the travel offer that is best suited to them. The tool that makes all this possible is the Travel Compass®, part of the company's orientation towards an 'advisory culture'.

Despite all the scientific research that went into its development, clients using the Travel Compass® do not get the feeling that it is a marketing tool designed to enhance customer relations and to solve the problem of uncovering and understanding consumer perceptions and preferences. On the contrary, loyal clients ask specifically for it, and it has generated word-of-mouth curiosity among new clients who are relieved to find a way to simplify their travel decisions. Couples, in particular, are grateful for the step-by-step process that allows each partner to participate and express themselves with thoughtful coaching by the PTA. In addition, contrary to what one may imagine, the Travel Compass® is useful for travellers at all budget levels, from budget holidays to the most luxurious. Through structured feedback it has allowed Kuoni to form a clearer picture of travel decisions, which already has borne fruit: the Travel Compass® now has new cards to represent the importance of sport and gastronomy, and will continue to be modified as consumer tastes and trends change. The successful adoption of the Travel Compass® in Switzerland prompted the company to roll out the concept in France and the Netherlands, and to a limited extent in the UK. Spain, Italy and possibly India are next (according to Kuoni's Nils Reisen). The company's Art Director Joël Walser made the analogy that the Travel Compass® is to a travel company what the stethoscope is to a doctor. For the moment, at least, no other travel provider has anything like it.

ABOUT KUONI

Kuoni is a leading leisure travel organization employing 13,000 people in 100 countries on five continents. In 2012 the company recorded the highest net profits in its 106-year history: CHF1.1 billion (almost US$1.2 billion). Kuoni Group's business activities are composed of three areas: tour operating, destination management and visa services. The company sells package holidays as well as premium individual holidays, which can be highly customized. The company sells through its own retail stores, third-party travel agencies, the internet, mobile devices, PTAs and call centres. For more information see www.kuoni.com/group.

DISCUSSION POINTS AND ESSAY QUESTIONS

1. To what extent do you think the Travel Compass® is a culture-specific tool? In what ways would Kuoni need to adapt it when using the compass in different countries?
2. Conduct an informal survey of your colleagues and friends to check if the Kuoni Travel Compass® segments detailed above correspond to their own 'travel longings'. Is there another potential segment that Kuoni does not currently identify?
3. Can you conceive of a tool (or process, or game) which, like the Travel Compass®, could be used to clarify travellers' interests and motivations online?

REFERENCES

Anon. (2011). Kuoni veut acquérir Gullivers Travel Associates. ATS-*Le Temps* 4 March.

Anon. (2013). La Boussole de Kuoni est en ligne. *Travel Inside* 15 May. www.travelinside.ch/traveltip/search/index.php?we_objectID=27486&pid=0

Dao, J. (2010). Réinventer le voyage en agence. *L'Hebdo* 15 December. www.hebdo.ch/reinventer_le_voyage_en_agence_76974_.html

Davis, P. (2013). Passengers stranded amid chaotic scenes after Nairobi airport fire. *Travel Weekly* 8 August. www.travelweekly.co.uk/Articles/2013/08/08/44932/passengers-stranded-amid-chaotic-scenes-after-nairobi-airport.html

CHAPTER 13

The marketing mix and tourist behaviour

Introduction

Once they have obtained their research data on consumer behaviour, tourism organizations have to manipulate their marketing mix – the four Ps: product, price, place, promotion – to reflect the nature of their target markets. In this chapter we explore the ways in which tourist behaviour influences the four Ps, and the ways in which tourism organizations seek to exploit market trends through the use of the marketing mix variables.

This will mean covering a range of issues relating to the four Ps, including:

- product – tangible aspects, service element, branding
- price – discounting, value for money
- place – the role of intermediaries, direct sell
- promotion – advertising, brochures, sales promotions.

When a tourism organization has identified its target customers, it must try to understand their behaviour and try and reflect this in its marketing programmes. The marketing mix is the set of variables which an organization can alter in the short term and the long term in order to satisfy its customer requirements. The four components, as listed above, can be amended separately or in combination with one or more of the other components. The marketing mix is therefore like a set of levers that the organization can adjust to meet its aims.

This chapter looks at each element of the marketing mix and discusses the important aspects of each in relation to consumer behaviour for tourism organizations.

Product

The tourism product must be designed or amended to reflect consumers' needs and wants. One of the key objectives for any tourism organization is **product positioning**, which is defined by Kotler and Armstrong (2004) as: 'The way in which the product is defined by consumers on important attributes – the place the product occupies in the consumers' minds.'

The correct positioning of a product will mean that the consumer can recognize it as being distinct from competitors' products because there will be unique, often intangible elements associated with it, which will allow the organization to differentiate its offerings.

An organization must understand its consumers' needs and wants before it can correctly position its products and services in relation to competitors' products. It will also have to study the market and the competition before it can effectively spot a gap in the marketplace to exploit. Organizations often use positioning maps to help them spot an opportunity in a particular marketplace. An example of a positioning map for the hospitality industry prior to the development of the budget hotels is shown in Figure 13.1.

Consumer preferences were moving towards being more budget-conscious as a result of the recession that had gripped the country during the early 1990s. Consumers wanted better value-for-money products and were prepared to sacrifice high levels of service to achieve this. The hospitality organizations developed their ranges of budget hotels under various brand names to reflect this demand (Horner and Swarbrooke, 1996). The correct positioning of the product to reflect consumer behaviour is therefore vital for the organization.

The position of the product in the product life-cycle (PLC) also means that a particular type of consumer will be attracted to the product, and that the marketing programme should reflect consumers' needs and wants. The product life-cycle model incorporates four main stages: induction, growth, maturity and decline. This model has been criticized as a forecasting model; it does, however, allow organizations to identify

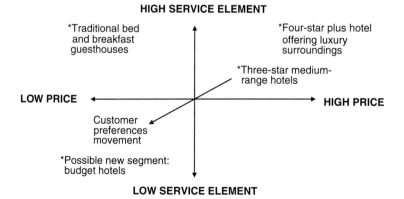

Figure 13.1 Positioning map of the UK hospitality industry prior to the development of the budget market

Source: Horner and Swarbrooke (1996)

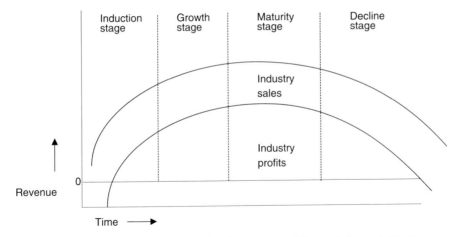
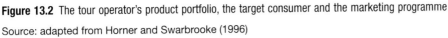

Figure 13.2 The tour operator's product portfolio, the target consumer and the marketing programme

Source: adapted from Horner and Swarbrooke (1996)

different types of consumers who are attracted to their products, according to where they are in the life-cycle.

A tourism organization will probably have products and services in different parts of the product life-cycle. It will attract different types of consumers to each of its products, and the marketing mix will have to be designed around their needs. This concept is illustrated in Figure 13.2, which refers to a tour operator that markets products at three different stages in the product life-cycle. The marketing programme for each product is different because it has to reflect the needs and wants of the particular group of consumers in the market segment. It can be seen from Figure 13.2 that each product requires a particular marketing strategy to reflect the target group's needs and wants.

Branding

A key aspect of differentiation for a product or service is branding. Kotler and Armstrong (2004) define branding as: 'a name, term, symbol or design or combination of them, intended to identify goods or services of one seller or group of sellers and to differentiate them from those of their competitors'.

Brand names, logos or trademarks encourage consumers to buy products and services because they give them the benefits that they are seeking. These benefits range from familiarity and safety to status and self-esteem (Horner and Swarbrooke, 1996).

Tourism organizations find branding particularly useful because a brand adds tangible cues to a service that is largely intangible in nature. This idea is explored in more depth in Figure 13.3, which explores the benefits that a strong brand name brings to an organization marketing a fully inclusive tour product.

The strong brand identity allows the organization to give the right types of message to their target consumers. A powerful brand will also allow the organization to develop its product or service on an international basis since a strong brand will give messages

Product	PLC stage	Consumer	Marketing programme
Summer sun holidays or FIT's	Maturity	Middle majority family clientele	Reassuring promotion emphasizing brand Relaunching activity with new destination
Long haul holidays or FIT's	Introduction	Innovators Outer directed individual	Promotion to build awareness Sales promotion (with distributors) Emphasis on product excitement
Flydrive holidays to the USA	Growth	Families in middle-income bracket seeking new experiences	Brand building promotion Work on distribution Reassurance on safety in brochure

Figure 13.3 The importance of a strong brand name on consumer choice for a fully inclusive tour

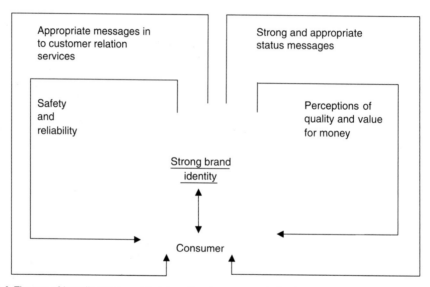

Figure 13.4 The use of branding to appeal to international consumers in tourism

of quality. The major airlines have used powerful brands to develop their business, appealing to international consumers. The use of branding by tourism organizations to appeal to an international tourism consumer and reflect their needs and wants is explored in Figure 13.4.

Price

Pricing is a key principle for any organization when marketing products and services. The price that an organization charges for its products and services must strike a balance between what the organization is trying to achieve in financial terms and, most importantly, the needs and wants of consumers from the target group. The pricing decisions of organizations will be affected by a number of factors including the pricing objectives, legal and regulatory issues, the competition and costs. The most important factor in terms of this book, however, is the consumer's perception of price in relation to quality and value for money. For non-profit-making organizations, the objectives are often to encourage new users. This can be achieved by using **differential pricing strategies**, where different prices are charged for different market segments.

The consumer must see a link between the price charged and the product quality. Many tourism organizations charge a high price which is a reflection of the special features of the product in terms of design or service delivery. Small, specialist tour operators can charge relatively high prices for the special features of the holiday on offer, their attention to detail and their high levels of personal service.

The airlines charge different prices for different levels of service. This relationship is explored in Figure 13.5. It can be seen from this diagram that the price of each product in the airline industry links to the perceptions of the market segments, and is reflected in the levels of service and product offerings. The most important issue here, for the airline, is whether customers perceive that the price they are paying represents good value for money in relation to the service delivery.

Tourism is a service industry, which means that it sells products that are, by their very nature, perishable. This means that organizations must work hard to obtain maximum usage or occupancy. The airline or train that departs when it is only half full will be losing valuable revenue. The tour operator that is relying on high volumes to maximize profits will have to work hard to gain sales. Pricing is used as a competitive advantage

Sector	Example	Comments
1. Destinations	Spain – 'España Passion for Life' 'Smile, you're in Spain'	To attract new up-market customer seeking cultural experience and to promote an image of Spain as a fun destination
2. Transport	British Airways	To attract international customer seeking reliability and customer service
3. Attractions	Disneyland Europe The Magic Kingdom	To attract children interested in the Magic of Disney
4. Tour operator	TUI – Sustainable Programme	To attract environmentally conscious post-modern tourist
5. Accommodation	MGM – Las Vegas	To attract the customer interested in combining entertainment and gambling

Figure 13.5 The relationship of price to consumer perception of quality for a major airline

Product	Customer	Customer expectations
First class Highest price	High socioeconomic group Customers with high status	• High levels of personal service • Rapid check-in • Large amount of space on board
Business class Medium price	Business traveler Medium/high socioeconomic class	• Some personal service • Reliable and quick check-in • Good space allocation on board • Business services on board
Economy class Lower prices	Families Low/medium socioeconomic class Students/single people	• Little personal service • Limited menus • Little space on board • Services for children

Figure 13.6 The ways in which price is used in tourism to influence consumer behaviour

tool in tourism in a number of ways to try to influence consumers in their purchasing patterns. A summary of some of these ways of using price to influence consumer behaviour is shown in Figure 13.6.

It can be seen from Figure 13.6 that different pricing strategies will encourage consumers to enter the market or, in certain circumstances, remain loyal to an organization. Pricing strategies can also encourage consumers to enter a market, and can be used to discourage consumers from abusing natural resources or facilities.

Place (or distribution)

A distribution channel (or place) has been defined by Kotler and Armstrong (2004) as: 'the set of firms and individuals that take title, or assist in transferring title, to the particular good or service as it moves from the producer to the final consumer'.

Place is of great significance to consumers because they might like the product and be able and willing to pay the price asked, but if they are unable to gain access to it no sale will result. Consumers are affected by the intermediaries in the distribution chain. It is often the retailer who has the most powerful effect on consumers when they are making their purchase decisions. The retail travel agent, for example, has a primary function in the relationship with consumers on behalf of the package holiday operator. This function was summarized by Horner and Swarbrooke (1996) and is shown in Figure 13.7.

It can be seen from this diagram that travel agents perform an important function in relation to the consumer. They can act as powerful persuaders in relation to consumer choice. They also act as points of contact for customer complaints if problems occur with holidays.

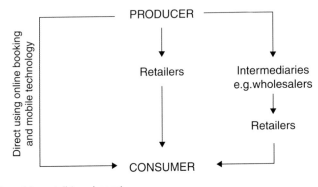

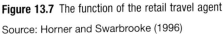

Figure 13.7 The function of the retail travel agent

Source: Horner and Swarbrooke (1996)

The special nature of tourism has led organizations to develop special distribution systems including consortia, central reservation systems, affiliations, and specialist operators such as tour operators and travel agents.

The tourism industry has been very active in the development of direct-selling operations. Computerized reservation systems have allowed service organizations such as airlines and hotels to communicate directly with the customer and cut out the intermediaries. This brings the organization distinct advantages with regard to the consumer because it is able to negotiate a sale directly with the consumer. It also allows the development of a relationship between the supplier and the consumer and facilitates sales promotion activity.

However, tourism organizations do tend to use direct-selling methods, encouraged by the development of multimedia systems, which will be increasingly important in the industry. Point of information (POI) systems are multimedia computers that stand alone and provide the customer with interactive services. Point of sale (POS) systems allow customers to buy their tickets and use electronic fund transfer (EFT POS) systems to make direct payments. These systems increasingly will be linked to POI systems and will mean that the customer can purchase tickets in shops, at departure points, or even in the home. Developments in ICT have allowed tourism organizations to develop a more sophisticated direct marketing business and travel agents will increasingly become redundant.

All these developments, however, depend on the attitude of the consumer. Consumers may resist the new technology and still feel happier being sold tourism products in a face-to-face experience within a retail shop. Their attitudes may well be determined by the market segment into which they fit.

A good example of organizations that use a combination of different sorts of distribution systems are the international airlines. This is explored in Figure 13.8.

The airlines sell directly to the customer using their own in-house online booking systems which link directly to their revenue and yield management systems. Consumers

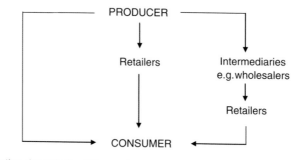

Figure 13.8 The distribution channels for airline seats

are now increasingly able to access these sites through their mobile devices. Airlines continue to also sell seats through online travel agents and traditional high street travel agents. Telephone bookings are now much diminished due to the use of ICT, although in some countries telesales are still significant. Budget airlines in particular also use their own websites to upsell to consumers through the offer of add-on services such as seat selection and different baggage options, as well as partner products such as hotels and car hire. The use of ICT by airlines also gives them powerful tools for database marketing.

The distribution of tourism products is being revolutionized by the development of new electronic databases which can be incorporated into telecommunication systems. These include computer reservation systems (CRS) and global distribution systems (GDS). Many tourism organizations see the development of global sales and distribution systems as a key strategic objective. These systems will allow organizations to communicate directly with customers on a worldwide basis. These developments have allowed many tourism organizations the opportunity to develop direct marketing distribution channels.

The growing use of ICT has reinforced, and acted as a catalyst for, the trend towards direct sales and the removal of travel agents from the distribution chain. It is now easy for tourists in many countries to buy airline seats and hotel beds online, as well as hire cars, and even to book excursions.

However, while the internet has allowed tourists to bypass high street travel agents, it has also created a different type of travel agent – the online travel agent. These include brand names such as Expedia, Lastminute.com, Travelocity, and so on. These online travel agents have helped stimulate the rise of the independent do-it-yourself traveller. These agents have intensified competition between airlines by showing consumers the prices of all airlines on a route where a traditional agent would have given the customer much less choice.

At the same time, some online agents, such as Expedia, have almost become tour operators because they enable tourists to create their own tailor-made package, including flights, hotel, transfers and excursions.

Meanwhile, many traditional tour operators and travel agents have struggled to come to terms with the internet, and their websites are often inferior to those of companies such as Expedia. This might be because they are in two minds about the internet as they also own a lot of high street travel agency outlets.

Promotion

The final part of the marketing mix – promotion – is the way in which the tourism organization communicates in an effective way with its target customers. Promotion is used by organizations to affect the ways in which consumers behave, and is therefore a vital motivator for any tourism organization. Tourism organizations use a variety of methods for marketing communication, which are summarized in Figure 13.9.

The methods of marketing communication that a tourist organization uses depend on the type of product, the aims of the campaign and the market characteristics. The definitions and aims of the main types of promotion are explored in Figure 13.10.

It can be seen from Figure 13.10 that there are a variety of marketing communication techniques, which will have different effects on consumer behaviour. The tourism organization will use press or public relations techniques when it wants to create a favourable impression of the organization in the consumer's mind. An example of this type of activity is the long-running public relations campaign for British Airways as the 'World's Favourite Airline'.

- **Brochures** are used by tourism organizations when they are trying to initiate sales. The brochure should be used to reassure consumers about the product offering, which is particularly important in a market where there is a high spend feature. A good example of a tourism organization using a brochure to inform and reassure potential customers of their products is the technique used by Thomson, a tour operator in the UK, where they show customer ratings for every aspect of the holiday (e.g. food, accommodation and location) based on market research with returning customers from the previous year.

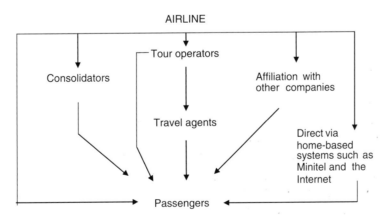

Figure 13.9 Methods of marketing communication

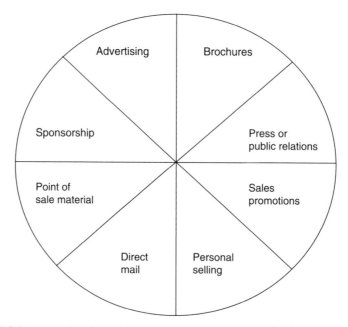

Figure 13.10 The definitions and aims of the main types of marketing communication in relation to consumer behaviour

- **Advertising** is used by tourism organizations when they want to reach large audiences in an efficient manner. Television advertising is often used by tourism companies at the beginning of the booking season to encourage early interest and bookings. Advertising is often used to repeat the marketing communication messages in an attractive and appealing manner. The logic here is that repetition of messages will have a greater positive effect on the consumer. An important innovation for the tourism and hospitality sectors has been the rise of satellite television. Tourism is an occasional rather than a regular purchase, so if one advertises during a popular soap opera with 10 million viewers, perhaps only 50,000 are thinking of buying a holiday at that moment, yet the cost of advertising will reflect the size of the audience and will be very expensive. Satellite television has created a market for low-production-cost television programmes and channels that are targeted to niche markets. For example, in the UK there are several channels just selling cruise holidays, so virtually every viewer is a potential customer and advertising costs are low, reflecting the small audience numbers. Satellite television has also led to the growth of global news channels such as CNN and BBC World. These are perfect vehicles for tourism and hospitality advertisers as their viewers are nearly all travellers who are watching in hotels while on their travels.
- **Sales promotion** is often used by tourism organizations to try to encourage potential consumers to buy a product for the first time, or to repeat a purchase. Package holiday companies in the UK have used sales promotion techniques extensively in their marketing programmes to influence consumer behaviour. Sales promotions such as 'free child places' target certain market segments at the beginning of the

season and produce frenzied purchasing behaviour because places are strictly limited.

- **Personal selling** is very important in tourism because services, by their very nature, involve a high degree of face-to-face selling activity. Personal selling is used by tourism organizations either directly or indirectly to initiate sales or encourage consumers to buy more. The large exclusive hotels, for example, use personal selling at reception and throughout the hotel to sell the guest more products and services during their stay.
- **Point of sale material** will help the tourism organization to encourage consumers to enter the market or to buy more of a particular product or service. It is very important that the point-of-sale materials and merchandizing materials in general meet consumer expectations. Styling and colouring of the materials should be attractive to the consumer and should reflect the organization's image and brand identity. It is also important that the styling of materials should be updated with new themes and colours according to customer perceptions. The theming of public houses by big breweries in the UK on an Irish theme is one example of point-of-sale and merchandizing activity. It is likely that the Irish theme will become unfashionable over time, and restyling along another theme will be necessary.
- **Direct mail** is being developed extensively by tourism organizations because the use of sophisticated databases will allow the development of customized promotional offerings. The large hotel chains, for example, can talk directly to their corporate clients. They may even communicate directly with individual business clients to inform them of new products and services on offer within their operation.

The intangibility of services means that the promotional techniques used by tourism organizations often have special characteristics. Organizations often use symbols to stress the nature of the service to the consumer. This makes it easier for consumers to identify with the organization and to recognize its products and services. The symbols developed by organizations are often linked to strong brand identities. The Thomson bird-in-flight symbol, for example, helps consumers to identify with feelings of freedom associated with their holiday products. The company more recently adopted the TUI logo.

The link of promotion to lifestyle has been extensively developed in markets such as alcoholic drinks and the car industry. There are signs that the tourism industry is beginning to develop similar styles of advertising to reflect consumer lifestyles. Tour operators' brochures, for example, are becoming more like designer lifestyle magazines, and it is likely that this type of development will continue in the future. The development of niche tourism products designed to appeal to distinct market segments will mean that these types of selective promotional literature based on consumer lifestyles will become increasingly popular.

The internet is now also a crucial part of the promotional mix, as even people who will not buy products online see it as a major source of information. Destination websites are a popular source of information for tourists, but they are often very weak, being static and with little concrete information and few links to sites where tourists can actively buy products.

Company websites can also often be rather static, without moving images or sound, or updated information, which negates the advantages the internet has as a promotional tool. Many tourism organizations' sites also lack a reservations facility so that tourists can book online.

At the same time, tourism organizations need to be aware that their product will also be featured on other people's websites, over which they have no control. These are well used by travellers but are largely beyond the control of tourism organizations and their marketing departments.

ICT is not just a new promotional tool – it has changed many of the old traditional methods. For example, electronic media advertising has affected traditional advertising media as it is perceived to be more cost effective.

Conclusions

In this chapter we have looked at the key issues involved in the development of each part of the marketing mix in relation to consumer behaviour. In general, tourism organizations should:

- consider each element of the marketing mix separately and evaluate the relationship of each part to consumer behaviour
- ensure that the different components of the marketing mix interact effectively to produce the desired effect on target consumers and their behaviour patterns
- consider how their total portfolio of products affects their consumers' behaviour patterns – construction and manipulation of an effective marketing mix to reflect consumer behaviour patterns is vital for tourism organizations.

Tourism organizations need to recognize the importance of the internet which, by potentially combining promotion and distribution in one transaction, theoretically turns the four Ps into two Ps plus a combined internet category that combines place and promotion. It is also important to recognize that the use of the internet is not the same all over the world. In many countries people are still concerned about online security, while in others they simply do not have reliable internet access. Nevertheless, there is no doubt that the internet will continue to play an increasingly important role in the marketing mix for tourism organizations.

Discussion points and essay questions

1. 'Customers purchase benefits not products.' Discuss this statement in relation to the design and implementation of effective marketing mixes for tourism organizations.

2. Outline the role of promotion within tourism marketing, particularly in relation to consumer behaviour.

Exercise

Choose one tourism product or service. Consider how each element of the marketing mix for the chosen product or service has been designed to reflect consumers' wants and needs. Are there any improvements that could be made to any element of the marketing mix, in your opinion?

References

Horner, S. and Swarbrooke, J. (1996). *Marketing Tourism, Hospitality, and Leisure in Europe*. International Thomson Business Press.

Kotler, P. and Armstrong, G. (2004). *Marketing Management: Analysis Planning, Implementation*, 4th European edn. Pearson Education, Upper Saddle River, NJ.

CASE STUDY 13.1: First Choice Holidays' all-inclusive package

INTRODUCTION

First Choice Holidays was formed as a result of an extensive re-launch of the Owners Abroad company in 1994. The company is part of TUI Group along with rival brand Thomson. The company offers a full range of package holidays and uses a range of sub-brands. It piloted the idea of an all-inclusive holiday during the 1995 season, which led to the successful introduction of the all-inclusive brochure for the 1996–97 season. Since 2012, following a decision by parent TUI, First Choice offers only all-inclusive holidays, styling itself in 2015 on its Facebook page as 'the home of All Inclusive'.

THE ALL-INCLUSIVE PRODUCT

The all-inclusive holiday concept was developed in the 1990s to respond to growing demand from consumers for a holiday priced to include all food, accommodation and activities for the duration of stay, although the concept harks back to the British holiday camps established in the 1930s, with the French Club Méditerranée being considered the first all-inclusive resort in the 1950s (Mintel, 2014). The all-inclusive concept offers the customer all transport, accommodation, drinks and sporting activities included in the price, that is, it includes the majority of expenses involved with a holiday. In 1996, First Choice Holidays was the first package holiday operator to introduce the all-inclusive holiday into the UK mainstream market with the introduction of a wide range of all-inclusive deals to popular summer Mediterranean destinations. From then it has continued to focus on providing 'all-inclusive-only' travel with over a million people travelling each year (Mintel, 2014).

In the 1990s a National Opinion Poll (NOP) survey revealed that 40 per cent of people did not understand the concept of the all-inclusive holiday and thought that it was 'too good to be true'. A survey carried out in 1995 revealed that the majority of interviewees thought that 'all-inclusive meant simply a standard package holiday, including only accommodation, flight and transfer'. But by 1996 it became apparent that the all-inclusive package holiday had become one of the fastest-growing types of holiday in the UK.

Initially the all-inclusive concept was well received by British consumers, who were keen to make their pound stretch further. In a 1996 survey, 73 per cent of interviewees stated that there were particular benefits to be gained from purchasing an all-inclusive holiday. They made such statements as:

- 'It would make financial planning easier.'
- 'It provides better value for money.'

Just over a decade later came the 2007–08 global financial crisis and once again travellers became cautious and budget-aware. This led to an exponential rise in this sort of holiday offering across the industry as providers struggled to compete (Mintel, 2014).

THE ALL-INCLUSIVE CUSTOMER

By the summer of 2013, all-inclusive holidays made up 55 per cent of the holidays sold by First Choice. Demand for this type of holiday had risen from 17 per cent of the UK market in 2007 up to 34 per cent in 2010 (Tui Travel plc); similarly for The Co-operative Travel a third of its 7 million package holidays between 2007 and 2011 were for 'all-inclusive' breaks (Mintel, 2014). 'The all-inclusive market has been a major beneficiary of the downturn' (ABTA, 2013) with popularity increasing into the 2015 market (ABTA, 2015).

Early customers in the UK for all-inclusive packages tended to be married and largely from the 30–50 age group. A large proportion of customers were from a higher socioeconomic group such as professional/senior managers. Single people also represented an important part of the target group.

The all-inclusive range of holidays also offers free child prices, discounts for children and groups, and special offers for tropical honeymooners. Exhibit 13.1.1 details the key customer groups that favour all-inclusive holidays.

Exhibit 13.1.1 All-inclusive holidaymakers

The largest group of consumers are middle-income couples and families.

All-inclusive holidays are popular with:
  pre-/no-children couples
  empty-nesters (adult children have left home)
  retirees
  families with younger children (4–12)
  occasion travellers (destination weddings, honeymoons)

All-inclusive holidays are not popular with:
  Single travellers (due to price supplements)
  Tourists who do not like beach holidays (most provision is beach-related)

Source: Mintel (2014)

As can be seen in Exhibit 13.1.1, the all-inclusive customer today comes from a range of specific market segments. These market segments are explored in Exhibit 13.1.2.

Exhibit 13.1.2 Niche market segments that are attracted to the all-inclusive product

Lifestyle	Health tourists
	Naturists
	Sports tourists
Behavioural	Weddings and honeymooners
	Gay couples
	Business travellers

Source: adapted from Mintel (2001)

The increase in the number of niche holiday-makers – such as health, sport and naturist, and gay all-inclusive – is an increasingly important part of the market. It is important to consider the reasons for the growth in the all-inclusive product in relation to trends in consumer behaviour.

WHY CHOOSE AN ALL-INCLUSIVE PACKAGE?

The choice of an all-inclusive holiday has been attributed to a number of factors that are associated with consumer behaviour. These factors are explored in Exhibit 13.1.3.

Exhibit 13.1.3 Reasons for choosing an all-inclusive package holiday

Cash rich/time poor customers	Consumers with decreasing amounts of leisure time but increasing income seek shorter/fuller experiences
Security issues	Worries about crime and the risks associated with unknown destinations mean that all-inclusive is a safe option
Relaxation	Increased stress levels mean that the all-inclusive resort offers a quick-fix experience with no hassle; the experience offers total relaxation
Budget certainty	The all-inclusive package allows the customer to have the security of paying for everything before departure and there are no worries associated with extra money or currency change
Increased availability and choice	The all-inclusive package is increasingly being offered in a wider choice of destinations and across different types of holiday accommodation – from individual hotels to all-inclusive resorts – with some hotel chains specializing in all-inclusive accommodation (e.g. Ola Hotels in Mallorca)
Hassle-free	While the internet has opened up the ability to search and create bespoke holiday elements, doing so through all-inclusive offerings allows freedom to search but without the complications of having to put together all the elements of a personalised package

Source: Mintel (2001, 2014)

The original growth of interest in the all-inclusive type of package was a result of changes in consumer lifestyles. Individuals, couples and families were increasingly finding themselves earning plenty of money but having very little time to spend it. There was also a desire to purchase easy and quick fixes in the holiday market with the desire to experience a hassle-free, relaxing holiday.

The post-financial crisis period from 2008–14 led to a growth in interest driven by budget constraints and the desire for certainty of costs. The requirement for value for money is played on by suppliers such as First Choice in their advertising: 'All you can is all we do'; 'All you can imagine', 'All you can unwind', and 'All you can whoosh!'.

THE SUPPLY SIDE OF THE ALL-INCLUSIVE PRODUCT

The development of the all-inclusive package holiday has allowed countries, regions, tour operators and hospitality companies to develop business that targets this type of consumer from across the world. Customers from the USA, Canada, Japan and European countries (Germany, UK, France, Netherlands, Austria, Switzerland and Italy) have continued to purchase all-inclusive packages. We will now look at examples of a hotel chain, a tour operator and a country that have explored the all-inclusive holiday product.

EXAMPLES OF ALL-INCLUSIVE INITIATIVES

The tour operator: First Choice

First Choice Holidays is a leading international leisure travel brand which operates in 26 countries; TUI Group, its parent organization, employs 77,000 staff. The group had the original desire to develop and operate a high-quality, mass-market package holiday business in the UK and American markets through the use of a portfolio of brands that have been developed over the past decade.

First Choice was one of the first in the UK to develop the all-inclusive package holiday and to recognize the potential for this type of product in the mainstream holiday sector. Following its incorporation into the TUI Group it became the first UK provider to offer only all-inclusive holiday packages.

The current all-inclusive package on offer by First Choice Holidays is shown in Exhibit 13.1.4.

Exhibit 13.1.4 Seven great things about First Choice all-inclusive holidays

The home of the all-inclusive	We're the all-inclusive experts – but you don't have to take our word for it. In 2013 we were named Best Large All Inclusive Holiday Company at the British Travel Awards
Dining	On top of a buffet or two, loads of hotels have *à la carte* restaurants plus extra treats like beach barbeques, crêpe stations and afternoon teas
Drink	Local drinks are part and parcel of our all-inclusive holidays. But some hotels up the ante with premium spirits and swish cocktail menus. At some, you'll even find optics in the bedrooms
Carefree indulgence	An all-inclusive holiday is about treating yourself without having to fork out every five minutes. And the set up can actually save you money, too
Essentials	With all our holidays, your flights, transfers and luggage allowance are included in the price, so you can relax knowing all the essentials are covered
24-Hour All Inclusive	Sign up for this and you won't have to set foot outside your hotel if you get an attack of the midnight munchies, or fancy another cocktail in the wee small hours
Ultra All Inclusive	On top of 24-Hour All Inclusive, this set up gives you extras like premium branded spirits and a bumper crop of activities, entertainment and water sports

Source: www.firstchoice.co.uk

New destinations are constantly being added and the range extended. Exhibit 13.1.5 shows the countries (as for the 2015 season) within which First Choice destinations are offered.

Exhibit 13.1.5 First Choice international destination list 2015

Aruba	Barbados	Bulgaria
Cape Verde	Costa Rica	Croatia
Cyprus	Dominican Republic	Egypt
Greece	India	Italy
Jamaica	Malta	Mauritius
Mexico	Montenegro	Morocco
Portugal	Spain	Thailand
Tunisia	Turkey	

Source: www.firstchoice.co.uk

The hotel group: Sandals, Jamaica

All-inclusive hotels and resorts in Jamaica have largely been developed by local entrepreneurs rather than international companies. This includes Gordon 'Butch' Stewart who founded the Sandals Resorts International (SRI) company, and the Issa family who founded the Issa Resorts Group and SuperClubs with the adult-only resort Hedonism II (Mintel, 2001).

The initial concept of the Sandals resort was to develop a hotel that catered for couples only and offered a full range of hospitality and leisure facilities. The group also developed wedding and honeymoon packages as part of the product offering.

A later development was carried out in 1999 when Sandals launched its new 'Beaches resort', which brought the all-inclusive idea to a wider range of market segments including singles, couples and families. The company has developed 'Kids Kamp' which caters for children and 'Ultra-Nannies' which offers a babysitting service to customers. This change in direction in 1999 has meant that the company can now target a wider customer base.

Jamaica relies on these chains to promote the island as a tourist destination and they are therefore critical to tourism receipts for the country as a whole. Since its founding in 1981, SRI has grown to encompass five brands: Sandals, Beaches resort, Grand Pineapple, Fowl Cay resort and Your Jamaican Villas. From a single hotel in Montego Bay it has expanded to cover 24 different locations across Caribbean countries – Antigua, The Bahamas, Grenada, Barbados, Saint Lucia, Turks and Caicos, and of course Jamaica.

THE COUNTRY: CUBA

The largest island in the Caribbean, Cuba lies off the south coast of Florida. It has used the development of the all-inclusive package as a major part of its tourism development strategy.

Fidel Castro took control of the island in 1959 and since then the island has been under communist rule. Cuba has a blend of cultural tourism and beach destinations, and there has been a growth in the number of hotels on the island over the past decade. Much of this development has been in the form of three-, four- and five-star all-inclusive hotels in key beach destinations such as Varadero, Cayo Largo, Cayo Coco and Santa Lucia. International hotel chains such as Super Clubs, Club Med, Sandals, Sol Melia and Iberostar have been active in the development of all-inclusive resorts in these areas of the island. Specialist tour operators such as Captivating Cuba have been active in promoting all-inclusive trips to Cuba with the optional extra of a cultural visit to Havana, the island's capital.

The normalization of US–Cuban diplomatic relations in July 2015 may have a profound effect on the Cuban economy and especially its tourism industry, which is likely to grow significantly in the future.

CONCLUSIONS

The growth of the all-inclusive holiday package has been due to a response by the tourism and hospitality sector to a changing pattern of consumer behaviour. It will be interesting to see whether this concept develops further, given that the drivers for the original growth – people's interest to travel and explore new destinations – has been replaced by an interest in value for money and control of expenditure.

DISCUSSION POINTS AND ESSAY QUESTIONS

1. Critically evaluate the reasons for the growth of consumers' interest in all-inclusive types of package holiday.
2. Carry out an in-depth study of a destination, tour operator or hotel chain that has used the all-inclusive concept as a major part of its strategic development. Assess the role of the all-inclusive concept in the future development of the chosen destination or organization.
3. Critically discuss the implications for the Cuban tourist industry of the normalization of diplomatic relations with its near neighbour the United States of America.

REFERENCES

ABTA (2013). *Travel Trends Report 2013*. ABTA, London. www.abta.com
ABTA (2015). *Travel Trends Report 2015*. ABTA, London. www.abta.com
Mintel (2001). *Adventure Travel. Global.* November. Mintel.
Mintel (2014). *All Inclusive Holidays.* June. Mintel.

CASE STUDY 13.2: See the bigger picture: positioning Burbank for tourists as the media capital of the world

Saskia Faulk

This case study details the behind-the-scenes strategy through which Burbank, California has emerged as a tourism destination over the past few decades, and how the city continues to attract tourists despite the draw of its better known neighbour, Hollywood. This surprising story begins during the Second World War, when the Lockheed aircraft plant in Burbank, California became one of the most strategic sites in the USA.

During the 1940s, in order to protect the aircraft manufacturer's massive installations from airborne attacks like that on Pearl Harbor, it was decided to disguise the entire Lockheed Corporation site, much as the British had done with their key military installations during the Battle of Britain. An army camouflage expert drafted to conduct the operation recruited artists, painters and set-designers from nearby movie studios Disney, Paramount and 20th Century Fox. They worked together for more than a year to secretly design a life-size 'set' made from sturdy tarpaulin which was fixed over the factories, air terminal and parking lots to give the illusion – from the air – of a large residential neighbourhood. In order to guarantee invisibility of the Lockheed plant and its 90,000 employees from enemy bombers, the attention to detail was impressive. The gardens surrounding the tidy rows of burlap houses were planted with trees made from bent wire and green- and brown-painted chicken feathers set on telephone poles. Full-size plywood cars were circulated on painted streets complete with fire hydrants which were disguised air-ducts for the factory below. During break times, Lockheed employees climbed onto the 'set' to walk around and hang up (or take down) what looked like laundry on garden clothes-lines. The initiative was so successful that, from a cockpit at cruising altitude, one of the world's leading military aircraft manufacturing plants looked like a peaceful California suburb (Lockheed Martin, 2013).

The plant escaped war-time bombing, and went on to employ some of the decommissioned military personnel returning from the war who came to settle down in Lockheed's company town. Yet within half a century the Lockheed plant closed, leaving many unemployed and a polluted industrial site in its stead. Since the 1920s, Burbank had grown in step with Lockheed. The aircraft giant still employed an estimated 66,500 workers (City of Burbank, 1999) until closure procedures set in for Lockheed aerospace in the 1980s. At century's end, with the disappearance of its main employer and core identity, the city of Burbank had lost its sense of direction and was economically stagnant. Lockheed Corporation's plant was dismantled and became a shopping mall, and its adjoining airfield became the Bob Hope Airport. Clearly, it was urgent to identify a new strategy for relaunching the city's business and tourism base.

RELAUNCHING BURBANK'S TOURISM BASE

It was an interesting twist of fate to realize that the real engine of Burbank was once again hidden behind the scenes, just as the Lockheed plant had been during the war. And the same kinds of people who designed the Lockheed 'set' were once again of prime importance. This new engine was the movie and entertainment sector which had discreetly grown to play the leading role in Burbank's economy.

Of course everyone knows about Hollywood, the iconic byword for entertainment. Hollywood is Burbank's immediate neighbour to the south. From a positioning standpoint, Hollywood was first into the entertainment tourism attraction game. Already in the 1920s Hollywood had extravagant hotels and the landmark Chinese Theater. Other movie-centred attractions such as The Walk of Fame were developed for tourists in the 1950s, while fans made pilgrimages to see movie stars' homes, hang-outs and shops. Today Hollywood still draws huge crowds for the same old haunts as well as for the frequent world film premieres and awards ceremonies such as the Oscars.

Yet by the 1990s Burbank had, without any fanfare, become the functional nerve centre of US movies and television productions. Hardly any productions were coming out of Hollywood any more, with the notable exception of Paramount Studios movies. Today Hollywood has far fewer soundstages and production facilities than Burbank. Confusion results from the general tendency to call everywhere relevant to movies 'Hollywood' if it is in California, regardless of the real address. The facts speak for themselves. Burbank is home to more than 1000 entertainment industry headquarters and offices. These include world leaders such as ABC Television Network, Cartoon Network, Nickelodeon, The Walt Disney Company (World Headquarters), Warner Bros, and other entertainment and creative industry players, which is why it is often called the 'media capital of the world'. Yet the general public remains largely ignorant about Burbank's central role in the movie business, apart from serious movie and series fans who read all the credits at the end of productions.

The time had come for Burbank city leaders to make manifest all that has been happening while the public remained fixated on 'Hollywood'. Their job was to guide interested visitors towards Burbank's authentic, living attractions in the wellspring of today's entertainment industry. For this reason, too, Burbank marketing strategy planners had their work cut out for them: how to adjust perceptions to this reality without being tedious.

Help came from an unexpected quarter: the mocking banter of a television talk-show host. Some older readers might remember *Tonight* show host Johnny Carson, who frequently made sarcastic mention of 'beautiful downtown Burbank'. The city could have been insulted by that perception, which in the 1970s and 1980s may have held a grain of blue-collar truth. Instead, the city recognized that it already had – unwittingly – national brand recognition. Brand equity, even. As Burbank's Mayor Marsha Ramos said: 'The Tonight Show put us on the map. Without that line from Johnny Carson . . . most people wouldn't even know that we exist' (James and Gold, 2007). All city planners needed to do now was align the statement's adjective 'beautiful' with the city's reality.

IDENTIFYING A POSITIONING STRATEGY

Even with such clear communications and branding tasks in mind, it was nonetheless a very difficult marketing proposition to create a positioning strategy for Burbank, which is overshadowed by the stellar reputation of its world-famous neighbour Hollywood. In 2011 the city's destination management organization, Visit Burbank, decided to meet this exceptional challenge head-on with a comprehensive tourism strategy centred on the idea that Burbank is the beating heart of movie and television production. The impetus for the idea came from grafting a tourism reputation on its existing national reputation within the entertainment business, 'Capitalizing on what we really already have, but restating it for the tourism market', as a Burbank marketing staffer puts it. It is an explicit positioning next to Hollywood, which until then had remained implicit.

Thus, with this clear vision, Burbank worked to bring the city's reality on the ground in line with growing public awareness of the city as the home of many favourite movies and shows. A number of areas were identified for improvement, such as:

- identification and analysis of local attractions consistent with the theme of being an entertainment industry centre
- interpretation and packaging of attractions and their communication
- renewed efforts to improve and then maintain the city's attractiveness to visitors, particularly its 'downtown' commercial area, including the elaboration of a downtown events programme to include comedy, movies and cars, consistent with the entertainment industry theme
- improved communication of hospitality offerings in Burbank, to include meetings and convention facilities, resulting in the foundation in 2011 of the Burbank Hospitality Association, which is behind the Visit Burbank initiatives (see www.visitburbank.com).

IMPROVING THE ATTRACTIVENESS OF THE DOWNTOWN DISTRICT

So that tourists enjoy their visit to Burbank, plan prolonged stays and indulge in retail and entertainment, city planners realized that the downtown area needed revitalization. In 2003 the Downtown Burbank Partnership (DBP) was founded to 'Create a vibrant and exciting commercial district with strategic capital improvements, enhanced maintenance and security, innovative marketing, and numerous events year round' (DBP, 2013). Thanks in part to the work of the DBP, the city-centre downtown district boasts more than 400 stores and restaurants as well as a shopping mall. There are more than 9000 free parking spaces, which is an unusual boon for drivers compared with other city centres on the west coast. The Partnership's mission is as follows:

> To promote Downtown Burbank as a vibrant entertainment and shopping destination with a dynamic street scene, enticing restaurants and an authentic urban vibe. This is accomplished by modernizing the physical infrastructure, keeping the District clean and

safe, establishing a brand identity, and advocating for the best interests of businesses and property owners in downtown Burbank.

(DBP, 2013)

Much work has gone into augmenting the impression of safety and cleanliness for visitors, such as maintaining an extra level of street cleaning with power washers. In addition, improving the flow of cars and pedestrians is a constant concern for any city centre, which is partially alleviated by the parking programme delivering thousands of easily accessible and free parking spaces. Currently nine electric vehicle charging stations are installed, and many more are programmed in order to encourage less polluting alternatives for visitors.

Through the DBP, free WiFi is offered in the downtown area, including the train station, used by 180,000 visitors yearly. The DBP actively encourages improvements to storefront facades, awnings and display windows, and sidewalk planters. These initiatives are pleasant for tourists, yet they have further-reaching consequences too: they become additional reasons to relocate to (or stay in) Burbank for business owners because life is improved and facilitated for both customers and employees. This is all very well, one might say, but what does Burbank have to offer visitors?

HOLLYWOOD IS FAMOUS BUT BURBANK IS WHERE IT REALLY HAPPENS: LIVING ATTRACTIONS

Over recent years, Burbank has earned nicknames like 'media capital of the world' and 'animation capital of the world'. Consistent with this reputation, visitors can participate in the life of productions and mingle with the human resources involved, both directly by being present at the taping of a live show, for example, or indirectly by going to the local cafés and restaurants packed with actors, directors, production people and script writers. About 100,000 employees make a living in Burbank – it is a working city, not a landmark (which some would say Hollywood has become), and thus a 'mecca' for movie and television fans.

Movie and television fans can find information, maps and GPS coordinates, and download mobile apps to find Burbank locations. They can dine at the historic Bob's Big Boy restaurant, featured in the film *Heat*, where Robert de Niro's character recruited the restaurant's dishwasher. They can book a room at The Safari Inn, which featured in *Apollo 13*. When the tyrannosaurus rex in Steven Spielberg's *The Lost World* prowled a city, it was in downtown Burbank. Parts of car chases in *Terminator 2: Judgement Day* were filmed in the city's concrete flood-control channels. Other movies and series that feature Burbank locations include *Behind the Candelabra*, *Chuck*, *Father of the Bride*, *Harlem Nights*, *Parks and Recreation*, *Reservoir Dogs*, *The Big Bang Theory*, *The Mentalist*, and *The Office*. Websites such as seeing-stars.com and filmaps.com provide such information. Visitors can also take tours of the different studios located in Burbank, which include Disney world headquarters, Warner Bros and NBC (now known as 'The Burbank Studios'). Warner Bros is the oldest studio in Burbank. Visitors on this studio tour can see backlot sets from *Rebel Without a Cause*, *Casablanca* and *Spiderman*, as well as viewing sound stages where actual filming is taking place. Burbank is home, since 1940, to the grandiose Disney world headquarters designed by Michael Graves, which features classic landmarks including a water tower, iconic gate, seven dwarves on its façade, and a sorcerer's hat. For the most part, the studios limit visitors because they are fully functioning facilities. The Walt Disney Studios feature in a number of films including *Saving Mr. Banks*, in which Tom Hanks brings Walt Disney to life.

When you are a fan, probably the most exciting experience is to see where your favourite TV shows are made. Burbank offers lots of choices to join the live audience at studio tapings. At Warner Bros Studios, for example, one can watch live shows like *2 Broke Girls*, *Friends*, *Mike & Molly*, *Mom*, *The Big Bang Theory*, *The Mentalist* and *Two and A Half Men*. Other big draws include the *Ellen DeGeneres Show* and *Conan*.

Although a number of studios do not permit tours to take place, they give an idea of what calibre of actors, singers, artists, animators, producers and directors work and walk the streets of Burbank, such as Nickelodeon Animation Studios (makers of *Sponge Bob SquarePants*, *T.U.F.F. Puppy* and more) and Cartoon Network (makers of *Star Wars: Clone Wars*, *The Powerpuff Girls*, and others), just to name two of many.

Just as important as the physical sites, attractions and entertainment opportunities is the excitement that visitors feel when breathing the same air as movie stars, sipping at a bar where everyone is talking about movies, and enjoying a meal where people at the next table are industry insiders discussing creative opportunities. Incidentally, Burbank boasts one of the top five highest-grossing cinemas in the US, another illustration of the importance of entertainment there. It is also important to many visitors to live their holiday-sized slice of the California dream and laid-back glamour lifestyle, and maybe even see a star or two. Many of entertainment's big names were born and bred in Burbank: Blake Lively, Elijah Wood, Debbie Reynolds and Tim Burton to name a few.

EVENTS IN BURBANK: A SAMPLE

Downtown Burbank Car Classic attracts visitors, vintage car fans and movie buffs with its unique 'Hollywood angle'. The outdoor exhibit and associated events held on the streets of the Downtown have presented the Batmobile, celebrity cars and vehicles that featured prominently in movies.

The Burbank Arts Festival showcases the city's own digital artists and production companies. More than 130 artists of all kinds exhibit, demonstrate, sell artworks and books, and participate in the events taking place. Some of the artists have contributed their ideas, art or visual effects to some of the most successful animation films in history for Burbank hometown companies Disney, Cartoon Network, Nickelodeon and others.

The Burbank Comedy Festival brings together more than 200 emerging comedy stars with national headliners for a week-long celebration of comedy packed with special events highlighting different comedy genres, including showcases, workshops, industry panels and live podcasts.

The Burbank International Film Festival focuses on the film-makers of tomorrow as they struggle to emerge today with their first cinematographic works. It is a great opportunity for ambitious talent working at Burbank studios, production companies and related entertainment companies to showcase themselves and network with industry leaders.

The Rink in Downtown Burbank makes ice-skating part of month-long holiday season themed evenings.

CTN Animation Expo brings together more than 6000 animators, studio executives, students, stars and fans from all over the world for workshops, exhibits, discussions and screenings. During the Expo, by official proclamation, Burbank citywide celebrates 'Animation Week'.

Magnolia Park is not an event, but a Burbank neighbourhood for serious vintage shopping in a preserved, lush 1950s atmosphere . . . and possible star-spotting too.

A CLOSE NETWORK OF ATTRACTIONS

Burbank has its own airport, the Burbank Bob Hope Airport, founded on the former Lockheed site described above. It is used by more than 5 million passengers a year, and is a stress-free alternative to the bustling Los Angeles airport. Burbank is also fortunate in being close – but not too close – to downtown Los Angeles thanks to the Metrolink train to LA and 54 other stations in the area. Downtown LA is 12 miles away and Hollywood is 5 miles away. For die-hard fans, Universal Studios is even closer, and Beverly Hills (star home tour) is 12 miles away. Natural beauty is also close at hand in Griffith Park, a massive urban green space, and in the Verdugo Mountains and Hollywood Hills, where there are miles of hiking and horse-riding trails, as well as million-dollar homes.

TOURISM DIVERSIFICATION STRATEGY

According to focus groups conducted by the Burbank Hospitality Association, a primary reason for tourists wanting to visit Burbank is the entertainment industry. Yet the city aims to diversify its visitors to conventions and business tourism in other sectors, showcasing its 50,000 square feet of convention space. The Burbank Hospitality Association was founded in 2011 with the primary mission of stimulating economic development through tourism, and promotes Burbank as a premier business and leisure destination. Around the world probably the best known event held in the city is the biggest yearly animators convention, CTN Animation Expo.

BURBANK'S CREATIVE COMMUNICATIONS STRATEGY

The destination management organization Visit Burbank works to communicate the attractions and benefits of visiting Burbank. Among the marketing materials developed by this association are a website, a Twitter feed, a Facebook page, and a multi-year marketing campaign reaching more than 31 million consumers via print and digital media outlets.

The organization works actively in cooperation with the Los Angeles Tourism and Convention Board to increase access to the massive market of visitors heading to LA.

The materials developed in 2012 used the tagline 'The town behind the tinsel' to position Burbank as the place where the entertainment industry lives and breathes. This is in implied comparison with Hollywood, or 'Tinseltown'. The website visitburbank.com features star-quality photos and movie-style jargon, with titles such as 'In Burbank, you're set for action'; 'How will you script your unforgettable stay in Burbank?'; and 'Get behind the scenes'. It features trip ideas with itineraries and several personalized stories developed to showcase different visitor interests: California car culture, vintage shopping, star-spotting and family fun. In these stories, complete with photos and itineraries, different characters have been developed to humanize the different tourist interests, such as car fanatic Tony, who recounts his experiences cruising around town and visiting the Downtown Burbank Car Classic. Kristine gives advice on various Burbank child-friendly attractions and activities, such as the Warner Bros Studio Tour Hollywood, and Pickwick Gardens. Daphne gives tips about vintage shopping in Magnolia Park as she seeks an outfit for a *Mad Men*-themed party. Visitors are invited to submit their own 'Burbank stories' too.

THE NEXT STAGE IN BURBANK'S BRANDING EVOLUTION

In 2015 the Burbank Hospitality Association decided to work on communicating how close it is to Los Angeles, and that it has its own airport. It determined that Burbank could be better positioned as a convenient base to experience the southern Californian lifestyle and explore Los Angeles without getting into that city's infamous traffic jams and stress: it is very close to many key attractions in and around LA.

In light of these findings and recommendations, it was decided to change the tagline from 'The town behind the tinsel' to 'See the bigger picture', thus avoiding the association of Burbank with the connotations of 'town'. This new tagline gives Burbank star status in its own right rather than working from an implied comparison with Hollywood. In addition, the use of the verb 'see' is an invitation, a call to action to see all there is to see in the Burbank area, and associates Burbank directly with the movie industry. Finally, due to the clear trend towards booking online, it is a major priority of the organization to enrich the current site with more itineraries and ideas, and integrate a more interactive aspect to the site. Go to visitburbank.com to see the latest version of this site.

WHAT TOURISM BOARDS CAN LEARN FROM BURBANK

The story of Burbank demonstrates the importance of identifying potential attractions that exist outside the public eye but may not have been identified as such, interpreted or used to position the destination in a unique and powerful way. In this case the professional identity of the city, as a world reference for the entertainment and creative industries and as the world media capital, was identified and packaged as a reason to visit for non-industry-insiders. Interestingly, in the case of Burbank this concerns companies and industrial sites, such as studios, to which visitors have no access but in which they are interested nonetheless. A marketing strategy like Burbank's demonstrates the necessity of identifying and unearthing sources of value for visitors.

It also crystallizes the importance of determining how to showcase these attractions and communicate about them in a compelling and integrated way.

DISCUSSION POINTS AND ESSAY QUESTIONS

1. Identify a town, city or region near you with which you are familiar. List its potential attractions – whether or not they are currently identified as such. Analyse your list and classify the potential attractions into categories or themes. Identify which categories or themes have the most potential to serve a market need, such as sports, cultural, family, nature or other activities.
2. Once you have inventoried potentially interesting sites, entertainment or attractions for visitors, consider how you could group these attractions together to form a thematic itinerary, or several possible themes. Identify how a tourist board could package them and communicate around them in order to constitute a new selling point for the town, city or region.
3. Now consider what kinds of potential attractions or destinations exist that are not currently considered attractive: sites where locals might even say 'no-one would be interested to see that!'. Reflect, as Burbank did, about how to communicate their value to visitors, even if a 'niche' market. Define a profile of potential visitors who would be interested in these sites.
4. As this case study was being written, Burbank was undergoing its branding evolution encapsulated by the new tagline 'See the bigger picture'. Go to visitburbank. com to see what the website has become. Given the history recounted in this case, critically analyse the website according to how it expresses brand values implied by this new tagline and the stated goal of being seen as the 'media capital of the world'. Present your findings.

REFERENCES

City of Burbank (1999). *Historic Preservation Plan*. Prepared by San Buenaventura Research Associates. www.burbankca.gov/home/showdocument?id=3014
DBP (2013). *Annual Report 2013*. Downtown Burbank Partnership, Burbank, CA.
James, M. and Gold, M. (2007). NBC Socks it to Burbank. *Los Angeles Times* 11 October. http://articles.latimes.com/2007/oct/11/business/fi-nbc11
Lockheed Martin (2013). *Lockheed during World War II: Operation Camouflage*. www.lockheedmartin.com/us/100years/stories/camouflage.html

Topical issues in consumer behaviour

This part highlights topical issues in consumer behaviour in the tourism field which are currently exercising the minds of academics and practitioners alike. The subjects are as follows:

- the debate about the 'ethical tourist' and the extent to which such a market segment exists
- the emergence of new markets and types of demand, and the reasons that underpin their growth
- the rise in use of the internet and social media in tourism.

In all cases we endeavour to present a balanced discussion that makes the key issues clear. At a time when the tourism industry and tourist behaviour is changing so rapidly, it is vital that all those involved in tourism are aware of these topical issues.

CHAPTER 14

The 'ethical tourist': myth or reality?

Since this book was first published, in 1999, there have been major developments in the debate about ethical issues in tourism and their relationship with tourist behaviour. In this chapter we revisit the concept of the 'green tourist', which was a major topic of debate in the 1990s, particularly among academics. We then go on to look at other developments that have taken place in the field of ethical tourism in the past few years.

But let us begin, back in the 1990s, with the concept of the green tourist that was in vogue in that decade.

The green tourist?

In a debate where terms are used frequently but are rarely defined, we should perhaps begin by talking briefly about what we mean by the term 'green'. Most definitions of the term focus on the natural physical environment. This is in contrast to the now more fashionable term 'sustainable', which tends to be concerned with the future and with the balance between the environment, society and the economic system. In recent years, environmental or green issues have come to the forefront of public debate in many countries. These have included global warming, animal welfare and wildlife conservation, organic food, pollution and the recycling of waste products. In the late 1980s and early 1990s a view developed that there was now a green consumer, who considered environmental issues when deciding which product to buy or not to buy. One of the first illustrations of this was a consumer boycott of aerosol-based products that contained chlorofluorocarbons (CFCs) in the late 1980s, after the media and pressure groups alerted consumers to the environmental impact of these CFCs. This led to companies replacing CFCs with other ingredients.

Another example of the so-called green consumer was seen to be the growing concern with food safety and quality and an increase in demand for organic food. Politicians, too, recognized the rise of the green consumer in the late 1980s and early

1990s, and rushed to endorse policies that were seen to be environmentally friendly. In its most extreme manifestation, this development in public opinion led to the growth of green political parties in the UK and France, for example. Since the 1990s, however, in the UK at least, public concern with environmental issues appears to have lessened.

It is important to recognize that most of what we have been discussing has been largely viewed from a UK perspective. Consumers have been interested in a range of environmental issues for many years in Germany, for instance, and the general level of public concern with these issues there is consistently higher.

Tourism, green issues and sustainability

While there has been relatively little explicit evidence of concern over green issues on the part of tourists, that is not to say that there has been no interest in the subject from anyone. In the 1980s and 1990s there was considerable debate worldwide on the environmental impacts of tourism and on the links between green issues and tourism. It became a high-profile subject in these years because of a number of factors:

- the writings of academics about the impacts of tourism, including the highly influential book by Mathieson and Wall (1982)
- popular, if rather subjective, books that have set out to influence the behaviour of tourists themselves, including Wood and House (1991); Elkington and Hailes (1992)
- proactive action on behalf of North American hospitality organizations such as Intercontinental and Canadian Pacific, designed to make their activities more environmentally friendly
- the work of pressure groups, notably Tourism Concern
- high-profile policy statements and initiatives by government agencies such as those made in the UK in the early 1990s.

As the debate developed, the term 'green tourist' did not achieve the acceptance that the phrase 'green consumer' has in general. The whole debate became complex, with a series of different terms being used.

Figure 14.1 shows some of the other words and phrases that were often used instead of the term green in relation to both tourists and tourism.

Although these words are used apparently interchangeably with the term green, some of them are different in subtle ways.

- **Eco-tourists** are largely motivated by a desire to see the natural history of a destination. In addition they may or may not be interested in protecting the environment of the area, but it is certainly not their main concern.
- **Alternative tourism** usually means tourism that is less packaged and is smaller scale. It is assumed that this will mean it is 'greener' than mass-market package tourism, but this is not necessarily the case.
- **Intelligent tourism** is related to the growing desire of some tourists to learn

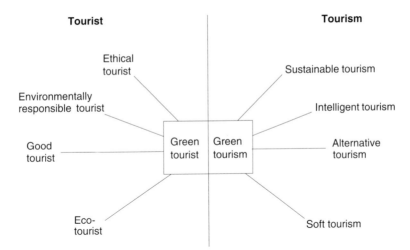

Figure 14.1 Alternative terms for green tourists and green tourism

something new while they are on vacation. It is thus associated with particular forms of tourism that might be seen as educational, including cultural
tourism and study holidays. Again, there is nothing inherently green about such
holidays.

- **Sustainable tourism** is concerned with social justice and economic viability as
well as the physical environment, and is also about the future. Both of these differentiate it from mainstream green issues and green concerns.
- **Ethical tourists** will be concerned with a broader range of issues than the arche-
typal green tourist. For example, they may be interested in human resource policies in the tourism industry, such as pay levels and the employment of local labour,
as well as the ways in which the economic benefits of tourism are distributed
throughout the economy. The term 'ethical tourist' is now the most commonly
used.

Figure 14.2 shows some of the influences that informed and interested tourists about
green issues in the 1990s.

Issues of concern to green tourists

Figure 14.3 identifies a selection of issues that might be expected to be of concern to
green tourists.

Clearly, many of these are interrelated, such as transport and pollution; and wildlife
and conservation. However, it is important to recognize that they can be seen from
different perspectives and they can exist in more than one 'box' at a time.

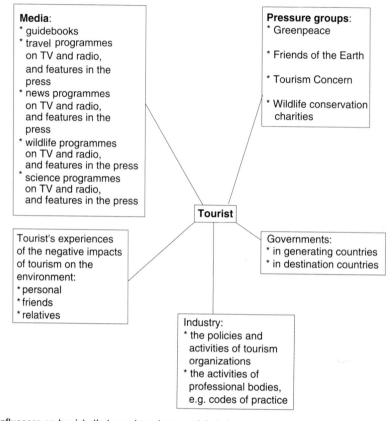

Media:
* guidebooks
* travel programmes on TV and radio, and features in the press
* news programmes on TV and radio, and features in the press
* wildlife programmes on TV and radio, and features in the press
* science programmes on TV and radio, and features in the press

Pressure groups:
* Greenpeace
* Friends of the Earth
* Tourism Concern
* Wildlife conservation charities

Tourist's experiences of the negative impacts of tourism on the environment:
* personal
* friends
* relatives

Tourist

Governments:
* in generating countries
* in destination countries

Industry:
* the policies and activities of tourism organizations
* the activities of professional bodies, e.g. codes of practice

Figure 14.2 Influences on tourists that may have increased their interest in green issues in the 1990s

Shades of green tourists?

As in any complex market, one cannot really talk about green tourists as if they were a homogeneous group. Tourists will each have their own views, which will determine their behaviour and differentiate them from other tourists. It is therefore perhaps better to talk in terms of 'shades' of green tourist, from dark green tourists to those with no hint of green whatsoever.

Figure 14.4 offers a representation of this concept and suggests some hypothetical examples of what it might mean in practice, in relation to tourist behaviour.

The different shades of green may reflect differences between consumers in terms of their:

* awareness and knowledge of the issues
* attitudes towards the environment in general
* other priorities in life such as making a living
* health, family commitments and housing.

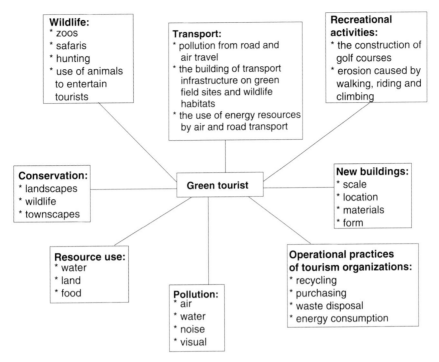

Figure 14.3 Issues that may concern the green tourist

Motivations of green tourists

Green tourists might be influenced by a number of motivators, including:

- an altruistic belief in the need to protect the environment
- a desire to feel good about their behaviour as tourists
- a wish to improve their image among friends and relatives by being seen to be concerned with environmental issues.

Whatever the motivation to be a green tourist, it may not always be converted into actual behaviour due to the influence of a range of determinants.

Key determinants of behaviour

The main determinants that may prevent tourists from being able to behave in a greener manner include:

- information obtained from the media and pressure groups
- amount of disposable income and other concerns such as poor housing or unemployment

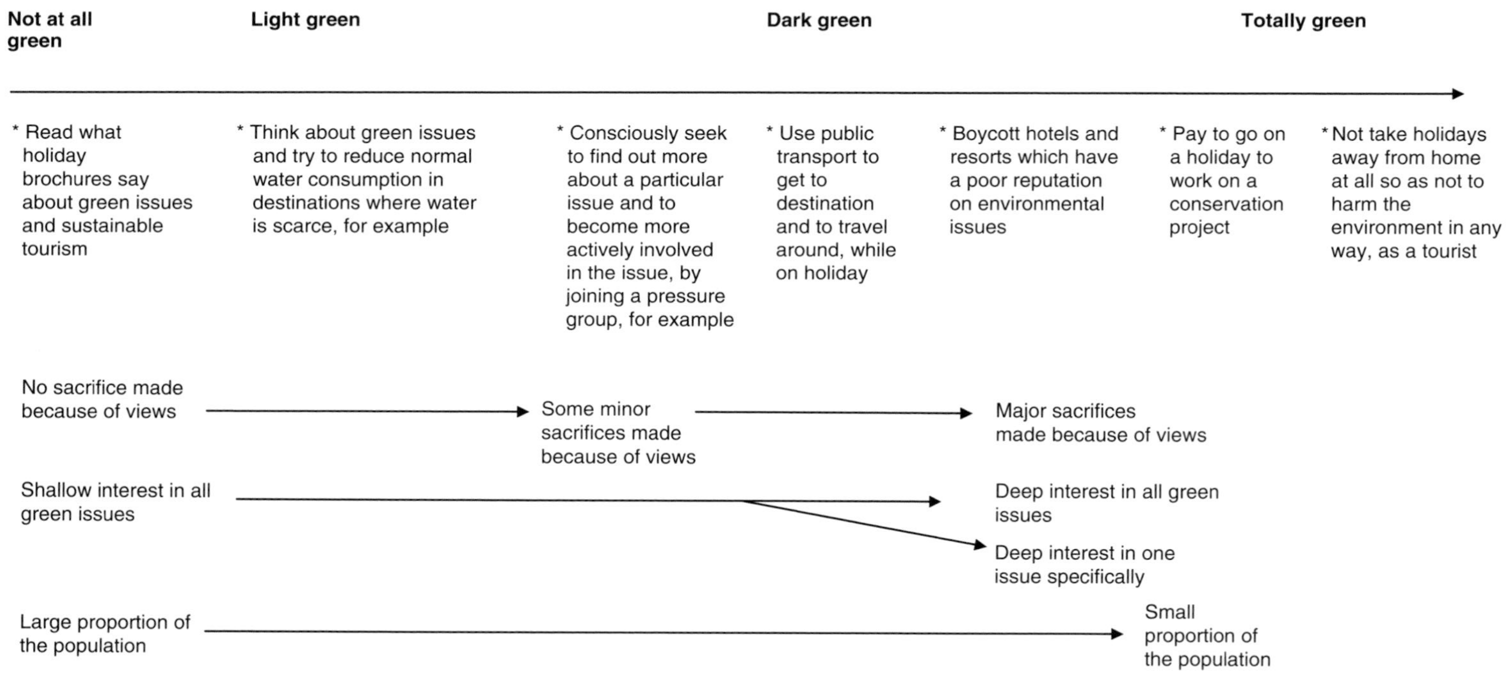

Not at all green	Light green	Dark green	Totally green
* Read what holiday brochures say about green issues and sustainable tourism	* Think about green issues and try to reduce normal water consumption in destinations where water is scarce, for example	* Use public transport to get to destination and to travel around, while on holiday	* Not take holidays away from home at all so as not to harm the environment in any way, as a tourist
	* Consciously seek to find out more about a particular issue and to become more actively involved in the issue, by joining a pressure group, for example	* Boycott hotels and resorts which have a poor reputation on environmental issues	* Pay to go on a holiday to work on a conservation project

No sacrifice made because of views ————→ Some minor sacrifices made because of views ————→ Major sacrifices made because of views

Shallow interest in all green issues ————————————→ Deep interest in all green issues

Deep interest in one issue specifically

Large proportion of the population ————————————————————→ Small proportion of the population

Figure 14.4 'Shades of green consumer' in tourism

- personal previous experience or that of friends and relatives
- ownership or non-ownership of a private car
- interest in particular issues such as animal welfare or activities such as riding and climbing
- preferences for particular types of holiday – beach, sightseeing, touring – and different destinations
- membership of particular environmental pressure groups and conservation organizations such as Greenpeace and the Worldwide Fund for Nature
- advice received from the industry, notably tour operators.

It is now time to see how these motivators and determinants are, or are not, reflected in actual tourism demand.

Evidence for the existence of green tourists

Although much was written about the green tourist in the 1990s, there was relatively little empirical research to establish the existence of this market segment. However, there seems little doubt that tourists have been interested in the environmental quality of the destination areas where they spend their holidays since the early 1990s.

A report by BAT Leisure Research Institute in 1993, for example, claimed that 'of ten criteria for a quality holiday listed by consumers, seven related to the environment' (Opaschowski, 1993). Guest surveys conducted by the German tour operator TUI also showed that, for German tourists at least, environmental quality did affect their satisfaction with their holiday. Figure 14.5 clearly demonstrates this fact in relation to five ecological criteria, which were identified by TUI, in relation to Cyprus. However, this was more about consumers' vested interest in the environment as a key determinant of the quality of their holiday experience than about tourists' concerns with the impact of tourism on destinations in general. The green tourist should surely be interested in tourism in all destinations, not just where they are holidaying that year.

If the latter definition is used then there would appear to be relatively little explicit evidence for the existence of the green tourist. In most cases, tourists either seemed unaware of the issues, or had some awareness but did not seem to modify their behaviour or demands as a result. In general, there appeared little evidence for consumers boycotting certain pursuits in tourism because of their concerns over environmental issues. Few visitors to Spain, Greece or Turkey appeared willing to forego the pleasure of a swimming pool, for instance, to reduce pressure on scarce local water resources.

Likewise, relatively few tourists seemed to make decisions based on environmental concerns. For example, very few tourists appeared to:

- choose an airline based on the effectiveness of its environmental management practices

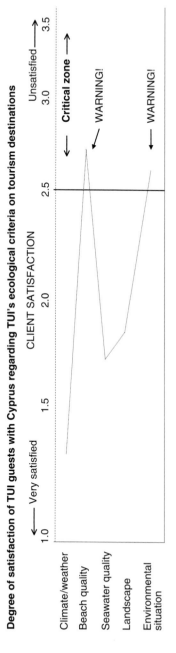

Figure 14.5 Guests' views on the environmental quality of their resort in Cyprus, 1992 (reproduced by kind permission of TUI)

- boycott hotels which did not recycle waste, or which provided complimentary toiletries that had been tested on animals in their bathrooms
- campaign against the building of new theme parks and accommodation units that destroyed wildlife habitats.

By the end of the 1990s, the only real examples of tourists' concern with environmental issues, among British tourists at least, related to wildlife. Tourists responded, to some extent, to appeals to:

- not buy souvenirs made from parts of animals
- not be photographed with monkeys and bears that are kept in captivity and 'exploited' by resort photographers
- not attend bullfights or festivals that are alleged to involve cruelty to animals.

Interestingly, these issues to which tourists responded to some degree were ones that had been highlighted by the media and animal welfare pressure groups.

However, at the other extreme, we can recognize the growth of a small, distinct niche of 'dark green' tourists. One manifestation of this development is the growth of conservation holidays, where tourists spend their holiday doing voluntary work on environmental projects. This trend began to develop in the early 1990s and has continued to grow.

The wellknown guidebook author Arthur Frommer (1996) identified a number of such holidays, including:

- the Sierra Club in the USA and its projects to protect wilderness areas in areas such as the Adirondack Forest Preserve in New York State
- the American-based La Sabranenque Restoration Project organization which operates in Europe to restore decaying villages
- Earthwatch, based in Massachusetts, USA, which organizes holidays whose volunteers work on environmental research projects.

Such projects also exist in the UK, for both adults and children, run by organizations such as the British Trust for Conservation Volunteers and the National Trust.

Some commentators also seem to view the growth of ecotourism as evidence for the rise of the green tourist. However, while there is no doubt that eco-tourism has been growing rapidly, it is questionable whether those who take such trips can be viewed as green tourists.

They are motivated mainly by a desire to experience the ecology of destinations at close quarters and to get off the beaten track. This is different from being committed to taking holidays that are environmentally friendly. In some ways one could argue that, by going off the normal tourist routes, eco-tourists are responsible for spreading the negative environmental impacts of tourism to new areas. Therefore their activities may be harmful even though their intentions are good.

It appears that there seemed to be little interest in green tourism among most tourists in the 1990s, except for a small niche market of dark green tourists.

The tourism industry and the 'green challenge' in the 1990s

While there is little evidence of widespread environmental concern among tourists in the 1990s, the tourism industry has sought to take initiatives on the environment in recent years. This interest dates in most cases from the late 1980s or early 1990s when the general debate on the environment reached its zenith with the consumer boycott of CFC-based aerosols and the highly publicized concerns over global warming.

Governments, keen to appear responsive to the concerns of voters, sought to show that they too were concerned about the environment. This is the context in which many tourism organizations began to take an active interest in the environment. They were responding to the perceived threat of potential government regulation of the tourism industry.

Industry action took a number of forms.

- Tour operators began to include information on environmental issues for their clients and have started to encourage them to become more concerned about the environment.
- Hotel chains such as Grecotel adopted environmental management policies and devised campaigns to raise tourists' awareness of environmental issues in destinations in Greece.
- Organizations began to sponsor award schemes for environmentally friendly tourism, such as British Airways' sponsorship of the 'Tourism for Tomorrow' awards.

Many people criticized the tokenistic approach to the environment taken by many tourism organizations. For example, planting a new tree for every guest who stayed at a hotel, or giving a few pennies to an environmental charity for each tourist who booked a holiday, can certainly be viewed as cosmetic. However, perhaps it could be argued that in taking such action the industry was just reflecting the general lack of in-depth interest in environmental issues of most tourists.

At the other end of the spectrum, new organizations sprung up targeting dark green tourists and tried to sell them green holidays such as eco-tourism packages.

From green tourism to ethical tourism

Since the 1990s there has been a fundamental change in the debate about so-called 'sustainable tourism'. The change has been so profound that now one rarely hears anyone talking about 'green tourism' or 'green tourists', and those who do are seen as odd and not as tourists.

The terms used in Figure 14.1, which were so trendy in the 1990s, now look outdated. In the debate over ethics in tourism, the new in-terms and buzzwords are:

- **ethical tourism**, which focuses on the impacts and behaviour of tourists, and attempts to apply moral values and concepts more to the practices of tourism

- **responsible tourism**, which implies restraint and a sense of responsibility on behalf of both tourists and the tourism industry and its activities and impacts
- **fair trade tourism** and the idea that tourists should pay a fair price for the vacation they enjoy and that their vacation should not be enjoyed at the expense of local people; this has mirrored the growing concept of fair trade in relation to commodities such as coffee and tea
- **pro-poor tourism** where the emphasis is on using tourism as a vehicle to reduce poverty and stimulate social and economic development.

These developments in terminology reflect a fundamental shift in the debate over the ethics of tourism and tourist behaviour, notably:

- a move away from being concerned just about the physical environment towards a broader interest in the social and economic impacts of tourism
- a switch from seeing tourism as something with negative impacts that have to be managed to something that can also have positive impacts
- a reduced reliance on government action and regulation and greater emphasis on the potential role of the industry and tourists themselves as positive agents of change.

This idea is underpinned by the rise of the concept of **corporate social responsibility**, which is now so fashionable in the business world.

These changes in thinking in tourism mirror developments in industry and society as a whole, which have seen:

- pressure groups changing from outright opposition to companies and their actions, to engaging in partnerships with these companies in an endeavour to influence their behaviour
- a loss of faith and confidence in governments and their ability to achieve positive changes in the impacts of tourism in destinations
- greater emphasis on the behaviour of tourists themselves, particularly in terms of where they are seen to behave unethically.

The issues

In recent years the ethical issues that have been most prominent have been those defined by the media. Media coverage of issues has meant that they come to the attention of the tourists themselves, and this makes governments and industry organizations want to be seen to be addressing them.

The highest-profile ethical issues in the past few years have included:

- **climate change, global warming** and the **carbon footprint** of tourists, particularly when they travel by air

- **sex tourism** and **child exploitation**, particularly in relation to mega-events such as the World Cup and the Olympics
- the **wages and working conditions** of those who work in the hospitality sector in destinations
- the negative impact of tourism on **indigenous wildlife** in destinations
- **water resources** and their apparent over-use by tourists in destinations that experience water shortages
- the **leakage of economic benefits** in some destinations which means that local people gain relatively little from the presence of tourists in their community
- relations between hosts and tourists and the apparent lack of **mutual respect** in many destinations
- the allegedly **unethical marketing** undertaken by some sectors of the tourism industry, such as timeshare operators and some budget airlines.

Industry takes the lead

An interesting development in recent years has been the drivers of the limited improvements we have seen in the ethics of the tourism industry.

Although supra-governmental bodies such as the European Commission and the UNWTO have issued policies and strategies, the impact of their actions appears to have been limited. The evidence about the attitudes of tourists themselves is limited and sometimes contradictory. However, there appears to be little evidence that ethics is a major factor in the vacation decisions of the overwhelming majority of tourists, nor do most seem willing to pay more for what is supposedly a more ethical product. This may reflect a lack of commitment, or perhaps a lack of confidence in the claims made by the industry about their products. It may also be a reflection of the global economic crisis, for we often find that when economies enter recession, consumers' interest in ethical tourism wanes as they have other more pressing concerns on their mind.

It is interesting therefore that it is the industry itself that has taken the lead, running ahead of pressure from either governments or consumers. Many companies have gone farther than either the law requires or consumer demand suggests they should.

Accor, through its Planet 21 initiative and the research that has driven it, has identified the scale of the problem of water consumption in the food chain; and some of the most innovative work on child sexual exploitation has been undertaken by the tour operator TUI in the Netherlands. Many tour operators now encourage customers to buy souvenirs that are made locally to maximize the economic benefits of tourism for local people.

Perhaps companies believe that action they take today will either prevent the need for future government regulation, or improve their media image, or bring them long-term rewards in terms of attracting new customers or increasing customer loyalty. However, that looks, today, more like an act of faith than an outcome backed by concrete evidence.

The rise of the concept of responsible tourism

Authors such as Harold Goodwin (2011) have argued that the term 'responsible' is a better one to use than 'sustainable'. His idea is that the ethical challenges in tourism can be solved only if every stakeholder accepts their responsibility for the outcome. These stakeholders include tourists themselves, the tourism industry, destination communities, governments, and so on.

For consumers this means being responsible for their own actions and impacts and regulating their own behaviour for the greater good of society and the environment. However, this may be a particular challenge in tourism – for many tourists their vacation is the one chance a year they have to escape from their everyday worries and responsibilities.

Volunteer tourism

A small segment of the population has gone beyond the concepts of ethical behaviour and responsible tourism, seeing tourism itself as an opportunity to 'do good'. In recent years we have seen the rise of volunteer tourism, where volunteers pay to go to other countries to do voluntary work such as working in an orphanage or teaching English to local children. This has now grown to the point where there are specialist operators managing these activities, some of whom are charging volunteers large sums of money and are making considerable profits from volunteering. This has raised questions about whether such volunteering is itself ethical despite its apparently good intentions. There have also been suggestions that some projects are of little value to the host communities so that the whole thing seems more about making tourists feel good about themselves rather than actually benefiting the destinations. Whilst this apparently rather cynical analysis is not true of all programmes, it has certainly tainted their image.

Lack of credible accreditation schemes

For the individual tourist who does want to take a more ethical vacation, it is very difficult to know which product to choose. There are a few respected operators, such as Responsible Travel in the UK, which focuses on ethical travel. In general, however, the market is full of companies making claims that are not substantiated, and most importantly there are no widely known and credible accreditation schemes for ethical vacations. So consumers have no independent and reputable source for obtaining details of companies that meet a particular set of ethical standards. In the face of this, many consumers who in principle want to be more ethical in their travel behaviour may give up the attempt.

Sustainability overload

There may be a bigger challenge facing efforts to make tourism more responsible – 'sustainability overload'. In some countries, at least, we begin to detect signs that people feel overwhelmed by the constant barrage of stories about global warming and climate change, water shortages and poverty-ridden tourist destinations. They feel that nothing they do will make a difference and they are weary of constantly being made to feel guilty about their behaviour. This, if it continues, could be a major threat to our ability to construct more responsible forms of tourism.

Emerging markets

Much of the discussion above relates to the mature outbound tourism markets of Northern Europe and North America. However, that is not where future growth will take place – that will be Asia, Africa, and South America, where at the moment the outbound markets are largely made up of economic elites. For most of the populations of these regions, taking a foreign vacation is a dream rather than a reality. If they are able to take a vacation, ethical issues are probably low on their list of priorities, not least because of cultural differences in the concept of ethics, and the lack of media attention paid to ethical travel in these emerging markets. It will be interesting to see how this situation develops over time as these markets mature.

Conclusions

In this chapter we have identified a wide range of ethical issues related to tourist behaviour. We have seen that while some tourists appear concerned about these issues and are willing to modify their behaviour, others seem disinterested, or feel that vacations are for fun not ethics. There is little evidence that consumers are, on the whole, becoming committed to being more ethical in their behaviour. Indeed, even those who are sympathetic may become apathetic due to feeling impotent and unable to make a real difference. Indeed, we fear there may even be a backlash in some small segments that will see 'unethical' tourism become almost fashionable.

Discussion points and essay questions

1. What do you consider are the most important ethical issues relating to tourists' behaviour, and why do you think this?
2. Critically evaluate the idea that eco-tourists are practising an ethical form of tourism.
3. Discuss why the tourism industry appears to be driving the development of responsible tourism rather than consumer demand or governments.

Exercise

Devise and carry out a survey of *either* tourists in a destination *or* people in your local area who take holidays, to establish the extent to which the 'ethical tourist' is a reality. Your survey must be methodologically sound and your report should cover:

- how you selected the sample of people you surveyed
- how you selected the questions you asked
- your interpretation of the results
- any problems you experienced that you feel made your results less reliable than they might otherwise have been
- advice for researchers who may want to carry out similar projects in the future.

References

Elkington, J. and Hailes, J. (1992). *Holidays that Don't Cost the Earth*. Victor Gollancz, London.

Frommer, A. (1996). *Arthur Frommer's New World of Travel*, 5th edition. Macmillan, London and New York.

Goodwin, H. (2011). *Taking Responsibility for Tourism*. Goodfellow Publishers, Oxford.

Mathieson, A. and Wall, G. (1982). *Tourism: Economic, Physical and Social Impacts*. Longman, London.

Opaschowski, H. (1993). *European Tourism Analysis*. BAT-Leisure Research Institute.

Wood, K. and House, S. (1991). *The Good Tourist: A Worldwide Guide for the Green Traveller*. Mandarin, New York.

CASE STUDY 14: British Airways: environmental policy

BACKGROUND

British Airways is one of the world's leading airlines and one of the most profitable. The company's financial results continue to set standards for the whole industry. The conversion of British Airways from the public sector to a profit-motivated business and the accompanying long-term operational and marketing campaign which accompanied this turnaround have been documented by Horner and Swarbrooke (1996).

> *Sustainability is a core element of our business plan and we recognize that at British Airways we are expected to set the standard on responsible aviation. We believe that by doing everything we can to mitigate our environmental impact, enrich livelihoods and communities which we serve and be a responsible business and employer, we will deliver on our promise of responsible flying for everyone.*

> British Airways (2013)

INTRODUCTION

British Airways is now part of International Airlines Group (IAG), along with Spanish airlines Iberia and Vueling, among others. Willie Walsh, the IAG CEO, said in the IAG Annual Report for 2014:

> We're always looking to improve our environmental performance. At IAG it's something that we very much want to do. We've been leaders in the industry in terms of the need to improve and address our environmental impact and we've made good progress in 2014. Initiatives we've started – like the joint business with Solena to develop a truly sustainable bio-fuel from household waste – will make even greater progress in 2015. I think it's critical in an environment where the oil price has fallen, that we show that we are still looking to improve our environmental performance. Some people are sceptical about the industry's commitment and expect us to row back. We will not do that. We will build on the progress to date, honour the commitments we've made and make new efforts to improve performance still further.

A summary of the 2014 financial position for British Airways is shown in Exhibit 14.1.1.

Exhibit 14.1.1 British Airways key statistics* 2012–14

Total Group continuing operations		12 months to 31 December		
		2014	2013	2012
Traffic and capacity				
Revenue passenger km (RPK)	m	138,431	131,333	126,436
Available seat km (ASK)	m	170,917	161,444	158,247
Passenger load factor	%	81.0	81.3	79.9
Cargo tonne km (CTK)	m	4,458	4,646	4,891
Total revenue tonne km (RTK)	m	18,198	17,767	17,597
Total available tonne km (ATK)	m	27,185	24,536	24,152
Overall load factor	%	72.3	72.4	72.9
Passengers carried	000	41,516	39,960	37,580
Tonnes of cargo carried	000	706	733	788
Operations				
Average manpower equivalent (MPE)		39,710	38,592	38,761
ASKs per MPE		4,304	4,183	4,083
Aircraft in service at year end		279	278	273
Aircraft utilization (average hours per aircraft per day)		10.44	10.61	10.89
Punctuality – within 15 minutes	%	79	76	79
Regularity	%	99.2	98.6	98.9
Financial				
Passenger revenue per RPK	p	7.55	7.71	7.51
Passenger revenue per ASK	p	6.12	6.27	6
Cargo revenue per CTK	p	13.41	14.82	15.07

Total Group continuing operations		12 months to 31 December		
		2014	2013	2012
Financial				
Average fuel price (US cents/US gallon)		301.50	314.84	317.85
Operating margin	%	8.3	6.2	2.2
Operating margin before exceptional items	%	8.3	5.7	2.5
Earnings before interest, tax, depreciation, amortization and rentals (EBITDAR)	m	1,886.00	1,515.00	1,051.00
Net debt/total capital ratio**	%	48.1	44.5	66.2
Total traffic revenue per ATK	p	43.9	44.1	42.4
Total traffic revenue per ASK	p	6.5	6.7	6.47
Total expenditure before exceptional items on operations per ASK	p	6.29	6.67	6.67
Total expenditure before exceptional items on operations excluding fuel per ASK	p	4.23	4.35	4.32
Total expenditure before exceptional items on operations per ATK	p	42.6	43.9	43.7

*Operating and financial statistics (not forming part of the audited financial statements. The table shows BA statistics, not IAG.

**Operating statistics do not include those of associate undertakings and franchisees.

Source: British Airways plc Report and Accounts year ended December 2014

British Airways is an international airline which has developed as a result of global strategic alliances with other airlines. Details of these are shown in Exhibit 14.1.2.

Exhibit 14.1.2 British Airways links, alliances and franchises

Group airlines (IAG subsidiaries)	Iberia (former Spanish flag carrier)
	Iberia Express
	Vueling – Spanish low-cost airline
	IAG Cargo
	Avios – Travel reward scheme operator
	Aer Lingus? (Summer 2015 IAG has submitted a recommended share offer)
British Airways subsidiaries	BA City Flyer – UK domestic flights from London City Airport
	Open Skies – non-stop services between Paris Orly and New York's JFK and Newark
British Airways franchises	ComAir (South Africa)*
	SUN-AIR of Scandinavia
Oneworld Alliance Partnership	airberlin, American Airlines, Cathay Pacific, Finnair, Iberia, Japan Airlines

Partnership across the Atlantic	LAN Airlines, Malaysian Airways, Quantas, Qatar Airlines, Royal Jordanian
	S7 Airlines, SriLankan Airlines, TAM Airlines
	British Airways, American Airlines (inc. US Airlines flights), Finnair, Iberia
Partnership between Europe and Japan	British Airways, Finnair, Japan Airlines
Codeshare – shared flights and seat selling	Oneworld alliance and IAG airlines plus Aer Lingus, airBaltic, Bangkok Airways, Flybe, Loganair, Meridiana fly, WestJet

*Kalula is the African low-cost carrier owned by ComAir – it is not a BA franchise.

Source: www.britishairways.com partners and alliances 2015

British Airways has a strong commitment to its social and environmental responsibility. In July each year it releases a British Airways Sustainability Report for the previous year (Exhibit 14.1.3).

Exhibit 14.1.3 Keith Williams, Executive Chairman, British Airways

I see our sustainability programme as a core part of our business. Aviation plays a vital role in the global economy by providing the opportunity for people to build better businesses and also to connect people and places to build better lives. At British Airways we are fully committed to playing our part in helping our industry achieve sustainable growth through our renewed sustainability programme 'Responsible Flying for Everyone'.

Our sustainability programme and this report are organised along three dimensions: mitigating our environmental impact, enriching livelihoods and communities, and being a responsible business. We have sought to follow the guidelines established in the latest Global Reporting Initiative, version four, as we recognise this represents best practice in sustainability reporting.

We work closely with regulators at a national, European and international level to help develop appropriate regulation to support the sustainable growth of our industry.

In particular, in relation to the important issue of climate change we support and welcome the progress made at last year's ICAO General Assembly in committing to develop a global solution for aviation to achieve the goal of Carbon Neutral Growth from 2020. We will continue to support these important activities.

I believe that sustainable alternative fuels will play an important part in enabling the aviation industry to meet its long term goal of a 50 percent reduction in net carbon dioxide (CO_2) emissions by 2050. I am proud of the progress we have made with our technology partner Solena to build Europe's first biomass-to-liquid biojet plant which is on track to begin production of biofuel by 2017.

We are also committed to ensuring that our operations and the aircraft we purchase will enable us to continue to reduce the environmental impacts on the communities local to airports, particularly in relation to the issue of aircraft noise. The arrival of the first of our 12 Airbus A380 and 42 Boeing 787 Dreamliner aircraft in 2013 has enabled us to reduce the noise impacts of our flights as they are at least 50 percent quieter than the aircraft they replace.

I recognise that improving the sustainability performance of our industry is best achieved through working collaboratively with our industry partners. I am very pleased with the progress we have made through the UK industry Sustainable Aviation Group. I am particularly impressed with the launch of the UK Aviation Noise Road Map in 2013, the first of its kind, which shows that we can reduce the noise impacts of our flights despite forecast growth. I look forward to the development this year of the Sustainable Alternative Fuels road map which will show the role that these fuels can play in reducing our climate change impacts.

Our flagship charity programme, Flying Start with charity partners Comic Relief goes from strength to strength raising more than £6 million since its launch in 2010.

I truly believe that through continued perseverance we can create a sustainable aviation industry. This means our customers will be able to continue to enjoy the incredible benefits that come from flying and enable British Airways to continue to set the standard for safe, responsible aviation.

Source: Chairman's Foreword, British Airways (2013).

AVIATION AND THE ENVIRONMENT

The potential for damage to the environment as the demand for air travel increases has been recognized and documented by many commentators. A summary of the types of damage that aviation travel can cause to the environment is listed in Exhibit 14.1.4.

Exhibit 14.1.4 Environmental damage caused by air travel

Noise	Aircraft noise affects the local community
	Noise from the ground power units
	Noise from the engine running
Waste	Waste from the aircraft and catering
	Hazardous waste from engineering
	Effluent
	Office waste
Emissions to atmosphere	Atmospheric impact of aviation
	Local air quality affected by ground transport
	Emissions from ground vehicle fleet
	Emissions from maintenance processes
Congestion	Congestion in the air
	Traffic pressures on the ground
Tourism and conservation	Impacts at destinations including waste, congestion, emissions and noise
	Conservation issues including protecting local environments and wildlife

Source: Aviation Environment Federation and British Airways.

Exhibit 14.1.4 shows that, although air travel is an integral part of the modern world, with tourism and business travel making a major contribution to economic development, it has tremendous potential for damaging the environment. It has been recognized by British

Airways that managing the impact on the environment in a responsible and acceptable way is central to the long-term survival of the airline. To help with this process, the Aviation Environment Federation has been established, which is concerned with all the environmental and amenity effects of aviation.

The European Community's programme of policy and action on the environment, 'Towards Sustainability' (the Fifth EC Environmental Action Plan of 1993), specifically targeted five sectors, including both transport and tourism, as critical to development of a strategy for sustainable development. Over the intervening years there have been reviews and updates to European Policy. 'Europe 2020' is the European Commission's strategy for 'smart, sustainable and inclusive growth', which was set out in March 2010. Europe 2020 put forward three mutually reinforcing priorities:

- **smart growth**: developing an economy based on knowledge and innovation
- **sustainable growth**: promoting a more resource-efficient, greener and more competitive economy
- **inclusive growth**: fostering a high-employment economy delivering social and territorial cohesion.

British Airways' 'Responsible Flying' can be said to link in to the second Europe 2020 priority of efficient use of energy and resources, promoting mobility through greener operations.

There has been regulation on aspects of airline operations such as noise, emissions and waste. Fiscal measures have also been applied and may be expanded further. Local noise charges at airports is one example of a fiscal measure. The self-interest of the airline companies involved can lead to environmental measures being taken. Fuel economy in aircraft, for example, can save the airline money in the long term, as well as having environmental advantages.

BRITISH AIRWAYS ENVIRONMENTAL POLICY

British Airways sets out to be 'the most admired airline' and thus it aims to 'set the standard for safe, responsible aviation' (British Airways, 2013; see Exhibit 14.1.5). British Airways explains its approach to sustainability as follows.

We recognise the importance of having an integrated sustainability strategy and business plan. Our right to do business is earned through responsible management of our operation and positive engagement with communities. British Airways' approach to sustainability is guided by the views of its stakeholders and awareness of our impacts on society, the environment and economy.

These two interdependent elements [. . .] inform the basis of our strategy: a commitment to mitigate our impact on the environment, run a responsible business and enrich livelihoods and communities.

We have shaped our renewed commitment to sustainability around simple principles:

- *a focused agenda*
- *effective co-ordination of our initiatives*
- *meaningful engagement with our stakeholders.*

Exhibit 14.1.5 BA's three pillars of work – Responsible Flying

1 Mitigating our environmental impact	Emissions associated with climate change
	Noise and air quality impacts
	Waste and recycling
2 Enriching livelihoods and communities	Sustainable communities
	Being a good neighbour
	Education and talent development
3 Being a responsible business	Customer and colleague wellbeing
	Inclusion and diversity
	Responsible procurement
	Colleague relations engagement and support

Source: British Airways Sustainability Report 2013

British Airways guides its activity through its corporate business plan 'Set the Standard for Responsible Aviation'. Executive review is carried out through the Corporate Responsibility Review Board, which is made up of members of the company's Leadership Team. Governance oversight is undertaken by the Corporate Responsibility Board Committee, which comprises Leadership Team and Board members.

Exhibit 14.1.6 presents the 2013 report of British Airways' progress towards achieving its environmental goals and targets. British Airways has reported its progress against its environmental and sustainable targets since 1992 on an annual basis. As necessary, and in line with international developments, British Airways amends or adds new targets to its responsible approach. An example of this from the British Airways Sustainability Report 2013 is the addition of a new target, to 'work with industry and stakeholders to support detailed development of a global market-based mechanism by the 2016 International Civil Aviation Organization (ICAO) Assembly' – an organization tasked with establishing regulations of aviation emissions by multilateral agreement.

CONCLUSIONS

British Airways will continue its long-term environmental policy and will be trying to communicate its successes via different communication media, including its Annual Sustainability Reports. In setting out to be the world's most admired airline, it has set the sustainability bar high. But the annual reporting of its environmental targets, performance and development shows a clear leadership within the aviation field in 'responsible flying'.

Exhibit 14.1.6

ENVIRONMENTAL GOALS AND TARGETS

Goals	Targets and actions	Progress in 2013
Climate change: advocate a responsible global regulatory approach to the aviation industry on climate change that is cost-effective and minimises market distortions.	Collaborate with IATA to develop and promote pragmatic policy recommendations for a global market-based measure. **New target:** work with industry and stakeholders to support detailed development of a global market-based mechanism by the 2016 International Civil Aviation Organisation (ICAO) Assembly.	We played a key role in achieving global agreement at the International Air Transport Association (IATA) Annual General Meeting in June 2013 on detailed mechanisms for achieving Carbon Neutral Growth from 2020.
	Press for the EU ETS to evolve in a way that avoids distortions and disputes.	The EU has amended the ETS to cover only flights within the European Economic Area from 2013 until 2016. This reduces the risk of distortions and disputes. In 2016, the scope will be reviewed in light of progress at ICAO.
Climate change: accelerate the implementation of sustainable low-carbon fuels into the aviation industry.	Work with low-carbon fuel developers to implement sustainable supply chains for alternative fuels before 2020. Deliver our sustainable fuel facility called Greensky.	Continued to progress the Greensky project with key decisions on site, technology, financing.
	Influence UK and EU regulators to establish positive incentives for sustainable low-carbon aviation fuels.	Worked with a number of groups to lobby on the key role that advanced biofuels derived from waste can play in decarbonising aviation. These included Leaders of Sustainable Biofuels and the EU Flightpath in Europe and Sustainable Aviation in the UK.
Climate change: improve carbon efficiency through a programme of targeted initiatives.	25 percent improvement in carbon efficiency from 111g CO_2/pkm in 2005 to 83g CO_2/pkm in 2025.	101.7g CO2/pkm in 2013.
	48,000 tonnes CO_2 reduction due to fuel efficiency initiatives in 2013. **New target:** 96,000 tonnes CO_2 reduction due to aircraft fuel efficiency initiatives over 2014 and 2015.	43,278 tonnes CO_2 reduction in 2013.

ENVIRONMENTAL GOALS AND TARGETS (CONTINUED)		
Goals	**Targets and actions**	**Progress in 2013**
Climate change: improve carbon efficiency through a programme of targeted initiatives (continued).	A 5 percent reduction in ground energy use in our buildings for 2013 against 2012. **New target:** 20 percent reduction in ground energy use by 2020 compared to 2013.	During 2013, we reduced our like for like ground energy by 5.8 percent and saved 5,565 tonnes CO_2.
	Reduce the effects of climate change along our supply chain.	We have expanded data collection on forest risk commodities and included carbon efficiency targets into catering supplier contracts.
Climate change: improve information for, and discussion with, customers on climate change issues.	Provide option for customers to support low-carbon initiatives in the booking process on our main website, ba.com. Develop up to four projects a year.	Conducted customer research on climate communications and as a result upgraded the point of sale Carbon Fund offering. The Fund supported four community energy projects in 2013 with a combined community benefit of almost £750 thousand over the projects' lifetimes.
Noise and air quality: minimise impacts of aviation noise on local communities and aviation emissions on local air quality.	Reduce average noise per flight by 15 percent by 2018 compared to 2008.	We continue to liaise with aircraft manufacturers to achieve the earliest practical entry for our new aircraft.
Waste and recycling: minimise waste, reduce disposal to landfill and increase reuse and recycling.	60 percent recycling by 2015 at our main bases of Heathrow and Gatwick.	45 percent of waste recycled at Heathrow and Gatwick (this includes re-use, recycling, composting and liquid recovery).
	Increase level of recycling of onboard waste.	Segregation of aluminium cans on long haul flights into Heathrow and Gatwick.

Source: British Airways Sustainability Report 2013

DISCUSSION POINTS AND ESSAY QUESTIONS

1. Evaluate the reasons for an apparent lack of interest amongst consumers in the UK in environmental issues when purchasing holiday products.
2. British Airways is trying to communicate its environmental policies to customers with the aim of increasing interest and encouraging concern. Discuss the most appropriate way of communicating this information to customers, in your opinion.
3. British Airways is serious about its programme for 'Responsible Flying', but as a citizen of the world, isn't the responsible thing for the environmentally concerned flyer to simply not fly at all?

REFERENCES

Horner, S. and Swarbrooke, J. (1996). *Marketing Tourism, Hospitality, and Leisure in Europe.* International Thomson Business Press.

CASE STUDY 14.2: TUI, Germany: environmental policy

INTRODUCTION

In 1997 a German industrial business called Preussag AG started to enter the tourism market through the purchase of Hapag-Lloyd, a leading German tourism company. Over time the company bought more tourism-related businesses, including British tour operator Thomson, and divested from industrial operations to become TUI (Touristik Union International), one of the world's leading tourism groups, listed on the Frankfurt Stock Exchange. In 2007 TUI AG merged its tour operating businesses with the UK listed tour operator First Choice Holidays plc, which was quoted on the London Stock Exchange, though TUI AG still held a controlling 54 per cent shareholding. The new group was known as TUI Travel plc. In 2014 the two entities TUI AG and TUI Travel plc merged to become a single dual-listed (London and Frankfurt) organization, TUI Group, creating the world's number one tourism business: a business of 77,000 staff, a turnover of €18.7 billion and operating profits of €869 million. The business operates across four broad sectors: tour operators (e.g. First Choice and Airtours); airlines (e.g. TUIfly and Corsair); hotels (e.g. Riu and Robinson Clubs); and cruises (e.g. Hapag-Lloyd Kreuzfahrten and Thomson Cruises). The TUI Group is shown in Exhibit 14.2.1.

Exhibit 14.2.1 TUI Group 2015 business operating sectors*

Northern Region
(UK & Ireland), Nordics, (Sweden, Norway, Finland, Denmark), Canada, Russia

United Kingdom: *First Choice, Thomson Tailormade, Crystal Ski, Thomson Lakes and Mountains, Thomson Sport, Hayes and Jarvis, Austravel, Intrepid Worldwide*

Nordics: *TEMA-resa*

Central Region
Germany, Austria, Switzerland, Poland & TUI Destinations Services

Germany: *TUI, 1-2-FLY, Airtours, Boomerang-Reisen, Gebeco, OFT REISEN, TUI Wolters, Berge & Meer, FOX-TOURS. L'TUR*

Austria: *RIU, Sensimar, Magic Life, TUI best FAMILY, Puravida, Robinson, GULET*
Switzerland: *TUI Reisewelten*

Western Region
Belgium, the Netherlands, France

Belgium: *Jetair, Jetaircenter, jetairfly, sunjets.be, vip selection, VTB*
Netherlands: *TUI Nederland, Arke, Kras, Goed Idee Reizen, Holland International, Extravacanza en Wedding Unlimited*
France: *Club Marmara, Splashworld, SuneoClub, Club Magic Life, Hôtels Couples*

Hotels and resorts	*Grupotel, Atlantica, Iberotal, Jaz, Sol Y Mar, TUI Magic Life, Nordotel, Dorfhotel aQi, Toskana Resort Castelfalfi, TI Hotels, Gran Resort, Karisma, Barut*
Cruises	TUI Cruises, Hapag-Lloyd Cruises, Thomson Cruises

*Note: Brand reorganization and simplification: following the creation of TUI Group in 2014 the business structure has been under a strategic and operational review. In May 2015 TUI Group announced that it was merging tourism and airline brands into a single TUI brand and simplifying its brand structure across the group to eventually trade under a single TUI brand. The well known Thomson brand dating from 1965 will be a casualty of this strategy. The strapline for this strategy is 'One Brand – Local Roots'.

Source: TUI Group websites

Exhibit 14.2.2 TUI Group key facts June 2015

Global company – domiciled in Germany
A FTSE 100 business:

 €10 billion market capitalixation (@13 May 2015)

 €18.7 billion revenues (financial year 2013/14)

 €869 million underlying EBITA* (financial year 2013/14)

77,000 staff	140 aircraft
130 countries	13 cruise ships
300 hotels	30,000,000 customers
210,000 hotel beds	from 31 source markets
1,800 retail shops in Europe	travelling to 180 destinations

Earnings before interest, taxes, and amortization.

Source: TUI Group Corporate Presentation June 2015

TUI ENVIRONMENTAL POLICY

TUI AG's early environmental policy had been developed as a central group strategy (Horner and Swarbrooke, 1996), the environmental strategy being an integral part of TUI's quality strategy. The TUI corporate policy stated: 'the protection of an intact nature and environment are of outstanding importance to us'.

 TUI AG appointed Dr Wolf Michael Iwand in 1990 as its environment manager to manage the Group's environmental policy, reporting directly to the board of directors. This recognized that it is key for any major tourism business that it makes major efforts to minimize effects on the natural environment that holiday-makers are visiting. It is only by taking a positive approach to environmental planning that tourism companies will continue to be successful in the future. The Group established short-, medium- and long-term objectives in relation to the environment in the late 1990s. These planning objectives are shown in Exhibit 14.2.3.

Exhibit 14.2.3 TUI AG's original planning objectives

Time period	Ecological objectives	Measures	Economic objectives
Short term	• Reduction of environmental pollution and impairment	• Education/consulting • Programme organization • Hotel management	• Quality control • Product optimization • Ensuring returns
Medium term (up to 2005)	• Environmental relief • Prevention of environmental pollution and impairment	• Environmental standards/eco-labelling • Environment information systems • Environmental quality goals	• Management of risk and opportunities/ innovation
Long term (up to 2030)	• Environmental relief • Prevention of environmental pollution and nuisance • Environmental improvements	• Eco-controlling • Ecological product control • Environmental impact assessment	• Securing the future • Securing and improving revenues

Source: Department of Environment, TUI (1997)

It can be seen that this programme outlined a series of measures which the Group hoped to achieve up to the year 2030. This includes moves towards 'eco-labelling' and 'eco-auditing' which originate from Brussels. The Group had four main aspects to its drive for sustainable tourist development. The first of these involved reducing pollution by all means and by low-cost activity. The second aspect was the establishment of financial and technical feasibility at the destinations. The third aspect was to stimulate environmental awareness among vacationers and clients, and to achieve satisfaction through environmental quality. The final aspect was to ensure that a measurable return on investment was secured.

In the first stages of its environmental initiatives, TUI worked with experts and environmentalists, local authorities and hotel partners to ensure that the holidays on offer were as environmentally friendly as possible. The Group established environmental criteria for its destinations, hotels and carriers. Details of these are shown in Exhibit 14.2.4.

Exhibit 14.2.4 Holiday-making and environmental friendliness – the late 1990s

TUI destination criteria:

• Bathing water and beach quality
• Water supply and water-saving measures
• Wastewater disposal and utilization
• Solid waste disposal, recycling and prevention

- Energy supply and energy-saving measures
- Traffic, air, noise and climate
- Landscape and built environment
- Nature conservation, species preservation and animal welfare
- Environmental information and offers
- Environmental policy and activities

TUI hotel criteria:

- Wastewater treatment
- Solid waste disposal, recycling and prevention
- Water supply and water-saving measures
- Energy supply and energy-saving measures
- Environmentally oriented hotel management (focus on food, cleaning and hygiene)
- Quality of bathing waters and beaches in the vicinity of the hotel
- Noise protection in and around the hotel
- Hotel gardens
- Building materials and architecture
- Environmental information and offers of the hotel
- Location and immediate surroundings of the hotel

TUI carrier criteria:

- Energy consumption
- Pollutant and noise emissions
- Land use and paving over
- Vehicle/craft, equipment and line-maintenance techniques
- Catering and waste recycling and disposal
- Environmental information for passengers
- Environmental guidelines and reporting
- Environmental research and development
- Environmental cooperation, integrated transport concepts
- Specific data: vehicle/craft type, motor/power unit, age

Source: General information brochure, TUI Travel, 1997

THE MOVE TO SUSTAINABILITY

As with British Airways (Case Study 14.1) there has been a change in emphasis over the years towards 'sustainability', an emphasis reflecting not simply tourist impact, but also the operational impacts of the corporations concerned.

From the UK side, TUI Travel produced Sustainability Reports and TUI AG included a dedicated 'sustainable development' section in its corporate magazine. As the combined TUI Group, TUI restates its commitment in the 'Sustainability' section of the Group's home page (2015):

Our approach

As the world's largest integrated leisure tourism business, we are proud of the positive role our industry plays around the world. The travel and tourism sector accounts for 9% of the world's GDP and 6% of its exports*. It is responsible for one in 11 jobs globally* and is the main source of foreign exchange in one-third of developing countries**.

There are also significant challenges. Travel and tourism accounts for around 5% of global carbon emissions** – half of which is attributable to aviation. We are committed to reducing carbon emissions which is a key challenge for TUI.

Both TUI Travel and TUI AG have a strong history of sustainability and the coming together of these two Groups will ensure that sustainability continues to be a priority for TUI as well as the rest of our industry. Our vision is to make travel experiences special whilst minimising environmental impact, respecting culture and people and bringing economic benefits to communities.

* United Nations World Tourism Organization, 2014
** United Nations Environment Programme, 2014

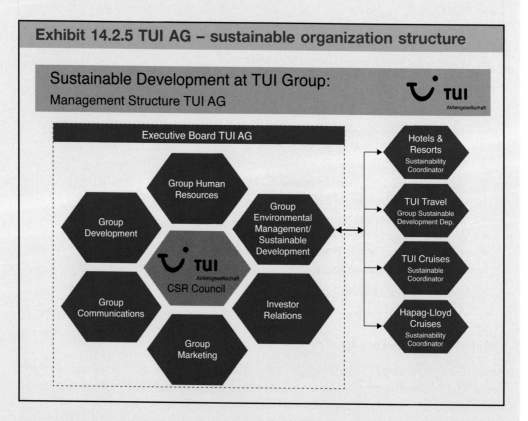

Exhibit 14.2.5 TUI AG – sustainable organization structure

Around the mid-2000s both TUI AG and TUI Travel plc started to change their environmental reporting towards an emphasis on sustainability. Both have been producing regular reports since then through both independent documents and reports, and incorporation into their investor/analyst briefings and annual reporting.

Exhibit 14.2.6 TUI Travel plc – approach to sustainability management

Sustainability management	Commitment at the most senior level is vital for us to achieve our goal of leading the leisure travel sector in sustainable development.
Senior Management Commitment	The Deputy Chief Executive Officer is responsible for reporting on sustainable development to the TUI Travel plc Board. The Group HR Director is responsible for reporting on sustainable development to the Group Management Board. There is also a Director of Group Sustainable Development.
Steering Committee	The Group Management Board acts as the Steering Committee, setting the strategic direction and long-term objectives for sustainable development.
Group Sustainable Development	The Group Sustainable Development department's role is to drive change towards a more sustainable company, to forge sector leadership. The department works closely with other Group departments and the TUI Travel network of Sector Coordinators, meeting regularly to tackle issues and develop action plans.
Sector Coordinators	Each TUI Travel sector has a Sustainable Development Coordinator, reporting on these issues directly to the Sector Managing Director. Mainstream businesses have a Sector Coordinator in each major geographical region. Sector Coordinators are responsible for identifying Group and sector-specific targets, collating performance data, and developing and implementing sustainable development strategy within their sector.
Champions Network	Sector Coordinators are responsible for appointing champions in each TUI Travel business to support them in the delivery of their Sector's sustainable development strategy.

To review our performance and to measure progress, we have incorporated sustainable development questions into regular colleague surveys at Sector and Group level. We also conduct an annual Sustainable Development Evaluation of TUI Travel tour operating businesses, as well as specific surveys of airlines, hotels and water transport operations.

Source: Tuitravelplc.com website 2015

An example of this is the 2013 Sustainable Holidays report from TUI Travel. Exhibit 14.2.7 is taken from this report setting out the context and linking policy to customer expectation.

CUSTOMERS AND THE TUI SUSTAINABLE TOURISM POLICY

As can be seen in Exhibit 14.2.8, one detailed target was for TUI Travel to improve external communications on sustainability through its focus on the issues that customers care

Exhibit 14.2.7 TUI Travel's Sustainable Holidays document 2013

We can make a real difference

Globally, 1 in 11 jobs are in the travel tourism industry and it accounts for 9% of global GDP. This is particularly important in developing countries.

Our customers expect it

89% of customers expect us to be working to reduce our impact on the environment and support local communities in our destinations.

Risks from climate change

Climate change will increase the intensity of tropical storms and rainfall, and cause more severe droughts, so it's really important for us to play our part by reducing our carbon footprint and supporting our suppliers to do the same.

It is making us more efficient

In 2012 TUI Travel saved £16 million due to eco-efficiencies, so investing in sustainability definitely makes sense for our business from a financial perspective.

It's important to our colleagues

80% of 13–25-year-olds want to work for a company that cares about its impact on society, and colleague engagement is 50% higher when sustainability culture is strong.

Global water shortages

Many of our destinations are facing water shortages so we need to become more efficient and reduce the amount of water we use. This is especially important because water is such a vital part of our product – just think of all the swimming pools!

Source: TUI Travel (2013)

Exhibit 14.2.8

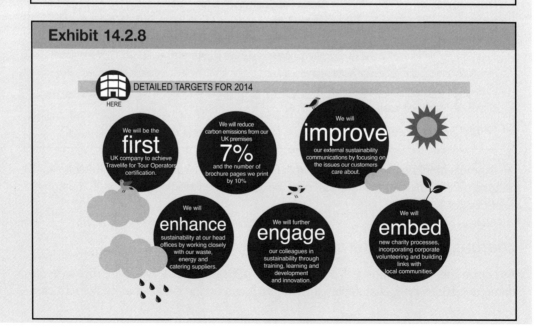

about. Their targets additionally tied in local stakeholders and communities through charity activities and staff volunteering. TUI Travel's goal for 2015 was to create demand for sustainable holidays by engaging with 5 million holidaymakers about sustainable holidays; all customers would have improved information on sustainability; and TUI would look to promote greener and fairer holidays through online communications, all through its 'holidays forever' commitment.

Additionally, TUI was involved with research enquiry on tourism and sustainable development. In July 2015 TUI, along with PricewaterhouseCoopers (PwC) and the tourism charity the Travel Foundation, released the findings of a research pilot study: 'Measuring Tourism's Impact: A Pilot Study in Cyprus'. The report was undertaken by PwC for the Travel Foundation through the access to hotels and suppliers facilitated by TUI Group. The research approach used by PwC was its Total Impact Measurement and Management (TIMM) approach. Exhibit 14.2.9 details the elements of the approach used in the pilot study.

The key findings of the Cyprus pilot study are listed in Exhibit 14.2.10. It should be noted that this case study is undertaken over only one year of activity so it does not identify impacts of infrastructure activity or longer-term social and environmental impacts; but it does highlight the economic impacts of tourism to the local economy. Greenhouse gas emissions are the most significant environmental cost, and the report emphasizes the need for tourism operations to be effective in how they plan not only their operation, but also the impact of their tourists. In addition to the impact on the local economy, tourism has a social impact in terms of skills and social development within the local community. Interestingly the report specifically highlights degree-related work placements as yielding the highest personal social impact.

Exhibit 14.2.9 What is Total Impact Measurement and Management (TIMM)?

The pilot study used TIMM, an impact measurement and valuation framework developed by PwC, which provides a comprehensive and balanced evaluation of a business' impacts on society, the economy and the environment. It is a holistic approach to 'impact' measurement:

- **Total** because it provides a holistic view of social, environmental, tax and economic dimensions – to see the big picture;
- **Impact** because it looks beyond inputs and outputs to outcomes and impacts to understand the footprint
- **Measurement** because it quantifies and monetises the impacts to value in a common language
- **Management** because it enables the options to be evaluated and the trade-offs optimised to make better decisions.

TIMM considers four key categories of impact:

- **Economic impact** covers the effect of an activity on the economy in a given area by measuring the associated output or value added (and changes in employment)
- **Tax impact** covers the associated tax contribution

- **Environmental impact** measures the value of the impacts on society of the emissions to air, land and water and the use of natural resources
- **Social impact** values the consequences of the activities on societal outcomes such as livelihoods, skills and cultural heritage.

TIMM involves estimating the value of each impact so that different impacts can be compared to each other. This enables decision makers to assess the total impacts and to compare alternative strategies, investment choices and operating plans. Business decisions can then be made with more complete knowledge of the overall impact they will have and a better understanding of which stakeholders will be affected by which decisions.

For a more detailed explanation of TIMM refer to PwC (2013).

Source: Travel Foundation (2015)

Exhibit 14.2.10 Cyprus pilot study – key findings

Groundbreaking pilot study reveals impact of tourism on host community, environment and economy

07/07/15

Today (7 July) the Travel Foundation, with PwC, has published the results of what is thought to be the most comprehensive destination impact assessment of tourism operations ever undertaken, examining the impact of 60,000 TUI Group customers who visited 8 hotels in Cyprus in 2013.

Key findings

- The positive economic and tax benefits are by far the greatest impact – amounting to €84 per guest per night – far exceeding the negative environmental (–€4) and social (–€0.2) costs. However, this is a one-year (2013) snapshot and does not take account of the construction of the hotels. In addition, many environmental and social impacts will accumulate over a longer timeframe.
- Greenhouse gases (GHG) are the most significant environmental cost – although this represents less than 0.01% of total GHG emissions in Cyprus. GHG impact more than doubles if flights to/from Cyprus are included.
- The most significant social benefit identified across all of the social impact areas is that associated with 'on the job' experience, with an upper estimate of €6.2 per guest night. This highlights the tourism sector's significant role in developing skills in the Cypriot workforce, which is important in the context of the Cypriot economy where unemployment has increased in recent years, particularly among young people.
- Work placements, where a placement is a condition of an individual's degree, yielded the highest social impact per person (€8,800 per work placement student). However, its relatively small overall impact is primarily driven by the small number of Cypriot work placement students currently benefiting at each hotel.

Source: Travel Foundation (2015)

CONCLUSIONS

TUI Group is the largest tour operator in the world and has been active in pursuing an ambitious environmental policy for all its tour operation businesses, which has developed into a sustainability policy linked to performance indicators, monitored outcomes and engagement with research and communities. The company considers this as an important part of its future strategy, linked to its position on corporate governance and corporate social responsibility.

DISCUSSION POINTS AND ESSAY QUESTIONS

1. 'Mass tourism and ecological soundness do not go together – but there is much one can do to lessen the impact of one on the other' (Dr Iwand, TUI). Discuss this comment in relation to TUI consumers.
2. The desire for consumers to travel to exotic destinations has been accompanied by an almost total lack of interest in the environment. Discuss the reasons for this and explore the actions that a mass tour operator, such as TUI, can take in response to this situation.
3. The Cyprus pilot study (Travel Foundation, 2015) suggests that tourism can bring important economic benefits to the local economy. Discuss the potential societal positives and negatives from tourism development.

REFERENCES

British Airways (2013). *Responsible Flying for Everyone. Sustainability Report 2013*. British Airways, Harmondsworth. http://responsibleflying.ba.com/wp-content/uploads/British-Airways-Sustainability-Report-2013.pdf

Horner, S. and Swarbrooke, J. (1996). *Marketing Tourism, Hospitality, and Leisure in Europe*. International Thomson Business Press.

PwC (2013). *Measuring and Managing Total Impact: A New Language for Business Decisions*. PricewaterhouseCoopers. www.pwc.com/totalimpact

Travel Foundation (2015). *Measuring Tourism's Impact: A Pilot Study in Cyprus*. Travel Foundation in association with PricewaterhouseCoopers. www.thetravelfoundation.org.uk/projects/destinations/cyprus/measuring_tourisms_impact

TUI Travel (2013). *Sustainable Holidays Here, There and In The Air*. TUI Travel plc. www.tantur.com.tr/pdf/TUI-UK-and-I-Sustainable-Holidays-update.pdf

Quality and tourist satisfaction

The concept of quality

Quality is a buzz word in all modern industries, and is seen as the key to achieving customer satisfaction. In this chapter we explore what the concepts of quality and satisfaction mean in tourism. First, we begin by looking at some standard definitions of quality.

Gummesson, writing in 1989, divided definitions of quality into two types:

- **technology-driven and product-oriented** definitions, which define quality in terms of conformance to requirements based on company specifications
- **fitness-for-purpose definitions**, which are market-driven and customer-oriented, and which focus on customer utility and satisfaction.

In general, the first type of definition tends to be used in manufacturing industries where the main aim is usually standardization and reliability. The second type, with its emphasis on customers and their satisfaction, is more commonly used in service industries.

Service quality is a more complex concept than manufacturing industry quality because of the unique characteristics of service products, or what Frochot (1996) described as the 'intrinsic services nature of heterogeneity, inseparability of production and consumption and intangibility'.

Because of these characteristics, the standardization of product that is the aim of manufacturing companies is impossible to achieve in tourism. In any event, in tourism the customer wants to feel that their experience will be different from other people's and tailor-made to match their tastes.

In many people's minds, quality is an absolute that is either present or absent from a product. It either is, or is not, a quality product. However, in reality it is more of a continuum from little or no apparent quality to high or even, in theory at least, total quality.

Furthermore, it has often been assumed that quality means premium-priced products at the top end of the market. This is clearly not true if we take the fitness-for-purpose view of quality, where any product can be seen as a quality product if it meets the needs of the purchaser. Therefore a simple youth hostel could be a quality product for a young walker on a limited budget looking for an inexpensive bed for the night. At the other end of the scale, for the tourist who enjoys being pampered, only a five-star hotel with a high staff-to-guest ratio will meet their desires.

This brings us to the crucial issue at the heart of quality in service industries and the fitness-for-purpose definitions. They are customer-oriented, and every customer is different. Quality is not a fact or a reality in such industries; it is a perception in the mind of the customer. In other words, quality is in the eye of the beholder. Whether or not a tourist will perceive a product as a quality product will depend on:

- their individual attitudes, expectations and previous experiences as a consumer
- the benefits they are looking for from the particular purchase in question.

These needs and desires are closely linked to motivators and determinants. In terms of a holiday they might include:

- looking for a low-cost vacation because of a lack of disposable income
- a desire to gain status from purchasing a particular holiday
- searching for a destination where the tourist will feel safe and secure
- a wish to take a type of holiday that will make it easier to make new friends
- a deeply held desire to meet local people, see the 'real' country and get off the beaten track
- a need to relax and reduce stress levels.

Tourists might be seeking more than one benefit from a holiday, and these might be conflicting or even contradictory.

The quality jigsaw in tourism

Because of the complex nature of tourism, product quality can be seen as a jigsaw, with many equally important but different-sized pieces that must all fit together perfectly in order to satisfy the tourist. The jigsaw is illustrated in Figure 15.1 in relation to the purchase of a family's annual summer holiday in a resort hotel.

The importance of tourist satisfaction

It has been suggested (Conway and Swift, 2000) that tourist satisfaction comes from a series of variables:

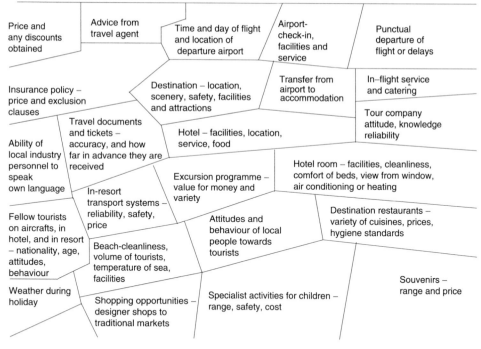

Figure 15.1 The quality jigsaw

- commitment
- trust
- customer orientation/empathy
- experience/satisfaction
- communication.

Satisfying the consumer in tourism is important for three main reasons.

- It leads to positive word-of-mouth recommendation of the product to friends and relatives, which in turn brings in new customers.
- Creating a repeat customer by satisfying them with their first use of the product brings a steady source of income with no need for extra marketing expenditure.
- Dealing with complaints is expensive, time-consuming and bad for the organization's reputation. Furthermore, it can bring direct costs through compensation payments.

The tourist satisfaction process

Figure 15.2 illustrates a simplified view of the process by which tourists are satisfied or not.

The tourism product	The satisfaction factor	The outcome
* Tangible element * Service element * Role of intermediaries and agents	* Perceptions of the tourist experience * Tourist attitudes and expectations * Uncontrollable factors such as strikes	* Tourist satisfaction * Tourist partial satisfaction * Tourist dissatisfaction

Figure 15.2 The tourist satisfaction process

Key models and techniques

There a number of models and techniques used in service industries in relation to quality and customer satisfaction. Several of these have been applied to tourism by various authors.

The SERVQUAL technique

The SERVQUAL scale was first introduced by Parasuraman, Zeithaml and Berry in 1985. They attempted to develop an instrument that would measure service quality across a range of service industries. It was based on empirical research, albeit not in the tourism industry. They stated that service quality has five dimensions (quoted in Frochot, 1996):

- **reliability**: the ability to perform the promised service dependably and accurately
- **assurance**: knowledge and courtesy of employees and their ability to convey trust and confidence
- **tangibles**: physical facilities, equipment and appearance of personnel
- **empathy**: caring, individualized attention the firm provides to its customers
- **responsiveness**: willingness to help consumers and provide them with prompt service.

The scale is often described by the acronym for the five dimensions: RATER.

Based on this idea they developed this technique whereby customers are asked questions and on the basis of their answers a score is calculated for each of the five criteria, and for subcriteria within these five groups. Service quality is defined as the gap between customers' expectations of service and their perceptions of the service experienced. However, the model has been criticized on various methodological grounds.

A number of writers have attempted to apply the SERVQUAL technique to tourism services. One particularly interesting attempt was made in 1996 by Frochot, who was studying its application to heritage sites.

The service gap concept

This concept is based on the idea that dissatisfaction in services such as tourism is caused by gaps between expectations and perceived outcomes. Parasuraman *et al.* (1985) identified five such potential service gaps as differences between:

- consumer expectations and management perceptions of consumer expectations
- management perceptions of consumer expectations and service quality specifications
- service quality specifications and the service actually delivered
- service delivery and what is communicated about the service to consumers
- consumer expectations and perceptions of the quality of the service received.

Eric Laws (1991) has applied this concept to the airline business:

> In airline advertising, passengers are often shown seated, or reclining in relaxed comfort in spacious cabins. They are attended by elegant and calm stewardesses (more rarely by stewards) and are featured enjoying delicious, carefully presented meals and fine wines. The reality is often very different. The point is that marketing communications are educating passengers to expect a level of service which it is beyond the ability of a carrier to deliver in all but the most favourable conditions. These might occur when there were no strikes, no mechanical failures, the cabin crew were on their peak performance, the plane was less than full, and all passengers were relaxed.

The aim therefore must be to use our marketing activities to create realistic expectations in the minds of our customers or else dissatisfaction may well result, however good we feel our product is. The SERVQUAL model has also been customized to suit the quality of hospitality and tourism services in particular; examples of this are DINESERV (Stevens, Knutson and Patton, 1995) and HOLSAT (Tribe and Snaith, 1998).

The critical incident approach

The critical incident approach to quality and consumer satisfaction is based on the idea that a tourist's satisfaction or otherwise with their experience of a product or service is a result of so-called 'critical incidents'. These incidents are concerned with the interaction between the organization's employees and customers, which can be termed the 'moment of truth' or 'the service encounter'. It assumes that there is a 'zone of tolerance' (Parasuraman *et al.*, 1985). In other words, customers will not notice a situation where the perceived experiences deviate only slightly from their expectations. Critical incidents are those that go beyond this zone of tolerance. 'A critical incident is one that can be described in detail and that deviates significantly, either positively or negatively, from what is normal or expected' (Bejou, Edvardssen and Rakourski, 1996).

Clearly an organization will wish to rectify the problems that caused a negative incident and to pacify the customer, while at the same time building on the strengths that contributed to a positive incident.

Bejou *et al*. (1996) carried out an interesting study of negative critical incidents in the airline industry in Sweden and the USA. In the hotel sector, such critical incidents could include:

- whether or not the check-in process goes smoothly
- if a meal ordered via room service appears quickly and meets the customer's expectations
- whether or not the concierge can provide an item which the guest has forgotten to pack.

These three models or techniques are based largely on the organization's perspective on service quality. This leads us to the issue of the service staff themselves.

The human resource management dimension

In a service industry such as tourism, human resource management is clearly of great significance in relation to quality and tourist satisfaction. Tom Baum has described the role of staff as 'making or breaking the tourist experience' (quoted in Ryan, 1997).

Tourist satisfaction depends on effective human resource management. This will occur only if staff:

- have the technical skills to carry out their job effectively
- have a positive attitude towards their job and are committed to pleasing their customers
- operate as a team and there are good working relations between frontline staff and managers
- are reliable in terms of attendance at work
- deal with complaints promptly, sympathetically and effectively.

However, in tourism, clients often complain about the quality of service and staff performance, particularly about waiting staff and tour operator representatives. This is probably not surprising as they are often employed as poorly paid temporary staff, with little training and working long hours.

Nevertheless, many tourism organizations have sought to put in place customer care programmes and other measures designed to improve the quality of service for customers. The fashionable technique of 'empowerment' has been used by companies such as the hotel chain Marriott to encourage staff to take more responsibility for satisfying customers' needs.

The role of marketing intermediaries

In tourism, a vital role is performed by marketing intermediaries, most notably travel agents. Their service is of great importance to most tourists and has a major influence on their ultimate satisfaction or dissatisfaction because they:

- provide advice on destinations and hotels, and their suitability for the client
- handle bookings and the issue of tickets
- advise the tourist on health issues and immigration formalities at the destinations
- take the client's money on behalf of the tour operator
- deal with complaints on behalf of the client.

Each of these factors can either enhance or diminish the quality of the tourist experience.

Work carried out in New Zealand by Cliff and Ryan in 1994 (quoted in Ryan, 1997) outlined consumer concerns about the reliability and performance of travel agents. They identify three dimensions to the travel agent's service quality, as follows.

- Tangible elements, such as the decor of the premises and the dress of the staff. If these do not satisfy the potential client they will not even think of using that travel agent.
- Reassurance that the agent is reliable and competent. If this reassurance is not given to the client, they may enter the premises but they will not book via the agent.
- After travel, if the tourist is not satisfied with the arrangements made by the agent they are unlikely to use them again.

Furthermore, inadequate performance by the marketing intermediary also affects the reputation and custom of the tour operator. If an agent recommended that a family should visit a particular resort and apartment complex in a certain resort that is lively, loud and not suitable for people with young children, the tourists would be dissatisfied with the holiday they had purchased from a particular operator. Yet it could have been a perfectly good holiday package, ideal for a young single person. It was just that the agent recommended it to clients for whom it was not designed.

The importance of problem-solving

The test of any quality management system is what happens when something inevitably goes wrong and the customer complains. Tourists do not expect perfection, but they do expect prompt action when problems occur.

Dealing effectively with difficulties and complaints can actively enhance tourist satisfaction. If everything on a holiday goes to plan, tourists tend not to notice. However, if something goes wrong and the organization handles the situation well, then the organization's reputation can be enhanced in the mind of the tourist. However, for this to happen, some basic guidelines need to be followed:

- Problems have to be put right as soon as possible. On a two-week holiday, the whole experience can be ruined if clients are not moved from inadequate to satisfactory accommodation within the first day or two.
- Make it easy for clients to contact resort representatives so they do not spend hours of their precious holiday trying to locate the person who is supposed to be there to help them.
- Ensure that any offer of compensation is fair and reflects the gravity of the problem.

Personal factors and satisfaction

There are two important personal factors which affect a consumer's satisfaction or otherwise, notably stress and arousal, and we will now briefly consider both of these.

Stress and tourist dissatisfaction

Stress caused by any aspect of the vacation experience tends to lead to tourist dissatisfaction. This stress can result from a variety of sources, as we can see from Figure 15.3.

We could have listed many others but those shown in Figure 15.3 give a good indication of the range of such factors. The tourist industry is constantly seeking to ameliorate these stresses, particularly at the higher end of the market.

Tourist satisfaction and arousal

In tourism, satisfaction is clearly connected to the concept of arousal. Too little arousal can cause boredom and dissatisfaction. According to Ryan (1997): 'The distinction

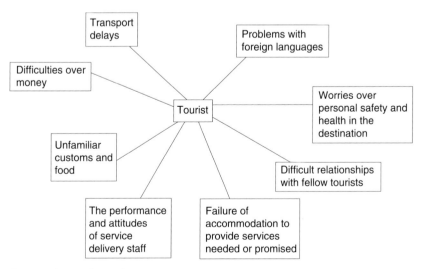

Figure 15.3 Sources of stress for tourists

between relaxation, a common motivation for holidays, and boredom is, from this viewpoint, dependent upon a level of arousal that is sufficient for relaxation, but is not so low as to induce boredom.'

At the other extreme, there is the concept of 'hyper-arousal, producing panic, frenzy and possible collapse' (Yerkes-Dodson Law, quoted in Ryan, 1997). A classic case of this in tourism might be the fear of flying experienced by some travellers. Hyper-arousal is likely to cause dissatisfaction in general.

However, in recent years the growth of so-called adventure tourism – white-water rafting and bungee-jumping, for example, has been based on hyper-arousal. This search for hyper-arousal is the exception though, for hyper-arousal in tourism normally arises when something goes wrong or there is an unforeseen occurrence such as an aircraft delay, and is seen as negative. Hyper-arousal is closely related to the concept of stress in tourism.

Changing expectations of quality over time

Tourists' expectations, in general, have risen over time in response to two influences:

*   an improvement in their everyday standard of living and housing amenities which make them always demand something extra when they are on holiday
*   product innovations by organizations that are then copied by competitors and become the norm.

We can see the way in which the consumer expectations of the accommodation product have developed over the years in response to both these factors.

At one time, hot and cold running water and shaving points in bedrooms were the height of sophistication. Then in-room radios were introduced and interior-sprung mattresses. After that came televisions, en-suite bathrooms, minibars and automatic alarms. These were followed by cable movie systems and, eventually, satellite television, jacuzzi baths and in-room pc links and Wi-Fi. Each of these was state of the art when first introduced but have now become the norm.

The interesting point is that while established generating markets such as the UK have passed slowly through all these stages, the recently developed markets such as Korea and Russia have demanded the latest state-of-the-art facilities from the beginning. At the same time, there are still consumers who are satisfied with less sophisticated in-room facilities, or rather they are willing to accept them in return for a low price.

The importance of uncontrollable factors

The factors that influence product quality or customer satisfaction, yet are outside organizations' control, are a major problem for the tourism industry. These include:

- weather, such as unseasonal rain in Mediterranean resorts in the summer or lack of snow in Alpine ski resorts in the winter
- strikes that affect tourists, such as air traffic controllers and ferry crews
- harassment of tourists by beggars and traders
- poor transport infrastructure in the destination country
- poor hygiene and sanitation standards and disease
- the perhaps unrealistic expectations of tourists; for instance, some people hope that a romantic weekend in Paris will put life back into a failing and doomed marriage
- the behaviour of other tourists in the resort or accommodation establishment
- government bureaucracy and bureaucratic factors, such as visa restrictions and departure taxes.

Any of these may cause tourist dissatisfaction with a holiday experience but they are outside the control of the tour operator that sold the holiday.

A good example of uncontrollable factors and tourist dissatisfaction comes from Las Vegas. The *Las Vegas Visitor Profile Study* showed that 5 per cent of visitors were dissatisfied because they did not win enough money in the casino! There is absolutely nothing the tour operator can do to solve this problem.

Subjective factors

Another difficulty in relation to quality and tourist satisfaction is that tourists have different attitudes, standards and prejudices. Often their satisfaction or otherwise is based on subjective views about an issue that is important to them, and that they judge in their own unique way.

Again, the *Las Vegas Visitor Profile Study* shows that:

- 10 per cent of visitors found the people in Las Vegas rude and unfriendly
- 8 per cent thought it too expensive
- 7 per cent said it was too hard to get to
- 4 per cent felt it was too intense
- 3 per cent claimed Las Vegas was dirty.

All these factors are subjective opinions based on individual interpretations of experiences as tourists. It is difficult to see how the tourism industry can respond effectively and in concrete terms to such views.

National differences in quality standards and tourist satisfaction

There is clear evidence that there are national differences in tourist expectations in relation to quality standards. It is widely recognized, for example, that German tourists are more concerned with the environmental quality of resorts than their British counterparts.

The authors' discussions with airline marketing executives also show that passengers of different nationalities have different quality standards. The consensus appears to be that passengers from countries such as Japan and the USA have higher expectations than those from more recently industrialized countries. These national differences in tourist expectations are obviously of great significance to organizations that operate transnationally, such as hotel chains and major airlines.

There are also national differences in the supply side, in terms of the quality of the product offered. These can lead tourists to modify their expectations if they are planning to visit a particular country, or even to decide not to visit a country. The different quality standards can cover elements of the product such as:

- food hygiene in restaurants
- fire safety in hotels
- public transport in destinations
- interpretation techniques in museums
- technical competence and attitudes of guides at heritage sites.

When considering the issue of national differences in product quality and tourist expectations, it is important to distinguish facts from the clichés and stereotypes that exist.

Quality management systems

The implementation of quality management systems in the tourism industry is crucial if tourists are to be satisfied in the longer term. This is also coupled with the fact that there have been worldwide changes in destinations and consumer taste (Tribe, 1999), accompanied by increased competition amongst tourism providers (Testa and Sipe, 2006; Briggs, Sutherland and Drummond, 2007; Pereira-Moliner, Claver-Cortés and Molina-Azorín, 2010). The International Organization for Standardization (ISO) has been successful in getting a large number of organizations in the world, including those in the tourism field, to adopt two of the main categories of their classification system: ISO 9001 for quality management systems and ISO 14001 for environmental management systems. There also a plethora of quality labels that have been developed for the tourism sector with little standardization across national boundaries, including labels for environmental quality, hotel star systems and beach quality levels (El Dref and Font, 2010). This does not help consumers make decisions, and just confuses them. That is why they are even more likely to make use of user-generated content review sites as well as word of mouth when making decisions.

Conclusions

We have seen that quality and tourist satisfaction are inextricably linked. However, they are both subjects about which we still have much to learn. In many cases we find airlines trying to apply models and techniques to tourism which were developed for service industries in general. We have yet to develop convincing models and techniques based on large-scale empirical research in tourism. This will not be easy, for we have also seen that many of the factors that affect satisfaction are uncontrollable, and quality is a highly personal and subjective concept.

Discussion points and essay questions

1. Discuss the idea that the most important factors which determine whether or not tourists will be satisfied are beyond the control of tourism organizations.
2. Critically evaluate the SERVQUAL technique and its potential use by tourism organizations.
3. Discuss the suggestion that quality means high price.

Exercise

Select a small sample of people, perhaps ten, who have recently taken a holiday. You should then interview them to see:

- how satisfied they were with their holiday
- which factors influenced their satisfaction or otherwise.

Produce a report of your findings, indicating what you have learnt from the survey about quality and tourist satisfaction, while recognizing the limitations of your survey.

References

Bejou, D., Edvardssen, B. and Rakourski, J.P. (1996). A critical incident approach to examining the effects of service failures in customer relationships. The case of Swedish and US airlines. *Tourism and Travel Research* Summer, 35–40.

Briggs, S., Sutherland, J. and Drummond, S. (2007). Are hotels serving quality? An exploratory study of service quality in the Scottish hotel sector. *Tourism Management* 28 (4), 1006–1019.

Conway, T. and Swift, J.S. (2000). International relationship marketing. The importance of psychic difference. *European Journal of Marketing* 34 (11/12), 1391–1413.

El Dref, M. and Font, X. (2010). The determinants of hotels' marketing managers' green market behaviour. *Journal of Sustainable Tourism* 18 (22), 157–174.

Frochot, I. (1996). Histoqual: the evaluation of service quality in historic properties. In *Tourism and Culture Conference Proceedings: Managing Culture Resources for the Tourist Volume*, eds M. Robinson, N. Evans and P. Callaghan. Business Education Publishers, Sunderland, UK.

Gummesson, E. (1989). Nine lessons on service quality. *TQM Magazine* 1, 2.

Laws, E. (1991). *Tourism Marketing: Service and Quality Management Perspectives*. Stanley Thornes, Kingston upon Thames, UK.

LVCVA (published annually). *Las Vegas Visitor Profile Study*. Las Vegas Convention and Visitors Authority.

Parasuraman, A., Zeithaml, V.A. and Berry, U. (1985). A conceptual model of service quality and its implications for future research. *Journal of Marketing* 49 (4), 41–50.

Pereira-Moliner, J., Claver-Cortés, E. and Molina-Azorín, J. (2010). Strategy and performance in the Spanish hotel industry. *Cornell Hotel and Restaurant Administration Quarterly* 51 (4), 513–528.

Ryan, C. (ed.) (1997). *The Tourist Experience: A New Introduction*. Cassell, London.

Stevens, P., Knutson, B. and Patton, M. (1995). DINESERV: A tool for measuring service quality in restaurants. *Cornell Hotel and Restaurant Administration Quarterly* 36 (2), 56–60.

Testa, M. and Sipe, L. (2006). A systems approach to service quality. *Cornell Hotel and Restaurant Administration Quarterly* 47 (1), 36–51.

Tribe, J. (1999). *Economía del ocio y el turismo*. Síntesis, Madrid.

Tribe, J. and Snaith, T. (1998). From SERVQUAL to HOLSAT: holiday satisfaction in Varadero, Cuba. *Tourism Management* 19 (1), 25–34.

CASE STUDY 15: The Savoy Hotel, London

INTRODUCTION

The Savoy Hotel is located on The Strand in the heart of the West End theatre district of London. The Savoy has played host to eminent men and women and provided the setting for glittering social occasions for over a century.

The Savoy Hotel was built with every luxury in mind. It was sold in 2005 to the Fairmont Hotels and Resorts Company. The ownership of the other hotels in The Savoy Group – the Berkeley, Claridge's and The Connaught – remain unchanged. More recently the hotel was reopened in 2010 after a complete refurbishment.

The original Savoy Group of Hotels and Restaurants were located in London. The company also owned The Lygon Arms in Broadway, in the Cotswolds. The hotels in the Group were represented by 'The Leading Hotels of the World' group. In 1995 the Group embarked on a major programme of work to re-establish itself as the world's leading luxury hotel chain. This programme of work involved a major period of refurbishment which has tried to maintain the old charm of the hotels, but introduced new comfort and facilities. The programme also involved an extensive programme of management restructuring and training, and new approaches to sales and marketing.

A BRIEF HISTORY OF THE SAVOY GROUP

The Savoy Hotel was built by theatrical impresario, Richard D'Oyly Carte. In 1881 he built the first theatre in the world with electric lights, The Savoy Theatre, and proceeded to commission operettas. Gilbert and Sullivan wrote the operetta *Trial by Jury* for Richard D'Oyly Carte, and it proved to be an instant smash hit when it was staged at the theatre.

D'Oyly Carte began to realize that theatre customers often needed overnight accommodation, and in 1885 he began to resurrect The Savoy Hotel on the banks of the River Thames. He recognized that he needed people with considerable talent to run the hotel. He brought César Ritz from Switzerland and Escoffier from France to convert the cooking at The Savoy to an art form. Society flocked to the new creation to try out the new dishes and soak up the luxurious ambience. The Savoy has been at the heart of the arts in London for over a century. It continues to be the home of leading artists and is a meeting place for journalists, captains of industry and politicians.

D'Oyly Carte quickly decided to expand his interest in hotels, and refurbished Claridge's in Mayfair in 1899. It opened with a flourish and quickly became a favourite hotel with royalty. Heads of state and royalty have stayed in the hotel ever since.

The Connaught was built in 1897 and rapidly became the hotel for the landed gentry. D'Oyly Carte also purchased The Berkeley which was located in Piccadilly. The area started to change after the Second World War, and the Managing Director, Hugh Wontner, was commissioned to seek out a new site. Land was found in Belgravia, a very elegant part of London, and the hotel was finally opened in 1972. The Berkeley has become a popular location for social, diplomatic and business gatherings.

The Group also purchased The Lygon Arms in the Cotswolds and Simpson's in the Strand. The Savoy Group of Hotels that existed before the sale of The Savoy is shown in Exhibit 15.1.

Exhibit 15.1 The Savoy Group of Hotels and Restaurants prior to the sale of The Savoy in 2005

The Berkeley, Wilton Place, Knightsbridge, London SW1X 7RL

Claridge's, Brook Street, Mayfair, London W1A 2JQ

The Connaught, Carlos Place, Mayfair, London W1Y 6AL

The Savoy, The Strand, London WC2R 0EU

The Lygon Arms, Broadway, Worcestershire WR12 7DU

Simpson's In The Strand, 100 Strand, London WC2R 0EW

Edward Goodyear Court Florist, 45 Brook Street, London W1A 2JQ

Savoy Theatre, The Strand, London WC2R 0ET

Source: The Savoy Group Promotional Literature

The Savoy Group's collection of hotels and restaurants has always epitomized excellence in service, style, elegance and cuisine. The combination of its rich history and distinguished cast list of guests and staff make it unique. It has also encouraged and trained thousands of young, career-minded people – it is a 'school' for learning to deliver quality of service.

We have always been at the very heart of innovation, a characteristic of The Savoy Group, and I am delighted to be in a position to help continue this tradition. I enjoy working with the staff, maintaining the existing high standards and enhancing them where appropriate. In this industry, the hotel business and the needs of our guests are constantly evolving, and our job is to make sure that we keep abreast of every change.

We aim to offer the best of both worlds – maintaining respect for the past and an understanding of the future. We have the very latest in technology and efficiency, giving modern comfort, which is combined with the original interiors and traditional standards of service.

The Savoy Hotel plc comprises a group of luxury hotels that is independent and answerable only to its Board of Directors. The Group's key objective is to maintain all the elements of style and service that have made it famous and envied throughout the world.

Ramon Pajares, Managing Director, Savoy Group, 1999

The Savoy Group, under the leadership of Ramon Pajares, began the painstaking process of restoring the hotels within the Group to be the most distinguished and individual hotels in England. The customer survey had noted some particular areas for attention such as general levels of comfort, improved business services and improved levels of personal service.

The Group spent £62 million on the refurbishment. The project affected all five hotels in the Group's portfolio and has combined careful restoration work with the installation of state-of-the-art technology. New bedrooms, penthouse suites, luxurious fitness facilities, meeting rooms and modern business amenities have all been incorporated in the ambitious programme. The programme summed up by Pajares' maxim: 'respecting the past and understanding the future'.

The refurbishment programme carried out at The Savoy and Claridge's is shown in Exhibit 15.2.

The Group paid particular attention to the needs of business executives in its refurbishment project. Business amenities and meeting rooms were upgraded. The refurbished rooms incorporate ISDN lines, video cameras, projection screens, high-quality sound systems and sophisticated audiovisual systems. Dual-line telephones, dedicated fax lines and modem points were incorporated. The rooms have individually controlled air-conditioning systems, a CD player and a CD library on demand, and the provision of US and European electrical points, voicemail and language facilities.

The refurbishment programme was followed by an extensive period of staff training including an intensive customer service training programme.

Exhibit 15.2 The refurbishment programme at The Savoy and Claridge's in the late 1990s

Claridge's

A London name to rank alongside Christie's, Harrods and the Victoria and Albert Museum, Claridge's, has all the style, elegance and sophistication of an English stately home.

Business at the top

A central element in the £32 million refurbishment programme at Claridge's has been the creation on the sixth floor of a self-contained conference suite comprising four inter-connecting meeting and dining rooms.

Olympian fitness

Claridge's magnificent new health and fitness centre, the Olympus Suite, is ideally suited for the international traveller.

Seventh heaven

Pride of place in Claridge's hotel-wide restoration programme is taken by the two new luxurious penthouse suites, one traditional, one Art Deco style, and seven Art Deco deluxe double bedrooms on the seventh floor.

Double award

In two separate readers' polls in 1996, Claridge's has been voted by *Travel + Leisure* magazine one of Europe's 25 best hotels, and by *Institutional Investor* magazine as one of the world's 25 best hotels.

The Savoy

The Savoy is a London landmark whose history and location are entwined with the capital's vibrant cultural and commercial past. Rich, elegant and flamboyant, the hotel's unique atmosphere makes any visit an event in itself.

Restoring the glory

The restoration of the famous Front Hall is just one element in an £18 million list of improvements which have brought a renewed sense of style to The Savoy.

Other public areas, including the American Bar, have been sympathetically restored to their former glory.

Big business

The magnificent Abraham Lincoln and Manhattan meeting and banqueting rooms, have been carefully restored to maintain their classical style whilst also incorporating the latest technology.

Past and future

Guest rooms have been redecorated, their architectural features painstakingly restored and bathrooms throughout upgraded.

Style vote

The Savoy's stylish interiors and elegance remain as popular as ever with readers of *Institutional Investor* and *Travel + Leisure* magazines, who voted it one of the world's 100 best hotels in their respective 1996 polls. It has just been named Egon Ronay's Hotel of the Year.

Source: The Savoy Group.

The Group also placed a new focus on sales and marketing. The first stage of this was to communicate the good news about the refurbishment programme across the world. The Group established a website and travelled to cities around the world, including Tokyo, Singapore and Hong Kong, to tell the trade about the dramatic improvements in the refurbished hotels.

The Group reorganized the sales and marketing departments. Specialists were appointed who were given the responsibility of regaining market share by developing key geographical markets (the UK, the USA, Europe and Japan) and by focusing on individual business and leisure segments. It was hoped that this quality marketing would help to re-establish the company as the first choice for customers who were looking for a luxury hotel in London.

The Savoy Hotel was bought by an American hotel company, the Fairmont Hotels and Resorts Company, on 19 January 2005. The ownership of the other members of the group – Claridge's, The Berkeley and The Connaught – remain as they were. Since this time the hotel has developed further with a change of ownership, and a summary of the most recent changes in the hotel's history is shown in Exhibit 15.3.

Exhibit 15.3 Recent developments at The Savoy

19 January 2005	The Savoy is purchased by a consortium headed by HRH Prince Al-Waleed Bin Talal bin Abdulaziz al Saud, who hands the management contract to Fairmont Hotels and Resorts
15 December 2007	The Savoy's general manager Kiaran MacDonald rings a bell at midday in the Front Hall, and declares The Savoy officially closed for the first time in its 118-year history, in order to begin a complete restoration of the entire building. At the time this is slated to cost around £100 million and take about 15 months.
10 October 2010	On 10-10-10 The Savoy finally reopens to the public after what has become a £220 million restoration project that has taken almost three years to complete. The opening is marked by the arrival in The Savoy's own Rolls-Royce Phantom of the first guest to check in to the hotel after reopening, the actor, writer and broadcaster Stephen Fry.
2 November 2010	HRH Prince Charles declares The Savoy officially (re)open after having been closed for almost three years. He unveils a plaque to commemorate the event in the presence of the hotel's part owner, HRH Prince Al-Waleed Bin Talal bin Abdulaziz al Saud, and his wife Princess Amira.
2014	The Savoy celebrates its 125th anniversary year. A variety of events mark the occasion, including historical tours with The Savoy's archivist, a special exhibition of press cuttings of reviews of the hotel from 1889 in The Savoy Museum, anniversary cocktails created by both the American Bar and the Beaufort Bar, and a new edition of The Savoy Cocktail Book.

Source: extracts from www.fairmont.com/savoy-london/hotelhistory

---

THE SAVOY TODAY

The Savoy has a long history of development and has maintained the Art Deco touches that have made it so famous. The hotel now has an array of modern amenities that make the hotel attractive to the business and leisure traveller. Visitors to The Savoy come from the UK and worldwide, with a large amount of custom from male business travellers. The Far East is an important market, with Japanese visitors being a particularly important segment. Both business and leisure customers look for high levels of individual service, and business guests particularly look for conference facilities, individual meeting rooms and business technology. The challenge for The Savoy is how to keep updating these services without changing the ambience of the hotel. An important part of The Savoy's hotel customer base is the special features that guests received with the reopening of the hotel in 2010, described in Exhibit 15.4.

Exhibit 15.4 Press release for the re-opening of The Savoy Hotel, 2010

The most ambitious hotel restoration in history is complete

November 22, 2010 – The Savoy, A Fairmont Managed Hotel, reopened its doors on Sunday, October 10, 2010. One of this year's most eagerly anticipated openings, The Savoy has undergone one of the most ambitious restorations in British history. The hotel closed in December 2007 for a restoration program that encompasses the entire building from the iconic entrance and the American Bar to Savoy Grill and the 268 guestrooms and suites.

'We are very excited to reopen The Savoy', comments Kiaran MacDonald, General Manager. 'It is fair to say that this project has not been without its challenges, but we are immensely proud to unveil the results of nearly three years of hard work and dedication. We are very aware of the place that The Savoy holds in many people's affections and we firmly believe that the hotel will exceed people's expectations and reclaim its position as one of the world's great hotels.'

Source: extracts from www.fairmont.com/savoy-london/press-room/thesavoyreopened

---

CONCLUSIONS

The Savoy Group has had to respond to demands from its guests to see improved facilities and services. A major investment programme, coupled with staff training programmes and renewed sales and marketing efforts, attempted to reverse a downward trend in sales experienced in the 1990s. The initial results of the programme of work indicate that it was successful. Particular emphasis was put on the use of new technology, improvements in public rooms, and leisure and business facilities. A change of ownership and continued market research led to the company closing for three years for a major refurbishment programme and reopening.

The focus on particular market segments, designing products to suit their needs and wants and communicating these developments to them, has been a major part of the continued strategy by the Fairmont Hotel Group.

DISCUSSION POINTS AND ESSAY QUESTIONS

1. The restoration programme in the 1990s at The Savoy Group was based on the maxim: 'respecting the past and understanding the future'. Discuss the importance of this statement in relation to the needs and wants of customers of The Savoy.
2. The Savoy carried out marketing research with guests to inform its most recent

refurbishment programme. Prepare a detailed plan of the marketing research programme that you would carry out for The Savoy prior to another programme of redevelopment. Suggest an ongoing programme of marketing research with guests that you would implement at the hotel.

3. The change of ownership led to the closure of the hotel for three years for refurbishment. Discuss the effect this would have had on guest loyalty and how the quality of the new hotel can be communicated to these guests.

CHAPTER 16

The emergence of new markets and changes in tourist demand

Introduction

This chapter aims to give a flavour of the emerging trends and discussions that are currently under debate in both the academic and commercial worlds of the hospitality and tourism sector. It does not attempt to give the reader the underlying principles of consumer behaviour, which are well covered in the second edition of our consumer behaviour book (Swarbrooke and Horner, 2007). It is clear from Chapter 15 that researching consumer behaviour is a topical issue in both the commercial and academic arenas of tourism, but before a research programme is designed, we should consider the underlying concepts and ideas that underpin this design process. It is also important to consider new thoughts on this area and contemporary academic research since this will provide the necessary insights to enable the development of efficient and effective products and services.

This chapter starts by going back to the psychological state of travel and discusses the underlying reasons for this. The second part of the chapter considers the apparent balance of power in the tourism market, and discusses how the consumer appears to have gained power in the buying relationship. The third part of the chapter will consider topical issues in relation to market segmentation, including the impact of age, culture, socioeconomic state and the values of tourists in relation to climate change and environmental issues. Within the chapter we will consider concepts such as psychological state, postmodernism, motivators and determinants, and market segmentation.

Why do people travel?

A tourist destination is not a simple product but an amalgam of different tourist products, services and public goods that are presented to the consumer as a total package. This offering should provide the tourist with a good experience. Early researchers often

	Major themes (number of articles)	Minor themes (number of articles)
Directly related (drawn from psychology)	Decision-making/consumer behaviour (14)	Perceptions and memories (4)
	Motivation (10)	Psychological benefits (3)
	Satisfaction and attitudes (8)	Tourist experiences (3)
	Social interaction (5)	Destination image (3)
Indirectly related (drawn from other fields, e.g. education, geography)	Knowledge and understanding (6)	Humour (1)
	Heritage and interpretation (6)	Involvement and interest (1)

Figure 16.1 The number of recent articles linking psychology and tourism themes featured in the *Annals of Tourism Research* 2007–11

Source: adapted from Pearce and Packer (2013)

described this experience in terms of a geographical area, such as a country or city (Hall, 2000), but more recent contemporary researchers have viewed destinations as a mixture of the consumers' space and the tourism products that provides tourists with a holistic experience based on their travel itinerary, their cultural background, their purpose of visit and their past experiences (Fuchs and Weirmair, 2003). This new set of ideas means that the underlying psychological state of the tourist has become more prominent in academic research and has begun to be explored in contemporary research programmes (Pearce and Packer, 2013).

A literature review of the *Annals of Tourism Research* carried out in 2012 showed that there has been growing interest in research on tourist behaviour using psychology, or a topic related to psychology such as education, geography or cultural studies, as the conceptual underpinning for the research. It is also interesting to note the topic areas on which researchers focused because this can give a feel for contemporary topics. The results of this work are shown in Figure 16.1. It can be seen that consumer behaviour and motivation are of major importance, although issues such as perception and memories, benefits, identity and destination image also constitute an important focus (Pearce and Packer, 2013). So if we accept that the reasons why tourists travel are due to the individual's psychological state, what factors have an influence on that state, and why do tourists select certain destinations?

Academic research on tourist behaviour

A great deal of the commentary concerning consumer choice in tourism is grounded in an old concept by Abraham Maslow (1943), the hierarchy of needs, where five levels of a pyramid can be seen as playing a role in the determination of a motivational profile for tourists, and those who have reached the top of the pyramid are viewed as being in a state of self-actualization and seeking deeper more authentic experiences (Hsu and Huang, 2008). More recent researchers have suggested that status- and

Destination choice	Satisfaction research
Relevance of memory to decision-making	Relevance of personal growth to decision-making
Concept of cautious borrowing – the tourist will try to balance the positive aspects of the past and the things that troubled them before making a decision	

Figure 16.2 The main focus of research on tourist behaviour

Source: adapted from Pearce and Packer, 2013

relationship-informed patterns of consumer behaviour are more appropriate, and there is a need to consider cultural groups, especially Asian consumers, which were not considered in Maslow's original work (Pearce and Panchal, 2011).

A number of academic commentators suggest that it is necessary to consider the multiple motivators of tourist behaviour so that accurate predictive patterns can be developed that are based on empirical research (Bowen and Clarke, 2009; Hsu and Huang, 2008; Pearce, 1992). Despite this, it is interesting to consider the types of areas that have emerged as key areas for debate over the past few years. These are summarized well in the recent article by Pearce and Packer (2013), and are listed in Figure 16.2. More detail of the literature in these areas is covered well in this article.

Main weaknesses in consumer behaviour research in tourism

A shift in the balance of power

The marketing of products and services in developed economies has seen a gradual shift in the power relationship from the provider to the consumer. Developed countries have been characterized by Vrontis and Thrassou (2007) as having the following features:

- high economic productivity and per capita income, and low inflation
- high labour costs and quality
- regulation of working conditions
- relative freedom in business activity
- high levels of education and administration
- excellent transport and communication infrastructures
- technological superiority
- increasing emphasis on service delivery rather than products
- emphasis on knowledge and information
- general stability
- socio-cultural environment that supports personal and collective development and expression.

In the developed countries it has been recognized that the influence of consumers has been growing over the past few decades, and now they are viewed as the sovereign force shaping the general business environment (Kotler *et al.*, 2005; Blackwell, Miniard and Engel, 2001). The new consumers in these countries feel informed and confident in their own decision-making, in contrast to the situation in the less developed countries (Teng, Laroche and Zhu, 2007; Laroche, Kim and Matsui, 2003). It is predicted, however, that in the process of globalization consumers in the developing countries will also mirror this movement in the longer term.

The reasons for this growth in apparent consumer power are probably many and varied. Many cite rising education levels as a key factor, along with the fact that in many countries tourists are becoming ever more experienced travellers. More experience leads to knowledge and confidence.

However, perhaps the main factor in the perceived swing of power to consumers has been the rise of new information technologies, primarily the internet (these are considered in more depth in Chapter 17). The internet:

- means that consumers now have far more choices available to them and can access products and services from a wider range of sources than previously
- has facilitated the rise of global consumer-generated media which allows travellers to take advice from fellow travellers whose opinions they may trust more than travel professionals who have a commercial motivation for the products and services they recommend.

The internet, with its focus on price, has also encouraged consumers to believe they can negotiate or 'haggle' with suppliers, particularly hotels. Customers may argue that a hotel should offer them the best rate they have seen online rather than a quoted rate and/or they may ask for 'extras' such as breakfast or parking to be included in the price. Companies obsession with brand loyalty means they make themselves more susceptible to this kind of consumer negotiation.

However, we have to be careful before we fully accept that the internet has led to consumers taking power from the industry. After all, the online travel agents control the supply and prices, and travel companies own some consumer-generated media sites. And the ICT equipment that consumers use is all developed by mega IT corporations for which tourism is just a revenue stream.

And even if some of this new consumer power is real, it can also have an unethical dimension. It is not unusual these days for hotel guests to threaten to post a bad review on TripAdvisor or a similar site if they are not given an upgrade or some additional benefit for which they have not paid.

How do consumers choose?

The choices consumers make regarding holidays are complex and involve a series of inter-related stages. The tourist has to think about decisions on different levels of participation, has to choose the destination, has to decide on their level of spending, and is motivated by a number of motivators and determinants (Swarbrooke and Horner, 2007). As we have seen above, the power of the consumer in this decision-making process has grown over the past decade in the developing countries. Despite this, they are influenced by many different factors and it can be suggested that their decision can be spontaneous rather than meticulously planned as some commentators would suggest. A full review of the literature on tourists' decision-making is given by Smallman and Moore (2010). A further complication of the choice process occurs when the tourist visit is being purchased on behalf of someone else as a gift. This adds further to the complexities of the decision-making process and often adds to the emotional influence from both donor and recipient (Clarke, 2008).

Although advertising vehicles have changed, there is still a heavy influence exerted by brands and advertising according to the product or service sector. A piece of research carried out in 2012 indicated that advertising significantly influences tourist decisions, with several variables (age, income, distance and internet usage) moderating decisions dependent on the decision stage and product type. It appears that the effect of advertising on the propensity to visit certain destinations, and the purchase of particular tourism services such as attractions, restaurants, events, shopping, hotels and outdoor activities, all varied, and this was made more complex when tourists were purchasing these items separately using the internet (Park, Nicolau and Fesenmaier, 2013).

There appears to have been little research in the new emerging markets on this topic. One piece of research with tourists at Taiwan Taoyuan International airport considered the subject of hesitation in tourism choice, which is considered a problem in this market. The research showed a strong correlation between the perceived risk of travel to a particular destination and hesitation in choosing the destination. The input of tourism knowledge about the destination had a positive impact on reducing this hesitation and increased the propensity to buy. This means that the creation of educational materials for new destinations delivered by different advertising media is particularly important in this market (Wong and Yeh, 2009). Another piece of research carried out at the same airport mirrored these findings, showing that airport shoppers sought information both before and during their experience to make the shopping experience both more reliable and convenient. This became a more satisfactory experience when they travelled as a group rather than on an individual basis (Chung, Wu and Chiang, 2013).

Tourism organizations try to segment markets using demographic, geographical, behavioural and psychographic variables in order to be able to target consumers more effectively, the idea being that consumers in particular groups will share common characteristics that can be targeted more effectively by tourism organizations (Swarbrooke and Horner, 2007). There are a number of contemporary issues related to market segmentation, discussed in the next section.

Contemporary issues in market segmentation

This part of the chapter investigates a number of contemporary issues in relation to market segmentation and tourist behaviour. The first of these is a demographic issue and concerns generational differences in travel behaviour.

Demographic variables – generational theory

It is widely recognized that the world's population is ageing, and that this is a phenomenon that is particularly apparent in the developed areas of the world. The United Nations has stated that more that 2 billion people in the world will be 60 years or over by 2050. The direct consequence of this is that older consumers will become increasingly important and will contribute significantly to the overall tourism spend. Many older people also have fewer commitments and higher disposable income, so have the potential to spend large amounts of money on tourism products and services. Even in countries such as China and India, the population is ageing, there is a burgeoning middle class, and the economies continue to grow. A significant proportion of Chinese and Indian people are also being educated in the West, which contributes to their global outlook and makes them ideal targets for tourism destinations and organizations.

This situation has fuelled recent interest in these consumers, and a number of pieces of research have taken place in different parts of the world to investigate how these consumers make their travel plans, and most importantly what influences them to purchase particular tourism products and services. Much of this research is based on the underlying concept of generational cohort analysis, which suggests that people in the same country who fit in a particular age group will demonstrate purchasing behaviour that is discrete and different from other generational groups (Cleaver and Muller, 2002; Prideaux, 2007). This interest has also grown in the business press, and terms have been derived that have come to be recognized in the mainstream literature, such as the 'silent generation', 'baby boomers', 'generation X' and 'generation Y' (see Figure 16.4)

Research was carried out in the US to compare and contrast the travel behaviour of these different groups, and a summary of the results of this research suggests that each group demonstrates different buying patterns in terms of influences on choice, destination preferences, and type of holiday preferences. This has implications for marketers in the US, however, because of the cultural setting of the research, the ideas will not necessarily be mirrored in other markets.

A piece of research carried out in Australia (Gardiner, King and Grace, 2013) added to the debate by showing that, regardless of generational group, the respondents in different groups did demonstrate distinct behaviour patterns. These patterns were a result of their own personal background, which partly reflected their formative years and society's values at this time. Their employment record, education and economic conditions during their formative years also contributed to their behaviour. They concluded that both societal and personal influences had an effect on tourism purchase behaviour.

The baby boomers as a special group

Baby boomers are defined as the group born between 1946 and 1964. They are major spenders on tourism products, and thus are a target for tourism organizations. Academic research has been conducted over recent years to consider what these consumers are looking for, how they seek information, and how they purchase products

Customization	Convenience and speed
Spiritual enlightenment	Authenticity
Service quality	Nostalgia
Experiences	Learning and enrichment
Environmental awareness	Health consciousness

Figure 16.3 Features that travelling baby boomers look for

Source: adapted from Hudson (2010)

and services. It has also been important to consider what brings them satisfaction. Another term has also been coined in the commercial world to emphasize the buying patterns of this generation – 'zoomers' – baby boomers who want to get the most out of life and live life to the fullest, in other words, baby boomers with zip (Hudson, 2010).

Recent research has considered what these zoomers look for in terms of their travel behaviour, summarized by Hudson (2008) on the basis of a literature review (Figure 16.3).

Baby boomers like to feel that their travel packages can be customized. They can either do this themselves on the internet or use a travel company that offers a bespoke and customized tour offering. This group also looks for convenience and a stress-free experience, so the company that arranges to pick them up from home at the start and end of the holiday will be at an advantage, for example. They tend to be interested in spiritual enlightenment, so cultural tourism experiences will offer these travellers a premium. Service quality levels will also have to be of a high standard and will have to be visible in the marketing literature. It is also important to engage in nostalgic experiences. This may range from going back to a destination visited earlier in life, to more sophisticated versions of nostalgia where visits are made to re-created towns, villages or industrial sites. They want new experiences and to be given the opportunity to learn, so the idea of incorporating lectures, or practical activities such as learning to cook or paint, are excellent product offerings. Environmental awareness and health consciousness are at a premium so the move to healthy slow food and environmentally friendly hotels will be attractive to this type of consumer.

Other research has considered the places where baby boomers look for information before booking a holiday, and the style of advertising that they prefer. Organizations have tried to use mass media to target this group, but research has shown that word-of-mouth communication with family and friends is much more important. This group also like feature stories in magazines, newspapers and television documentaries (Patterson, 2007). The baby boomers do not like to see older people in advertising messages because they tend to feel that they are younger and more vibrant than they actually are (Patterson, 2007). A model for marketing communication to baby boomers has been suggested by Hudson (2010) as incorporating the following features:

- emphasising youth
- using nostalgia as a theme

Group	1	2	3	4
Generation	Silent generation	Baby boomers	Generation X	Generation Y
Born	prior to 1945	1946–64	1965–80	1981–2000
Values	Conformity, discipline, conservative, distrust of change	Optimistic due to increased educational and social opportunities; seek exploration and achievement; are influenced by television; seek personal fulfilment	Entrepreneurial spirit, loyalty, creativity and information focus; value both work and life, put more emphasis on work–life balance despite desire to get on in life	Most globally oriented group, adapt rapidly, crave change, smart, creative, technically savvy, loyal
Holiday patterns	Moderate spenders, tend to take longer holidays out of peak season	Biggest spenders in developed markets; take more leisure and business trips a year; are often the most affluent consumers	Take moderate numbers of trips in a year, often travel with others, particularly children	Average spenders; more interested in activity and adventure

Figure 16.4 A brief summary of the key characteristics of the four generations

Source: adapted from Li, Li and Hudson (2013)

- promoting the experience and not the product
- showing how to improve baby boomers' lives
- providing detailed information and telling a story
- using a wide range of media and features, including online media, which is critical.

A stereoype exists that baby boomers who have reached the age of 50 have fewer needs, are unwilling to try out new products and services, and have little buying power (Coleman, Hladikova and Savelyeva 2006). This could not be farther from the truth as baby boomers redefine retirement and seek new products and services from the travel industry.

THE RUSSIAN TOURIST

Historical background

Numbers of Russian tourists started to grow in the 1880s, and in 1885 the first tourist agency was established in Petersburg. Russians continued to travel as hedonistic and cultural tourists. By 1858 many prominent members of the younger generation had been on a 'grand tour'. Tourism continued to grow but there was an ongoing debate in Russia about the growth in hedonistic rather than cultural tourism. In the Soviet period the state sought to limit personal travel and to make its citizens' tourism a cohesive force of socialist nation-building. In recent times, especially since the fall of the Iron Curtain and since the 1990s, Russians have been freer to travel and tour operators have flourished in Russia to encourage outbound tourism. Russian tourists are now seen as an attractive target market for many destination marketing organizations.

The past 20 years

The past 20 years have seen a dramatic growth in the number of trips made by Russian citizens abroad. There has been a large growth in numbers since the late 1990s, and Europe is seen as a particularly attractive destination. In 2010 Russians made 25,487,000 trips to non-CIS countries. Countries that attract Russian tourists in Europe include Finland, Italy, Germany, Greece, Czech Republic, Bulgaria, France and Cyprus. High-spending tourists also like to visit Switzerland and London.

What do Russian tourists look for?

- They want to go to the seaside in summer for sun, warmth and sea.
- They want luxury, particularly in relation to accommodation, facilities and food.
- They value their accommodation and facilities in the destination.
- They like service staff to speak Russian.
- They also like cross-border shopping, particularly to Poland.

Sources: Bar-Kolelis and Wiskulsi, 2012; Furmanov, Balaeva and Predvoditeleva, 2011; Vespestad, 2010; Choi, Tkachenko and Sil, 2009; Layton, 2009

Geographical segmentation and the effects of culture

One of the most commonly used methods of market segmentation in tourism is geographical segmentation, where individuals, usually from one country, share common characteristics based on their culture. Values are probably the most important manifestation of culture, along with heroes, rituals and symbols (Hofstede, 2001; Hofstede and Hofstede, 2005). It is suggested that these values influence tourist behaviour in a fundamental way. We shall now consider one new target market to illustrate some key points.

The illustration of 'The Russian tourist' provides a short summary of the history of Russian tourism and the key factors that Russian tourists look for when booking holidays. According to research by Hofstede and Hofstede (2005), Russia is considered to be a collectivist culture, which assumes that Russians will be more interested in socially consumed products rather than products that are highly individual. Despite this, tour operators in Russia have reported that some of their clients seek activity and nature holidays, which could be seen as suiting individualist societies where people seek self-actualization and renewal (Vespestad, 2010). If this is a growing trend, it suggests that geographical segmentation is a dangerous proposition. After all, how can one nation of so many individuals from different geographical locations across Russia fit into one discrete market segment? It seems more appropriate to use multi-variate

International tourist arrivals (overnight visitors) worldwide exceeded the 1 billion mark for the first time ever in 2012, with 1,035 million tourists crossing borders, up from 995 million in 2011
Asia and the Pacific recorded the strongest growth with a 7 per cent increase in arrivals, followed by Africa (+6 per cent) and the Americas (+5 per cent)
International tourist arrivals in Europe, the most visited region in the world, were up by 3 per cent; the Middle East (−5 per cent) has not yet succeeded in returning to growth
With a 4 per cent increase in real terms, the growth in international tourism receipts matched the growth in arrivals
International tourism receipts reached US$1,075 billion worldwide in 2012, up from US$1,042 billion in 2011
China became the number one source market in the world in 2012, spending US$102 billion on international tourism
Forecasts prepared by UNWTO in January 2013 point to growth of 3–4 per cent in international tourist arrivals for 2013, only slightly below 2012's level and in line with UNWTO's long-term forecast
By UNWTO region, prospects for 2013 are stronger for Asia and the Pacific, followed by Africa

Figure 16.5 International tourism in 2012 – key trends and outlook

Source: UNWTO (2012)

market segmentation techniques to obtain a more sophisticated picture, although this type of research has yet to be done in Russia.

Socioeconomic segmentation – the effects of the recession

The United Nations World Tourism Organization (UNWTO) has predicted that the global picture on worldwide tourism data is positive, with growth being shown in particular areas of the world. Details of its predictions can be seen in Figure 16.5. These figures seem to indicate that the economic crisis of 2010 is over, although they do mask some areas of the world where tourism has been particularly badly hit and is hoping to recover soon. One example of a country that it still trying to recover at the time of writing is Greece.

It is interesting to reflect on the world economic crisis that has just occurred and consider what consumers in particular socioeconomic groups did as a result of finding themselves in difficult economic situations. As tourism spend is discretionary, a reduction in personal wealth and income will by definition reduce the amount of money available to spend on tourism products and services. The situation is more complex than this, however, because different patterns of behaviour are shown depending on the individual's personal circumstances and the market conditions. During the economic crisis consumer spending was influenced by a range of factors, including inflation, insecurity of savings, declining values of housing and pensions, and reduced incomes. The effects continue to be a problem up to the present time, and were particularly severe in countries such as Greece, Italy and Spain. Other countries, such as the UK and the Netherlands, also experienced difficult times. Little was known about the effects of this global recession on tourism buying behaviour, so research was carried out to collect data to accompany the many anecdotal accounts that were appearing in the media. It is considered important to collect information about consumers' attitudes to spending on travel during an economic recession so that future decision can be better informed (Sheldon and Dwyer, 2010).

A piece of research was carried out in the Netherlands during 2011 to investigate what had happened to tourist purchase behaviour at an individual level during the crisis (Bronner and de Hoog, 2012). It was based on the premise that tourist behaviour in a crisis has two main dimensions – the first being the **range of scope** (the more widespread the crisis, the more severe will be the reaction in terms of purchasing behaviour), and secondly the **depth** (which reflects on the severity of the effect at the local level). It was also suggested that consumers tend to take four courses of action, depending on the range of scope and the depth, as follows:

- **substitution**, where alternatives are sought – so tourists may go to a free museum rather than an expensive visitor attraction
- **cheese-slicing**, which is a way of economising on certain aspects – tourists may choose a cheaper hotel, or spend less on extras at the destination
- **pruning**, mainly giving up on holidays, cancelling them or delaying making a decision – previous research has shown that tourists tend to do this when the crisis is seen as severe and deep
- **day trips from home**, where tourists economise by not booking accommodation but just going on day trips.

The research in the Netherlands showed that the predominant model tourists adopted was cheese-slicing rather that the expected pruning, so they still went on holiday but tried to economise on certain aspects once there (Bronner and de Hoog, 2012). The authors suggested that the reason is that holidays have become such an important feature of life in general that tourists will do anything rather than cancel a holiday, even when the economic situation is dire. They also suggested that tourism organizations could provide more information to tourists on how to economise rather than just allowing them to do their own research on social media sites.

Little of this type of research has been done in Asia, but one piece of research carried out in Japan showed that Japanese tourists are influenced a great deal in their tourism research behaviour by level of prosperity and income, although their household size and travel distance also had an effect on their purchase behaviour (Wu, Zhang and Fujiwara, 2013).

Psychographic segmentation – environmentalism and the effect of climate change

The final new trend that this chapter reviews is the new consumer interest in environmentalism and issues in relation to climate change. Sustainable tourism behaviour is a topic that has dominated the minds of both academics and practitioners over the past few decades. There are signs that tourist provision can be improved in terms of resource consumption, waste management, transport optimization and local communities (Budenau, 2007). Consumers have shown a growing interest in the topic, but until recently have been reluctant to spend the extra money that organizations often demand for sustainable products and services (Swarbrooke and Horner, 2007). Consumers now seem to have a growing interest in this area and are demonstrating new values and lifestyles that demonstrate their commitment to sustainability. This growing interest is spilling over into their tourism behaviour, where the topic of climate change is also beginning to have an impact on their purchase patterns and behaviour.

Despite the growing interest and declared positive attitudes towards sustainable tourism, only a few tourists buy responsible tourism products, choose environmentally friendly methods of transportation or behave responsibly to the local environment or the local community. This low support from customers is the main barrier to the introduction of sustainable tourism principles and practice, and as such is worthy of research. Various pieces of research have considered tourists' behaviour in relation to the environment in different regions of the world. The position in Britain demonstrates the dilemma that tourists have in this area. A large majority of tourists consider it is fairly important that their holiday choices do not damage the environment, with 85 per cent thinking that their holidays should not damage the environment, and 71 per cent thinking that tourism should benefit the local community (Budenau, 2007). However, another piece of research showed that only 32 per cent of British tourists have chosen holidays that were deliberately designed to reduce the impact on the local environment (Goodwin and Francis, 2003). Since this piece of research was carried out, following the world economic crisis, it is likely that this situation will have deteriorated due to falling incomes and the cheese-slicing behaviour discussed above.

The situation in relation to accommodation choices seems a little better, particularly in countries where a green labelling system for hotels leads to more positive choices. For example, research has shown that 69 per cent of Danish tourists are willing to pay for an eco-labelled hotel (Chafe, 2005). In another piece of research, 62 per cent of Italians and 42 per cent of Germans see the environmental impact of hotels to be important; 86 per cent of Dutch tourists would welcome a star system for hotels that combines the environment and quality performance; and 90 per cent of Italian tourists are in favour of an eco-labelling system for hotels (CREM, 2000).

Tourists can damage or protect the environment at various stages of the tourism experience, as well as just at the obvious accommodation stage. A summary of these different stages is shown in the illustration of 'Tourist holiday choice stages', along with possible barriers that can prevent tourists choosing a sustainable option.

Tourist holiday choice stages, environmental impact, and possible barriers to positive action

Stage	Negative outcomes	Possible barriers
Choice of holiday	Air pollution, noise	Economic situation
	Congestion	Inconvenience

Choice of accommodation	Environmental damage Employee damage	Lack of knowledge Confusion of labels
Visitor behaviour/ entertainment	Upset locals by causing a nuisance, prying into their private lives, damaging outdoor spaces and indoor environments	Lack of cultural awareness Lack of education Hedonistic tendencies Peer group pressure
Choice of products and services	Choice of imported goods Smuggling of endangered species	Lack of knowledge Economic priorities Desire for international brands

Source: adapted from Budenau (2007)

It can be seen from the illustration that tourists have a wide variety of opportunities to cause environmental damage. Environmentally friendly alternatives may be difficult to access for tourists as they may be less comfortable or less convenient. Taking a train rather than a flight, for example, may cost more, be less convenient and be much more time-consuming. The desire for numerous convenient short holidays rather than one long summer holiday, for example, has fuelled the growth of budget airlines travelling over relatively short distances at prices that are cheaper than the alternatives.

A very important limiting factor for tourist choices is the availability of financial resources. The choice of the annual summer holiday is one of the most important expenses in the year, involving a long-term evaluation of options in terms of price, service quality and time (Swarbrooke and Horner, 2007). The average family will make rational decisions on the basis of perceived understandings of price, value and quality. So the influence of altruistic arguments pleading for better attitudes may have limited effect on behaviour due to limited financial resources. Acting as an environmentally friendly tourist may therefore just be a pipe dream rather than a reality, apart from for a relatively few determined individuals. After all, the development of the cheap mass market package tour has embedded the idea of cheap-and-cheerful holidays in the psyche of large numbers of consumers in western economies, and this is a scenario that will probably be repeated in other areas of the world where tourism is in the early stages of development.

If we do not accept this gloomy prediction, then there are things that the tourism and hospitality sectors can pioneer to lead to modifications in tourist behaviour. We will return to this later in the book, but for now we should give an outline of some of the influences that research has shown can have a positive effect on tourist behaviour. The most common tools for changing tourist behaviour that have been used to date are informative ones rather than economic instruments such as taxes and fees. The slow uptake by tourists of new environmental product offerings has raised questions as to whether governments and the EU should do more to foster good behaviour. In the meantime, there are two main types of initiative that are used to try to alter tourist behaviour.

The first of these is the use of **eco-labels** to inform potential tourists of good practice in the area. There is a lot of confusion about the different eco-labels because there has been no standardization applied across geographical boundaries, which has led to the proliferation of different versions in a plethora of markets. In 2001, for example, it was estimated that there were 70 tourism eco-labels in Europe alone (Font and Tribe, 2001). One example of an organization that promotes eco-tourism in the UK and accredits organizations on the basis of set criteria is Green Tourism (see the illustration 'Green Tourism'). Organizations can apply for accreditation for anything from a large, company-wide initiative to a small, discrete initiative by smaller companies. One example is shown in the illustration 'Combe House', in which a small hotel has applied for certification on the basis of growing its own food and using it in the operation, adopting the principles of 'slow food'. These are very worthy initiatives but the problem can be that tourists from outside the UK do not recognize or are not able to judge the quality standard of a UK-based label. On the other hand, it is a good start.

GREEN TOURISM

The mission

Green Tourism has been running since 1997. We are a not-for-profit organization.

We have more than 2000 members across the UK, Ireland and Canada, making us the largest and most established sustainable national grading programme in the world.

Green Tourism is recognized by UK national and regional government as a crucial part of its drive towards sustainability. Our aim is to build on this strong position and ensure that the UK remains at the forefront of sustainable tourism in the future whilst extending our work around the world.

Green Tourism is independently validated by the International Centre for Responsible Tourism (ICRT) on behalf of VisitEngland, VisitWales and the Northern Ireland Tourist Board and endorsed by VisitScotland and Fáilte Ireland.

'GTBS [the Green Tourism Business Scheme] provides excellent value for money to a wide range of tourism firms with first class environmental advice and auditing. Satisfaction rates of certified firms are very high and dropout rates low, both for the smallest of tourism firms and increasingly at corporate level.'

Xavier Font, ICRT

Source: www.green-tourism.com

The second method of improving tourist choice is by using a variety of awareness-related tools. The work by TUI (Case study 14.2) is a good example of this type of move. Recent evidence suggests that consumers would prefer to purchase from socially responsible companies as long as the quality is not affected (Goodwin and Francis, 2003; Miller, 2003).

COMBE HOUSE

Combe House Devon is an independent, privately run Grade 1 Elizabethan Country House Hotel and Restaurant. Combe House's environmental project to restore the old Victorian garden has led to the on-site production of 60 per cent of the hotel's seasonal fruit and vegetable needs. It has a GOLD Green Tourism Business Scheme award, and Condé Nast Johansens National Award 2010 awarded it the 'Most Excellent Innovation in Sustainable Hospitality'.

Combe House Hotel and Restaurant has identified that the cost of restoring the old Victorian Gardens and developing the fruit and vegetable project has been approximately £12,000. This has brought about an estimated saving of 30 per cent on the fruit and vegetable bill, giving a payback period of approximately 3 years. The activities have also increased the hotel's status with guests as a place that is truly developing its food quality and local sustainability potential. The decision has led to the development of improved soil condition. The soil is now organic and has resulted in a significant increase in the number and varieties of birds and insects. There is less dependence on factory produce, less waste from the kitchens, and pests have also been reduced by investing in frames, insect- and bird-netting. Growing produce locally has also reduced the need for van deliveries, resulting in a reduction in carbon emissions and traffic congestion on small country roads.

Source: www.green-tourism.com/go-green/sustainable-business-case-study/combe-house-devon/case-11/

The influence of climate change is also predicted to have an effect on tourism demand, but the complexity of the subject and the lack of research means that little is known as to how far-reaching this will be in the future. It is considered essential that this is researched in much greater depth so that predictions can be made concerning potential geographical and seasonal shifts in tourism demand, as well as predictions about tourism markets that will grow and decline in the future (Gössling et al., 2012). These authors have also recognized that there are a number of characteristics related to tourist perceptions of climate change, and these are shown in Figure 16.6.

A full debate about the complexities of these characteristics is given in the full article. There is also a debate about the fact that, although there has been a substantial amount of research carried out on the effect of climate change on tourism markets, little is known about the complexity of demand responses and more research is therefore required (Gössling et al., 2012).

Conclusions

This chapter offers some new insights into the issues and complexities of consumer behaviour in tourism at the present time. Many factors are currently having a profound effect on tourists, leading to new patterns of tourist behaviour. Many of these changes

Perceptions vary by holiday type and role	Perceptions change with age, culture and other socio-demographic variables
Differences in individual preferences, values and personalities	Perceptions are comparative
Differences between *ex situ* and *in situ* perceptions	Perceptions are heavily influenced by the media
Media will increase interest in 'last-chance' tourism	Single events can have wide-ranging consequences for perceptions
Perceptions are complex, adaptive and hierarchical	Perceptions are context-dependent
Accurateness of the understanding of climate variables and resources (e.g. weather parameters) is insufficiently understood	Adaptive behaviour is insufficiently understood
Public perceptions of climate change may be ill-informed and highly polarized	

Figure 16.6 Issues surrounding tourists' perceptions of climate change impacts

Source: Gössling *et al.* (2012)

are understood merely at an anecdotal level, and further research is necessary on the demand side of tourism to enable a deeper understanding to be developed. Research on consumer behaviour in the areas of the world where tourism is developing rapidly, such as the BRIC countries (Brazil, Russia, India and China), is even less well developed and there is a desperate need for both academics and commercial organizations to carry out this much-needed research in both cross-sectional but more importantly longitudinal pieces of research.

Discussion points and essay questions

1. Discuss the effects that the global world recession has had on the tourism market in a chosen country or region.
2. Critically analyse the effect that a person's culture has on their tourism behaviour.
3. Analyse the premise that a person's generation leads to different tourist behaviour regardless of cultural background.
4. Review the effect that climate change has had on tourist behaviour to date. Debate how this will develop in the next 10 years.

References

Bar-Kolelis, D. and Wiskulsi, T. (2012). Cross-border shopping at Polish borders. Tri-city and the Russian tourists. *GeoJournal of Tourism and Geosites* 1 (9), 43–51.

Blackwell, R.J., Miniard, P.W. and Engel, J.F. (2001). *Consumer Behaviour*, 9th edn. South Western-Thomson Learning, Cincinnati, OH.

Bowen, D. and Clarke, J. (2009). *Contemporary Tourist Behaviour: Yourself and Others as Tourists*. CABI, Wallingford, UK.

Bronner, F. and de Hoog, R. (2012). Economizing strategies during an economic crisis. *Annals of Tourism Research* 39 (2), 1048–1069.

Budenau, A. (2007). Sustainable tourist behaviour – a discussion of opportunities for change. *International Journal of Consumer Studies* 31 (5), 499–508.

Chafe, Z. (2005). *Consumer Demand and Operator Support for Socially and Environmentally Responsible Tourism.* Center on Ecotourism and Sustainable Development (CESD), International Ecotourism Society (TIES), Washington, DC.

Choi, J.G., Tkachenko, T. and Sil, S. (2009). On the destination image of Korea by Russian tourists. *Tourism Management* 15 (1), 1–12.

Chung, Y.S., Wu, C.L. and Chiang, W.E. (2013). Air passengers' shopping motivation and information seeking behavior. *Journal of Air Transport Management* 27 (1), 25–28.

Clarke, J. (2008). Gifts of tourism: insights to consumer behaviour. *Management Science* 35 (2), 25–28.

Cleaver, M. and Muller, T. (2002). The socially aware baby boomer: gaining a lifestyle-based understanding of the new wave of ecotourists. *Journal of Sustainable Tourism* 10 (3), 173–190.

Coleman, L.J., Hladikova, M. and Savelyeva, M. (2006).The baby boomer market. *Journal of Targeting, Measurement and Analysis for Marketing* 14 (3), 191–210.

CREM (2000). *Feasibility and Market Study for a European Eco-label for Tourist Attractions (FEMATOUR).* Consultancy and Research for Environmental Management, Amsterdam.

Font, X. and Tribe, J. (2001). Promoting green tourism: the future of environmental awards. *International Journal of Tourism Research* 3 (1), 9–21.

Fuchs, M. and Weirmair, K. (2003). New perspectives of satisfaction research in tourism destinations. *Tourism Review* 58 (3), 6–14.

Furmanov, K., Balaeva, O. and Predvoditeleva, M. (2011). Tourism flows from the Russian Federation to the European Union. *International Journal of Tourism and Hospitality Research* 23 (1), 17–31.

Gardiner, S., King, C. and Grace, D. (2013). Travel destination marketing: an empirical examination of generational values, attitudes and intentions. *Journal of Travel Research* 52 (3), 310–324.

Goodwin, H. and Francis, J. (2003). Ethical and responsible tourism: consumer trends in the UK. *Journal of Vacation Marketing* 9 (3), 271–284.

Gössling, S., Scott, D., Hall, C.M., Ceron, J.-P. and Dubois, G. (2012). Consumer behaviour and demand response of tourists to climate change. *Annals of Tourism Research* 39 (1), 36–58.

Hall, C.M. (2000). *Tourism Planning: Policies, Processes, Relationships*. Prentice Hall, Upper Saddle River, NJ.

Hofstede, G. (2001). Culture's Consequences: Comparing Values, Behaviors, Institutions and Organizations Across Nations. Sage, Thousand Oaks, CA.

Hofstede, G. and Hofstede, G.J. (2005). *Cultures and Organizations: Software of the Mind*, 2nd edn. McGraw-Hill, New York.

Hsu, C.H.C. and Huang, S. (2008). Travel motivation: a critical review of the concept's development. In *Tourism Analysis, Behaviour and Strategy*, eds A. Woodside and D. Martin. CABI, Wallingford, UK, pp. 14–27.

Hudson, S. (2010). Wooing zoomers: marketing to the mature traveller. *Marketing Intelligence and Planning* 28 (4), 444–461.

Kotler, P., Armstrong, G., Saunders, J. and Wong, V. (2005). *Principles of Marketing*, 4th European edn. Pearson Education, Upper Saddle River, NJ.

Laroche, M., Kim, C. and Matsui, K. (2003). Which decision heuristics are used in consideration set formation? *Journal of Consumer Marketing* 20 (3), 192–209.

Layton, S. (2009). The divisive modern Russian tourist abroad: representations in self and other in the Early Reform Era. *Slavic Review* 68 (4), 848–871.

Li, X., Li, X. and Hudson, S. (2013). The application of generational theory to tourism consumer behaviour: an American perspective. *Tourism Management* 37, 147–164.

Maslow, A.H. (1943). A theory of human motivation. *Psychological Review* 50 (4), 370–396.

Miller, G. (2003). Consumerism in sustainable tourism: a survey of UK consumers. *Journal of Sustainable Tourism* 11, 17–39.

Park, S., Nicolau, J.L. and Fesenmaier, D.R. (2013). Assessing advertising in a hierarchical decision model. *Annals of Tourism Research* 40, 260–282.

Patterson, I. (2007). The effects of prior and recent experience on continuing interest in tourist settings. *International Journal of Consumer Studies* 31 (5), 528–533.

Pearce, P. (1992). Fundamentals of tourism motivation. In *Tourism Research: Critiques and Challenges*, eds D. Pearce and R. Butler. Routledge & Kegan Paul, London, pp. 85–105.

Pearce, P. and Panchal, J. (2011). Health motives and travel career pattern (TCP) model. *Asian Journal of Tourism and Hospitality Research* 5 (1), 32–44.

Pearce, P.L. and Packer, J. (2013). Minds on the move: new links from psychology to Tourism. *Annals of Tourism Research* 40 (1), 386–411.

Prideaux, B. (2007). Potential impacts of generational change on destinations. In *Advances in Hospitality and Leisure, Volume 3*, J.S. Chen ed. Emerald Group Publishing, Bingley, UK, pp. 39–54.

Sheldon, P. and Dwyer, L. (2010). The global financial crisis and tourism: perspectives of the academy. *Journal of Tourism Research* 49 (1), 3–4.

Smallman, C. and Moore, K. (2010). Process studies of tourists' decision-making. *Annals of Tourism Research* 37 (2), 397–422.

Swarbrooke, J. and Horner, S. (2007). *Consumer Behaviour in Tourism*, 2nd edn. Elsevier Butterworth-Heinemann, Oxford.

Teng, L., Laroche, M. and Zhu, H. (2007). The effects of multiple-ads and multiple brands on consumer attitude and purchase behaviour. *Journal of Consumer Marketing* 24 (1), 27–35.

UNWTO (2012). *UNWTO Tourism Highlights*, 2012 edn. World Tourism Organization, Madrid.

Vespestad, M.K. (2010). Tour operators' insight into the Russian nature-based experience market. *European Journal of Tourism Research* 3 (1), 38–53.

Vrontis, D. and Thrassou, A. (2007). A new conceptual framework for business–consumer relationships. *Tourism Management* 25 (7), 789–806.

Wong, J.-Y. and Yeh, C. (2009). Tourist hesitation in decision making. *Annals of Tourism Research* 36 (1), 6–23.

Wu, L., Zhang, J. and Fujiwara, A. (2013). Tourism participation and expenditure behavior: analysis using a Scobit based discrete-continuous choice model. *Annals of Tourism Research* 43, 662.

CASE STUDY 16: The environmental activist traveller: new dimensions

Saskia Faulk

PROFILES OF ECO-TOURISM

Condensed report based on analysis of transcript of eco-tourism focus group discussions conducted by European consumer research firm with affluent and educated travellers.

Client profile: European market-leader tour operator and travel agent in the mid- to upper-price segments.

Target population: self-employed professionals, managers, successful entrepreneurs and similar 35–60 years of age (see participant profile below).

Objectives determined by client to build on preliminary focus group research:

1. to explore perceptions of and attitudes towards eco-tourism
2. to establish factual knowledge levels on eco-tourism and related topics
3. to understand motivations for preferring and purchasing eco-tourism products

FOCUS GROUP PROTOCOL

1. Moderators introduce themselves and outline the aims of the session and rules of discussion
2. Participants introduce themselves
3. Questions asked explicitly; probing questions used additionally to draw participants out
4. Discussion duration: 2 × 45 minutes (10-minute break with hot and cold beverages and snacks provided)

PARTICIPANT PROFILE AS REQUESTED BY CLIENT

Total participants in study: 73 (seven focus groups of nine to eleven participants)
Mean age: 39.7
Mean income (estimated): €47,000
Other socio-demographic criteria:

*   married/divorced with minimum one child
*   Master's or postgraduate education attainment
*   50 per cent female
*   Western European permanent resident.

Behavioural criteria: travel internationally for leisure at least three times per year.

Have purchased at least two eco-tourism or environmentally friendly hospitality products per year.

OVERVIEW OF PARTICIPANTS WHOSE INPUT IS PROFILED IN THIS REPORT

1. Carlos (Basque Region, Spain), restaurant chef, age 32
2. Sanjay (London, UK), university lecturer and communications specialist, 38
3. Anne (Brussels region, Belgium), veterinary surgeon, 37
4. Florian (Berlin, Germany), small business consultant, 46
5. Lise (Copenhagen, Denmark), self-employed beautician, 57
6. Amandine (Nîmes, France), financial analyst with global firm, 49

Extracts follow of respondents' comments that analysts judged to be typical of certain types of views on the topics explored in each question.

QUESTION 1: WHAT DOES 'ECO-TOURISM' MEAN TO YOU?

Sanjay: It means holidays that don't harm the environment.

Anne: All kinds of travel that help the natural environment and local people.

Carlos: For me it's an indicator that this destination won't harm my health.

Amandine: I think it's a good example how companies think: it's just like bait to make us feel less guilty about having fun on holiday.

Lise: I think it's a lot more than just 'holidays'. An immense amount of tourism is not about holidays at all: what about business travellers? People going to conferences? And how about travelling for educational purposes? I get annoyed when I'm flying to a conference or planning a trip to go to a workshop that all the eco-fuss is about holidays: people splashing about on lovely beaches and riding bicycles with their children. Business travellers are probably the worst polluters of all! And yet they seem to be excused from the whole debate.

Florian: I think it's a marketing label designed to make people think one place is better than another. It's the new 'luxury'. Unfortunately.

QUESTION 2: ARE CERTIFIED ECO-FRIENDLY HOTELS AND TRAVEL PACKAGES CREDIBLE? DO YOU BELIEVE THEIR CLAIMS THAT THEY ARE ECO-FRIENDLY?

Anne: Look, it depends. In Europe there are so many different 'eco' labels that most people honestly don't know what they mean any more. When you get outside of Europe it is impossible to know which 'eco' labels are genuine. I've been to quite a few eco-certified hotels, resorts and restaurants that are not actively damaging the environment but they aren't helping it either, so for me the 'eco' label is either a minimum standard that all businesses today should adhere to, or it's just a marketing gimmick. Do I believe them? No I don't. I prefer to judge for myself but it's hard to do that when reserving a hotel or planning a trip in a faraway country. Basically in that case I rely on recommendations of friends and trusted websites. I'll give you a few examples of these later. However, when it comes to organic labels for food products at the supermarket or restaurant, I do buy them. Absolutely. Because organic certification – in many countries at least – is a legally-protected label with pretty good inspections, and checks and balances. Therefore I believe their claims. I want to support organic farmers, definitely, so show me a hotel chain or tour operator that deals only or mostly with hotels that serve organic food and I'll believe them: I'll be their most loyal client!

Lise: I honestly don't know who to believe, but let's say I wouldn't go to a hotel or on a tour that doesn't even bother to have a certificate or clearly set-out environmental policy you can read on the website or request from the company directly. I read it myself and decide if I agree with it or not. But let's be clear that I think the most damage to the environment doesn't come from hotels: air travel is the real killer. I wanted to go to a conference in Australia last year and checked what my ecological footprint would be on that flight (it's so easy to do online using the WWF carbon footprint calculator) and found it was more than 7000 pounds of carbon dioxide! That's as much as the carbon footprint of my entire house for three months. I was amazed and decided because of that not to go to the conference, even though I had found a great little ecological hotel to stay in there. I suppose I could have paid for carbon offset, which would have cost about US$50, but I just don't trust that these carbon offset companies are really effective in helping our planet.

Amandine: Excuse me, but when I go on holiday the last thing I think about is checking the mattress to see if it's made of sustainably-farmed coco fibres. A holiday is a holiday, not a time to be worrying about this and that. Most people take holidays to *get away from* worries, not to go somewhere and worry about how much pollution the safari vehicle makes or about the animal welfare concerns in production of the ham on the buffet. It seriously annoys me to see these little stickers in the bathroom telling us to save water or switch off the lights: people should realize it's just the hotel owners trying to cut costs. That's all. Switch off your lights at home if you're worried: doing it three weeks a year while you're on holiday won't make any difference!

Carlos: One thing I like about travel companies is that I can get a feel for if they are honest about their environmental policy because I experience the service myself. I wouldn't go to the factory to see how my clothes are manufactured and I can't go to each farm to check how the grapes are grown for the wine I serve at my restaurant, but when I travel I am literally 'going to the factory' and can see lots of things for myself. I remember once in Bali, when travelling with a tour operator that makes a big fuss about how environmentally friendly they are, there was Italian milk on the breakfast table and Italian fruit juices in the bar. I complained. Milk. . . OK maybe there aren't many local dairy farms but don't tell me there isn't Indonesian or Asian pasteurized milk. . . And as for the fruit juice let's not even comment on that. Flying stuff like that around the world for the tourists is just ridiculous from any point of view and of course environmentally it's catastrophic. So I would say that everyone should pay more attention to the 'details' and also use more common sense. Doesn't it make more business-sense too?

Florian: I think that you can't believe them once you start getting too far from your home base. If you don't understand the political and social problems in a country, let alone the language, how can you possibly understand things like environmental attitudes? The problem is that in the tourism industry you have to look way behind the scenes. The hotel might be truly ecologically friendly, but whose land is it on? Just one example, but I'm sure there a hundreds of others. I was reading a Peace Brigades report that in Chiapas, Mexico the local government hired paramilitary thugs to terrorize local indigenous people to give up some really pristine land so they could build an eco-tourism development on it. Then the tourism developers were planning to use the same 'colourful' locals as a kind of bait to attract tourists. Worse, there were plans to import employees from elsewhere. In a situation like that, the local people lose out in so many ways when tourism is developed. Or what about Tunisia? Or Egypt? After all the so-called 'Arab Spring' revolutionary dust has settled, everyone agrees that these countries were ruled by repressive dictators. . . but for decades no-one said a word while we Europeans flocked there *en masse* for cheap beach holidays.

How can you or I, as tourists, have such background knowledge? See, on the face of it the growth of eco-tourism seems like a good thing: how could it be bad? But when you really look at it you realize that usually the wrong people are profiting from it because developers are looking for always more 'virgin' territories to build on. I always check what the activists say when deciding where to go now.

Sanjay: I don't know if it's for me to judge if their claims are true or not! I mean, I'm not an expert: they are the experts, so I basically have to take them at their word. Yeah, but we're not as blind as those companies think we are, I mean we notice that most of the staff is Northern European, and all the managers are in destinations far away from home. . . while one reason we chose to go far away on holiday was to get away from these stressed types we work with every day in our usual jobs. I want to see more local people staffing and managing these places. I mean I want to literally see my money going to them and their families rather than some anonymous hotel company headquarters in Utah. . .

QUESTION 3: IF THE PRICE IS THE SAME, WHY WOULD YOU PREFER TO CHOOSE AN ENVIRONMENTALLY FRIENDLY OPTION OVER ONE THAT IS NOT?

Amandine: People who pay more for so-called environmentally friendly goods are suckers. Sorry, but that's just not what business is about. Businesses are about making money, not saving the planet! I do buy environmentally friendly products, but I buy them for reasons other than their eco-friendliness: they just so happen to be good quality.

Question: So what about tourism in particular?

People should take care of the environment every day in their own homes and own lives if that's what they care about. If the price is the same, why not – and I have bought – but I wouldn't pay a centime more for a trip or hotel night that claims to be better for the environment. I mean, where's the proof? Environmentalists themselves, and even governments, can't agree on what global warming means, so who are customers to believe?

Who am I, a financial analyst, to say what is right or wrong about complex environmental issues! Especially when it comes to a complex phenomenon like tourism. . . forget it!

Lise: I buy all kinds of supplies for my business and I care a lot about their environmental impacts. I know that lots of beauty products are already not good for nature (like nail polish for instance), so I think it's good to send a message to companies that there is demand for less damaging formulas. By the way, I don't even believe some of the environmentally friendly claims on the packaging, but that's not the point. You can see it this way: it's probably better for our health too if it's better for nature! Basically you could say that I create demand for less toxic products and if everyone did, we would have. . . less toxic products!

Question: So what about tourism in particular?

Well, the same goes for 'eco-friendly' hotels, restaurants, packages and so on: even if I know they are not perfect, by choosing them I am part of a consumer movement demanding better, safer products and services.

Florian: Whatever I buy, I usually go for the less damaging choice. But you choose your poison, you know.

Question: So what about tourism in particular?

I'll give you a tourism example because the very concept of a 'holiday' is flawed. Some people don't want to spend their free time wallowing in self-indulgence on holiday. In fact, you don't even need to go far from home to really rest. There was a great study done by the Worldwide Fund for Nature a while back that found how people were happy before going on holiday: that the mere thought of escaping somewhere gave happiness. Then happiness levels fell as the actual trip took place. It makes sense really with the Western concept of holiday, which is basically another opportunity to consume more. Several times now I have done volunteering activities instead of a 'holiday'. Once I joined a group that was building a schoolhouse in Kenya and came back feeling like a new person. Another time I took my family to Fiji where I volunteered to teach English to a group of local entrepreneurs. It's true that simply flying there we polluted a lot, but there was no other choice! In any case, once on the ground we lived with the locals, like the locals, and we really made a difference to people's lives. My kids had a great time too. Now *that's* being friendly to the environment!

Anne: I *always* choose the environmentally friendly option. I'm even more likely to choose it if it's more expensive. Why? Because an ecologically sound and ethically produced item costs more to make. It's simple. Imagine you as an entrepreneur make minimum efforts to be environmentally friendly (which means basically that you follow the law, which companies do anyway to avoid legal costs). Imagine you concentrate all your efforts on cutting costs and being more and more profitable: then you cut down on 'luxuries' like taking into account the natural, ethical or social factors. That's the typical business model today. There are some companies, a few, that manage to be socially or environmentally responsible with that business model, and that's great. It costs money though. And where is that money going to come from? From us: the consumers. So if we want a better, cleaner, more just and safe world, we in affluent countries simply have to pay for it and stop running around looking for bargains. A 'bargain' does not exist. I should probably make clear that if an environmentally friendly option is priced the same as a conventionally produced option, it makes me suspicious because I know it costs more to make. I'll think that they cut corners if they're managing to sell cheap. There is actually a great short film you can watch that explains this really well, called the *Story of Stuff*. It's about products, not services like tourism, but still it makes the point.

Question: So what about tourism in particular?

It's true that tourism is more complicated to understand, but I would say the same simple rule applies: send the right messages to travel suppliers and be prepared to pay the true cost!

Sanjay: Yeah, sure I would, but the problem is that usually an 'ecological' option costs more. Personally, I can afford it and I think it's just the right thing to do when I can, so yeah. However, when it's more expensive most people just can't afford to even if they'd like to. You know, people are worried about keeping their jobs at the minute so saving a bit of money on holidays and other luxuries is just common sense, right?

Question: So what about tourism in particular?

Let me tell you what really annoys me about some of these travel packages that claim to be environmentally friendly: they have a snob factor marketed into them and I don't want to be paying for that. If I'm paying more for an ecologically friendly holiday then I want my money to be going to the right places and people, not to the marketing department that's trying to add an aura of prestige to my holiday thank you very much.

QUESTION 4: IF YOUR SPOUSE OR COMPANION SURPRISED YOU ON YOUR BIRTHDAY WITH AN ECO-TOUR IN YOUR FAVORITE COUNTRY, HOW WOULD YOU FEEL ABOUT IT? HOW WOULD YOU FEEL ABOUT TELLING YOUR FRIENDS?

Sanjay: I would be right pleased but I would hope she wouldn't spend our hard-earned money for an illusion, thinking that she is helping anybody (or anything) on this planet apart from me.

Anne: That would really be nice . . . I think he knows me well enough to take very seriously any environmental claims and check them out before booking any tour. Anyway, he shares my worries about this planet. I think my friends would respect his and my choice. If we are impressed by where we go, we will make sure that we spread the word among our friends as much as possible!

Carlos: I doubt that she would because she would be worried about getting it right. She would probably give me some other kind of surprise and let me plan a trip! Let's say she did, though. It would probably be with a company we travelled with in the past about which I didn't complain too much. You know, the problem with 'environmentally friendly' anything is that it attracts really demanding customers, like me. There hasn't been one company we travelled with that made us 100 per cent happy about their environmental performance.

About telling my friends, sure, I would talk a lot about it. Actually I always do (they know me for that) when we come back from holiday and my holiday pics are all over the internet on photo-sharing sites. I would write all about it on my blog, too, all the good and bad points about my trip, so I can help educate people both travellers and travel companies.

Amandine: [*laughs*] It would never happen. But if he did, I wouldn't refuse it, of course: it's kind of cute. I wouldn't be so proud to tell my friends about it though because they wouldn't think so highly of my boyfriend for falling for that trick!

Lise: I don't have a partner right now but this exact thing happened in the past and we argued about it during the whole trip. We just couldn't agree on the idea that going on holiday doesn't mean taking all your affluent-country junk and gadgets with you around the world to pollute the whole planet. That can be a serious problem for a couple, when one partner thinks the environment is important while the other doesn't. Tell my friends about it? I sure did. Now they all know to be careful about what kinds of gifts to give me: I don't like anything that pollutes or is made in bad or dangerous conditions!

Florian: She would definitely do some research first: we don't take any chances when travelling with our kids. She would check out those websites I told you about first. Sure we would talk to our friends about it, particularly online to spread the word about a company that does things right.

Researcher's conclusions

1. There are big individual differences in this affluent, educated segment about what constitutes eco-tourism, ranging from different perceptions of it to a perceived lack of credibility in the concept.
2. No-one really knows what eco-tourism means and travellers bring all kinds of factors, including social and political ones, into their definitions.
3. Travellers have very strong views and feelings about eco-tourism and related issues; some input was quite emotional.
4. Better communication – and more unified communication – is needed on this topic from travel and tourism companies.

Links

WWF carbon footprint calculator	footprint.wwf.org.uk
Global Code of Ethics for Tourism by the World Tourism Organization	www.unwto.org/ethics/index.php
National Geographic Center for Sustainable Destinations	http://travel.nationalgeographic.com/travel/sustainable/about_geotourism.html

ResponsibleTourism, a leading informational and showcase site for travel companies to provide information about their offerings	www.responsibletravel.com/copy/responsible-tourism
The *Story of Stuff*, film about life-cycle analysis	www.storyofstuff.org
Tourism Concern 'fights exploitation in tourism and campaigns for more ethical, fairly traded forms of tourism'	www.tourismconcern.org.uk
The Eco-Tourism Society is dedicated to educating travellers about the impacts of tourism and how to minimize the negative impacts.	www.ecotourism.org/site/c.orLQKXPCLmF/b.4832143/k.BD87/Home.htm

DISCUSSION POINTS AND ESSAY QUESTIONS

1. What travel choices do Florian, Sanjay and Anne make? What is your travel profile? Do you see yourself in any of the participants? If so, who? In what ways do you differ and what do you have in common? Is there anyone in the class who resembles Lise, Amandine, Carlos. . ..? If so, take time to ask them about their brand preferences and choices generally and about tourism particularly.
2. Who really knows what 'green' means? Write an answer to the following questions on your own or in a small group.
   (a) Define 'carbon footprint', 'organic', 'green tourist', 'nature-based tourism'.
   (b) What exactly are the issues regarding 'responsible tourism'?
   (c) What are the differences between 'responsible-' 'sustainable-' and 'eco-' tourism?

Three steps:

1. Write an answer that the group agrees on for each question without looking online or in a book.
2. Conduct quick research online, using some of the resources provided above, to check your answers to question 2.
3. Make a comparison and check whether your answers were correct and in agreement with 'expert' definitions.
4. Present your findings. You might be surprised!

ACKNOWLEDGEMENT

This case was written based on research conducted with Kraisorn Chaichana, Lise Grottenberg, Ingimar Ingimarsson, Stephanie Muller, Bianca Prado and Thien Tri Truong.

CHAPTER 17

The role of information and communication technologies in tourism

This chapter explores the rapidly growing role of information and communication technologies (ICT) in tourism, a phenomenon that has truly revolutionized the sector since the first edition of this book was published in 1999. It explores the chronological development of ICT in tourism, including the evolution of ICT tools. The chapter then goes on to look at the rise of consumer-generated media as a means of sharing tourist experiences and evaluating customer satisfaction. Next we discuss the growing importance of virtual reality and augmented reality in tourism. And finally, we hypothesize about what may happen in the future in relation to ICT and tourism.

Introduction

In the previous editions of the book we talked about likely changes in the ways in which we purchase tourism products. We predicted that technological innovations were going to continue to change how we purchased tourism products, in several ways, as follows.

1. The development of the internet and interactive television will stimulate the growth of direct marketing and direct booking. People will increasingly be able to access information and make bookings from their own home or office. Tour operators, airlines and hotels will help encourage this trend as the internet is a relatively inexpensive promotional tool and direct selling takes away the need to pay commission to travel agents.
2. The growth of ever more sophisticated global distribution systems will help tourists put together individual, tailor-made itineraries, by giving them access to the detailed product information which they require.
3. Smart-card technologies will bring with them the benefits of ticket-less travel which will stimulate the growth of last-minute purchases of tourism products.

We were certainly correct about the internet, but we were wrong about interactive television because we did not anticipate the rise of the mobile phone and tablet devices as the preferred method of accessing the internet. Point two was correct, and the final point was also fairly accurate.

We correctly predicted the fact that the dividing line between promotion and distribution would become increasingly blurred as ICT developments encourage people to gather information and make bookings at the same time.

However, we also made the following predictions that turned out not to be right, although the final point has been seen to some extent:

> we might also see changes in the future in terms of who we buy holidays from, as the role of travel agents declines and other organizations take their place. These could be:
> - high street retailers who will combine selling holidays with the sale of goods needed by tourists, such as clothes, sun protection creams and luggage
> - tele-shopping networks that may simply add holidays to the portfolio of products they sell
> - banks that provide loans for holidays and sell currency might go on to sell the holidays themselves
> - telecommunications companies which may become involved in selling holidays as their systems play more and more of a role in the distribution of the tourism product.

The historical development of ICT in tourism

Throughout its history, the evolution of tourism has been shaped by technology, notably the introduction of jet aircraft more than 50 years ago. It is only in the past 20 years that ICT has made a major impact on how tourists book their holidays, how they experience their vacations, and how they remember these experiences and share them with others. Before that, ICT was used primarily by the industry to improve the efficiency of its operations. In the 1990s we saw ICT transforming the airline sector as the internet permitted airlines to market directly to tourists without the need to go through intermediaries such as travel agents. The new budget airlines drove this change because it facilitated their business model, which was based on squeezing costs out of the system, and this development meant no more commission payments to travel agents. It could be argued that without the internet, the budget airlines would not have been able to exist. It took a while for traditional airlines to embrace online booking as they relied heavily on travel agents for their bookings and could not afford to upset them.

Over time, the internet became an increasingly important part of the promotion and distribution strategies of tourism organizations, including tour operators, visitor attractions and destination marketing organizations.

In the early days, the main role of the internet was in helping organizations in their marketing and to reduce their distribution costs. From day one it was seen as a threat by conventional travel agents, but by and large it was viewed positively by the tourism industry and was under its control. As we will see later in this chapter, there has been a subtle change in use of the internet whereby consumers have used it to leverage more influence and even power in the supplier–consumer relationship. This was foreseen by O'Connor (2010), who wrote that 'the internet is evolving from a push marketing medium to one where peer-to-peer generation and sharing of data are the norm'.

Before we go on to explore that phenomenon, let's return to the earlier days of the role of the internet in tourism. Sadly there is not enough reliable empirical data on consumer behaviour in tourism related to ICT, but several commentators have put forward convincing arguments about why consumers have embraced ICT, and about some of the barriers to the adoption of ICT by consumers.

Buhalis (2003) identified a series of factors that motivated tourists to use the internet. These included:

- richness and depth of information
- ease in identifying information
- self-service and economical
- available at all times
- products offered at discounted prices as suppliers pass distribution savings on to consumers.

He went on to say that the typical online tourist tends to be a well-educated and well-travelled individual, and typically comes from the baby boomer generation, although there has also been an explosion in the younger generation X and generation Y categories using the internet for travel purposes (see Chapter 16). In fact, travel planning and booking has been recognized as one of the most appropriate sectors for the development of online applications (Buhalis, 2003). Research has also shown that early adopters of mobile phone technology were more likely to be younger, higher-earning and unmarried, and these consumers were engaging with online travel booking sites to a higher degree (Munnukka, 2007). Research in the US supported this, where it was found that generation X-ers (aged 27–40) were much more likely to use mobile technology and apps compared with the baby boomers (41–50 years old), although baby boomers think that mobile technology is critical and therefore are likely to try to learn how to use it (Yang and Jolly, 2008). This is probably due to the fact that generation X-ers have been exposed to mobile phones from an early age, whereas baby boomers have had to learn how to use them later in life and therefore are less used to the technology.

A number of factors also slowed the adoption of the internet by tourists, some which were identified by Buhalis (2003):

- cost of the fee for the internet service provider (ISP) – the higher the cost of internet access, the less likely individuals are to search and book online
- lack of trust, especially if the names are unfamiliar
- lack of security

- fear of making mistakes
- would rather talk to a real person
- concerned about privacy
- do not own a credit card
- confusing and complicated
- a business booking travel may prefer to use a travel agent even if the cost is higher.

We also need to recognize that there were geographical differences in adoption, which could be based on anything from governments blocking access to the internet for their citizens to the lack of an effective internet infrastructure in the country. In Asia, too, travel agents were respected and many citizens who were not experienced travellers preferred to use their services as a 'comfort blanket'.

Therefore in the 1990s and early 2000s, the main impact of the internet was felt in Northern Europe and North America, where there were experienced travellers and a good internet infrastructure.

We also need to understand that what was happening with the internet and travel was also being seen in other sectors of the economy – tourist behaviour does not exist in isolation.

Buhalis (2003) sought to identify the factors that encouraged people to embrace online information searching and booking in tourism, and identified the following:

- reduction of the gap between expectations and perceived experience due to more information being available
- consumers have more information and therefore more choice
- better understanding of consumer needs due to research, interaction and data mining
- consumers feel empowered
- pricing is more flexible, organizations can match supply with demand more accurately and offer discounts
- new business models where consumers can pay what they want – e.g. lastminute.com
- new added-value services on offer
- a reduction in bureaucracy and paperwork
- personalized services
- better integration of departments and functions in organizations
- user-friendly and customized interfaces
- language barriers are reduced through the use of automatic translations
- development of sophisticated loyalty schemes
- accurate and much richer market research that can be used to improve services and customer loyalty.

As tourists embraced the internet, their appetite for it grew and they developed a hunger for it, whilst the rate of adoption surprised many in the tourism industry. Organizations had to redesign their information systems, booking approach, and service design and delivery systems. Tourism organizations had to develop new and exciting online

Stage 1	Pre-purchase	Searching for holiday possibilities in the initial stages – consumers search online, view holiday programmes online, look at travel blogs, and consult with friends, family and colleagues
Stage 2	Purchase	Consumers use a wide range of online booking sites to book their total package or individual components of their holiday, including transport, visitor attractions, festivals and music events, dining and restaurant booking, insurance
Stage 3	During the holiday experience	Consumers use technology-based systems to check in, and for added services during their holiday; share experiences with others e.g. via blogs and user-generated content; contact holiday providers during their stay to praise or complain
Stage 4	Post-purchase	Consumers may do all of the above on return from holiday and this activity may continue for some time; organizations may contact them with follow-up communication e.g. customer reviews, complaints processes, repeat offers

Figure 17.1 Consumers' use of the internet – stages of the holiday experience

product offerings to capitalize on these new opportunities and provide increased competitive advantage, or face competitive disadvantage.

It soon became clear that consumers used the internet through all the stages of their holiday experience and a summary of these different stages is shown in Figure 17.1.

Academic research is continuing in all these areas of the purchase-decision process to try to define a detailed profile of what consumers do, why they do it and, importantly, how organizations can capitalize on this new and developing behaviour. A range of current research in the area is summarized in the following parts of this chapter. Case study 17 also helps to illustrate the points made.

Changing relationship between industry and consumers due to ICT

In recent years we have seen a subtle but very clear change in the power relationship between the demand and supply sides in tourism in relation to ICT.

Demand side

As we saw above, at the beginning the internet was a tool for the industry to reduce its costs and target customers more effectively.

However, two factors have combined to change this situation irrevocably.

Firstly, there have been a number of developments in ICT that have impacted heavily on tourist behaviour, including:

- the smartphone, allowing consumers easily to access information and make bookings anywhere, anytime
- tablet devices, with the same impact on behaviour

- the explosion of social media, a perfect vehicle for consumers to share their experiences with fellow travellers and give feedback to tourism organizations
- the 'selfie stick', which has made it much easier, and more fashionable, for tourists to take photos on vacation and share them with the world.

Secondly, as more and more people use the internet to plan their travels and share their experiences, they have become more experienced and confident, and more willing to use it.

We have also seen a growth in usage by older travellers, which is very important – while young people may have a desire to travel, they often lack the money to travel widely. Their parents and grandparents are the core of the tourism market as they often have more disposable income.

So one aspect of this changing relationship between consumers and the tourism industry relates to how the internet has empowered consumers to plan their own trips and comment on their experiences to a wider audience.

Supply side

We have also seen an interesting change in the supply side of the industry as a result of ICT. We now see a new generation of tourism businesses developing purely as a result of ICT, including Airbnb and Uber. The former has grown at a phenomenal rate and is now a serious competitor for the hotel sector. In August 2015 luxury hotels in Paris complained that they were losing business to Airbnb as owners of luxury apartments used the website to rent them to city visitors.

It is almost as if there was a conspiracy between these new types of enterprises and consumers to squeeze traditional hotels, tour operators and travel agents out of the market. For example, today very few UK tourists buy a city-break package to a European city offered by a traditional tour operator. The majority book a flight and accommodation independently online, as well as activities, fine dining meals and excursions. Increasingly, particularly for younger travellers, the accommodation is likely to be some form of private rather than commercially owned accommodation, which tourists feel gives them a more authentic experience.

So the industry is struggling to compete with the rise of do-it-yourself independent travel and is desperately trying to provide more flexible products to attract consumers – except in the beach holiday market, where the traditional package holiday is still popular.

As well as having to cope with competition from new types of competitor and the rise of the independent traveller, the tourism industry also has to contend with the constant scrutiny of consumer reviews.

Consumer-generated media, tourism and the obsession with reviews

There has been a proliferation of online sites and opportunities to review hospitality and tourism organizations over the past decade, but the interesting question to ask is – how influential this is in relation to tourists' planning and decision-making in general? Research has indicated that consumers consider online hotel reviews when they are booking a holiday, and consider both positive and negative reviews when forming an opinion about hotels. This is particularly marked when the hotel is less well known to them (Vermeulen and Seegars, 2009). Online travel communities are an increasing phenomenon and, because travellers prefer to consider unbiased information, these have become an important source of information when making travel purchase decisions. Recent research, however, found that the effect online discussion had on consumers was directly related to the perceived usefulness of the advice, the trust in the online community, and the personal characteristics of the consumer (Casaló, Flavián and Guinalíu, 2010). Research carried out in the same year indicated that online user-generated reviews had a significant impact on online sales, with a 10 per cent increase in traveller reviews boosting online sales by more than 5 per cent (Ye *et al.*, 2011).

The desire for an increased level of rankings and league tables has also infiltrated the tourism and hospitality sector. The online travel website TripAdvisor and its hotel ranking system is a prominent example of this type of review site. The 'independent traveller' is increasingly turning to the site when forming impressions during the early planning stages of their holiday. It has been suggested that TripAdvisor is an example of an internet-mediated abstract system (Giddens, 1991) that draws on calculative process (Miller, 2001) to construct trust (Jeacle and Carter, 2011). Younger travellers are also using web-based map services such as Google maps, Yahoo maps and Microsoft Virtual Earth to plan their own travel itinerary. This has become even more complex as individuals can collaborate in this planning process by using various social media sites including Facebook and Twitter, and research has shown that these types of systems are attractive to younger consumers (Sigala, 2010).

There is also growing interest in sharing information online in terms of online communities and the benefits these can bring to individuals and consumers. Research has shown that for members who actively participate in an online community during the booking process, this experience fortifies their sense of belonging, and members can support the community by sharing knowledge, community promotion and even behavioural changes. It seems that an online community can result in trust and feelings of belonging that can bring very positive benefits to individuals and groups (Qu and Lee, 2011).This sense of belonging can be used in destination marketing where the community can work together in sharing ideas and creating online communities to help to promote the destination, as well in obvious commercial applications in the more commercial areas of the sector.

Although the power of the internet as a search engine is without doubt, other researchers have shown that users are not always using consumer-generated media for travel planning, and behaviour is often determined by the nationality and background of the consumer (Ayeh *et al.*, 2013). Despite this, there has been a proliferation of online communities such as VirtualTourist, IgoUgo, TripAdvisor, and social networking sites such as Facebook and Twitter, that all can be used to stimulate discussions about travel and have changed the behaviour of tourists in relation to travel planning and purchase (Ayeh *et al.*, 2013). User-generated travel reviews are used when travellers decide which destination to choose, where to stay, and what to do in terms of activities (Arsal *et al.*, 2008). A recent piece of research by the World Travel Market in 2010 showed that only one in three individuals who embarked on holiday planning in 2010 consulted some form of social media, although it can also be suggested that since 2010 things have moved forwards at a rapid pace, with more individuals becoming used to using user-generated sites. Organizations have had to react to the growing number of online reviews and the relationship of these to perceptions of trust. Research shows that consumers are influenced by both negative and positive reviews, and the fact that they are still influenced by brand names has meant that some large organizations have developed blogs and other social media platforms to try to build up trust and loyalty in the increasingly competitive market. The illustration of Bill Marriott and his blog is an example of this type of development.

MARRIOTT INTERNATIONAL USES A BLOG TO DEVELOP AN ONLINE COMMUNITY

Welcome to my blog, Marriott on the Move!

It seems that today, the business world is becoming much more transparent, thanks in large part to the internet.

All this got me thinking, 'Why do I blog?' I've found it's a great learning experience and I've had a lot of fun doing it. I'm sure you probably have learned a lot about me. I do value family, work and community, and I'm not afraid to tackle controversial topics such as reforming our immigration policy or putting our non-smoking policy in our hotels in the United States and Canada. I like to talk about good news, but I'm not afraid to talk about the bad news, such as my blog about the bombing of our Islamabad hotel.

Businesses must have values and I've tried to communicate some of ours in my blog. We certainly do have a growing commitment to saving the environment. Many of you offered praise in your comments; others want us to do even more.

How do I blog?

I sometimes handwrite my blogs because I don't know how to type. An assistant from our global communications team helps me with all the technical aspects of my blog. When I want to do a blog, they come to my office with an digital recorder and record what I say.

Sometimes I write it out, sometimes I use notes and sometimes I speak off the top of my head. I come up with a lot of the ideas, but people in our company also have topics for me to consider. When I'm through recording, it's transcribed and the text and the audio file are uploaded. The comments are viewed and printed out for me to read. If there are any I feel I should respond to, I dictate what to say.

As you can see, being a technophobe like me adds a lot of steps, but I make it work because I know that it's a great way to communicate with our customers and stakeholders in this day and age. When your family's name is on the building or you are the person clearly identified with the company, everything you say or do affects the business, good or bad. In this fascinating information age, you have to be transparent.

I'm Bill Marriott and thanks for helping me keep Marriott on the move.

P.S. I think you'll enjoy The Washington Post story: An Old Dog Learns to Write a New Blog.

Source: www.blogs.marriott.com

Ethical consumption and authenticity

Consumers are also increasingly using social media and user-generated content as a vehicle to measure the quality of providers. This relates to their personal factors and satisfaction or dissatisfaction.

There are two important personal factors that affect a consumer's satisfaction or otherwise – stress and arousal. We will now briefly consider both of these in relation to social media and user-generated content. Stress caused by any aspect of the vacation experience tends to lead to tourist dissatisfaction. This stress can result from a variety of sources, as we saw in Chapter 15. The tourist industry is constantly seeking to ameliorate these stresses, particularly at the higher end of the market. The use of social media to achieve this is a new avenue of development. For example, adventure tourism based on hyper-arousal (see above) benefits from internet communities sharing the same interests.

Tourists' expectations, in general, have risen over time in response to two influences which we discussed in Chapter 15. The internet allows the sharing of views of hotels and other components of the travel experience across national boundaries and at a much more rapid rate.

The factors that influence product quality or customer satisfaction, yet are outside their control, are a major problem for the tourism industry. The source of this dissatisfaction was discussed in Chapter 15. There is absolutely nothing the tour operator can do to solve this problem, but organizations can communicate about uncontrollable factors via the internet.

Another difficulty in relation to quality and tourist satisfaction is that tourists have different attitudes, standards and prejudices. Often their satisfaction or otherwise is based on subjective views about an issue that is important to them, and that they judge in their own unique way. It is difficult to see how the tourism industry can effectively respond in concrete terms to such views. Perhaps the use of the internet and social media is a way to respond to subjective comments?

There is clear evidence that there are national differences in tourist expectations in relation to quality standards. It is widely recognized for example, that German tourists are more concerned with the environmental quality of resorts than their British counterparts. There are also national differences in the supply side in terms of quality of the product offered (see Chapter 15).

When considering national differences in product quality and tourist expectations, it is important to identify that the sharing of information via the internet is likely to mean that these differences will be reduced and expectations will rise.

Online reviews and the rating obsession

Research has shown that dissatisfaction, rather than satisfaction, increases consumers' motivations to write reviews on hotel websites (Öğüt and Cezar, 2012). Electronic word of mouth (eWOM) has become a recent obsession with consumers who turn to social media sites to express their delight or disgust with the products, services and organizations they have experienced. This phenomenon is relevant not just for the hotel sector – consumers have also become used to posting reviews of restaurants on social media sites. Research has shown that online reviews written by consumers in this market are much more positively associated with the online popularity of the restaurant compared with the effect of editors' views (Zhang *et al.*, 2010).

Research has shown that a growing number of individuals are showing a tendency to spread negative word of mouth via social media sites, compared with the numbers complaining directly to a provider. This is probably due to the fact that, once a person becomes used to social media sites, it is easier to complain in this way compared with approaching the provider, and they may also feel that the results are more profound (Wei *et al.*, 2012).

Research carried out in Italy showed that consumers were using Facebook more as a vehicle for complaining rather than as an informational source about products and services. The authors suggested a shift from the phenomenon of e-tourism to one of f-tourism given the power of Facebook as a vehicle for eWOM (Pantano and Pietro, 2013). It seems that where a site has personal information about the respondents, the content is seen as being more credible. A piece of research with young consumers showed that when an ambivalent review about a hotel was posted online accompanied by personal information about the respondent, then this led to a significant lowering of booking intention. In other words, if you think you know the person then you tend to trust them more and their views will impact on yours (Xie *et al.*, 2010). The use of TripAdvisor as a vehicle for complaining and offering advice to fellow tourists is also an important phenomenon that is providing a focus for researchers (Vásquez, 2011).

However, perhaps more importantly, the 'TripAdvisor phenomenon' – the obsession with reviews – is creating new tourist behaviours that are quite worrying. There is clear evidence from industry sources that some travellers are now using the threat of posting a bad review as a lever to try to gain discounts or upgrades, a form of blackmail in truth. There is also anecdotal evidence that some hotels are giving in to such pressure, which will surely cause this behaviour to grow.

Social media and the sharing of tourist experiences

Social media have transformed the way in which tourists record and share their vacation experience and memories. Traditionally the holiday postcard and the holiday photo or video taken on an expensive camera were the only ways of recording and sharing vacation experiences. They were seen by just a few friends and family, and their quality deteriorated over time. Then we saw the introduction of smartphones and tablets with integrated high-quality cameras, 'selfie sticks', and social media such as Instagram which are picture-based. Suddenly anyone can take great photos and share them with people across the world in a form that theoretically should last for many years without deterioration. Photoshopping has also allowed us to modify reality in our photos, so that now the camera actually can lie! For some people, this process of recording and sharing vacation images has become a virtual obsession, and sites such as Facebook are filled with 'this is me in x' pictures and stories. We need to recognize that this is important because vacation memories and the sharing of these memories has always been a massively important part of the tourist experience.

The use of ICT in different tourism sectors – airlines, hospitality, tour operations and destinations

The illustration of Bill Marriott and his blog is an example of a hotel company that has engaged with the emerging social media agenda in the tourism and hospitality sector. This section examines the adoption of ICT by different areas of the sector and provides examples to illustrate the points.

As noted above, airlines were the earliest adopters of ICT developments in tourism, starting with their use of computer reservation systems and then global distribution systems. They then went on to use ICT to facilitate development of the strategic alliances that have been so important in the airline sector. They have used ICT to move towards ticketless travel and online check-in to further reduce their costs and offer greater convenience for customers.

The hospitality industry has been a more recent convert to the use of ICT, and its use in revenue management is now well established. However, in terms of the customer interface it has been more limited. Online check-in is still quite rare, as is virtual billing, with most guests at checkout still receiving a bill in an envelope. On the other hand, restaurants are making increasing use of ICT both for booking a table and using tablets for ordering. Furthermore, ICT has opened up the possibility for new types of enterprise to enter the market, such as real-time restaurant reservation sites like the San Francisco-based OpenTable site. ICT has helped larger companies to benefit from multi-channel distribution strategies and e-procurement which have the potential to cut costs. But ICT also has potential for SMEs as it can help them compete with larger companies and focus on communicating their points of differentiation.

Tour operators depend on ICT to provide them with the opportunity to differentiate themselves from competitors. Use of the internet allows them to research and develop their product more effectively by deploying the readily available market research data from their reservation data systems. By utilizing ICT, companies can offer a more sophisticated range of products and services, including insurance, weather forecasts, in-destination additional services and shopping opportunities for their customers. Furthermore, it allows them to be more flexible and to cooperate with other related partners in a more efficient and effective way. The use of ICT also permits tour operators to show customers images and 360-degree panoramic views of destinations, properties and individual rooms. This means that the customer can have a much more informed view of what to expect and takes away some of the problems related to the intangibility of the product. It allows tour operators to show a more realistic view of what is on offer and reduce feelings of insecurity in travel, which is becoming increasingly important due to recent terrorist attacks and natural disasters. Tour operators can also communicate messages related to the sustainability of the destination and tourism organizations via ICT systems, and this can be a particular priority depending on the market.

Tour operators have responded to the trend towards more independent travel caused by ICT by developing so called 'dynamic packaging'. In other words, they now allow customers to buy individual elements as well as a complete package – it is better to at least sell people a flight than nothing at all. The illustration shows how the German tour operator TUI has changed its distribution systems to offer unique holidays in a mass market using online booking systems.

TUI TRAVEL CHANGES DISTRIBUTION INCREASINGLY TO UNIQUE HOLIDAYS AND ONLINE BOOKING

Over two-thirds of mainstream holidays booked are now unique holidays, an increase on last year that has been steadily rising since 2007, when this became the focus of our strategy. The main benefits of unique holidays are five-fold. They provide higher margins, are often booked earlier leading to better yield management and efficiency and we receive excellent customer feedback that, in the majority of cases, leads to repeat bookings and advocacy within our customer base.

Our direct distribution channels are key to the Group's success and enable us to increase margin and improve results. The number of holidays booked through our mainstream websites continues to increase and this remains the core contributor for direct sales. Of our direct sales, 35 per cent is online which equates to £3.7 billion in revenue. There is still ample opportunity to increase direct distribution channels which will help us gain further margin across all our source markets.

We are an online business but we continue to drive further enhancements through technologies that amplify the customer experience at the front-end and drive further efficiencies in the back-end processes. In May this year we launched the award-winning TUI Digital Assistant in the UK as the 'MyThomson' mobile app which was very well received by customers achieving a five star rating in the Apple App Store and topped the free download travel app chart shortly after launch. Since then, we have had in excess of 180,000 downloads proving we understand what our customers want and need from their travel provider. Post year end, we began the TUI Digital Assistant international roll-out with the 'Meine TUI' mobile app launch in the German source market.

Peter Long, Chief Executive

Source: TUI Travel Annual Report 2013

E-travel agencies have also developed as a result of the new technology. Companies such as ebookers (www.ebookers.com), Expedia (www.expedia.com) and lastminute. com (www.lastminute.com) have established considerable market share in a market that was considered to be crowded with conventional high street travel agents. However, in many countries, ICT and this new competition has seen a decline in the number of high street travel agents. The latter were too slow to respond to ICT, seeing it as a threat rather than a potential opportunity. Only those agents that have focused on high service quality and added value have been able to compete effectively with online agents.

Two interesting impacts of the rise of online travel agents are:

- the selling power of the online agents, which is greater than that of any high street agent, has allowed them to impose tough contractual terms and commission rates on hotels, which has stimulated many hotel companies to try to maximize their own direct sales to guests to reduce dependence on online agents
- the plethora of online agents, hotel wholesaler sites and airline sites has led to the rise of comparison sites such as TravelSupermarket, where consumers can see the offers of a range of providers on a single screen.

Destinations can use ICT to develop their relationships with internal stakeholders and tourists. ICT has also given them new more dynamic multi-media ways of marketing the destination, although many have still failed fully to take advantage of this opportunity. National tourism organizations, which are usually public service organizations that are tasked with the development and marketing of regions or countries, have used ICT in a variety of ways to communicate with their stakeholders in a more effective way. This has included:

- development of a well recognized brand and unique selling point
- provision of information search areas about different components, including amenities, attractions, activities, accessibility, available tourism packages and ancillary services
- itinerary planning for visitors
- customer database information
- market research and analysis of data
- image libraries and materials for the press

- financial management systems
- economic impact analysis data
- access to third-party sources such as weather forecasts, transport timetables, and theatre and event-planning websites.

The development of a destination management system using the internet is a specialized area, and the World Tourism Organization (UNWTO) has given advice to destination marketing organizations about their development. Some destinations have been much more effective than others at using new technology, and have developed excellent marketing platforms and ideas incorporating blogs and social media as well as well designed websites and other unique offerings. It is interesting to compare different destinations and their websites, as well as the other techniques they have used to create competitive advantage. The illustration on VisitScotland shows how the country has used social media and blogs as well as the more standard website and marketing communication methods. Further examples of good practice include Cape Town's use of Facebook, Visit Norway's use of social media, and VisitBritain's Top 50 Places campaign.

USE OF ONLINE MARKETING AND SOCIAL MEDIA BY VISITSCOTLAND

The main aim of VisitScotland, the national tourism organization for Scotland, is to contribute significantly to the advancement of Scottish tourism by giving it a real presence in the global marketplace, benefiting the whole of Scotland.

Target markets

Over half of the people in many of our target markets are online – for example around 75 per cent of Swedes, 70 per cent of Americans and 61 per cent of Germans are internet users.

Use of the internet is now spread throughout all types of people. Affluent older people using the internet – 'silver surfers' – are increasingly common, while younger people are also enthusiastic adopters of the new mobile and wireless technologies. As this e-generation gets older, the proportion of people who do not use the internet will become smaller and smaller.

The popularity of internet communications and shopping is partly driven by people's increasingly busy lives. The internet allows people to shop 24/7, and gives them a feeling of control, as it enables quick and easy comparison of products and prices. The wider availability of broadband connections allows people to do more of their daily tasks online.

Travel planning and booking is one of the most popular uses of the internet. For many internet users, the internet is the most important source of information on their holidays. Business travellers are also major users of the internet for organizing their trips.

brilliantmoments

Scotland is a land of Brilliant Moments: the sights, sounds and experiences that make your break memorable and make you want to return. It might be tasting your first whisky cocktail, teeing off on our world-class golf courses or hearing the dramatic music of the pipe band at a Highland games. Whatever your own brilliant moments in Scotland might be, share them with the world using #brilliantmoments.

Source: www.visitscotland.org

Virtual reality

When we were working on the first edition of this book, there was a lot of debate about virtual reality (VR) and what it might mean for tourism. Idealistic voices saw it as a way of encouraging people not to travel, but instead to have a VR experience of tourist destinations. This, it was argued, would reduce carbon emissions and benefit the environment.

Then VR seemed to become focused on the more profitable world of gaming, aimed primarily at young males, or it became part of the entertainment industry. VR had been attracting less interest from ICT developers for a number of years.

However, at the time of writing there has been a flurry of activity with new VR products coming to market or announced, including the Oculus Rift, Samsung Gear VR, Google Cardboard and Jaunt VR. Tourism and hospitality organizations are utilizing some of these developments, notably airlines such as Qantas and Emirates, while in 2014 Marriott launched its own 'Teleporter' VR product.

Now the emphasis is on using VR to enhance the tourist experience rather than the use of VR to encourage the substitution of trips by VR experiences.

Augmented reality

The *Oxford English Dictionary* defines augmented reality (AR) as 'a technology that superimposes a computer generated image on a user's view of the real world thus providing a composite view'. In other words, what a consumer sees in the real world can be supplemented by further information from other sources in real time.

AR has developed enormously across consumer society in recent years, starting with phenomena such as QR (quick response) codes, for example. Companies in most industries have seen the potential of AR as a marketing tool or as a way of enhancing the consumption experience.

Tourism is no exception, and indeed is an ideal sector for AR particularly in the short-break city tourism market where tourists want to get the maximum value from their limited time in a destination with which they are unfamiliar.

Those wishing to learn more about AR in tourism would be well advised to search out the work of Dimitrios Buhalis and the E-Tourism Lab at Bournemouth University and Timothy Jung at Manchester Metropolitan University, both in the UK.

However, AR could never have developed without the rise of the smartphone and other tablet devices which have provided a convenient way of accessing the growing number of AR applications.

On the other hand, this is still a field where technological developments are not always an instant success. The first generation of Google Glass, a wearable technology incorporating an optical head-mounted display, was withdrawn in 2015, although Google is committed to producing further versions in time.

The role of ICT in the tourism market of the future

We return to this issue in Chapter 19 as the future of ICT will be a major factor in the future evolution of tourism. At this stage we will just make a few observations, beginning with the recognition that if we were to produce a new edition in five years' time, we would be talking about technologies that have not even been thought of yet. There are, however, a number of points we can make about the future at this stage, as follows.

- ICT will become an even more important part of the tourism industry and will be adopted by most people in most countries. It will become increasingly difficult to be a tourist unless one engages with ICT, as processes like face-to-face airport check-in disappear altogether.
- Organizations will seek to make more use of the information they have in their databases to increase sales and brand loyalty.
- Social media will be used more for co-creation between tourism organizations and consumers, rather than simply companies sending messages and consumers responding with reviews. Organizations will encourage consumers to give them ideas for new products, for example.
- ICT will change the way we pay for tourism products, with contactless payment making paying more convenient and quicker.
- The obsession with consumer reviews will continue to grow – but maybe organizations will start to review their customers in return!
- Virtual reality and particularly augmented reality will grow in tourism as ways of enhancing the tourist experience.
- The issue of consumer privacy and security will become an ever more important issue and organizations that do not protect their clients' data and privacy will face both legal action and a loss of business. In this respect, social media raises particular concerns. ICT increasingly allows organizations to collect sensitive information such as the location of customers using mobile technology, and the control and use of this type of information has interesting ethical dimensions. There are also ethical questions related to the use of collected data and whether an organization should share this with other organizations, and even governments, if requested for reasons that are outside the organizational remit. All of these ethical issues can be viewed simply as an extension of previous issues related to marketing practice in

general, but the rise of social media and mobile technology has made the issues more complex and harder to understand both for consumers and organizations.

Finally, are we going to see a backlash against ICT in the future that may affect tourism? Will some segments want to spend at least two weeks a year practicing 'slow tourism' or 'retro tourism' without mobile devices and computers? For these people, the pleasure of travel will be in discovering places like an explorer, rather than knowing everything about the place you visit in advance thanks to ICT. If so, we predict these will be segments at the high end of the market price-wise, and with older people predominating. This remains to be seen, but it is something we believe will happen over the next few years, albeit as a minority activity.

Discussion points and essay questions

1. Discuss how destinations can use ICT to develop their competitiveness in the future.
2. Discuss how hotels should respond to the increasing use of TripAdvisor by their guests.
3. Critically evaluate the factors that will determine the future development of virtual reality and augmented reality.
4. Discuss the strategies that high street travel agents could use to compete with online travel agents.

Exercises

1. Compare and contrast the quality of the websites of two different destinations. What does this analysis show you?
2. Evaluate the use of blogs by a chosen tourism or hospitality organization.
3. Consider the comments that have been posted on TripAdvisor for a chosen hospitality or tourism organization. Evaluate how effectively the organization has responded to the comments, and suggest improvements.
4. Conduct a focus group with a small group of young tourists to determine their beliefs and attitudes to the use of social media and applications in their own tourist behaviour. What does this exercise tell you about likely future tourism behaviour?

References

Arsal, I., Backman, S. and Baldwin, E. (2008). Influence of an online travel community on travel decisions. In *Information and Communication Technology in Tourism 2008: Proceedings of the International Conference in Innsbruck, Austria, 2008*, P. O'Connor, W. Hopker and U.Gretzel, eds. Springer, Dordrecht, the Netherlands, pp. 82–93.

Ayeh, J.K., Au, N. and Law, R. (2013). Do we believe in TripAdvisor? Examining credibility perceptions and online travelers' attitude toward user generated content. *Journal of Travel Research* Online, 11 February.

Buhalis, D. (2003). *eTourism: Information Technology for Strategic Tourism Management*. Pearson Education, Harlow, UK.

Casaló, L.V., Flavián, C. and Guinalíu, M. (2010). Determinants of the intention to participate in firm-hosted online travel communities and effects on consumer behavioural intentions. *Tourism Management* 31 (6), 898–911.

Giddens, A. (1991). Modernity and Self-Identity: Self and Society in the Late Modern Age. Polity Press, Cambridge.

Jeacle, J. and Carter, C. (2011). In TripAdvisor we trust: rankings, calculative regimes and abstract systems. *Accounting, Organizations and Society* 36 (4), 293–309.

Miller, P. (2003). Governing by numbers: why calculative practices matter. *Social Research* 11 (1), 17.

Munnukka, J. (2007). Characteristics of early adopters in mobile communications markets. *Marketing Intelligence and Planning* 25 (7), 719–731.

O'Connor, P. (2010). Managing a hotel's image on TripAdvisor. *Journal of Hospitality Marketing and Management* 19 (7), 754–772.

Öğüt, H. and Cezar, A. (2012). The factors affecting writing reviews in hotel websites. *Social and Behavioural Sciences* 58, 980–986.

Pantano, E. and Pietro, L.D. (2013). From e-tourism to f-tourism: emerging issues from negative tourists' online reviews. *Journal of Hospitality and Tourism Technology* 4 (3), 211–227.

Qu, H. and Lee, H. (2011). Travelers' social identification and membership behaviors in online travel community. *Tourism Management* 32 (6), 1262–1276.

Ryan, C. (ed.) (1997). *The Tourist Experience: A New Introduction*. Cassell, London.

Sigala, M. (2010). Measuring customer value in online collaborative trip planning processes. *Marketing Intelligence and Planning* 28 (4), 418–443.

Vásquez, C. (2011). Complaints online: the case of TripAdvisor. *Journal of Pragmatics* 34 (3), 1707–1717.

Vermeulen, I.E. and Seegers, D. (2009). Tried and tested: the impact of online hotel reviews on consumer consideration. *Tourism Management* 30 (1), 123–127.

Wei, W., Miao, L., Cai, L. and Adler, H. (2012). The influence of self-construal and co-consumption others on consumer complaining behaviour. *International Journal of Hospitality Management* 31 (3), 764–771.

Xie, H., Miao, L., Kuo, P. and Lee, B. (2011). Consumers' responses to ambivalent online hotel reviews: the role of perceived source credibility and pre-decisional disposition. *International Journal of Hospitality Management* 30, 178–183.

Yang, K. and Jolly, L.D. (2008). Age cohort analysis in adoption of mobile services and generation Xers versus baby boomers. *Journal of Consumer Marketing* 25 (5), 272–280.

Ye, Q., Law, R., Gu, B. and Chen, W. (2011). The influence of user-generated content on traveller behaviour: an empirical investigation on the effects of e-word-of-mouth to hotel online bookings. *Computers in Human Behaviour* 27 (2), 634–639.

Zhang, Z., Ye, Q., Law, R. and Li, Y. (2010). The impact of e-word-of-mouth on the online popularity of restaurants: a comparison of consumer reviews and editor reviews. *International Journal of Hospitality Management* 29 (4), 694–700.

CASE STUDY 17: A never-ending process: the role of guest reviews online in the provision of quality service

by Saskia Faulk

In August 2013 a guest from the UK wrote the following on TripAdvisor (www.tripadvisor. com):

> We had read the great reviews on Trip Advisor and were a bit skeptical – could the hotel really be this good? I am pleased to tell you that we found it even better than the reviews suggested!

The Oceania Club Hotel is an 'Ultra all-inclusive' beach hotel in Nea Moudania, Halkidiki, Greece. According to an informal estimate by Oceania Club's General Manager, at least 95 per cent of its guests critically appraise reviews they read online before booking. One key source for such reviews is travel information website TripAdvisor ('the world's largest travel site'), as well as major online booking portals such as Booking.com and even those of tour operators, who prominently feature user-generated content such as positive or negative reviews and photos. With so much consumer emphasis on these trusted reviews, hotels need to be careful how they shape guest expectations and how they deliver quality service on-site. Oceania Club is no exception to these dynamics, with 814 TripAdvisor reviews (of which 592 rated the property as 'Excellent' in August 2013), three consecutive Certificates of Excellence, and 2013 Traveller's Choice in the luxury category.

The hotel has 298 rooms, four restaurants, six bars, two pools, a shop, a spa with fitness centre, and a private beach. It is 30 minutes from Thessaloniki International Airport and 60 km from Thessaloniki's Central Business District (www.oceaniaclub.gr). Oceania Club is owned by Sani S.A., a hotel holding company that also owns four other hotels in the region. It is located in the scenic Halkidiki region of northern Greece, where the weather is sunny, the sea is crystalline, the coast is covered in fragrant pine forests, and Mount Olympus presides majestically in the background. There is an abundance of ancient, and even prehistoric, sites in the region – as well as city attractions in and around historic Thessaloniki. Unique Mount Athos and a string of scenic coastline villages are a short drive away. Yet guests do not need to leave the property to experience an active holiday, as on-site they can enjoy the beach and programmed activities or participate in watersports.

The hotel first opened in May 2005 and operates only from April to October due to the seasonal nature of tourism in the area and the cold, northern-Greek winter. It is an 'ultra all-inclusive' hotel: all services and activities are included. All-inclusive hotels are a growing trend, with guests citing their convenience compared with more traditional packages. For families, particularly, everyone can be kept happy with multiple activities, while food and drinks are available all day without one having to carry a wallet around. Thus travellers know exactly how much their holiday will cost as they do not have any further charges after their arrival.

Oceania Club is known to be one of the best all-inclusive hotels in Europe and has won many awards from the travel site TripAdvisor such as Certificate of Excellence each year since 2011, 'Top 25 All-inclusives in Europe' and Top 25 Family Hotels in Greece (both in 2012), and 'Luxury Winner' in 2013. A list of other prizes and distinctions is shown in Exhibit 17.1.

Exhibit 17.1 Awards and distinctions Oceania Club has won since 2006	
2013	Holiday Check for Leading Hotels in Europe
	TripAdvisor Travellers' Choice 2013 Luxury Winner
2012	Gold medal by TUI UK
	Good Food Award by Saga UK
	Top Performer – Stay by Saga UK
	Top 25 All-inclusive Hotels in Europe by TripAdvisor's members (5th Position)
	Top 25 Family Hotels in Greece by TripAdvisor's members (15th Position)
	Green Key eco label
	Travelife Gold Award UK
	Good Food Award by Saga UK
2011	Top Performer – Stay by Saga UK
	Gold medal by TUI UK
	Certificate of Excellence by TripAdvisor's members
	Green Key eco label
	Travelife Gold Award UK
2010	Holly Award, Top 100 Hotels of the world – TUI
	Top Stay – Saga Tours
	Good Food – Saga Tours
2009	Gold Award – First Choice
	Gold Award – Thompson
	Top Stay – Saga Tours
	Good Food – Saga Tours
2008	Marque of Excellence – Thomas Cook
	Gold Award – First Choice
	Top Stay – Saga Tours
	Good Food – Saga Tours
2007	Best hotel in the world – First Choice
	Good Food – Saga Tours
2006	Marque of Excellence – Thomas Cook
	Holly Award, Top 100 Hotels of the world – TUI

Competition in the hotel sector is fierce. Greece has 8900 hotels and 352,000 rooms. In the all-inclusive hotels segment there is a direct competitor very close by, and also elsewhere around the country, mainly on the islands of Crete, Kos and Rhodes. Further afield there are hundreds of direct competitors in Italy, Portugal and Spain. In particular, neighbouring Turkey has seen marked growth in all-inclusive hotel openings with lower rates due to comparatively low operating costs. On a global scale, if one takes similar luxury all-inclusive beach resorts into consideration, a large number of direct competitors exist in Latin America and the Caribbean, and Egypt, Morocco and Tunisia. Yet, with recent media coverage of civil unrest and political instability in some of these destination countries, Greek holidays may be perceived as a relatively safe option.

Due to the high level of competition, it is vital for Oceania Club's marketing team to clearly differentiate the hotel, so targeted segments understand that the level of services and quality is worth the higher price compared with competitors. Therefore the accent is on going the extra mile to make guests feel welcomed and happy. One example of this is the bar service offered directly poolside at all pools and on the beach, while at competing hotels guests need to fetch their own drinks. Other services and facilities that add value compared with competitors include *à la carte dining* offered at no extra charge, free wireless internet in all areas of the hotel, and international branded spirits in all bars.

GUEST PROFILE

In 2011 most guests were European, with 37 per cent from Great Britain, 29 per cent from Russia and the Ukraine, and 18 per cent from Germany. Guests from countries in the neighbouring Balkan region were from Bulgaria (6 per cent), Serbia and the Former Yugoslav Republic of Macedonia (both 2 per cent each). Greeks composed 2 per cent of guests, which reflects their reduced spending power during the current crisis. The next markets Oceania Club plans to enter are France, Israel and Italy, but this is not imperative due to the continued growth of British and Russian markets. From June to August, most guests are young, affluent families with children, while during the shoulder season there are more elderly couples. In terms of reason for travel, approximately 80 per cent of guests cite family holidays, 19 per cent are couples (mostly older) wishing to spend time together, and 1 per cent are on their honeymoon. Typically, guests say they are happy to pay higher Oceania Club rates in order to be insulated from stereotyped beer-swilling soccer-fan tourists who populate certain cheap holiday resorts around the Mediterranean. Thanks to this positioning strategy, Oceania Club maintains its position as a high-quality, luxurious hotel.

MARKETING STRATEGY AND GUEST LOYALTY

In terms of usage rate, Oceania Club has an exceptionally high proportion of returning guests: 30 per cent. Those who do receive many privileges, starting with extra discounts, upgrades, special services, extra bookings in the *à la carte* restaurants, and free massages in the spa. As a result, some are pleased to demonstrate that they have received exclusive services as well as having had privileged contact with hotel managers. This strategy increases their loyalty and encourages them to influence friends and family and write positive comments on social media sites such as TripAdvisor.

PRICING AND SALES PROMOTION

The price is all-inclusive and is calculated according to the room type (five categories ranging from double room to deluxe suite), number of guests accommodated, and dates/season. The first child booked is free, and there are extra discounts for early bookings. For guests who book directly online, Oceania Club offers free transfers to and from the airport.

MARKETING COMMUNICATION CHANNELS

The company uses a variety of marketing communication channels, including advertising online and in the press, contracting and joint marketing with tour operators, co-branding with certain high-end brands, working on new synergies with airlines, developing public relations to increase brand awareness, and maintaining good relationships with journalists.

A number of sales activities, special promotions, website updates, advertising campaigns, new brochures, events and special seasonal attractions are budgeted for each year. Working in tandem with tour operators, Oceania Club features in national newspaper classified and display advertisements, and travel and lifestyle magazine advertisements in the British, German and Russian markets, as well as increasingly in newer markets, such as France and Italy. The company also advertises using media channels such as National Geographic Travel, House & Garden Perfect Getaways, and special issues of *The Times* (UK) iPad editions. Online marketing strategies included targeted advertising and Google's Pay Per Click service, along with search engine optimization. Facebook is used rather casually for weekly postings of news and photos in an effort to engage fans, and many do respond by posting their own holiday snaps, comments and stories. Twitter is used in a similar way, also avoiding sales-type messages. More traditional brochures are sent to travel agents and tour operators, and emails regarding special offers are sent to former guests.

The hotel's website is in English, French, German and Russian, where special offers are also promoted and direct booking is available. TripAdvisor is widely used to gather information prior to booking, as well as HolidayCheck (www.holidaycheck.de) by German guests and Top Hotels (www.tophotels.ru) by Russians. Online and off, potential guests can find out about Oceania Club through tour operators such as TUI, Thomson and Thomas Cook. Tour operator guests evaluate the hotel through a questionnaire that allows operators to provide feedback rapidly to the hotel, potentially allowing Oceania Club to be awarded a place in the 'Top 10', 'Best of', or 'Most Popular' brochures (see Exhibit 17.1).

GUEST RELATIONS

At check-in, the reasons for the guest's trip are identified in order to begin catering to their wishes in a targeted manner (needs may be different if travelling for a honeymoon, senior trip or childhood-focused holiday). It is at this point that guests' email addresses enter the database. At check-out, guests complete a satisfaction questionnaire, which staff follow up in order to discuss any particularly good or bad points mentioned.

The staff is described generally on TripAdvisor as being motivated, multicultural and friendly. This may be due to the General Manager's stated preference to hire people 'with a genuine smile and warm manner rather than more experienced workers who bring their bad habits with them'. Because guest loyalty is so important for Oceania Club, staff members are trained to provide high-quality, personalized service, and a good number speak Russian, which is important for guests from that part of the world. The level of personalization is evident in reviews, where guests cite first names of staff in order to thank them or make their point. Loyal guests tend to write comments on social media sites such as TripAdvisor, which potentially influence thousands of other users to click through and book at Oceania Club. Marketing communication standards include guaranteeing a response within 24 hours to email or telephone requests.

DISTRIBUTION CHANNELS

Approximately three-quarters of guests make their reservations through a tour operator such as Thomson (a key account) or Saga, with a high proportion of these being Russian guests who benefit from the advantageous conditions tour operators offer them. It is important for the hotel to work on maximizing the currently low amount (25 per cent) of individually-booked reservations, due to the big cut taken by intermediaries. For online bookings, the most effective site is the hotel's own. This is followed by Booking.com, a commission-based online booking and review site owned by Priceline.com, with which the hotel has observed a 50 per cent year-on-year growth.

THE VIEWS OF OCEANIA CLUB

The following are answers to some of our questions by Timos Antonakis, General Manager of Oceania Club, about the importance of online travel reviews.

How important are online reviews for you, such as those on TripAdvisor?

We realized that TripAdvisor was an important marketing tool a few years back when more and more guests told us they relied on this tool to see previous holidaymakers' experiences before booking. We also realized that the risk of a bad review on TripAdvisor or elsewhere was one more reason to ensure that any potential issues at the property had to be taken care of without delay. We don't thank each person who writes a review online because then it just becomes meaningless. As for any negative comments, we don't address them on TripAdvisor because people reading may then just focus on the negative reviews and the management response will catch their attention. We do have a system in place to contact guests based on their check-out survey, so we can discuss one-to-one any issues that came up during their stay. For positive reviews, if we know who they are, we do send a personal email to thank them. Let's say that, overall, their importance lies in the fact that they're one more source of information about how we are doing. It's a never-ending process.

What do you learn from online reviews? Can you give us an example?

We have learned a lot from the reviews on TripAdvisor and elsewhere. For example, one thing I learned thanks to comments was to increase vegetarian options at the food outlets. Another example is to have a personal care package on hand for people who arrive having lost their luggage. It happens very rarely, but when it does we need to be prepared. Sometimes people don't like to tell you what they think face-to-face, and after all, they're on holiday so we don't want to press them for details. The bottom line is that, in order to be satisfied, we must meet or exceed guests' expectations. Guest comments on these social media sites can help us to do that . . . possibly as much as they can help potential guests to decide!

DISCUSSION POINTS AND ESSAY QUESTIONS

1. How should a hotel respond when a negative review is posted online? How would you define a policy for your hotel or destination in terms of:
    *   a response (or not) online – how should this be done and by whom?
    *   a response directly to the guest or visitor if possible – how should this be done and by whom?
    *   a response on-site, for example informing staff or guests, and possibly making a change to service standards
    *   other types of response, for instance direct marketing materials and other marketing communications.
2. Similarly, should the hotel respond when a positive review is posted? Look at some examples of this kind of interaction on TripAdvisor (or other online resource) and set out some pros and cons.
3. The presence of such accessible feedback raises the question as to what kinds of feedback should be considered when undertaking a service quality audit at the property. Should TripAdvisor and other types of spontaneous online customer feedback be viewed as valid sources of information? Identify the strengths and weaknesses of such information.

ACKNOWLEDGEMENT

This case study was based on interviews conducted in August 2013 with the General Manager of the Oceania Club, Mr Timos Antonakis, and Marketing Manager of Sani S.A. Hotels, Mr Antonis Avdelas.

7

Conclusions
and future

At the end of a long text dealing with a complex and only partially understood concept, it is now time to attempt to draw some conclusions and make predictions about the future.

In this part of the book we:

- identify the main conclusions that have arisen from the previous seventeen chapters
- highlight the need for further research and the development of new consumer behaviour models in tourism
- compare tourist behaviour with that of consumers in general
- suggest some ways in which tourist behaviour may evolve in the future.

CHAPTER 18

Conclusions

At the end of such a lengthy book on a very complex subject, it is difficult to try to draw general conclusions. Nevertheless, we highlight here some key points that have emerged from the preceding chapters.

- Tourist behaviour has a long **history**, dating back over 2000 years. Many 'modern' forms of tourism, such as health tourism, are simply a continuation of a tradition that dates back to Roman times. At the same time, some early forms of mass tourism such as Christian pilgrimages are now specialist niche markets.
- Many existing **models** of consumer behaviour in tourism are generally much simpler than general consumer behaviour models. Yet tourism is a particularly complex aspect of our modern consumer society, so perhaps they are too simplistic.
- Most of the **motivations** that make tourists want to take a particular holiday can be divided into six distinct, but related, groups:
  - physical
  - emotional
  - personal
  - personal development
  - status
  - cultural.
- The motivations of any individual tourist are **influenced** by their:
  - personality
  - lifestyle
  - past experiences
  - personal circumstances, including family situation and disposable income.
- Tourists may well have **more than one** motivator at any one time.
- Tourists may admit to a **socially acceptable** motivator while in reality they may be driven by a motivator that is less socially acceptable. They may be conscious or unconscious of this important distinction.

- Different types of tourism product are associated with different motivating **factors**, for example, museums and theme park visits are generally stimulated by different motivations.
- There are two types of **determinants** of tourist behaviour, those that are:
  - personal to the tourist
  - external to the tourist.
- Those determinants that are **personal** to the tourist are of four types:
  - their personal circumstances
  - their knowledge
  - their experiences
  - their attitudes and perceptions.
- The **external** determinants include the following five types:
  - views of friends and family
  - marketing activities of the tourism industry
  - influence of the media
  - national political, economic, social and technological factors
  - global political, economic, social and technological factors.
- The main **purchase decision-making models** used in tourism, as outlined in Chapter 6, tend to have a number of weaknesses, including that:
  - they are often based on little or no empirical research
  - many are now at least 15 years old and do not take account of recent changes in patterns of purchase behaviour such as the growing role played by ICT
  - most are based on experiences in traditional markets such as Europe and the USA, not the new markets such as South East Asia
  - they are too simplistic to explain the complex process of purchasing a tourist product.
- Many **academic typologies** of tourists are flawed in that they:
  - rarely differentiate between different nationalities and cultures
  - tend not to recognize that tourists can move between categories and rarely always remain in one category
  - do not usually recognize that holiday choice is often a compromise rather than an expression of the true desires of the tourist
  - often have methodological weaknesses, such as being based on small samples
  - pre-date the rise of the internet and therefore exclude its influence on tourist behaviour.
- Typologies of tourists are clearly similar to the concept of **market segmentation**, although the former are theoretical while the latter is concerned with applications and practice in marketing.
- In the global tourism market, the major growth in tourist arrivals is being seen in **Asia and the Pacific**, while Europe is experiencing relative decline in its share of world tourism.
- There are significant **differences between countries** in terms of tourist behaviour in domestic, outbound and inbound tourism.

- Tourism is not a single market but is rather a series of **submarkets**, all of which have their own characteristics. These submarkets include the following, and more:
  - family market
  - backpacker market
  - hedonistic tourists
  - visiting friends and relatives
  - day-trippers or excursionists
  - educational tourists
  - religious tourists
  - 'snowbird' market
  - ethnic minority tourists
  - tourists with disabilities
  - retired people
  - short-break takers.
- There are also variations in consumer behaviour within the different **sectors** of tourism:
  - accommodation
  - visitor attractions
  - destinations
  - transport operators
  - tour operators
  - retail travel.
- **Business tourism** is very different from leisure tourism in terms of consumer behaviour regarding:
  - frequency of trips
  - duration of trips
  - when purchase decisions are made
  - who makes purchase decisions.
- In business tourism we see the difference between **customers and consumers**. The former tend to be the companies that pay the bills, while the latter are the employees, usually the business travellers themselves.
- Research on tourist **behaviour** is weak in a number of respects, most notably:
  - the fact that much quantitative data is outdated and based on small samples, which mean the results are open to question
  - the relative lack of sophistication in terms of qualitative research on how and why tourists make their decisions.
- Consumer behaviour affects every aspect of **marketing**, in that it should influence:
  - product development
  - pricing strategies
  - distributive channels
  - promotional campaigns.
- There is no such thing as an **'ethical tourist'**; there are 'shades of ethical consumers' in tourism, and there are some tourists who are not at all interested in ethical issues.
- There are significant **differences between nationalities** in terms of tourists' attitudes towards the environment and other ethical challenges in tourism.

- The current era is seeing the growth of a number of **emerging markets** in tourism, including:
  - eco-tourism
  - direct booking
  - children-only holidays
  - all-inclusive vacations
  - budget cruising
  - outbound tourism from Asia
  - 'no-frills' airline travel
  - the international wedding market
  - couples-only holidays
  - visiting sites associated with popular culture, such as films and television programmes
  - visits to religious retreats
  - trips designed to improve tourists' health.
- There is no apparent evidence for the idea that we are seeing the emergence of the **'global tourist'** or even the 'Euro tourist'.
- **Quality** in tourism is a jigsaw where, if any piece is missing, the customer will be dissatisfied.
- Tourist **dissatisfaction** is largely a result of gaps between expectations and perceived outcomes, viewed from the perspective of the tourist.
- The concept of quality and the expectations of tourists **change over time**.
- There are many **uncontrollable factors** that influence tourist satisfaction:
  - weather
  - strikes
  - harassment of tourists by beggars and traders
  - difficulties within the destination such as hygiene problems, poor infrastructure and crime
  - behaviour of other tourists.
- **Information and communication technologies** have transformed tourist behaviour in recent years, and continue to do so in terms of what people buy, how and when they buy it, and how they record and share their experiences.

Hopefully this book has helped, in a small way, to focus attention on this important field in the study of tourism. As well as the main text we hope that the discussion points, exercises and case studies will help you to deepen your understanding of this crucial area of tourism management.

In the era of so-called 'consumer-led marketing', where organizations are told they must meet the demands of their consumers if they are to thrive, it is vital that we understand tourists and what makes them tick.

In Chapter 19 we gaze into our crystal ball and attempt to predict what might happen in the future. This is a risky activity at a time when consumer factors appear to be changing at an ever greater pace and new forms of tourism are continually emerging.

CASE STUDY 18: New Zealand's 'Home of Middle-earth' campaign

Saskia Faulk

'We especially like that we can tell our friends and family that we ate lunch in Rivendell.'
(comment from a tourist from Texas, USA)
'Oh, and after the tour for dinner, we ate at the Green Parrot and found out Peter Jackson hosted a party for the filming crew there and it was a favorite of Viggo Mortensen.'
(comment from a tourist from New Zealand)
'I'll never be stuck for a laugh again now that I have the photos of Chris posing as Legolas – priceless!'
(Comment from a tourist from England)

Tourists leaving these messages on a tour operator's site obviously feel strongly about their themed experiences. 'Isengard is on your left'. . . 'Just ahead you can see the vistas of Mordor'. . . 'See the smoke trails on your right? Those are the chimneys of Hobbiton'. . . Today, tour guides can be heard making these statements through coach loudspeakers because fictional place-names drawn from Tolkien's writings have become so real in New Zealand. If aliens were to discover this country today, they would definitely believe that hobbits, elves and dwarves really exist.

Beginning in 2001, filmgoers around the world were astounded by the vistas of unmatched beauty seen in the films *The Lord of the Rings* and, later, *The Hobbit*. It has been said that New Zealand is the unnamed star of the trilogies. While other well-known films such as *Avatar*, *The Chronicles of Narnia*, *Whale Rider* and *The Last Samurai* were also filmed in New Zealand, the tourist board made no specific efforts to target movie tourists until the global success of *The Lord of the Rings*. As the national tourist authority boasts on its website, 'New Zealand's popularity as an international film making destination means movie buffs are spoiled for choice when it comes to film locations to visit' (www.newzealand.com/int/film-locations). If Tolkien fans wanted to visit every film location, it would mean 150 destinations for *The Lord of the Rings* alone, not counting all those used in *The Hobbit*.

A BRIEF FOR THE UNINITIATED: ABOUT THE TWO TRILOGIES

The Hobbit (1937) and *The Lord of the Rings* comprise a fantasy epic written by scholar J.R.R. Tolkien between 1954 and 1966. The books were initially underestimated as a commercial success, but exceeded all expectations when they gained popularity among fans of literature as well as fans of the nascent fantasy genre who carried the books to 'cult' status (The Tolkien Society, 2015). A broader appeal was easier to attain for *The Hobbit* than *The Lord of the Rings* because it is a less complex story aimed at children, at least on the face of it. The mythical land where all the stories take place is 'Middle-earth', hence the name used in New Zealand marketing campaigns.

Several radio and film adaptations (including an animation version by US film-maker Ralph Bakshi) had already been made when New Zealand's own Peter Jackson began writing the screenplay with Fran Walsh and Philippa Boyens. It took eight years of work to make *The Fellowship of the Ring*, *The Two Towers* and *The Return of the King*, which were released between 2001 and 2003.

By all accounts, Sir Peter Jackson's initiative to make the films was ambitious. In 2003 Jackson said about *The Lord of the Rings*:

This is a giant undertaking, but I consider this a personal film. It's my film of a lifetime. I read the book when I was 18 years old and thought then, 'I can't wait till the movie comes out.' Twenty years later, no one had done it – so I got impatient.

IMDB (2015)

In terms of budget, box-office success and critical acclaim (which do not necessarily go together), the films were indeed 'giant'. The trilogy had a production budget of US$281 million, although that figure may be as high as US$331 million according to some estimates. The marketing budget was estimated at US$145 million (Mathijs, 2006). All three *Lord of the Rings* productions are in the top twenty of *Variety*'s top-grossing films of all time ranking. The films won, in total, 17 Academy Awards, four Golden Globe Awards, the MTV Best Movie Award for three consecutive years, 16 Saturn Awards and numerous professional and industry awards. The financial legacy of the films continues with DVD and merchandising sales, and was refreshed with the release of *The Hobbit* trilogy.

DID THE FILMS MAKE A DIFFERENCE TO NEW ZEALAND TOURISM?

New Zealand's top visitor market is Australia, followed by China, yet all eyes are on the US market in third place, whose visitor numbers jumped by 13.4 per cent in 2013. Visitors from the UK, Japan and Germany (in fourth, fifth and sixth places, respectively) were also increasing. One airport survey revealed that, whether due to the determination and initiative of Tolkien fans or thanks to state marketing activities, one in ten visitors to New Zealand in 2013 affirmed that their reason for visiting the country was having seen *The Lord of the Rings* or *The Hobbit* films. Hard data alone, however, point to a growth in international visitor numbers due to the films (Ministry of Economic Development, 2012). An estimated 47,000 tourists visit film locations each year.

Yet the data may not be showing the full picture, as tourists' motivations tend to be complex, and the initial inspiration felt while watching a film may merge with a broader set of factors over time. Some tourists may not have even been aware of the existence of New Zealand were it not for the films. In 2014, when the Ministry of Business, Innovation and Employment conducted in-depth research on the topic, it became clear that the Middle-earth campaign was a key driver of the growth in visitors from advanced economies. One analysis found that Hobbiton movie set credit card spends were disproportionate to those in the country as a whole, indicating a very high level of interest in the Hobbit-themed attraction. Can the economy of a country truly depend, at least in part, on the passion for hobbits and wizards of people half-way around the world? It is an important question, for the New Zealand economy benefits from tourism to the tune of US$6.5 billion per year. This represents 10 per cent of the country's GDP, while one-tenth of New Zealanders are employed in the tourism sector. Tourism is second only to dairy as the most important industry in New Zealand.

TOLKIEN TOURISTS – AS DIVERSE AS THE PEOPLES OF MIDDLE-EARTH

An informal analysis demonstrates that there are different types of Tolkien fan. This observation can be supported superficially in citing the diversity of his very public supporters: US President Barack Obama, author Marion Zimmer Bradley, Pope Francis, Queen Margrethe of Denmark and film director James Cameron. The existence of different Tolkien-inspired fan groups over recent history and in the present day is also indicative of a broad appeal which is fragmented according to subculture. These range from computer programmers, engineers and hackers (most famously at Stamford and MIT), to musicians (most famously Led Zeppelin and The Beatles), to hippies in the 1960s (Spangenberg, 2007).

There are those who consider themselves 'Tolkien geeks' or 'Ringers', and who may also be fans of the fantasy genre of literature and its offshoots in art, cosplay, live-action role-playing and gaming. Others are interested in the aesthetic, symbolic, magical and spiritual aspects of Tolkien's works, while yet others find sustenance in mythical and historical aspects rooted in northern European mythology. And others simply enjoy a good adventure and its skilful telling. Then there are younger fans who primarily know *The Lord of the Rings* and *The Hobbit* from film, and whose interests encompass mainly the locations, studios, special effects and celebrity aspects. It is thus difficult to generalize, yet clearly a number of Tolkien fans are getting older and thus more affluent. They may have their own family with whom they travel. This intergenerational aspect was emphasized by the general manager of Western long-haul tourism at Tourism New Zealand, Gregg Anderson. In his view, a main draw of New Zealand for fans is that parents, grandparents and grandchildren travelling together can each find what they are looking for at or near the same attraction: for example, hard-core fans can focus on movie trivia on location, while other family members can hike and enjoy the natural beauty of the sites (Pinchevsky, 2012). It is thus difficult to target any particular group, so Tourism New Zealand instead decided in 2010 to target 'Active considerers', who have the intention of visiting the country as part of a list of preferred destinations in the medium term, are over 18 years of age, and are willing to pay an allocated amount on their holiday. The tourism bureau then conducts in-depth research to 'tailor New Zealand's marketing messages to the interests and priorities of this group of people in each market, with the aim of converting their interest into purchase of travel'. (Tourism New Zealand, 2015a).

WHERE (AND WHAT) THE HECK IS NEW ZEALAND?

Simply being a movie location does not necessarily turn a country into a tourism magnet. New Zealand has much to offer movie fans outside its cinematic attractions, which is an important consideration, given the substantial travel distance required for Tolkien fans (unless they are coming from Australia, its closest market a 3.5-hour flight away). New Zealand is in the South Pacific Ocean, approximately 10 hours flight time from Pacific Rim countries, or 12 from the west coast of the USA (New Zealand Tourism Guide, 2015). Composed of two main islands and a multitude of small ones, the country has a land mass approximately the size of the British Isles or the state of California. Summertime is from December to February and winter is from June to August. This inversion of seasons can be a selling point, because while the tourist-generating markets in the Northern Hemisphere are shivering as they shovel snow, it is summer in New Zealand. The same may also be true in summer for Northern Hemisphere dwellers wishing to escape capricious weather or heatwaves.

Tourists, like film-makers, appreciate the diversity of New Zealand's topography. At turns dramatic mountains, active volcanoes, steamy rain forests, craggy plains and lush green rolling hills, let alone its brooding fjords and picturesque towns, the countryside mutates over relatively short distances. For long-haul tourists particularly, a New Zealand holiday can embrace such different ecosystems as to explore an entirely different setting each day.

One-third of the country is protected as parks, reserves and heritage sites. These assets, plus the national passion for sports and the outdoor lifestyle, combine to ensure there are many opportunities to enjoy nature. Nature is abundant and unspoiled in the main, which is due to a low population density of 15.8 per square kilometer (comparable with Finland, Argentina and the Republic of Congo) as well as concerted conservation efforts. There is a well-developed network of dedicated cycling routes (2500 kilometres of it, to be exact) as well as mountain-biking trails and several scenic railways, making environmentally friendly transport a real possibility for like-minded tourists.

Ancient forests and landforms, diverse ecosystems, rare birds and animals, snow-capped mountains and crystalline lakes, wild coastlines, and white- and black-sand beaches are all part of the country's wondrous natural heritage. Eco-tourism offers are myriad, often blended with soft or extreme adventure possibilities – commercial bungee jumping began in New Zealand. Yet these treasures were largely unknown to tourists until they were projected into movie theatres worldwide, with enthusiastic support from the star-spangled cast who found themselves often having to clarify that these were not digitally created landscapes, but real, untouched New Zealand.

The economy is powered by the food processing industry, primarily meat and dairy, and engineering. Forest plantation products, plastics, clothing and climbing equipment, electronics and telecommunications are areas where the country has a competitive advantage, while specialized lifestyle products such as film, wine and yachts have become increasingly important in recent years. The population is small, 4.5 million in 2014, but known for its innovative capacities. The culture is a unique blend of ancient indigenous Maori and immigration from English-speaking Europe, as one may glean from the country's place names, variously Invercargill, Canterbury and Christchurch; Whangaparaoa, Pukaki and Hari Hari.

CO-BRANDING OF NEW ZEALAND TOURISM AND TOLKIEN

As *The Hobbit* star Martin Freeman says, the backdrops seemed so perfect in the film that some viewers may think they are the result of special effects. Yet they are natural, and untouched, and really as beautiful as they appear. Leading cast members of the films are often seen vaunting the beauty of the country in an authentic and personal manner on online videos and DVD/Blu-ray bonus features. Such a branding strategy is coherent, because in Tolkien's books the landscape is so important that it becomes a major character in its own right: natural characteristics of mountains (Misty Mountains, stone-giants, Mount Doom), plains (Rohan, North Moors), green countryside (the Shire), forests (Fangorn, Mirkwood), and even living things in the environment such as trees (tree-men or Ents) take on great significance in the books, and subsequently in *The Lord of the Rings* and *The Hobbit* films.

NEW ZEALAND'S '100% MIDDLE-EARTH' CAMPAIGN: EXPLICITLY LINKING MOVIES WITH TOURISM

In 1901 New Zealand was the first country ever to initiate a government department dedicated to the promotion of tourism. By the end of that century, tourism had become the country's biggest export earner, and the '100% Pure New Zealand' campaign, launched in 1999, became one of the world's most successful tourism brands. Over the years since, the campaign has been redefined as '100% pure relaxation', '100% pure welcome', '100% pure adrenalin', and '100% pure you'. As the new millennium dawned, the trademark '100%' came to be applied to the fictional land superimposed on New Zealand's landscapes by Sir Peter Jackson in his two trilogies – Middle-earth.

New Zealand is, by all accounts, a most beautiful country on screen and off. Yet the nation does not simply rest on its lovely laurels. One strategy of Tourism New Zealand is to convert film interest into travel, an explicit goal since the 1970s when the New Zealand Film Commission began to fund local projects. Today, the tourism board works closely with the New Zealand Film Commission and Film New Zealand to identify opportunities relating to films made in the country that can help promote it as an exceptional travel destination. For the past 15 years, the tourism authorities have successfully marketed New Zealand as the home of Middle-earth. The 100% Pure Middle-earth, 100% Pure New Zealand marketing strategy aimed to convert into travel the international attention New Zealand drew from starring in the movie adaptations of Tolkien's books. A key point of the strategy is a website with interactive digital content on Middle-earth locations and experiences. The site was designed by Weta, the film effects specialists used by Sir Peter Jackson, with the result that the graphics, signature sounds and design meld seamlessly with the movie experience (see www.newzealand.com/int/feature/middle-earth).

When the New Zealand government signed an agreement with US movie-making giant Warner Bros stipulating that all *Hobbit* films were to be made in New Zealand, it initiated a government–Warner Bros strategic partnership to promote the country as both a tourism and a film production destination. Specifically, as part of the agreement, all *Hobbit* DVDs include a tourism marketing featurette, and world premieres will be held in New Zealand, among other provisions. Specific public relations and marketing activities agreed upon with Warner Bros included tactics prior to, during and after each film's premiere, including the following.

- Inviting major international media outlets to Middle-earth locations and experiences. These included CCTV (China, with 6.3 million viewers), TF1 (France, with 3.8 million viewers) and Sky Movies (UK, with 10.7 million viewers). High-profile celebrities were also invited, such as Chinese actress Yao Chen, whose visit generated 34,697 stories.
- Providing international media outlets with Middle-earth destination content (footage, imagery and text).
- Involvement in international venues such as red carpet presence of New Zealand Tourism at movie premieres, holding New Zealand food-and-wine events, and installing a Hobbit Hole at Claridge's Hotel, London.
- Creation of Middle-earth television commercials showing locations and experiences in New Zealand, and *New Zealand Home of Middle-earth* DVD featurettes with cast endorsements.

PARTNER PARTICIPATION IN THE MIDDLE-EARTH BRANDING STRATEGY

Successful tourism requires coordination between different sectors such as transport, food and beverage, hospitality, sports and events, among others. Therefore, if a national branding campaign is to succeed, these different participants need to sing the same tune. A most significant player is the country's 75-year-old national carrier, Air New Zealand, which has fully integrated the Middle-earth theme in its own marketing strategy, as the 'Official airline of Middle-earth'. Following the trend of unconventionally-themed passenger safety videos (featuring the adventurer Bear Grylls, fitness guru Richard Simmons and comedian Betty White, for instance), Air New Zealand struck gold with two of its most recent efforts. Firstly, *An Unexpected Briefing: Safety Video* (2012) featured elves as cabin staff and a Gandalf-like pilot. Dwarves, hobbits, orcs and the Witch-king of Angmar are among the passengers demonstrating safety compliance, as well as cameos by Gollum and Sir Peter Jackson. Within two years, the video was watched 12 million times on YouTube. It can be viewed at Air New Zealand's Hobbit Media Kit: www.tourism.net.nz/tours/hobbit-movie-set-and-location-tours

Secondly, timed to coincide with the third Hobbit film *The Battle of Five Armies*, the airline produced a new version, *The Most Epic Safety Video Ever Made*. This video uses a humorous story-telling mode to provide safety messages integrated into the adventures of two real-life Tolkien fans. *The Hobbit* stars Dean O'Gorman (Fíli),

Sylvester McCoy (Radagast) and Elijah Wood (Frodo) feature in the video, with a closing word from Sir Peter Jackson. Safety messages regarding seat belts, smoking and other airline-specific information are filmed in elaborate detail in several locations, using digital technology by Weta such as flying on the back of an eagle. Air New Zealand brand manager Jodi Williams explains: 'We set out to make the most epic airline safety video ever to celebrate our three-year partnership with *The Hobbit* films [. . .] The number of people watching it, the feedback from customers and the coverage generated by global media outlets has been outstanding'. The video earned 16 million views during its first week on Facebook, China's Youku and YouTube combined, and benefited from major media coverage. *The Most Epic Safety Video* can be viewed here: www.youtube.com/watch?v=qOw44VFNk8Y&feature=youtu.be

In a bold move, the company had two Air New Zealand Boeing 777-300 planes customized with Hobbit-themed images, one of Smaug the dragon and the other featuring the dwarves. They are the largest graphics ever applied to an aircraft. The Middle-earth theme was further integrated into the travellers' experience by the New Zealand Customs Service, which inks incoming passports with a 'Welcome to Middle-earth' stamp. Other initiatives include postage stamps featuring *The Hobbit* cast members, as well as coins.

INTERPRETATION OF MOVIE LOCATIONS AS TOURISM MARKETING COMMUNICATION

Another important tourism marketing partner is the Department of Conservation, which provides detailed information on Middle-earth filming locations, effectively repackaging natural attractions as filming locations. The Department divides the country into seven destination regions: Canterbury, Nelson/Marlborough, Otago, Southland, Tongariro/Taupo, Wellington and West Coast. For each, information is provided as in the example in Exhibit 18.1.

Exhibit 18.1 Filming locations in Tongariro/Taupo

Region name	Tongariro/Taupo
Film/story location name	Mordor
New Zealand location name	Whakapapa skifield, Tongariro National Park
Film/story sequence summary	Isildur cuts off Sauron's finger and the Ring
View of location	39° 14.116′ S 175° 33.529′ E – view in Google maps
Location	39° 14.114′ S 175° 33.522′ E – view in Google maps
Access	State Highway 48

Source: adapted from Department of Conservation (2015)

Many other lists and guides regarding filming locations exist, of which some are officially sanctioned by Tourism New Zealand, and others are the work of small businesses in the tour operating, entertainment or hospitality sectors. There are 150 *The Lord of the Rings* locations to visit, and around 37 for *The Hobbit* fans. Recommended itineraries include self-drive, cycling, hiking, horseback riding, helicopter, mountain bike, quad, off-road vehicle, boat and kayak modes. There are also many guided tours. Most of these start or end in New Zealand's capital Wellington, now also known as 'Wellywood' in a nod to her bigger Californian sister. This is where the production facilities are located, and there are a number of well-trodden city itineraries that follow in the footsteps of cast and crew to culinary, leisure and cultural attractions. Also in Wellington is the Weta Workshop, where models, miniatures, weapons and digital effects were made, and visitors can watch the staff at work and see the museum. On the same site is the Weta cave, a paradise for unique movie merchandise shoppers. Many fans go to Matamata to visit the minutely detailed Hobbiton movie set, an extensive built attraction, and have a drink or meal at the Green Dragon Inn. The numerous other fan attractions typically offer guided tours by people who can tell 'insider' stories. Because the films were produced relatively recently, guides often have first-hand experience on set, having worked as an extra or as one of the crew, which heightens the authenticity and uniqueness of the tourist's experiences. Guides often bring props, costumes and film footage on tablets with them to filming locations in order to bring them to life. Role-playing and posing is encouraged and filmed for the appreciation of absent family and friends, resulting in the comments at the beginning of this case study.

Exhibit 18.2 In-depth knowledge extra: development of the New Zealand movie industry

The New Zealand movie industry is growing rapidly, with sustained growth in year-on-year production revenues. A robust entrepreneurial spirit, a creative and productive workforce, and some government incentives enabled the development of the diverse sectors upon which film-makers rely, ranging from costume designers, conceptual artists, blacksmiths and other traditional artisans, to sound engineers and special effects designers, as well as state of the art digital technology developers, animators and post-production technicians. Unlike certain other stunning areas of natural beauty, New Zealand also has an excellent transport and communications infrastructure, which makes it relatively easy to access remote sites, land helicopters and allow for massive logistics shifting to take place from one location to another. The existence of unspoiled landscapes and large unpopulated areas means that film crews can use nature as an uncrowded stage. As Sir Ian McKellan tweeted when asked where else outside New Zealand the movies could have been filmed: 'There are plenty of Middle-earth locations in the UK, but they're not suitable because everywhere there is evidence of human activity. New Zealand has much fewer walls, fences, telegraph poles, etc.' On the same note, Sir Ian summarized his attitude to New Zealand thus: 'Why didn't I come here before, and when can I come back?' (McKellan, 2012).

A selection of films and television series made (even partially) in New Zealand:

1949	*Sands of Iwo Jima*
1993	*The Piano*
1994	*Heavenly Creatures*
1995–2001	*Hercules: The Legendary Journeys; Xena: Warrior Princess*

A selection of films and television series made (even partially) in New Zealand:

2001	*The Crooked Earth; The Lord of the Rings: The Fellowship of the Ring*
2002	*The Lord of the Rings: The Two Towers*
2003	*The Lord of the Rings: The Return of the King; The Last Samurai; Whale Rider*
2005	*King Kong; The Chronicles of Narnia: The Lion, the Witch and the Wardrobe; The World's Fastest Indian*
2007	*Bridge to Terabithia*
2008	*10,000 BC; Legend of the Seeker; Underworld: The Rise of the Lycans*
2009	*Avatar; Legend of the Seeker; Das Paradies am Ende der Welt; The Lovely Bones; Under the Mountain; X Men Origins: Wolverine*
2010	*Boy; Home By Christmas; Yogi Bear*
2012	*The Hobbit: An Unexpected Journey; The Red House; Ghost TV*
2013	*The Hobbit: The Desolation of Smaug; Eternity*
2014	*The Hobbit: The Battle of the Five Armies; Syrenia; What we do in the Shadows; Housebound; The Dark Horse*
2014	*Dawn of the Planet of the Apes*

Source: adapted from Film New Zealand (www.filmnz.com) and Wikipedia (https://en.wikipedia.org/wiki/List_of_New_Zealand_films#2010)

Developing the movie industry can have important direct benefits for the economy, such as the US$340 million spent during production and post-production for *The Hobbit* films (Milne, 2011). The importance of the film industry for the economy could be summarized by the fact that, of the six top-grossing movies ever, two were filmed in New Zealand: *Avatar and The Lord of the Rings: Return of the King.* In addition, there are 'spillover effects' from the movie industry to other sectors, whereby subcontractor companies in animation, production and post-production grow as a result. More broadly, the technological advancement and innovation necessary in the international movie market benefit the entire New Zealand economy. Such expertise increases attractiveness as a film-making destination, with repercussions for tax income, employment, foreign investment, infrastructure development and, not least, the business/research and development reputation of the country.

BEYOND HOBBIT-TOURING: NICHE TOURISM EXPERIENCES IN NEW ZEALAND

Once Tolkien fans have exhausted their wish-list of experiences, there are many tempting on-site experiences. Some visitors even go to New Zealand for these attractions alone!

- Destinations and activities include going offroad with a quad, hiking, and flying with the pilots who flew camera crews to film sweeping landscapes for *The Lord of the Rings* locations. There are a number of world-class theme parks, and one can go marine mammal watching or bird watching, or take the plunge and go snorkeling with the seals. Opulently comfortable hotels and spas relax visitors too.
- Wine tourism is increasingly important, as the reputation of New Zealand wines becomes ever better. There are wine tastings and courses, as well as cycling tours in the vineyards. Culinary experiences, including gastronomic tours, wine and food

pairing courses, and cooking lessons using New Zealand's exceptionally wide variety of fresh local produce, are easy to plan.

- Soft and extreme adventure and active tourism finds many breathtaking natural sites in the country for kayaking, canyoning, or cruising the rivers, lakes and coasts. Sky-diving, parasailing, bungee-jumping, mountain-biking, hiking and climbing are offered at many different sites. Diverse weather systems mean that local operators can 'guarantee' waves for surfers.
- Cultural tourism is nourished by a range of high-quality art and performance venues in New Zealand's larger cities. Yet an authentic, fascinating and completely unique culture exists also in New Zealand: that of the Maori people. An ancient civilization that arrived on New Zealand's shores one millennium ago, the Maori have a rich and complex culture with intricately beautiful art traditions that many visitors particularly appreciate. Immersion in the Maori culture is possible, with many culinary and accommodation offerings, as well as cultural discovery as part of activities showcased in the Indigenous New Zealand website. According to Tourism New Zealand, experiencing Maori culture is the second main motivator of tourists visiting the country (Tourism New Zealand, 2015b). Activities are varied and include forest treks, geothermal spas and healing, horse-riding, and observation of culture-specific ceremonies. The spiritual dimension so central to Maori culture is emphasized in many of these activities.

Exhibit 18.3 Selected New Zealand traveller (and fan) resources online

100% Middle-earth – *The Lord of the Rings* locations with descriptions, links and travel tips	www.newzealand.com/int/feature/lord-of-the-rings
Air New Zealand's Media Kit	www.airnewzealand.com/media-centre-about-us
Department of Conservation's guide to *The Lord of the Rings* locations	www.doc.govt.nz/parks-and-recreation/places-to-go/lord-of-the-rings-locations
Lord of the Rings Wiki ('One wiki to rule them all') – includes a directory of film locations and their book counterparts	http://lotr.wikia.com
Tolkien Gateway – includes a wealth of information including a guide to film locations and their book counterparts	http://tolkiengateway.net

---

REFERENCES

Department of Conservation (2015). *Lord of the Rings Locations*. www.doc.govt.nz/parks-and-recreation/places-to-go/lord-of-the-rings-locations/

Mathijs, E. (2006) *The Lord of the Rings: Popular Culture in Global Context*. Wallflower Press/Columbia University Press, New York.

McKellan, I. (2012). #AskGandalf. @IanMcKellan. www.facebook.com/notes/the-hobbit/sir-ian-mckellen-askgandalf-twitter-qa-transcripts/458451170857160

Milne, J. (2011). Scenery will make a splash in 'Hobbit'. *New Zealand Herald* 13 February. www.nzherald.co.nz/nz/news/article.cfm?c_id=1&objectid=10705880

Ministry of Economic Development (2012). *Growth and Dynamics of the New Zealand Screen Industry*. Discussion paper. www.filmnz.com/media/2700/discussion-paper-growth-and-dynamics-of-the-nz-screen-industry.pdf

New Zealand Tourism Guide (2015). Flight times. www.tourism.net.nz/new-zealand/about-new-zealand/flight-times.html

Pinchevsky, C. (2012). The impact (economic and otherwise) of *Lord of the Rings/Hobbit* on New Zealand. *Forbes* 14 December. www.forbes.com/sites/carolpinchefsky/2012/12/14/the-impact-economic-and-otherwise-of-lord-of-the-ringsthe-hobbit-on-new-zealand

Spangenberg, L. in Drout, M.D.C. (ed.) (2007). *J.R.R. Tolkien Enyclopedia: Scholarship and Critical Assessment*. Taylor & Francis, Abingdon, UK.

Tourism New Zealand (2015a). *New Zealand's target market*. www.tourismnewzealand.com/about/what-we-do/our-role-and-capability/

Tourism New Zealand (2015b). *Maori tourism*. www.tourismnewzealand.com/about/about-the-industry/m%C4%81ori-tourism/

IMDB (2015). *Peter Jackson – Biography*. www.imdb.com/name/nm0001392/bio?ref_=nm_ov_bio_sm

The Tolkien Society (2015). *The Author*. www.tolkiensociety.org/author/biography

DISCUSSION POINTS AND ESSAY QUESTIONS

1. Using a location with which you are familiar and which is the location of a film, book or game, consider how to best communicate the link between fiction and reality.

2. Consider the risks of excessive commoditizing around a story, an event or local heritage. A number of Tolkien fans find the '100% Middle-earth' marketing distasteful, and feel that these communication efforts cheapen their experience (which some even call 'sacred'). Discuss how destinations can avoid over-doing their attempts to generate visitor income to the point of irritation.

3. On its corporate website, Tourism New Zealand declares 'When films are produced in New Zealand it provides an opportunity for Tourism New Zealand to gain access to quality content, marketing opportunities and high impact media channels to promote New Zealand as a tourism destination.' Conduct some research into your government's (national, regional or local) view on attracting film-makers, and reflect on whether they are missing or capitalizing on business development and potential future tourism opportunities. Read Exhibit 18.2 about the movie industry in New Zealand to enrich your discussion. There is also more specific information at www.tolkiensociety.org/.

The future of tourist behaviour

In this chapter we consider how tourist behaviour might evolve in the future in terms of who will be travelling, what tourists will buy, and how they will buy tourism products.

This is the third edition of this book – and the third time we have written a chapter with this title. When the first edition was published in 1999, we were still in the twentieth century and September 11 was still to happen. It seems like a very different world from the one we inhabit now. The second edition was published in 2007, before the economic crisis, which has been part of all our lives now for such a long time.

Predicting the future is always fraught with danger, but we need to try. Governments and companies seek to anticipate future demand so they can plan infrastructure and develop new products.

The factors that drive change in the tourism market are many and varied. Some are factual and measurable, such as the distribution of wealth in a society, currency exchange rates, demographics and visa regulations. In Figure 19.1, taken from the 2007 edition of this book, some of these factors are identified.

However, others are much more difficult to identify and measure, and these are perhaps even more important influencers of behaviour. They include how people perceive destinations and, very importantly, how they perceive risks such as terrorism and how this perception affects their behaviour.

Some things do not change, such as the basic motivations that make us want to take vacations, nor does the geography of the world. However, most things do change, and that change takes place differently and at a different pace in different countries, which adds to the complexity of predicting future behaviour.

Perhaps we should start by briefly reviewing what we predicted would happen in the future in the 2007 edition and compare that with what actually happened. The original 2007 text is in a different font, with our commentary in normal typeface.

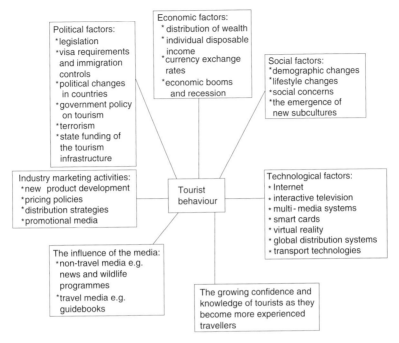

Figure 19.1 Factors influencing trends in tourist behaviour

New-generating countries

There are economic, political and social reasons why the major growth in outbound tourism in future years will be seen largely in countries which until recently have generated relatively few international tourist trips. These countries include:

• Eastern Europe, where political and economic change is slowly creating a growth in outbound trips
• Asia and the Pacific, where economic growth is rapidly expanding the market for outbound trips by the residents of those countries. For example, outbound trips from South Korea rose between 1986 and 1995 from 455,500 to 3,819,000, an increase of some 850 per cent in just ten years.

However, in both cases, the growth in outbound tourism will only continue if there is political stability and economic growth in both regions of the world. Past events seem to indicate that this may not be the case, with uncertainty over the future of Russia after Yeltsin left power and turmoil in the currency markets of South East Asia.

As yet, there is little outbound tourism from most countries in Africa and South America. This may change, however, as:

• some economies, such as Brazil, are growing rapidly
• political change in some countries may lead to a more equal distribution of wealth, which may make more of the population able to take a trip abroad.

In general terms this has proved to be fairly accurate, certainly in terms of growth in outbound tourism in Asia, although we should also have noted the rapid growth of domestic tourism within Asian countries.

On the other hand, we were over-optimistic about Eastern Europe, where the economic crisis and the political situation in Russia and the Ukraine have dampened the growth of tourist demand.

Whilst we were largely right about Brazil, we were over-optimistic about the extent to which political change in Africa would lead to a fairer distribution of wealth and thus an increase in outbound tourism.

Market segments which will grow in importance

Social change, the influence of the media and the actions of the tourist industry seem likely to have the following effects on segmentation in tourism:

1. Demographic change in Northern Europe, the USA and Japan will lead to growth in the importance of the elderly or 'third age' market. Conversely, in countries where the population is becoming more youthful – Southern Europe, South America and South East Asia – there will be a growth in the 18–30 market segment.
2. As children become ever more consumers in their own right, an increasing number of them will take holidays separately from their parents.
3. There will be more non-Christians travelling internationally in future which will have implications for the tourism industry worldwide.
4. We may see the growth of segments, which share similar characteristics, regardless of their nationality. Students may be the first example of such a segment.
5. As attitudes towards people with disabilities change over time, there should be a growth in the number of travellers who have disabilities. They will become a major market, which the industry will not be able to neglect.

We believe that all of these predictions were correct to an extent, but that the changes we predicted were over-optimistic in terms of the pace of change, largely due to the impact of the global economic crisis.

New types of tourism products

The development of any new types of tourism will result from:

- the changing tastes of tourists
- whatever the industry chooses to make available to tourists
- technological innovations
- social concerns.

In Chapter 16, we looked at some of the current trends in tourist demand and the products that are now in fashion.

The veteran travel writer, Arthur Frommer, writing in 1996, identified a number of types of tourism products that may grow in popularity in the future. These included:

- 'vacation resorts that stretch the mind and change your life'
- 'political travel' which allows tourists to visit countries which are often in the news and see for themselves what everyday life is like there
- 'volunteer vacations' where tourists work for nothing on projects which are good causes, such as conservation work or building a school in a poor country
- taking holidays that involve staying with an ordinary family in another country
- searching for new modes of travel, such as freighter ships and sailing vessels
- 'ethical holidays' where tourists are concerned about the impact of their trip on the host community and the staff who look after them
- health-enhancing holidays.

Frommer also talks about finding 'new ways to visit old destinations', where, he argues, tourists visiting well known destinations, perhaps for the third or fourth time, will look for new, more off-beat experiences.

It is also likely that the growing pressures of modern life will lead more people to use their holidays to reduce stress and/or gain spiritual enlightenment as an antidote to the materialism of modern life. This will increase demand for trips to 'retreats', even among those who do not have strong religious beliefs.

As well as the development of new products, many tourists will be encouraged by the industry to take similar types of holidays as they have before, but in new locations. This might include:

- European tourists taking short city breaks to places further afield, such as Cape Town, Samarkand, Tbilisi, Havana and Tehran
- beach holidays being taken in Namibia and Brazil
- skiing trips to Japan, Argentina and Chile
- cultural holidays in Myanmar, Laos and Nigeria.

In general, it seems likely that tourists will travel longer distances for their main vacations, even though their main holiday activity or motivation may be little different from the past.

We believe that the predictions by Frommer nearly 20 years ago, and our own, have proved fairly accurate. However, at this point we need to make an important point. These trends in vacation behaviour have been largely restricted to those who are affluent, well educated and well travelled. The gap between these people and the majority of the population of the world has probably grown in recent years. For those who have money there is a greater choice of experiences than ever before, but this is only a tiny proportion of the people who live on the planet.

Virtual reality and fantasy tourism

One of the major current debates in tourism revolves around virtual reality technologies, and the ability to create synthetic substitutes for real tourism experiences. The question is, will virtual reality (VR) reduce the demand for conventional tourism or increase it by stimulating even more people to want to take particular trips?

The potential application of VR in tourism, once the technologies themselves have become more sophisticated, is virtually unlimited. We could let people:

- feel the sun on their face, hear waves lapping on the shore, as they lie on a deserted beach on a Pacific Island, all in their own home
- experience a visit to the greatest of the pyramids in Egypt, without the fear of terrorist activities, stomach upsets or overbooked flights, because they would not need to leave home
- enjoy a romantic *bateaux-mouches* cruise on the Seine in Paris, with the love of their life, all from the comfort of their bed at home.

At the same time, virtual reality technologies, and other technological innovations, could help us to develop new forms of escapist tourism by allowing people to live out their fantasies. Already, the Russians are allowing tourists to experience what it is like to:

- be a cosmonaut training for their first space flight
- be a fighter pilot, on a sophisticated flight simulator.

In this case, it is a result of economic necessity and the desire to attract foreign currency, through the use of well-established VR technologies.

Alternatively, one day we will be able to create artificial environments, where tourists can experience holidays under the sea, or in gravity-less environments. Or perhaps, one day, tourism will be a wholly mental activity, with no need to travel; an activity which takes place purely within the tourist's own home and is limited only by the imagination of the tourist.

This area of virtual reality has been very interesting over the past few years. Its use in tourism has developed much less than we anticipated. This may be a function of the fact that those companies that would have developed the technology did not believe the market would buy the products in large enough quantities to make their development financially viable. It may be that they thought augmented reality (AR) had a broader appeal, so they focused their efforts on developing wearable devices on which AR apps could be used to enrich the experience of tourists and those going about their everyday lives in their home environment. We will return to this subject later.

Will tourism demand turn full circle?

It is often assumed that the evolution of tourism demand is a linear process of stages, which are passed through in a sequence. Figure 19.2 illustrates the widely accepted conventional wisdom about how the behaviour of many British tourists has changed over time.
There are several reasons why this apparent linear process may become more circular in future. It could perhaps turn full circle if:

• diseases such as malaria discourage tourists from taking trips to long-haul destinations, where the threat of infection is perceived to be high
• the Earth's resources become depleted and it either becomes difficult to justify long-haul trips or the cost of fuel makes such trips too expensive.

At the same time, the coastal resorts of Britain and Spain may begin to be seen as attractive as heritage tourism destinations, given that mass tourism is now part of our modern heritage.

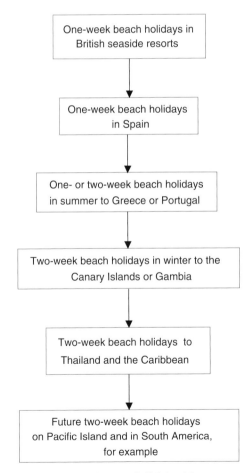

Figure 19.2 The evolution of beach holiday demand among British tourists

We already have examples of how tourism demand can turn full circle. Spa tourism reached its peak in Europe in the eighteenth and nineteenth centuries and then declined early in the twentieth century. Now, however, the spa resorts of Europe are experiencing a boom. Likewise, cruising which went into decline after the Second World War is currently experiencing a real renaissance.

This is an interesting subject and there still seems to be truth in the points we made in 2007. Spa tourism and cruising are still growing despite recent high-profile cruise ship accidents. In addition, in Europe there are signs that some of the old coastal resorts that declined dramatically with the rise of international travel, such as Margate in the UK, are regaining some popularity, riding the wave of nostalgia and the interest in all things retro. At the same time, across the world the economic crisis has forced many people to take a domestic rather than an international vacation or, as it is called in the UK, a 'staycation'.

Changes in the way we purchase tourism products

Technological innovations are going to continue to change the way in which we purchase tourism products, in several ways:

1. The development of the Internet and interactive television will stimulate the growth of direct marketing and direct booking. People will increasingly be able to access information and make bookings from their own home or office. Tour operators, airlines and hotels will help encourage this trend, as the Internet is a relatively inexpensive promotional tool and direct selling takes away the need to pay commission to travel agents.
2. The growth of ever more sophisticated global distribution systems will help tourists put together individual, tailor-made itineraries, by giving them access to the detailed product information, which they require.
3. Smart-card technologies will bring with them the benefits of ticket-less travel, which will stimulate the growth of last-minute purchases of tourism products.

Developments in technology such as multimedia systems and the Internet are blurring the dividing line between promotion and distribution in tourism. In other words, tourists, through these systems, can both gain information and make bookings at the same time, in the same place.

We might also see changes in the future in terms of who we buy holidays from, as the role of travel agents declines and other organizations take their place. These could be:

*   high street retailers who will combine selling holidays with the sale of goods needed by tourists, such as clothes, sun protection creams and luggage
*   tele-shopping networks that may simply add holidays to the portfolio of products they sell
*   banks who provide loans for holidays and sell currency, might go on to sell the holidays themselves

- telecommunications companies which may become involved in selling holidays as their systems play more and more of a role in the distribution of the tourism product.

This is where we have to say we were not so successful at predicting what would happen, but in our defence, perhaps no-one could have envisaged the ways in which technologies unknown ten years ago would change our lives, and thus our vacations. Interactive television and tele-shopping in tourism has all but disappeared in the face of the rise of sophisticated multifunction mobile phones and then tablets. We underestimated the extent to which online travel agents such as Expedia and Lastminute.com would come to dominate the market. We will return to the subject of ICT and tourist behaviour later in the chapter.

Towards a new agenda for consumer behaviour research in tourism

In Chapter 12, the authors provided a critique of current consumer behaviour research in tourism. If we are to better understand tourist behaviour and use this knowledge to improve marketing within the industry, we need to adopt a new agenda for research.

We went on in 2007 to identify a list of ways in which research on tourist behaviour could be improved. Sadly, the academic research in the field and academic theory in the area seems to have made very little real progress since then. Governments also still seem much happier measuring tourist flows and 'guesstimating' economic impacts than seeking to understand behaviour through qualitative research. This is a pity because only by understanding behaviour can you predict future behaviour. The industry, on the other hand, has made great strides in the quality of its marketing and approaches to segmentation based on sophisticated state-of-the-art research.

We hope you found this evaluation of our 2007 predictions interesting. Now it is time to look at what we did not predict!

What we did not forecast in 2007

In our defence, we believe that many of the changes in the market we failed to predict were things that were impossible for anyone to predict, and seem to have taken many people by surprise. Let us now explore them one by one.

Impact of the global economic crisis

The 2007 edition was published before the onset of the global economic crisis, which has had a profound impact on individual tourist behaviour and the tourism market as a whole. At its simplest, it has reduced the number of holidays taken and/or the amount spent on each vacation. However, it is perhaps a measure of how important vacations are to people now that the reduction in demand has been less than might have been expected. The economic situation has been fertile ground for the growth of budget air travel and budget hotels.

One aspect of the crisis has been its impact on people's pensions. With an ageing population in many key generating markets, we would have predicted a very bright future for the seniors market. The prospects are now less impressive as people realize they will have to work longer before they can retire, and that their pension may be lower than they once hoped.

Consumer-generated media

Perhaps the biggest omission from our original predictions was that we failed to foresee the explosion in consumer-generated media. Its impact in tourism has largely been twofold.

* Sites such as TripAdvisor, where tourists can read the opinions of other customers. It is clear that many tourists now rely heavily on such sites before making any decisions. This has meant that the advice of professionals such as travel agents is being sought less, as people now trust fellow consumers more than the so-called experts.
* Social media sites, where tourists can share their experiences, memories and photographs with friends and the wider world. This influences consumer behaviour but is totally outside the control of industry, although industry now tries hard to manipulate these media.

New types of service supplier

The rapid growth of smartphones and tablet devices has created opportunities for new types of entrepreneurs to enter the tourism market. We have seen this clearly in the case of Airbnb and Uber, which have had a massive impact in a relatively short period of time.

The impact of the media

We underestimated the influence of the media in 2007. The growth of satellite television and the rise of mobile devices that allow people to access media material 24 hours a day, anywhere in the world, has transformed the role of the media in our lives. The mobile phone also means that everyone is now a reporter, with tourists' footage of events often able to be on television screens around the world in minutes.

Experiential marketing and co-creation

In 2007 we recognized the fact that companies were starting to market experiences rather than products, but we underestimated how this concept would become embedded in the tourism sector. The rise of mobile device apps has turned every trip into an experience, and a co-created experience at that, as we download information and images as we travel and then upload our experiences for others to see. In this way, others become an important part of our vacation experience and *vice versa*.

Destination crises

In many ways, the most shocking change we failed to foresee in 2007 was the enormous increase in destination crises that now appear to be part of the everyday reality of the tourism industry. Firstly, terrorism that targets tourism and tourists as a deliberate policy. I am writing this days after 38 tourists were killed by terrorists on a beach in Sousse, Tunisia; this happened just months after an attack on tourists at the Bardo museum in the same country. Tourists are now high on the target list of terrorist groups, which themselves are becoming ever more ambitious, effective and well resourced.

We appear to also be seeing a growing number of natural disasters that affect tourism, such as earthquakes, volcanoes, and diseases and health epidemics. Perhaps there are no more of these than before, but their impact is magnified by the fact that we now have a truly global media, and tourists are now visiting pretty well everywhere in the world. These types of crisis affect tourist behaviour in ways we have barely begun to understand.

The economic situation has also led to some destination crises. As we write this, for example, tourists are being told to take euros with them when they go to Greece on vacation as the banks may run out of cash or even be closed due to the crisis around the Greek debt.

Industry crises

Since 2007 the travel industry has had its own crises, from the two air crashes that affected Malaysian Airlines in 2014, to the Germanwings crash of 2015, to the sinking of the *Costa Concordia* cruise ship. Accidents like these have always happened, but the world's media have covered these exhaustively. It remains to be seen how such events will influence the tourism market in the long term.

So what will happen in the future?

Our view is that the market will remain volatile for the foreseeable future thanks to both the political situation and the continuing economic crisis.

However, tourists have proved to be a resilient breed, and they seem committed to continuing to take vacations whatever happens in their lives. Therefore, while their choices may be influenced by everything that happens around the world, we remain sure that tourism will continue to grow on a global scale.

Five major predictions

- **Information and communication technologies** will play an increasing role in how we purchase, consume and remember touristic experiences. However, we can only guess at the nature of these technologies currently because by 2025 it is likely that the most influential technology will be one that we have not even seen yet! On the other hand, we feel confident that wearable technologies, whether watches, glasses or clothes, will become increasingly relevant to tourism over the next few years.
- **Consumer-generated media** will play an increasing role in how people buy and experience tourism, but the types of media are likely to come and go in fashion cycles. We will also have to deal with the ethical issues involved with social media such as privacy, and the impact reviews can have on a business and its staff – a phenomenon of power without responsibility.
- Tourists will be made ever more aware of the **ethical issues in tourism** thanks to the media, from low wages to the environmental impact of tourism. It seems intuitive that as people learn more about global warming and climate change, they will seek to modify their behaviour for the benefit of the planet and the future of their family. However, we think it is likely that most tourists, even those who are sensitive to environmental issues in their everyday lives, will not take their conscience with them on holiday. Instead, most of them will just want to enjoy their vacation without feeling guilty. We also sense there is a growing sense of 'sustainability fatigue', where people think there is nothing they can do that will make a difference, so they start to switch off when the word 'sustainable' is mentioned. On the other hand, there will continue to be a small market segment of 'ethical travellers' whose consumption decisions are based on ethical considerations. Ironically, we believe that ethical influences on behaviour are more likely to occur around issues such as child sexual abuse, poor treatment of staff and wildlife exploitation, rather than global warming and climate change.
- Sadly, we believe that **terrorism is now a fact of life** and something that can affect anywhere in the world, and we think that terrorists will increasingly try to attack tourists. Clearly, this means we will need to take more security measures as an industry. And more importantly, it means that we need a new approach to segmentation in which we identify customer types in terms of how they respond to the risk of terrorism. These types may include those who:
  - stop travelling if there is any perceived threat
  - could be persuaded to travel and take the risk if prices are dropped substantially
  - reassure themselves with thoughts – largely inaccurate – that 'terrorists never strike twice in the same place' or 'security will always be improved after a terrorist attack'
  - refuse to be intimidated by terrorist threats almost as an act of personal defiance
  - wish to show solidarity with the residents of tourist destinations where there are terrorist attacks
  - get a thrill from travelling to dangerous places.

Interestingly, I think we will need to take a similar approach to all risks, including diseases and natural disasters, as well as looking at how we communicate with tourists about these crises.

- We believe that **the market in Asia will continue to grow**, become more democratized and start to mature. At the moment most outbound tourism from China and India, for example, is undertaken by the middle classes, which have grown in both countries in recent years, but still represent only a minority of the population. They tend to travel to famous destinations and iconic attractions while buying high-value designer brands to take home from their trips. The search for status is clearly a key motivator in the behaviour of many of these tourists, who may be the first generation in their family able to take foreign vacations. This view is certainly stereotypical but not inaccurate. From South East Asia, tourists also tend to travel in groups, seeking out food with which they are familiar. In many ways, these patterns of behaviour have much in common with the upper-middle-class European travellers of 100 years ago, or the Northern Europeans who 'discovered' Spain half a century ago. As the economies of Asia continue to develop, it seems likely that we will see foreign travel becoming accessible to a wider range of groups within the society. Then we may see the current 'elite' travellers becoming more confident and experienced, and feeling less need to travel in-group, just eat familiar food and buy designer brands as proof of their wealth. They may also move on from the iconic 'must-visit' destinations of the world to explore lesser-known places off the beaten track. The destinations they no longer visit will then fill with the 'new' travellers from their countries, greater in number, lesser in per head spending. Again, this is what happened in the Northern European market, but there is no guarantee it will also happen in the markets of South East Asia.

Those are our five 'big' predictions. It may also be that some more of our 2007 predictions reach fruition over the next ten years.

We think that some of the trends we talked about earlier will continue, such as ICT facilitating the growth of new types of tourism enterprise and new ways of buying and selling tourism products – or should we say experiences, as we believe the idea of selling experiences rather than products will grow. However, it is for you to decide if this is reality or just marketing hype designed to sell more products.

There seems little doubt, though, that technological innovations will make it easier and easier to buy tourism products, starting with the current developments in contactless payment systems.

Will everything change?

The simple answer is 'no', or perhaps more accurately, 'it depends what you mean by change'.

Yes, we will be using different ways of choosing, paying, sharing and remembering our vacations thanks to technology, but there will still be many people travelling to the same destination to do the same things at the same time of year, every year. In addition, even if we go to new places, our motivations for doing so are unlikely to change any time soon.

Summary

Most importantly, we recognize the difficulties involved in predicting tourist behaviour whilst recognizing that this is something we need to do as an industry.

We have seen that a range of factors will lead, in the future, to changes in who tourists are, what they buy and how they buy it. However, we also believe that the behaviour of some individual tourists will not change noticeably. Even within the global tourism market as a whole, we will find that changes in behaviour will be evolutionary rather than revolutionary. We will also see variations in the pace of change between different:

- countries
- market segments
- sectors of the tourism industry.

Nevertheless, there is little doubt that tourist behaviour will change in fundamental ways in the years to come. That is why it is so important that we become better at researching consumer behaviour in tourism.

A final thought

When we wrote the first edition of this book, our son, also called John, was eight years old. By then he had already been on vacation with us to a number of countries, on trips planned months in advance using guidebooks and our own previous travel experience.

By the time we wrote the second edition, he was 16 years old and had been to four continents, but still with us, and still on trips booked well in advance by us using the internet.

Today, as we write, he is 24 years old, living and working in London, and taking several vacations a year despite having only a limited salary. Thanks to us, he is an experienced and confident traveller. And because of his age, all types of ICT seem natural to him. Unlike us, he seems to absorb new technologies rather than having to laboriously learn to use them as we do. He makes trips at short notice, and seems to think nothing of travelling 8,000 kilometres each way to Cape Town for a three-day break, or going to Paris for a night. He uses social media to help plan his trips and share his experiences, and is an enthusiastic user of Airbnb and Uber. He trusts these new styles of tourism enterprises and although he recognizes some of the ethical issues implicit around these enterprises and social media, he is still enthusiastic about them. Access to Wi-Fi appears almost as important as the presence of oxygen for John on vacation, but it seems to enrich his vacation experience to be able to instantly share his experiences with friends.

Fortunately for us as parents, he also enjoys travelling with us as well as with friends. This time away from work with John is really important time for us as a family. However, John also works very hard and has to try to live on a limited salary in an expensive city, so parental help with holiday costs is understandably welcome.

So why have we told you all this? Because if you want to understand how tourist behaviour will change in the future you should not ask us, you should talk to John and people of his age all over the world, for they are the tourists of the future!

Glossary of terms

This glossary is offered as a service to readers who may be unfamiliar with some of the terms used in this book. It is not meant to be a definitive set of definitions but rather a simple, easy-to-use interpretation of some key words and phrases.

ACORN – a method classifying residential neighbourhoods on the basis of who lives there, for use in marketing research or direct mail.

Advertising – any paid form of non-personal presentation of ideas, goods or services by an identified sponsor.

All-inclusive – a type of package holiday where one price covers everything that guests will require in the destination: accommodation, food, drink, activities and entertainment.

Allocentric – a term, coined in 1977 by Plog, which refers to those tourists who are adventurous, outward-looking and like to take risks.

Backpackers – term used to describe tourists (who tend to be younger people) who take relatively long trips seeking out places that are off the beaten track, making relatively little use of the mass tourism infrastructure, and trying to minimize their expenses.

Brand – the name, symbol or design, or combination of these, that is used to identify the products or services of a producer to differentiate them from competitors' products or services.

Brand loyalty – the propensity or otherwise of consumers to continue to purchase a particular brand.

Business tourism – tourist trips that take place as part of people's employment, largely in work time, rather than for pleasure, in people's leisure time.

Catchment area – the geographical area from which the overwhelming majority of an organization's or product's customers are drawn.

Commission – money paid by a producer to an external agent who helps the organization to sell its products, usually expressed as a percentage of the selling price.

Competition – the process by which two or more organizations endeavour to gain customers at the expense of another organization or organizations.

Concentrated marketing – the focusing of the marketing effort on just one or two of the available market segments.

Consumer – the person who actually uses or consumes a product or service.

Consumer behaviour – the study of which products people buy, why they buy these products, and how they make their purchasing decisions.

Critical incident – this concept suggests that the tourist's satisfaction or otherwise depends on what happens at times when something out of the ordinary occurs.

Culture – the sum total of knowledge, attitudes, beliefs and customs to which people are exposed in their social conditioning.

Customer – the person who actively purchases the product or service, and pays the bill. The term is often used interchangeably with 'consumer' but they are different. For example, in business tourism a company is the *customer* as it pays for the travel services, but it is the employee or business traveller who actively travels, and is therefore the *consumer*.

Demand – the quantity of a product or service that customers are willing and able to purchase at a particular time at a given price. Where there is a desire to purchase a type of product or experience which is not currently available, for whatever reason, we talk about *latent demand*.

De-marketing – action designed to discourage the purchase of particular products or services.

Demographics – the study of population structure and its characteristics such as age, sex, race and family status.

Desk research – the collection of secondary data in marketing research.

Destination – the country, region or local area in which a tourist spends his or her holiday.

Determinants – the factors that determine whether or not someone will be able to take a holiday and, if so, what type of holiday he or she will be able to take.

Differentiated marketing – the development of a different marketing mix for each market segment.

Direct marketing – selling directly from the producer to the customer without the use of intermediaries such as travel agents.

Discounting – a reduction in the list price of a product or service to encourage sales.

Disposable income – the money that remains once all expenditure has been subtracted from the income of an individual or family.

Distribution – the process by which products and services are made available to customers by producers.

Domestic tourism – tourism where the residents of a country take holidays or business trips wholly within their own country.

Eco-tourist – someone who is motivated by a desire to take a vacation that allows him or her see the natural history of a destination and meet the indigenous population.

Ethics – the moral values and standards that guide the behaviour of individuals and organizations.

Excursionists – people who take leisure trips that last one day or less and do not require an overnight stay away from home.

Family life cycle – the stages through which people pass between birth and death that are thought to influence their consumer behaviour.

FIT – fully-inclusive tour.

Geodemographics – an approach to segmentation which classifies people according to where they live.

Green issues – a commonly used term that is used as an umbrella for a variety of issues relating to the physical environment, from recycling to pollution, wildlife conservation to global warming.

Growth market – a market where demand is growing significantly.

Hedonism – the constant quest for pleasure and sensual experiences.

Heterogeneous – a market which consists of segments or subgroups that differ from each other significantly in terms of their characteristics and/or purchasing behaviour.

Homogeneous – a market made up of people whose characteristics and/or purchasing behaviour are wholly or largely identical.

Inbound tourism – tourist trips from a foreign country to one's own country.

Intangibility – the characteristic of a service by which it has no physical form and cannot be seen or touched.

International tourism – tourist trips where residents of one country take holidays or business trips to other countries.

Leisure – leisure is considered to be free time, the time that is not devoted to work or other duties. Some people also use the term to describe an industry that provides products and services for people to use in their spare time.

Leisure shopping – shopping as a leisure activity, not as a necessary task of everyday life. It implies that products are purchased for the pleasure involved in buying and consuming them rather than because of their utilitarian value.

Lifestyle – the way of life adopted by an individual or group of people.

Market – consumers who currently are, or potentially may become, purchasers and/or users of a particular individual or group of products or services.

Market leader – the product that has the largest share of a single market, that is, it is purchased by more people than any of its competitor products.

Market share – the proportion of sales of a particular type of product achieved by an individual product.

Marketing mix – the four controllable marketing variables – product, price, place and promotion – which marketers manipulate in order to achieve their marketing objectives.

Marketing positioning – the position in the market which a product is perceived to have, in the minds of consumers, in relation to variables such as quality, value for money and level of service.

Marketing research – the process of collecting, recording and analysing market-related information, including published or secondary data, or primary research. It is designed specifically to provide data that help an organization improve the effectiveness of its marketing activities.

Media – may refer to either the news media or the advertising media (the media in which advertisements may be placed).

Model – a representation that seeks to illustrate and/or explain a phenomenon.

Motivation – those factors that make tourists want to purchase a particular product or service.

Niche marketing – the targeting of a product and service at a particular market segment which is numerically much smaller than the total market.

NRS – National Readership Surveys Ltd (formerly JICNARS, Joint Industry Committee for National Readership Surveys).

Off-peak – a period when demand for a product or service is habitually lower than at other times, which are termed peak periods.

Outbound tourism – tourist trips from one's own country to a foreign country.

Perceptions – the subjective interpretation by individuals of the data available to them, which results in them having particular opinions of, and attitudes towards, products, places or organizations.

Perishability – a characteristic of tourism products whereby they have very limited lives, after which they no longer exist and have no value. For example, an airline seat is no longer an existing saleable product once the aircraft has departed.

Point of sale – refers to techniques used at the point when tourists actually buy products or services to encourage higher sales, such as window displays in travel agencies.

Postmodernism – a sociological theory that has major implications, if it is a valid theory, for the study of consumer behaviour in tourism. It is based on the idea that in industrialized, developed nations the basis on which people act as consumers has been transformed in recent years. The theory suggests the traditional boundaries, such as those between highbrow and lowbrow culture, and up-market and down-market leisure activities, are becoming blurred and are breaking down. Authors, notably John Urry, have looked at the implications of postmodernism for the tourism industry.

Post-tourist – a tourist who recognizes that there is no such thing as an authentic tourism product or experience. To post-tourists, tourism is a game and they feel free to move between different types of apparently totally contrasting holiday, from an eco-tourism trip to Belize one year to a sun, sand, sea and sex trip to Benidorm the next.

Product-service mix – the combination of tangible elements and service that is aimed at satisfying the needs of the target market.

Promotion – the techniques by which organizations communicate with their customers and seek to persuade them to purchase particular products and services.

Psychocentrics – a term coined in 1977 by Plog referring to inward-looking, low risk-taking, less adventurous tourists.

Psychographic – the analysis of people's lifestyles, perceptions and attitudes as a way of segmenting tourism markets.

Purchase decision – the process by which an individual decides whether or not to buy a particular type of product and then which specific brand to purchase.

Qualitative research – research concerned with customers' attitudes and opinions, which cannot be qualified.

Quantitative research – research concerned with statistical data that can be measured and expressed numerically.

RATER – reliability, assurance, tangibles, empathy and responsiveness – the five factors of SERVQUAL (see below).

Repositioning – the process by which organizations attempt to change the consumer's perceptions of a product or service.

Seasonality – the distribution over time of total demand for a product or destination, usually expressed in terms of peak and off-peak seasons to distinguish between those times when demand is higher than average and vice versa.

Segmentation – the technique of dividing total markets into subgroups whose members share similar characteristics as consumers.

Service gap – a concept coined by Parasuraman *et al.* which is based on the idea that tourist dissatisfaction is caused by perceived gaps between expectation and actual outcomes.

SERVQUAL – a technique developed by Parasuraman *et al.* which is designed to measure service quality (now more commonly known as RATER, see above).

Snowbird – a person living in an area that is cold in winter, who takes long trips to warmer destinations to escape the cold weather.

Social tourism – a broad area primarily concerned with providing opportunities to participate in tourism for those who would not normally be able to go on trips for primarily financial or health reasons.

Target marketing – marketing activity aimed at a particular group of consumers within the overall total population.

Tour operator – an organization that assembles package holidays from components provided by other sectors such as accommodation and transport. These packages are then sold to tourists, usually through travel agents.

Tourism – the activity in which people spend a short period, of at least one night, away from home for leisure or business.

Tourist – a consumer of tourism products.

Typology – a classification that subdivides a group into subgroups which share similar characteristics.

Undifferentiated marketing – a broad-brush approach to marketing in which the market is not subdivided into segments.

Up-market – Products aimed at the more expensive, higher-status end of the market.

Virtual reality – a set of technologies that replicate real-world experiences and can be developed as leisure products.

Visiting friends and relatives (VFR) – tourist trips where the main motivation is the desire or need to visit friends and relatives.

Visitor – a widely used term for someone who makes a visit to an attraction. Visitors are not all tourists in the technical sense in that they will not all spend at least one night away from home.

Visitor attraction – a single site, unit or entity which motivates people to travel to it to see, experience and participate in what it has to offer. It may be human-made or natural and could be a physical entity or a special event.

Word of mouth – the process whereby consumers who have experienced a product or service pass on their views, both positive and negative, about the product or service to other people.

Index